Hebrews

ΠΑΙΔΕΙΑ 🔲 paideia
COMMENTARIES ON THE NEW TESTAMENT

Hebrews

JAMES W. THOMPSON

Baker Academic
a division of Baker Publishing Group
Grand Rapids, Michigan

Published by Baker Academic
a division of Baker Publishing Group
P.O. Box 6287, Grand Rapids, MI 49516-6287
www.bakeracademic.com

Printed in the United States of America

Library of Congress Cataloging-in-Publication Data
Thompson, James, 1942–
   Hebrews / James W. Thompson.
     p.   cm. — (Paideia : commentaries on the New Testament)
   Includes bibliographical references and indexes.
   ISBN 978-0-8010-3191-5 (pbk.)
    1. Bible. N. T. Hebrews—Commentaries. I. Title.
BS2775.53.T77 2008
227'.8707—dc22
                                              2008024697

For Everett Ferguson and Abraham Malherbe,
teachers, mentors, and friends,
who introduced me to the cultural and philosophical world
of the New Testament,
encouraged me to pursue graduate studies,
and have continued the conversation throughout my academic career

Contents

List of Figures

Foreword

Paideia: Commentaries on the New Testament is a series that sets out to comment on the final form of the New Testament text in a way that pays due attention both to the cultural, literary, and theological settings in which the text took form and to the interests of the contemporary readers to whom the commentaries are addressed. This series is aimed squarely at students—including MA students in religious and theological studies programs, seminarians, and upper-divisional undergraduates—who have theological interests in the biblical text. Thus, the didactic aim of the series is to enable students to understand each book of the New Testament as a literary whole rooted in a particular ancient setting and related to its context within the New Testament.

The name "Paideia" reflects (1) the instructional aim of the series—giving contemporary students a basic grounding in academic New Testament studies by guiding their engagement with New Testament texts; (2) the fact that the New Testament texts as literary unities are shaped by the educational categories and ideas (rhetorical, narratological, etc.) of their ancient writers and readers; and (3) the pedagogical aims of the texts themselves—their central aim being not simply to impart information but to form the theological convictions and moral habits of their readers.

Each commentary deals with the text in terms of larger rhetorical units; these are not verse-by-verse commentaries. This series thus stands within the stream of recent commentaries that attend to the final form of the text. Such reader-centered literary approaches are inherently more accessible to liberal arts students without extensive linguistic and historical-critical preparation than older exegetical approaches, but within the reader-centered world the sanest practitioners have paid careful attention to the extratext of the original readers, including not only these readers' knowledge of the geography, history, and other context elements reflected in the text but also their ability to respond correctly to the literary and rhetorical conventions used in the text. Paideia commentaries pay deliberate attention to this extratextual repertoire in order to highlight the ways in which the text is designed to persuade and move its readers. Each rhetorical unit is explored from three angles: (1) introductory matters; (2) tracing the train of thought or narrative or rhetorical flow of the argument; and (3) theological issues raised by the text that are of interest to the contemporary Christian. Thus, the primary focus remains on the text and not its historical context or its interpretation in the secondary literature.

Our authors represent a variety of confessional points of view: Protestant, Roman Catholic, and Greek Orthodox. What they share, beyond being New Testament scholars of national and international repute, is a commitment to reading the biblical text as theological documents within their ancient contexts. Working within the broad parameters described here, each author brings his or her own considerable exegetical talents and deep theological commitments to the task of laying bare the interpretation of scripture for the faith and practice of God's people everywhere.

Mikeal C. Parsons
Charles H. Talbert

Preface

As interpreters have acknowledged for the past two generations, the dominant image for Christian experience in the Epistle to the Hebrews is that of the journey of the people of God. This commentary is a stage in my own journey with this mysterious book. Because I was intrigued by the artistry and complex argument of Hebrews during my graduate studies, I began the journey with my dissertation, "'That Which Abides': Some Metaphysical Assumptions in the Epistle to the Hebrews," in 1974. That work became the basis for the monograph, *The Beginnings of Christian Philosophy* (1982). Since that time, I have continued my work with Hebrews in lectures, classes, and journal articles. As with the people of faith in Hebrews 11, I have not yet reached the destination in my attempt to grasp the many nuances of this work. I am grateful to the editors of the Paideia series, Charles Talbert and Mikeal Parsons, for the invitation to continue my journey with Hebrews in this volume. I am also grateful to James Ernest and the editors at Baker Academic for the careful reading and editorial suggestions.

Others have contributed to this work. My wife, Carolyn Roberts Thompson, read drafts of the commentary and made suggestions for stylistic improvement. My graduate assistant, Michael Coghlin, also read earlier drafts and did valuable research. My colleague, Mark Hamilton, offered helpful insights into Old Testament and rabbinic texts. The careful reading of the commentary by students in a Greek seminar on Hebrews in the spring semester of 2008 frequently raised important questions about the translation and interpretation of specific passages. Any errors that remain are, of course, my own.

James W. Thompson
March 1, 2008

Abbreviations

General

b.	Babylonian Talmud	lit.	literally
ca.	circa	NT	New Testament
d.	died	OT	Old Testament
dub.	dubious	par.	parallel; and parallels
ed.	edition	rev.	revised
ET	English translation	sp.	spurious

Bible Texts and Versions

ASV	American Standard Version	NIV	New International Version
KJV	King James Version	NRSV	New Revised Standard Version
LXX	Septuagint		
LXXB	Septuagint (Vaticanus)	RSV	Revised Standard Version
MT	Masoretic Text		

Ancient Corpora

OLD TESTAMENT		Judg	Judges
Gen	Genesis	1–2 Sam	1–2 Samuel
Exod	Exodus	1–2 Kgs	1–2 Kings
Lev	Leviticus	1–2 Chron	1–2 Chronicles
Num	Numbers	Neh	Nehemiah
Deut	Deuteronomy	Esth	Esther
Josh	Joshua	Ps/Pss	Psalm/Psalms

Prov	Proverbs
Isa	Isaiah
Jer	Jeremiah
Ezek	Ezekiel
Dan	Daniel
Hos	Hosea
Mic	Micah
Hab	Habakkuk
Zeph	Zephaniah
Hag	Haggai
Zech	Zechariah
Mal	Malachi

Deuterocanonical (Apocryphal) Books

1–2 Esd	1, 2 Esdras
Jdt	Judith
1–4 Macc	1–4 Maccabees
Sir	Sirach
Sus	Susanna
Tob	Tobit
Wis	Wisdom of Solomon

New Testament

Matt	Matthew
Rom	Romans
1–2 Cor	1–2 Corinthians
Gal	Galatians
Eph	Ephesians
Phil	Philippians
Col	Colossians
1–2 Thess	1–2 Thessalonians
1–2 Tim	1–2 Timothy
Phlm	Philemon
Heb	Hebrews
Jas	James
1–2 Pet	1–2 Peter
Rev	Revelation

Dead Sea Scrolls and Related Writings

CD	*Damascus Document*
1QM	*War Scroll* from Qumran Cave 1
1QS	*Rule of the Community*
1QpHab	*Commentary on Habakkuk* from Qumran Cave 1
11QMelch	*Melchizedek* from Qumran Cave 11

Targumic Texts

Tg. Ps.-J.	*Targum Pseudo-Jonathan (Targum Yerushalmi I)*

Rabbinic Literature

Gen. Rab.	Genesis Rabbah
Lev. Rab.	Leviticus Rabbah
Midr. Tanh.	Midrash Tanhuma
Ned.	Nedarim
Pesiq. Rab.	Pesiqta Rabbati
Sabb.	Sabbat

Old Testament Pseudepigrapha

Apoc. Ab.	Apocalypse of Abraham
2 Bar.	2 Baruch
3 Bar.	3 Baruch (Greek Apocalypse)
As. Mos.	Assumption of Moses
Ascen. Isa.	Ascension of Isaiah
1 En.	1 Enoch (Ethiopic Apocalypse)
2 En.	2 Enoch
Epist. Ar.	Letter of Aristeas
Jos. Asen.	Joseph and Aseneth
Jub.	Jubilees
Mart. Isa.	Martyrdom of Isaiah
T. Dan	Testament of Dan
T. Jud.	Testament of Judah
T. Levi	Testament of Levi
T. Moses	Testament of Moses

Apostolic Fathers

Barn.	Barnabas
1 Clem.	1 Clement

Nag Hammadi Codices

Gos. Truth	Gospel of Truth

Ancient Authors

AELIUS ARISTIDES

Or.   *Orationes*

AESCHYLUS

Ag.   *Agamemnon*

ALBINUS

Didask.   *Didaskalikos (Handbook of Platonism)*

APHTHONIUS

Prog.   *Progymnasmata*

APOLLODORUS

Bibl.   *Bibliotheca*

ARISTOTLE

Eth. Nic.   *Ethica Nichomachea*

Mund.   *De mundo* (sp.)

Pol.   *Politica*

Rhet.   *Rhetorica*

CICERO

Off.   *De officiis*

DEMETRIUS

Eloc.   *De elocutione*

DIO CHRYSOSTOM

Or.   *Orationes*

DIODORUS SICULUS

Bib.   *Bibliotheca historica*

DIOGENES LAERTIUS

Vit.   *Vitae philosophorum*

EPICTETUS

Diss.   *Dissertationes*

EURIPIDES

Alc.   *Alcestis*

EUSEBIUS

Hist. eccl.   *Historia ecclesiastica*

PE   *Praeparatio evangelica*

GALEN

Adv. Lyc.   *Adversus Lycum*

Diff. febr.   *De differentiis febrium*

Temp.   *De temperamentis*

HELIODORUS

Aeth.   *Aethiopica*

HERMOGENES

Prog.   *Progymnasmata* (sp.)

HERODOTUS

Hist.   *Historiae*

HOMER

Il.   *Iliad*

Od.   *Odyssey*

ISOCRATES

Antid.   *Antidosis*

JOHN CHRYSOSTOM

Capt. Eutrop.   *Homilia de capto Eutropio* (dub.)

Hom. Heb.   *Homiliae in epistulam ad Hebraeos*

JOSEPHUS

Ant.   *Jewish Antiquities*

JW   *Jewish War*

JUSTIN

1 Apol.   *First Apology*

LACTANTIUS

Epit.   *Epitome of the Divine Institutes*

MINUCIUS FELIX

Oct.   *Octavius*

NICOLAUS

 Prog.   *Progymnasmata*

ORIGEN

 Cels.   *Contra Celsum*

 Hom. Exod. *Homily on Exodus*

OVID

 Metam. *Metamorphoses*

PHILO OF ALEXANDRIA

 Abraham *On the Life of Abraham*

 Agriculture *On Agriculture*

 Alleg. Interp. *Allegorical Interpretation*

 Cherubim *On the Cherubim*

 Confusion *On the Confusion of Tongues*

 Creation *On the Creation of the World*

 Decalogue *On the Decalogue*

 Dreams *On Dreams*

 Drunkenness *On Drunkenness*

 Embassy *On the Embassy to Gaius*

 Flaccus *Against Flaccus*

 Flight   *On Flight and Finding*

 Giants   *On Giants*

 Good Person *That Every Good Person Is Free*

 Heir   *Who Is the Heir?*

 Joseph *On the Life of Joseph*

 Migration *On the Migration of Abraham*

 Moses   *On the Life of Moses*

 Names *On the Change of Names*

 Planting *On Planting*

 Posterity *On the Posterity of Cain*

 Prelim. Studies *On the Preliminary Studies*

 QE   *Questions and Answers on Exodus*

 QG   *Questions and Answers on Genesis*

 Rewards *On Rewards and Punishments*

 Sacrifices *On the Sacrifices of Cain and Abel*

 Sobriety *On Sobriety*

 Spec. Laws *On the Special Laws*

 Unchangeable *That God Is Unchangeable*

 Virtues *On the Virtues*

 Worse *That the Worse Attacks the Better*

PINDAR

 Olymp. *Olympian Odes*

PLATO

 Crat.   *Cratylus*

 Gorg.   *Gorgias*

 Prot.   *Protagoras*

 Rep.   *Republic*

 Symp.   *Symposium*

 Tim.   *Timaeus*

PLINY

 Ep.   *Epistulae*

PLUTARCH

 Adul. amic. *Quomodo adulator ab amico*

 Cohib. ira *De cohibenda ira*

 Curios. *De curiositate*

 E Delph. *De E apud Delphos*

 Frat. amor. *De fraterno amore*

 Garr.   *De garrulitate*

 Is. Os.   *De Iside et Osiride*

 Pomp. *Pompeius*

 Quaest. conv. *Quaestionum convivialum libri*

 Thes.   *Theseus*

 Virt. mor. *De virtute morali*

POLYBIUS

 Hist.   *Historiae*

Abbreviations

PORPHYRY
    Abstin.   *De abstinentia*

QUINTILIAN
    Inst.   *Institutio oratoria*

SENECA
    Ep.   *Epistulae morales*
    Herc. Oet.   *Hercules Oetaeus*

SEXTUS EMPIRICUS
    Pyrr. hyp.   *Pyrrhoniae hypotyposes (Outlines of Pyrrhonism)*

STOBAEUS
    Ecl.   *Eclogae*

TACITUS
    Ann.   *Annales*

TERTULLIAN
    Modesty   *On Modesty (De pudicitia)*

THUCYDIDES
    Hist.   *Historiae*

XENOPHON
    Mem.   *Memorabilia*

Anonymous Ancient Works

Rhet. Her.   *Rhetorica ad Herennium*

Modern Works, Series, and Collections

BDAG   *Greek-English Lexicon of the New Testament and Other Early Christian Literature.* Edited by F. W. Danker. 3rd ed. Chicago: University of Chicago Press, 2000.

NPNF   *Nicene and Post-Nicene Fathers.* 2 series. Edited by P. Schaff and H. Wace. 28 vols. Repr. Peabody, MA: Hendrickson, 1994.

OTP   *Old Testament Pseudepigrapha.* Edited by J. H. Charlesworth. 2 vols. Garden City, NY: Doubleday, 1983–1985.

PG   Patrologia graeca [= Patrologiae cursus completus: Series graeca]. Edited by J.-P. Migne. Paris, 1857–1866.

SIG   *Sylloge inscriptionum graecarum.* Edited by W. Dittenberger. 4 vols. 3d ed. Leipzig: S. Hirzelium, 1915–1924.

TDNT   *Theological Dictionary of the New Testament.* Edited by G. Kittel and G. Friedrich. Translated by G. Bromiley. Grand Rapids: Eerdmans, 1964–1976.

Hebrews

Introduction

The Epistle to the Hebrews has played an important role in shaping the faith of the Christian church. Its rich imagery is evident in the church's hymnody, and its memorable phrases have shaped Christian discourse. To speak of drawing nearer to God, marching to Zion, entering the promised land, finding a place of rest, and approaching the divine mercy seat is to enter into the world of Hebrews. Its description of the work of Christ as the offering of the great high priest and its emphasis on the humanity of the one who was "tempted in every respect" (4:15) has been the basis for Christian theological reflection for generations. As the book with the longest sustained argument in the NT, Hebrews is one of the earliest examples of Christian theology as faith seeking understanding.

Despite its honored place in liturgy and theology, it is probably the most mysterious book in the NT. William Wrede labeled it "the riddle of the New Testament" (1906), and Erich Grässer described it (1993, 2:18), in words drawn from the book itself, as "the word that is hard to explain" (cf. Heb 5:11). This mystery includes the absence of information about the identity of the author or the original recipients and their location. Despite the title in early manuscripts, "To the Hebrews," and the title in later translations, "The Epistle of Paul to the Hebrews," the book identifies neither the recipients nor the author. Moreover, both the absence of the normal epistolary conventions, including the identity of the author and readers, and the distinctive literary form suggest that Hebrews can scarcely be included among the Epistles.

The book also includes mysterious modes of argumentation that contribute to the riddle. Its claim that "it is impossible to restore to repentance those who have fallen away" (6:4–6) has puzzled Christians since the second century. Its description of the mysterious figure of Melchizedek (7:1–10) has also been the source of endless speculation. Only the author of Hebrews describes the work of Jesus in high priestly and sacrificial terms. Thus the placement of Hebrews between the letters of Paul and the General Epistles reflects an awareness among earlier scholars of the work's distinctiveness.

The Historical Puzzle: Author and Audience

The Author

One dimension of the mystery of Hebrews is the authorship of the book. Although the book is anonymous, Hebrews has been included among the letters of Paul since ancient times. As early as the second century, Christians in the East attributed the letter to Paul. The oldest complete extant manuscript of Hebrews, $\mathfrak{P}^{46}$, placed Hebrews after Romans in the collection of Pauline writings, as did numerous later manuscripts. Indeed, no evidence is available to suggest that Hebrews ever circulated independently or in any collection other than that of Paul (Eisenbaum 2005, 218–19). In Alexandria, where Hebrews was most influential, church leaders attributed the work to Paul and attempted to explain the anonymity of the book. Pantaenus (d. ca. AD 190) suggested that Paul omitted his name because of modesty (Eusebius, *Hist. eccl.* 6.14.4), while Clement of Alexandria suggested that Paul omitted his name because, as the apostle to the Gentiles, he would evoke suspicion among Jewish listeners (Eusebius, *Hist. eccl.* 6.14.3).

Although ancient writers included Hebrews among the letters of Paul, many recognized problems in the attribution of Pauline authorship. The anonymity of the book and its refined Greek distinguished it from the Pauline letters. Clement of Alexandria recognized the stylistic differences between Hebrews and the letters of Paul and suggested that Paul wrote the letter in Hebrew and that Luke translated it into Greek (Eusebius, *Hist. eccl.* 6.14.2). Origen also recognized the stylistic differences between Hebrews and the Pauline letters,

Clement and Origen

Clement of Alexandria was born around AD 145 or 150 and died around 215–216 in either Athens or Alexandria (more likely the former). He became part of the catechetical school under Pantaenus ca. 190 and succeeded him as headmaster on his death, ca. 200. Origen (ca. AD 185–254), one of his students, succeeded Clement as head of the catechetical school. Origen possessed a powerful intellect and quickly gained a reputation as an exegete and theologian. He is best remembered for his major theological treatise, *De principiis*, the *Hexapla* (his parallel edition of Hebrew and Greek versions of the Old Testament), *Contra Celsum* (a lengthy rebuttal of an earlier pagan critic of Christianity), and his numerous commentaries.

concluding, "Who wrote the epistle, God truly knows" (Eusebius, *Hist. eccl.* 6.24.11–14). However, Origen commonly cited Hebrews as a letter of Paul (Koester 2001, 21, 41–42), and the Eastern church treasured this writing. The Western church, in its struggle with problems over those who lapsed in persecution and troubled by the references to the impossibility of repentance (6:4–6; 10:26–31; 12:16–17), contested Pauline authorship. Tertullian (ca. AD 160–225) proposed that it was written by Barnabas (*Modesty* 20; Koester 2001).

Although Pauline authorship was generally accepted during the Middle Ages and the Reformation, questions continued to be raised about the authorship of the book, leading scholars to speculate on the identity of the author. Luther, for example, suggested that Apollos might be the author of Hebrews. In the modern era, scholars are virtually unanimous in concluding that Paul was not the author, and some have suggested the names of possible alternatives, including Luke, Barnabas, Apollos, and Priscilla. However, since no evidence exists to support a specific name from a list of candidates known to us from the NT, the attempt to identify the name of the author is not a worthwhile task, for this search involves only speculation.

Although the name of the author is unknown, the book offers abundant evidence of the author's background, education, worldview, relationship to the readers, and period of activity. The masculine participle in 11:32 suggests that the author is male. He claims neither apostolic authority nor a place in the first generation. Unlike Paul, he never offers himself as an example or speaks autobiographically. He refers to the leaders of the community, but does not claim to be one of them (cf. 13:7, 17, 24). He speaks, not on his own authority, but argues on the basis of scripture. With the community that he addresses, he belongs to the second generation that received the message "from those who heard him" (2:3). More than any other writer of the NT, he speaks in hortatory subjunctives ("let us"), identifying himself with his listeners.

The postscript in 13:18–25 adds another dimension to the mystery surrounding the author, for this section not only mentions Timothy (Paul's co-worker?) but also contains the familiar phrases that are found in the Pauline letters. Here the author speaks in the first-person singular and offers information about himself. He requests the prayers (13:18) of the community and expresses his desire to be restored to them soon (13:19) along with Timothy (13:23), who has recently been released. The concluding greetings (13:24) and benediction (13:25) also correspond to the ending of Paul's letters. Scholars have interpreted this postscript in two different ways. Some have argued that the postscript belongs to the later hand of someone who desired to integrate this work within the Pauline letter collection (cf. Grässer 1997, 3:409). Others suggest that the reference to Timothy is an indication that the author, like Timothy, belongs to a Pauline circle.

Scholars have also examined the themes in Hebrews for evidence of dependence on the letters of Paul. The two writers occasionally cite the same texts

Periodic Sentence

A periodic sentence is a carefully structured statement in which a balance is created by the word order, or syntax, that may be described in terms of a path "around," literally going in a circle and returning to where the sentence began. According to the rhetorical handbooks, the building blocks of the periodic sentence are the clauses (*kommata* = brief phrases and *kōla* = complete clauses) that the orator weaves together. Some orators arranged clauses antithetically, while others employed parallelism or a series of subordinate clauses. Most of the rhetorical handbooks, including those of Aristotle, Theophrastus, Demetrius, and Cicero, gave attention to the periodic sentence. According to Demetrius (*Eloc.* 16–18), the periodic sentence is composed of two to four clauses (*kōla*). The refined style gives grandeur to a speech (45–47) but is inappropriate for letters (229). Although Paul occasionally exhibits stylistic refinement (cf. 1 Cor 13; 2 Cor 4:16–18), he does not employ the periodic sentence. The prologue of Luke is a good example of this style. Hebrews employs the periodic sentence in 4:12–13; 5:7–10; 7:1–3; 12:18–24.

(e.g., Jer 31:31–34 in 2 Cor 3:6; Heb 8:7–13; 10:16–17; Hab 2:4 in Rom 1:17 and Heb 10:38) and share such themes as the faith of Abraham (Rom 4; Gal 3) and the validity of the law. Nevertheless, the author's use of these texts rarely shares significant themes with Pauline usage. Thus the view that the author belongs to a Pauline circle remains inconclusive.

The evidence indisputably indicates that the author was well educated, displaying a linguistic refinement that is without parallel in the NT. Ceslas Spicq identified 152 words in Hebrews that appear nowhere else in the NT, of which most come either from the LXX or from educated Greek circles (Spicq 1952, 1:157). The author also speaks in complex periodic sentences (1:1–4; 2:2–4; 5:7–10; 7:26–28) that were characteristic of linguistic refinement. He delights in alliteration (cf. 1:1, *polymerōs kai polytropōs palai . . . patrasin . . . prophētais*), internal rhyme (5:8, *emathen aph' hōn epathen*, "he learned from what he suffered"), and anaphora (11:3–39, "by faith . . . by faith . . . by faith . . ."). He employs a sophisticated rhetorical vocabulary and uses metaphors that are derived from the law courts (cf. 6:16; 7:7), athletics (12:1–2), and education (5:11–14), all of which were at home among Greek philosophers and rhetoricians. He was also acquainted with Greek philosophical categories (see below, pp. 23–26).

The Audience

The identity of the recipients is as mysterious as the identity of the author, who gives few clues about their location or the date of the book. The final greeting, "Those who are from Italy greet you" (13:24), is the only reference to a location, but it is ambiguous, for it can mean either that the author is in Italy writing to a community in a distant place or that the author is writing to a community in Italy. Some scholars have argued vigorously that the community lives in Rome (Lane 1991a, lviii–lx; Weiss 1991, 76; Ellingworth 1993, 29), noting that Hebrews was first quoted by Clement of Rome at the end of the first century. Others (John Chrysostom; Westcott 1890; P. Hughes 1977; Isaacs 1992) have suggested a destination in Jerusalem, maintaining that the argument based on the sacrificial system would be most intelligible to a Jerusalem community. However, proposals for the location of the readers, like those identifying the author, reflect more the scholar's dissatisfaction with the mystery surrounding Hebrews than any supporting evidence.

Similarly, the author gives few clues about the dating of this homily. Since the central argument focuses on the sacrificial system, many scholars have attempted to correlate the argument with the destruction of the temple in Jerusalem, maintaining that the use of the present tense for the activities of the tabernacle suggests a date before the destruction of the temple in AD 70. On the other hand, Marie Isaacs (1992, 67) has argued that Hebrews was written between 70 and 90 in order to reassure the community that atonement is possible without animal sacrifices. Inasmuch as Hebrews argues on the basis of the tabernacle rather than the temple, one cannot draw conclusions about the date of Hebrews by referring to the destruction of the temple in AD 70. The fact that writers spoke of the cultic activities in the present tense after the destruction of the temple (Josephus, *Ant.* 3.151–224) suggests that we can draw no conclusions based on the use of the present tense. The date remains unknown and of only marginal importance for understanding the book, for our interpretation requires that we know not the location or the date of the composition of this work but the issues that the author confronts.

Ancient Christian writers assumed that the homily was addressed to Jewish Christians, as the title *To the Hebrews* suggests. The earliest identification we have after Clement and Origen comes from John Chrysostom (ca. 347–407), who located the addressees "in Jerusalem and Palestine" (Isaacs 1992, 24, 39). Nevertheless, we cannot be sure that *To the Hebrews* is an accurate description of its original recipients, for the author never refers specifically to the ethnic background of the readers. Although the superscription is to be found in all extant manuscripts, it probably reflects an inference based on the content of the work rather than information about the recipients of the book.

Some modern commentaries continue to maintain that Hebrews is a letter written to Jewish Christians who were tempted to return to Judaism. This conclusion is based on the author's consistent argument for the superiority of Christ to the institutions of the OT and his appeal to the authority of the OT. The author's argument for the superiority of Christ would, according to this view, be intelligible only to a Jewish Christian audience that was having difficulty breaking its ties with the Jewish tradition. However, this reconstruction ignores the numerous references in the book to the situation of the readers. As is the case with authorship, the best evidence for the historical situation of the readers is to be found in the numerous references in the exhortations. In references to their situation, the author mentions a need to correct false teaching (13:9) only once, and he never indicates that the readers are Jewish Christians who are tempted to return to Judaism. Instead, he gives a coherent picture of the issues that his community now faces. The community's current situation becomes evident in (1) the implied narrative of the community's history, (2) direct statements about their situation, (3) warnings about future dangers, and (4) possible allusions to their situation. We may combine this information with the insights drawn from historical and sociological analogies to gain a better understanding of the readers' situation.

1. The author refers to the narrative of the community's existence that extends from their conversion to the time of writing. He recalls the "earlier days" (10:32) when their original leaders had taught them the word of God (13:7; cf. 2:3). The readers were then "enlightened" (6:4; cf. 10:32), became "partakers of the Holy Spirit" (6:4), and experienced the powers of the coming age (6:5). Shortly after their conversion they experienced the trauma of persecution that resulted in imprisonment, public abuse, confiscation of property, and other forms of suffering (10:32–34; 12:4–11). Their suffering was probably not officially sponsored by civic authorities, but was not unlike the experience of new converts elsewhere who had alienated themselves from their relationships and shamed their families by their conversion. The readers responded with extraordinary community solidarity (6:10; 10:32–34) to this suffering.

Recent sociological analyses have illuminated the situation of this community by observing that its history conforms to common patterns within religious groups. At the beginning, many people accepted the Christian claim that the crucified and exalted Christ was the ultimate revelation of God and that the whole universe was subject to him. The one who stood in control of all reality demanded their total allegiance, separating them from all other loyalties and creating a new community of those who shared this view of reality. This all-encompassing claim created hostility among the populace, which responded by subjecting the new movement to abuse. Thus in a society that valued honor above all else, the readers have experienced the shame of losing their place in the world (DeSilva 2000, 18). Despite their alienation from society, they could maintain their commitment because their teachers had initiated them into an alternative symbolic world in which Jesus Christ is Lord and reinforced their commitment with the solidarity of an alternative family in the community of faith. Therefore, like countless other new religious movements, this community began with a period of enthusiasm that empowered it to adopt an alternative worldview that evoked the hostility of the populace (Salevao 2002, 132).

2. The current status of the readers is evident in the author's distinction between "earlier days" (10:32) and the time in which he writes (cf. 5:12). The

community belongs to the second generation after their original leaders have died (cf. 13:7), for the message was first declared to them "by those who heard him" (2:3). They now have drooping hands and weak knees (12:12). The author speaks of their current situation when he says, "You have become dull of hearing" and "you ought to be teachers because of the time" (5:11–12). Some are abandoning the assembly (10:25) and "need endurance" (10:36). Despite the history of alienation, he also indicates that no one has died (12:4).

The current situation of the readers also conforms to the common patterns among new religious movements, which with the passage of time lose their initial intensity and wonder if the price for commitment is too high. The recipients of Hebrews have experienced the dissonance between the Christian claim and the reality they experience, for they do not see the world in subjection to the Christ. Having experienced the loss of property and status without seeing rewards commensurate to their loss, the group now faces the loss of solidarity: "While they could accept their loss in the fervor of religious solidarity, living with their loss has proven difficult" (DeSilva 2000, 19), leading them to ask if it is worth it to be a Christian. The readers are grappling with the religious instruction that they received at the beginning in the context of their contemporary experience, trying to make sense of them both (Isaacs 1992, 13). According to David DeSilva, "From a sociological perspective, the

Persecution and Social Ostracism in the Early Church

Although the Roman government conducted no comprehensive persecution designed to crush Christianity before the one promulgated by the emperor Decius in AD 249–51, strong opposition to Christianity existed from the beginning, often leading to governmental intervention against the Christians. Both 1 Peter (cf. 4:4) and the letters of Paul (cf. Phil 1:28; 1 Thess 1:6; 3:3) refer to external opposition experienced by the community, while Revelation probably refers to extensive localized persecution (cf. 2:9–10, 13; 6:9–11). In recalling the persecution of Christians by Nero after the fire of Rome (AD 64), Tacitus (ca. AD 56–ca. 115) indicates Roman attitudes long after the event, referring to Christianity as a "superstition" and a "disease" and to Christians as a people "loathed for their vices" (Tacitus, *Ann.* 15.44).

Public hostility to Christians was based on several factors. The primary cause was their exclusive claim to religious truth, which led to extensive proselytizing. The confession that "Jesus is Lord" (cf. Phil 2:11) was an implicit challenge to the Roman imperial order. Conversions often resulted in division within families (cf. 1 Pet 3:1–7) and the breaking of social ties with close associates (Elliott 1981, 80). The rejection of pagan religion also led to withdrawal from civic life (1 Pet 4:4). As a result, rumors of Christian misdeeds circulated among the populace, and Christians inherited many of the same charges that ancient people made against Judaism.

crisis appears to be one of the survival of the integrity of the sect as a viable subculture within the host society. The cost of maintaining the identity of the sect is, for some members at least, rising above the value of such an enterprise" (1994, 10).

3. In the numerous paraeneses, the author warns his readers about the dangers he envisions. He is concerned lest they "drift away" (2:1), "fall away" (3:12), "fall short" (4:11), "fall" (6:6), "sin deliberately" (10:26), throwing away the confidence that they have gained in Christ (10:35). The fact that the references to the threat facing the community are not specific (Isaacs 1992, 27) suggests that the author is more concerned with the community's abandonment of the faith than with any alternative they might take.

4. Some allusions may provide further insight into the community's situation. When the author concedes in 2:8 that "we do not yet see all things in subjection to him," he is probably speaking for the community that struggles with the dissonance between its confession and the realities of alienation. The description of Jesus' solidarity with humanity in suffering (2:10–18) undoubtedly reflects the author's desire to address the community's painful situation. The imagery of the people who are being tested on the way to the promised land (3:7–4:11) also suggests that the readers are tempted to abandon their faith. The emphasis in Heb 11 on the people of God as "sojourners" and "aliens" (cf. 11:13–16, 38) who are homeless in this world and subject to abuse (11:26) probably reflects the situation of the readers. The reminder that Jesus experienced "shame" and endured the cross (12:2) suggests that the author is addressing a community that has a history of alienation and shame.

The Literary Puzzle: Genre and Structure

The mystery of Hebrews extends to its distinctive literary form and structure, which are essential elements in the author's attempt to persuade his audience to remain faithful. The genre is not merely the container for the author's message, nor is the structure merely the table of contents. Both the genre and the structure are intertwined with the message to have the maximum persuasive impact on the wavering audience. The analysis of the genre and the structure reveals the author's major emphasis and the relationship of the themes of the homily to each other.

Literary Genre

Except for the final chapter, the book lacks the essential characteristics of a letter. Unlike the Pauline letters, which commonly proceed from a recitation of prior events toward theology and exhortation, Hebrews is a series of biblical expositions, each followed by an exhortation that actualizes the passage for the audience. Although the author, like Paul, speaks directly to his audience

The Pauline Letter Form

Discoveries of ancient papyrus letters by Adolf Deissmann (ET 1965, 213–25) in Egypt revealed a pattern in ancient correspondence that Paul adopted in his own letters.

	Ancient letters	Paul's letters
Opening	Name of author and recipient Greeting Thanksgiving	Name of author and recipient Greeting Thanksgiving
Body	Disclosure formula ("I want you to know") Request ("I appeal to you")	Disclosure formula Autobiography Teaching Request/Ethical instructions Future travel plans
Closing	Greetings to individuals	Greetings to individuals Request for prayer Doxology

Hebrews contains only the final ethical exhortations, greetings, request for prayer, and doxology.

in a dialogical manner, stylistic features distinguish Hebrews from the letters. The author speaks frequently with the hortatory subjunctive ("let us"; cf. 4:14; 10:19–23, 24; 13:15) rather than the imperative or the first-person singular ("I appeal to you"). He emphasizes the actions of speaking and listening, as if he were speaking directly to an audience (cf. 2:5; 5:11; 6:9; 8:1; 9:5; 11:32). Only in chapter 13 does Hebrews have the familiar epistolary forms. The exhortations in 13:1–6 resemble the ethical section of Paul's letters in form and content. The conclusion in Heb 13:18–25 has elements characteristic of Pauline letters: the request for prayer (13:18; cf. Rom 15:30; 1 Thess 5:25), the expression of desire for a future visit by the author (13:19; cf. Phlm 22), a final benediction (13:20, 25; cf. Rom 15:33; 2 Cor 13:13; 1 Thess 5:23), and the final greetings (Heb 13:24; cf. 1 Cor 16:19–20). Thus the literary style of the first twelve chapters suggests that the author has employed a distinctive genre to persuade his audience.

The author describes this work as a word of exhortation (13:22), a term that is used in Acts 13:15 for the synagogue homily. Lawrence Wills (1984) has examined the word of exhortation in Acts 13:34–41 and noted its similarity to Hebrews and to other works of that period. The word of exhortation consisted of (1) *exempla* containing authoritative evidence to commend the points that follow, (2) a conclusion based on scriptural evidence, and (3) an exhortation that was joined to the presentation by "therefore." Wills observes that several speeches in Acts, including the speech of the town clerk in Ephesus (Acts 19:35–40), follow this pattern. Josephus records several speeches that follow a similar pattern (examples in Wills 1984, 295) that is also present in 1 Peter and *1* and *2 Clement*. Wills notes that the homiletic pattern of *exempla*/conclusion/exhortation is recycled in Hebrews in successive expositions.

Since this pattern exists in Jewish homiletical works, Hebrews is commonly identified as a synagogue homily. However, the pattern identified by Wills was not limited to synagogue homilies but was used also in the speeches of ancient Greek orators. The historian Thucydides (ca. 460–400 BC) also records speeches that have the pattern of *exempla*/conclusion/exhortation (*Hist.* 2.34–46; Black 1988, 14). Consequently, scholars in recent years have applied Aristotelian rhetoric to the analysis of Hebrews. Of the three types of speeches identified in the handbooks, two of them have analogies in Hebrews. Only judicial rhetoric, which calls for decisions about the past, does not fit into this form of rhetoric. With Hebrews' glorification of the status and work of Christ, it resembles epideictic rhetoric, which was intended to offer praise and reinforce the values of the audience. Since deliberative rhetoric called for decisions about future conduct, many scholars have identified Hebrews with this form of speech. Thus one can conclude that Hebrews has elements of both deliberative and epideictic rhetoric, for it contains both praise for the work of Christ and a call for action by the readers.

The author's use of rhetorical devices is evident in numerous respects. In the first place, the predominance of *synkrisis* in Hebrews, according to which the saving events in Christ are compared to the institutions of the OT, reflects the author's rhetorical training. In the second place, the author's mode of argumentation suggests rhetorical training, for he not only argues from scripture but also makes abundant use of terminology from logical

Rhetorical Persuasion and Rhetorical Handbooks

Ancient rhetorical theorists analyzed the components of effective persuasion in handbooks designed for practitioners in the law courts and other areas of public life. The two oldest extant handbooks, both from the fourth century BC, are Aristotle's *Rhetorica* and the *Rhetorica ad Alexandrum*, attributed to Anaximenes of Lampsacus (380–320 BC). All the handbooks from the fourth to the first century BC are lost. Later handbooks that included some are all of the major guidelines for orators included *De elocutione* by Demetrius (first or second century BC), several works by Cicero (*Topica, De inventione, Partitiones oratoriae, De oratore*) and the anonymous *Rhetorica ad Herennium* from the first century BC, and the *Progymnasmata* of Theon and *Institutio oratoria* of Quintilian from the first century AD (see Anderson 1999, 38–96). The handbooks delineated the types of speeches, appropriate arguments, and the arrangement and style most suitable for the audience.

Synkrisis

Ancient rhetorical theorists described *synkrisis* as comparison for the purpose of evaluation. Comparisons could involve (a) good with good, (b) bad with bad, and (c) good with bad. Thus *synkrisis* could be used in speeches of either praise or blame. According to Aphthonius (fourth century BC), one employed *synkrisis* to compare "fine things with good things or poor things beside poor things" (*Prog.* 31). According to Nicolaus, "Our subjects will be great when they seem greater than the great" (*Prog.* 61). Topics for comparison of individuals included birth, ancestry, education, health, strength, and beauty. Exercises in *synkrisis* were a part of the curriculum of teenage students of rhetoric. Plutarch's *Parallel Lives*, a comparison of Greek and Roman leaders, was a major example of extended *synkrisis*.

proof commonly in use by orators (cf. Thompson 1998; Löhr 2005). Frequent arguments based on what is "necessary" (7:12; 9:16, 23), "impossible" (6:18; 10:4), and "appropriate" (2:10) indicate the author's rhetorical training. Thus ancient readers would have recognized the author's training in both the homiletic tradition of the synagogue and Greek rhetoric.

Structure

Although most scholars agree that the structure of the homily is an indispensable part of the message, the artistry of this homily makes it a challenge for anyone who wishes to analyze its structure, as the widely divergent structural analyses of Hebrews demonstrate. The author's artistry is evident in the fact that he skillfully avoids displaying the scaffolding of his work as one topic blends into another. Consequently, scholars have identified multiple structural signals, resulting in a wide diversity of opinion. Views of the structure of Hebrews extend from structural agnosticism (e.g., Moffatt 1924, xxiii) to elaborate and detailed analyses. Some look for thematic signals to the structure of the book, while others identify either literary or rhetorical signals. The complexity of the problem is evident in the fact that several books have been devoted to the topic (Vanhoye 1976; Übelacker 1989; Guthrie 1994). No NT book has elicited a more rigorous examination of its structure.

Our view of the structure is also related to our understanding of the purpose of the book. A traditional structure of Hebrews locates the structural signals in Hebrews in the comparisons (*kreittōn*, "better than"), concluding that Hebrews is a series of comparisons intended to demonstrate that Christianity is better than Judaism. An example of this structure is found in the commentary by Philip Hughes (1977).

Christ Superior to the Prophets, 1:1–3
Christ Superior to the Angels, 1:4–2:18
Christ Superior to Moses, 3:1–4:13
Christ Superior to Aaron, 4:14–10:18
Christ Superior as the New and Living Way, 10:19–12:29
Concluding Exhortations, Requests, and Greetings, 13:1–25

This structure follows the themes of the book, focusing on the expositions but paying little attention to the exhortations that are interspersed throughout the homily. Inasmuch as the exhortations indicate that the author is not engaged in a polemic, but employs the expositions to lay the foundation for the exhortations, the thematic approach does not acknowledge the essential focus of the homily.

In the twentieth century, most scholars turned from the thematic approach to the literary aspects of Hebrews to identify the structural signals of the book. Most of the discussion has focused on two alternative approaches. Albert Vanhoye (1976) recognizes structural signals in (1) the announcement of the subject to be discussed (e.g., 1:4; 2:17–18; 6:20), (2) hook words that appear at the end of one section and the beginning of the next, (3) inclusions that demarcate the boundaries of units (e.g., 3:1 and 4:14), (4) variations of literary genre (exposition or exhortation; e.g., 2:1–4), and (5) words that are concentrated in a unit (e.g., angels in chaps. 1 and 2). Using these structural signals, he outlines Hebrews in five parts that are framed by an introduction (1:1–4) and conclusion (13:20–21):

   I. The Son superior to the angels (1:5–2:18)
  II. Christ's faithfulness and compassion (3:1–5:10)

Hook Words in Hebrews

Hook words in Hebrews link apparently unrelated topics together by concluding one section with the topic for the next unit of the book. Examples of hook words include the following:

- "Greater than angels" (1:4) introduces the extended comparison of the Son and angels in 1:5–28.
- "Faithful . . . high priest" (2:17) is a link to the comparison of the faithfulness of Jesus (3:1–6) with the unfaithfulness of the ancestors (3:7–4:11).
- "High priest after the order of Melchizedek" (6:20) introduces the discussion of Melchizedek in chapter 7.
- "My righteous one will live by faith" (10:38) is a link to the discussion of faith in chapter 11.

Table 1.
Matching Bookends for the Central Section of Hebrews

4:14–16	10:19–23
Therefore, having a great high priest	Therefore, having . . . a great priest
who has passed through the heavens	through the curtain
Jesus, the Son of God	by the blood of Jesus
let us hold fast to the confession	let us hold fast the confession
let us draw near . . . with boldness	let us draw near with a true heart

III. The central section on sacrifice (5:11–10:39)
IV. Faith and endurance (11:1–12:13)
V. The peaceful fruit of justice (12:14–13:19)

Vanhoye's structure then becomes an elaborate chiasm. The result is that the center of gravity becomes the central section on the high priestly work of Christ (5:11–10:39). Vanhoye's approach, despite its helpful insights, is not totally satisfactory. The focal point of the argument is not the high priesthood of Christ but the climactic exhortation at the latter part of the homily.

Recent scholars have insisted that any structural analysis must recognize that the theological expositions do not stand on their own but lay the foundation for the exhortation. For example, Wolfgang Nauck (1960) observed the *inclusio* in 4:14–16 and 10:19–23 and concluded that these passages form the "bookends" for the central section on the priestly work of Christ. (See table 1.) This *inclusio* results in a tripartite structure. Part 1 has an *inclusio* formed by the opening periodic sentence focusing on the fact that God "has spoken in his Son" (1:1–4) and the periodic sentence on God's word in 4:12–13. The bookends in part 2 (4:14–10:31) indicate that the exposition on the high priestly work of Christ builds the case for the exhortation to hold on to the Christian confession (4:14; 10:23). The final section (10:32–13:25) is composed primarily

---

Inclusio

Inclusio, a Latin word meaning "imprisonment, confinement," is a literary term for similar wording placed at the beginning and end of a section as a framing device. In some instances the *inclusio* marked the place for a digression from a subject to which the speaker returned, while in other instances the repetition was helpful as emphasis in oral address. Examples in Hebrews include 1:3, 13 (right hand of God); 3:12, 19 (unfaithfulness); 4:14; 5:10 (high priest); 8:7–13; 10:16–17 (new covenant). The first two major sections (1:1–4:13; 4:14–10:31) are framed in this way.

of exhortations that draw the consequences of the theological section and call for faithfulness. With the juxtaposition of the theological and paraenetic sections, the author shows that the center of gravity is in the exhortations. Thus the author of Hebrews demonstrates how theology serves preaching. Nauck's tripartite structure, which recognized the importance of paraenesis in the structure of Hebrews, has been widely accepted, often with minor variations, especially in demarcating the end of the central section and the beginning of the final section (Weiss [1991] places the end of the central section at 10:18; Hegermann [1988] places it at 10:31; and Michel [1966] places it at 10:39). This structure recognizes essential elements in the message of Hebrews.

The fact that Hebrews shows elements of epideictic and deliberative rhetoric (see above) suggests to many scholars that classical rhetorical patterns provide the model for the arrangement of Hebrews. However, despite the growing popularity of the rhetorical analysis of Hebrews, scholars have reached little agreement in determining how Hebrews fits the arrangement commended in the rhetorical handbooks. While they discover in Hebrews most, if not all, of the parts of the speech delineated by Aristotle, they do not agree on the identification of these units. For example, while some identify Heb 1:1–4 as the exordium, others extend it to include all of chapter 1 or even 1:1–2:4 (Koester 2001, 84). Scholars debate the boundaries of the *narratio*, which states the facts of the case. Übelacker (1989) and Nissilä (1979) place it at 1:5–2:18; Berger (1968) and Weiss (1991) at 1:5–4:13. The *propositio* is equally elusive. Übelacker (1989) places it at 2:17–18; Koester (2001) places it at 2:5–9; and Backhaus (1996) places it at 4:14–16.

Widespread disagreement does not, however, render rhetorical analysis impossible, for most of the disagreements involve the boundaries of each section. Scholars are in general agreement that rhetorical analysis is intended to determine the persuasive power of the argument by following its movement. Like orators who often used some, but not all, of the standard arrangement, the author has adapted numerous rhetorical strategies to persuade his audience. Thus the reader may analyze the sermon with the tools of rhetorical

Elements of the Rhetoric of Persuasion

Ancient handbooks on oratory recommended several standard elements, which speakers adapted for their own purposes, sometimes omitting one or more of them. The introduction (*exordium*) was intended to introduce the topic and make the audience favorably disposed. A narration (*narratio*) of the facts pertaining to the case commonly followed. The narration was then followed by a proposition (*propositio*) stating the case to be argued. The main body of the argument (*probatio*) offered the proofs, and the concluding section (*peroratio*) summarized the case, often with increased emotional intensity.

criticism. This commentary follows an approach that employs the tripartite division identified by Nauck and Aristotelian rhetorical analysis to determine the rhetorical effectiveness of the author.

Hebrews 1:1–4. The first four verses of Hebrews fit well with the Aristotelian definition of the exordium. The author makes the audience favorably disposed and attentive with the beautiful periodic sentence that suggests the importance of the message. He also introduces the major themes of the homily: God's speaking (1:1–2; cf. 2:1–4; 4:12–13; 12:25), the relationship between the many and the one ("in many and various ways . . . in these last days"; cf. 7:23–24; 9:26–27; 10:11–14), the purification for sins (9:1–10:18), the exaltation to God's right hand (1:3; 7:3; 8:1; 10:12), and the comparison of the superiority of the exalted Christ to everything on earth (cf. *kreittōn*, "greater than," in 6:9; 7:7, 19; 8:6; 11:16, 40; 12:24). In sum: God spoke the final word to us when the Son made purification for sins and sat down at God's right hand, becoming greater than angels (or any other object of comparison). The claim for the universal importance of the topic is a model for what one expects in the exordium (Lausberg 1998, 270). The remainder of the homily will elaborate and draw the implications for this claim as the author recycles these themes.

In the recycling of themes using *synkrisis*, or comparison, the author employs the rhetorical device of amplification, following the advice of Aristotle:

> And you must compare him with illustrious personages, for it affords ground for amplification and is noble, if he can be proved better than men of worth. Amplification is with good reason ranked as one of the forms of praise, since it consists in superiority, and superiority is one of the things that are noble. (*Rhet.* 1.9.38–39, trans. Freese 1939, 103–5)

Amplification was also a device for repeating points that had already been made (Aristotle, *Rhet.* 3.19.1–2). The remainder of the homily continues with a series of comparisons between the exalted Christ and the institutions of the OT.

1:5–4:13. The author supports and clarifies the exordium in 1:5–4:13 by extending the *synkrisis* (1:5–13; 3:1–6), clarifying its content (2:5–18), and drawing the paraenetic conclusions with examples from the past (2:1–4; 3:7–4:11). The clarification in 2:5–18 is necessary because the claims in chapter 1 do not correspond to the experience of the readers, who "do not see everything in subjection" (2:8) to the Son. Their experience of suffering and alienation has placed their most fundamental conviction in doubt. Consequently, the author introduces the humanity of Christ as a precondition for his status as exalted high priest (2:17–18). This clarification offers encouragement to the readers by interpreting their own struggle as a necessary prelude to the ultimate glory. They are following the leader who shared in their suffering in order that he might help them in their current struggles (2:17–18). Because the leader is faithful, the community should respond with faithful endurance in its present situation (3:1–4:11), knowing that it dares not reject God's ultimate word (1:1–2; 2:1–4; 4:12–13). God continues to speak through the scriptures, summoning the people to faithful endurance. The faithfulness of Jesus and the unfaithfulness of the fathers from the basis for exhortation to faithfulness. The word of God (cf. 1:1–2) has the power to expose the community's unfaithfulness (4:12–13).

Because 1:5–4:13 introduces all the themes that the author will unfold in the remainder of the homily it functions as the *narratio*, stating the facts of the case to be argued (Backhaus 2005, 58–59; Berger, 1984, 1368). The victorious christological claim (1:5–13) requires clarification in light of the community's present suffering (2:5–18). The description of Christ as the one who was "like his brothers in every respect" (2:17) anticipates the claim in 4:15 that he "was tempted in every respect." The author introduces the Son as the exalted high priest in 2:17 and develops that theme in 4:14–10:31. He indicates the dire consequences of rejecting God's ultimate word (2:1–4; 3:12–19; 4:12–13) and develops that theme throughout the homily (5:11–6:20; 10:26–31). His recollection of examples of unfaithfulness by Israel's ancestors (3:7–4:11) anticipates his summary of examples of faithfulness in chapter 11.

4:14–10:31. Since 4:14–10:31 develops the themes announced in 1:5–4:13, it conforms to what the rhetorical handbooks called the *probatio*, the major argument. The transitional exhortation in 4:14–16 is the *propositio*, introducing the main argument. The author develops in greater detail the themes of Christ's humanity and his path from suffering to triumph (4:14–5:10) as well as the exalted high priesthood (7:1–10:18), drawing the paraenetic consequences (5:11–6:20; 10:19–31). The "word" that is "hard to explain" (5:11) describes the sacrificial event that transcends earthly existence, guaranteeing the future and providing a reality to which the faltering community can hold firmly. Thus the author has built the case by the recycling of themes, employing the rhetorical device of *synkrisis* to compare the heavenly priesthood, sanctuary, and sacrifice with their earthly counterparts. As the *inclusio* of 4:14–16 and 10:19–25 indicates, this section is not meant as a polemic against a false teaching but is intended to demonstrate that the community's confession is firm and that the community can "hold on" (4:14; 6:19; 10:23). The sacrifice of Christ is the guarantee of God's covenantal promise. The central section elaborates on the purification for sins brought by Christ (cf. 1:3; 2:17–18), reassuring the community of the certainty of its confession. The guarantee of God's saving work provides access to God and the stability to persevere.

10:32–13:25. Having built his case for the superiority of the Christian confession to all alternatives, the author now reaches the climax of the homily, calling for the community to respond faithfully to the work of Christ in the heavenly sanctuary. The author builds on the previous two sections to show their relevance for his readers. The author's memory of the faithfulness of Jesus (2:17;

3:1–6) and the unfaithfulness of the ancestors (3:19; 4:2; cf. 4:11) in a time of testing corresponds to 10:32–12:11, in which the author exhorts the readers to be faithful (10:32–39; 12:4–11), recalls the faithfulness of the fathers in times of trial (chap. 11), and describes the faithfulness of Jesus (12:1–3). Similarly, the opening and concluding sections correspond in significant ways; the theme of God's speaking to the people provides the frame for the argument. The author's opening statement that "God has spoken in a Son" (1:2) and the call to pay attention to "what we have heard" (2:1) anticipate the author's "see that you do not refuse the one who is speaking" (12:25, recapitulating 1:1–4; 2:1–4; 4:12–13) and the reference to the "word of exhortation" (13:22), providing a frame for the entire letter. Those who hear the divine voice live obediently in the present (13:1–6) and follow the pioneer outside the camp, faithfully enduring abuse with him. The author recapitulates earlier ethical reflections (6:10–12) and the theme of following the pioneer (2:10) on the path of suffering. With its summary of the preceding argument and emotional intensity, the final section, therefore, conforms to the Aristotelian understanding of the *peroratio*, while the first two sections are the *narratio* (1:5–4:13) and the *probatio* (4:14–10:31), amplifying the

An Outline of Hebrews

Hearing God's word with faithful endurance (1:1–4:13)

Exordium: Encountering God's ultimate word (1:1–4)

Narratio: Hearing God's word with faithful endurance (1:5–4:13)

Paying attention to God's word (1:5–2:4)

The community's present suffering (2:5–18)

Hearing God's voice today (3:1–4:13)

Probatio: Discovering certainty and confidence in the word for the mature (4:14–10:31)

Drawing near and holding firmly: following the path of Jesus from suffering to triumph (4:14–5:10)

Preparing to hear the word that is hard to explain (5:11–6:20)

Grasping the anchor in the word for the mature: the sacrificial work of Christ as the assurance of God's promises (7:1–10:18)

The priesthood of Melchizedek as the anchor of the soul (7:1–28)

The sacrificial work of Christ as the assurance of God's promises (8:1–13)

The ultimate sacrifice in the heavenly sanctuary (9:1–10:18)

Drawing near and holding firmly in an unwavering faith (10:19–31)

Peroratio: On not refusing the one who is speaking (10:32–13:25)

Enduring in hope: the faithfulness of Jesus and the faithfulness of the ancestors (10:32–12:13)

Remembering the faithfulness of earlier days (10:32–39)

Remembering the faithful heroes of the past (11:1–12:3)

Enduring faithfully in the midst of suffering (12:4–13)

Listening to the one who is speaking from heaven (12:14–29)

Bearing with the word of exhortation (13:1–25)

author's opening words. With this rhetorical structure, the author confronts the discouragement of his community with a call to persevere.

Because the author lives between cultures, he has adopted elements from the Jewish homily and from Greco-Roman rhetoric. The ultimate test of structural analyses is the extent to which they illuminate the author's essential purpose. With this structural analysis we note that Hebrews is indeed a "word of exhortation," for the expositions lay the foundation for the exhortations. The center of gravity for Hebrews is not the exposition of the high priestly work of Christ but the call to endure articulated in the final section. The expositions serve to reestablish the community's symbolic world, and the emphasis on God's word indicates the seriousness with which the community should respond to God's word. The homily's central message becomes evident in the accompanying outline.

The Purpose of Hebrews

As the alternation between exposition and exhortation indicates, the purpose of Hebrews is to reorient a community that has been disoriented by the chasm between the Christian confession of triumph and the reality of suffering that it has experienced. The centerpiece of the author's persuasive effort is the claim that "God has spoken in these last days by a Son," which he announces in the opening line (1:1–2a) and amplifies throughout the homily (cf. 2:1–4; 3:6, 7–14; 4:2, 12–13; 5:11–6:3, 13–20; 12:18–29). The Son's coming to earth, death, and exaltation are God's ultimate word (cf. 12:24–25) to the community. As the elaboration on this theme in 4:14–10:31 indicates, this event is God's word of promise, the basis for the hope that is the "firm and steadfast anchor of the soul" (6:19), the confidence to draw near to God (4:16; 10:19), and the guarantee (7:22) of God's covenant. God's speech is both a promise and a summons "not to refuse the one who is speaking" (12:25). Thus the community that is the beneficiary of the certainty of God's ultimate promise can now live with the apparent uncertainty of its own situation, knowing that God's ultimate word is the guarantee of the future.

The author's frequent comparisons are not intended to engage in a polemic against Judaism or other competitors but to provide certainty for a wavering community and to rebuild their shattered world in order to ensure that they maintain their endurance. The theological sections indicate that the Christian experience is not only better than Levitical cultic practices but also superior to any alternative to the work of Christ. For people whose own world is shattered by disappointment and alienation from the world around them, the author offers an alternative reality that does not belong to the material world and is superior to the values of the dominant culture. In the examples of the faithful people—including Jesus himself—who endured shame and alienation because they could see what was invisible to the rest of the world (11:27), the author indicates that their suffering is not a misfortune but a sign that they have a place to belong among the people of God. While the readers may be a small minority in this world, they have a new family in the community of faith that shares their confidence in the alternative reality, providing support to them in time of need. Believers can live as strangers without seeing the ultimate triumph of God if they are able to see beyond the realities of this world.

The Story World of Hebrews

The community's own narrative, as we have seen above, involves the dissonance between its confession and the reality that it experiences. At the beginning the community learned the confession that the Son is at God's right hand, but it now lives within the sphere of alienation and testing and does not see "everything in subjection" to Christ (2:8). The author responds by reminding the community of its confession and placing its experience within all of reality.

In order to make his case, the author moves from the known to the unknown, appealing to traditions that the community shares and reminding them of their original confession (cf. 3:1; 4:14; 10:23), the common ground on which he builds his argument. This confession is consistent with early Christian traditions reflected in other NT witnesses. From early Christian tradition, the author and the community have received the confession that Jesus is the Son who has come "in these last days" (1:2), lived a sinless life (4:15; cf. 2 Cor 5:21), died on the cross to take away sins (1:3), was exalted to God's right hand (1:3, 13; 8:1), and will return (9:28). He has inherited an exegetical tradition, according to which Ps 110:1 and Ps 2:7 are interpreted in christological terms and linked with Ps 8 to describe the exalted Christ at God's right hand (1:5, 13; 2:6–8; cf. 1 Cor 15:25–27; Eph 1:20–23).

In continuity with other NT writers, the author confirms the Christian claims with an appeal to the OT, describing the readers as the heirs of Israel who hear God's voice through scripture. He assumes the biblical narrative that includes creation (1:1–3; 11:3), humanity's condition under the power of sin and death (cf. 2:14–15), and hope for a coming age (cf. 6:5) of a new covenant when God would "remember their sins no more" (8:12; cf. Jer 31:34). He also shares the prophetic hope for the consummation of the narrative when God will shake the heavens and the earth (12:26–27).

The author places the community within the story world of the Hebrew scriptures, indicating that they have experienced that for which Israel had hoped: the coming of the "last days" (1:2), the "powers of the coming age" (6:5), and the "new covenant" (8:7–13; 10:15–17; cf. 9:15–22). In contrast to God's ultimate revelation, Israel's means of atonement were a mere "shadow of the coming good things" (10:1), destined to be replaced. "Another priest" has replaced the Levitical high priesthood (7:11); the new covenant has rendered the old one obsolete (8:13); and the once-for-all sacrifice of Christ has replaced the sacrifices of the old covenant (10:1–10).

As participants in Israel's story, the community now lives between the coming of the last days (1:2) and the ultimate "day" (10:25) when Christ returns (9:27–28). He holds before the community the promise of (4:1; 6:12, 15, 17; 10:36; cf. 10:23; 12:26) and hope for (3:6; 6:11; 10:23) the reward that God once gave to the patriarchs. Indeed, the promised land that Israel did not enter is now available to the readers (cf. 4:9), and Israel's ancestors wait for the church to complete its course faithfully (11:40).

Like other NT witnesses, the author shares the apocalyptic understanding that anticipates the end of the narrative and awaits the consummation of history. Thus the apocalyptic dimension of Hebrews is an undeniable part of the author's mental furniture. Inasmuch as the community's original confession interpreted the coming of Christ in eschatological terms, one can assume that the author's community had already placed its confession within the framework of Israel's eschatological hope.

Because other dimensions of the story world of Hebrews are unique to the author, scholars have searched for the background that would have made his reflections intelligible. For example, the author's interest in the obscure figure of Melchizedek has analogies in the Dead Sea Scrolls (11Q Melchizedek) and in some strands of Judaism (2 Enoch). The author's metaphorical world of entering behind the cosmic curtain (6:19–20; 10:19) to draw near to God in the heavenly world belongs to another stream of Judaism. Ernst Käsemann argued in The Wandering People of God (1984; first published in German in 1938, and probably the most influential book on Hebrews in the twentieth century) that this imagery, along with the motif of being on the way to a homeland opened up by the forerunner (cf. 2:10; 6:20), is rooted in gnostic

Apocalyptic Literature

Apocalyptic literature, derived from the Greek apokalypsis, meaning "disclosure" or "unveiling," describes a heavenly or future reality revealed to humanity via divine messengers, dreams, or visions. Works of this kind were produced by a number of Jewish groups before and during the era of the New Testament, which shares a number of the characteristics of apocalyptic literature (see especially Revelation). Central to the apocalyptic worldview is the conviction that the world is presently in the final throes of rebellion against God, a situation that will be remedied in the near future when God intervenes dramatically to transform the world, punish the ungodly, vindicate the righteous, and establish his kingdom on earth. Most ancient apocalypses were written under the names of prominent people of the distant past (e.g., Enoch, Baruch, Ezra).

speculations. Käsemann's most important contribution was his identification of the pervasive theme of pilgrimage throughout Hebrews; his claim for a gnostic background is more problematic. Otfried Hofius (1970b) offered alternative suggestions for the background of this central theme in Jewish apocalyptic texts. Furthermore, the discoveries of the gnostic texts at Nag Hammadi have not supported Käsemann's view.

The author's reflections extend beyond the linear history of Israel's story, for he places these events on a larger canvas that includes all of reality. With the claim that the Son is at God's right hand, the author consistently demonstrates that Christian experience is the culmination of Israel's experience in time and sets out its ontological superiority. The author not only contrasts the old with the new; he claims that the new is ontologically superior to the old because it belongs to the transcendent world. The author's focus is evident in his use of comparisons, for what is "better" is ontologically superior to the object of comparison. The Son is better than angels (1:3–4, 13) because he is exalted above them. He is superior to earthly high priests (chap. 7) because only he is exalted. Consequently, the exalted high priest abides forever (cf. 1:10–12; 7:3, 24), in contrast to angels (1:7) and the Levitical priests (cf. 7:16, 23–24). Similarly, the contrast between the heavenly and the earthly dominates the author's description of the sacrifice of Christ. Christ is the minister in the "true tent" (8:2) rather than the "copy" and "shadow" (8:5). Levitical priests serve in an "earthly" sanctuary (9:1) "made by hands" (9:11) whereas Christ entered "the greater and more perfect tent" (9:11). The author associates Christian experience with those things that are invisible (11:1, 27), "not made with hands" (9:11), and "cannot be touched" (12:18), in contrast to the experience of Israel, whose institutions and leaders belonged to this creation.

The author's appeal to metaphysics is one of the dimensions of the mystery of Hebrews, for the irony is that the book most rooted in scripture uses the vocabulary of Hellenistic philosophy more than any other NT document. The distinction between the "true tent" and the copy echoes the language of Plato (*Rep.* 514–17) and his heirs. The distinction between the abiding transcendent world (1:10–12; 7:3, 24; 10:34; 12:27–28) and the transitory world also echoes the categories of Platonism (cf. Plato, *Tim.* 28–30). Moreover, the author's distinction between the one and the many (7:23–25; 10:1–14) would have been intelligible to one who had been shaped in the Platonic tradition, which distinguished the transcendent and eternal "One" from the earthly and mortal "many."

Since the seventeenth century, scholars have noticed the affinities between the argument of Hebrews and the biblical expositions of Philo of Alexandria (ca. 20 BC–AD 50), who consistently employed Platonic categories in his interpretation of the OT, maintaining that the Greek sages were indebted to the Pentateuch for their wisdom (*Spec. Laws* 4.61; *Alleg. Interp.* 1.108; *Heir*

> ## Plato
>
> Plato (427–347 BC) was born into an aristocratic family but abandoned politics for philosophy after meeting Socrates. He produced twenty-seven works in dialogue form. Central to Platonic philosophy as it was understood in the first century was the distinction between the heavenly world of "archetypes," which are unique, unchanging, and eternal, and the mundane world of "types," which are multiple, subject to change, and temporary. Only the heavenly, ideal world is ultimately real.

214). Philo and Hebrews share not only the insistence of the two levels of reality derived from the Platonic tradition; they also cite numerous passages (e.g., Gen 2:2; Exod 25:40; Josh 1:5; Prov 3:11–14) in ways found only in their writings (Runia 1993, 76). By far the most remarkable parallel is the way Heb 13:5 splices together Josh 1:5; Deut 31:8; and possibly Gen 28:15 in the same way that Philo does (*Confusion* 66; Schenck 2005, 81). Furthermore, as Spicq (1952, 1:39–91) has shown, the two writers share a common vocabulary, mode of exegesis, and major themes. Philo's description of the *logos* employs vocabulary that resembles the christological language of Heb 1:1–4 (cf. *Creation* 146; *Cherubim* 127; *Worse* 83). The two writers employ similar arguments to indicate the ineffectiveness of Levitical sacrifices (Heb 9:1–10; 10:1–18; *Moses* 2.107; *Spec. Laws* 1.257–261). Both Philo and the author of Hebrews present lists of examples (Heb 11; Philo, *Virtues* 198–225).

Despite the numerous parallels, there is insufficient evidence that the author of Hebrews was actually dependent on Philo. The two writers undoubtedly belonged to the circle of educated people schooled in both the LXX and Greek rhetoric and philosophy. The author is only a representative of many in the NT era who appropriated the categories of Platonism and Stoicism to explain the faith. Indeed, Philo is one of the major witnesses to the Middle Platonism of the period. He shares much in common with Plutarch (ca. AD 45–125) and other Middle Platonists who also employed philosophy to interpret inherited religious traditions. Both the author and Philo share with Middle Platonists a focus on the ontological distinction between the transcendent and the phenomenal world. For Middle Platonists, as for Hebrews, the individual "sees the invisible" (Heb 11:1, 27; Philo, *Unchangeable* 3; *Posterity* 15) but lives on earth as a stranger (Philo, *Cherubim* 120–121; *Dreams* 1.46). The individual searches for and finds stability only through access to the transcendent world.

The major debate in scholarship on Hebrews has been the determination of the author's intellectual worldview. We need not choose one over the other, as if the Jewish and Greek worlds existed in isolation from each other. The author lives between the world of scripture and that of Greek philosophy.

Philo of Alexandria and the *Logos*

Philo, who lived between approximately 30 BC and AD 50, was a leader of the Jewish community in Alexandria. Like other young men of the Jewish aristocracy, he received a comprehensive Greek education. He maintained his Jewish identity by keeping the laws, but he sought a philosophical interpretation of Jewish ceremonies, interpreting the laws allegorically with the philosophical categories derived primarily from Middle Platonism. He produced a large body of literature, composed primarily of commentaries on the Pentateuch.

Philo's combination of Jewish and Greek wisdom is evident in his elaborate *logos* speculation. *Logos* has a wide semantic range: word, thought, speech, meaning, reason, proportion, principle, standard, or logic. In Stoic philosophy, the *logos* was universal reason, governing and permeating the world. Some Jews and, later, Christians saw Greek philosophical speculation about the *logos* as compatible with their traditional understanding of the creative and governing function of God's "word." For Philo the *logos* is the head of all creatures, neither created not uncreated, but rather the creative word and mediator between God and creation. *Logos* functions similarly to "Christ" in Hebrews: the founder and sustainer of all things, the ultimate intermediary between God and humankind, and the exact representation of God to humanity. His *logos* speculation also offers a significant parallel to other New Testament claims that God created the world through the word (John 1:1–3) and that Jesus Christ is God's agent in creation (Heb 1:3; Col 1:15–20).

He is one among many early Jewish and Christian writers who struggled to describe their faith in the language of philosophy. His Christian confession that "God has spoken to us in these last days" through a crucified savior is irreconcilable with Platonism. Since his task is to be not a systematic theologian but a pastor encouraging his audience to hold fast to its confession, he uses Platonic categories in his claim that, although believers do not "see" the world in subjection, faithful people see the invisible. In this heavenly world of the exaltation, Christ has completed his work and now abides forever while Christians are strangers on the way to the transcendent reality. Like Clement of Alexandria, Origen, and other early Christian writers, he affirmed Christian convictions that could not be reconciled with Platonism while employing Platonic categories to interpret Christian existence. Thus while the author is not a consistent Platonist, he employs categories that were probably known to educated people throughout the ancient world. The Platonic distinction between the transcendent/eternal and the earthly/mortal could be easily incorporated into the biblical faith to provide the vocabulary for instructing believers that they should place their trust not in visible realities but in that which is beyond their perception. Christians

Middle Platonism

Middle Platonists combined aspects of Stoic and Platonic thought. According to Middle Platonists, all of reality may be divided into the two realms of the intelligible and the perceptible world. The former is characterized by "being," while the latter is characterized by "becoming." True "being" in the intelligible world exists in timeless eternity while the perceptible world is subject to constant "becoming." Consistent with this dualism, Middle Platonists distinguish between the One, which transcends the universe, and the Indefinite Dyad, the principle of duality, which is infinitely divisible. The One belongs to the intelligible world, while the latter can be seen throughout nature. For the author and for Middle Platonists, the "better" reality belongs to the transcendent world.

have access to this world, which is invisible, unshakable, untouchable, and not of this creation.

These arguments, which the author apparently expected to be convincing to his addressees, who did not "see the world in subjection to Christ," form the basis for his exhortation to hold fast. Thus the author places his readers within the sphere of totality in order that they "hold fast" to their possession. The assumptions of Middle Platonism provide him with a useful means to develop his argument, pointing his readers to the reality beyond what they see. Those who possess the invisible, eternal reality can have the courage to withstand the visible and temporary time of wandering through the wilderness.

Encountering Hebrews Today

Ghanaian theologian Kwame Bediako (2000) remarks, "Hebrews is our epistle" because its claim that the priestly work of Christ ends all sacrifices challenges a society that turns to tribal and national priests (28) to meet human needs. Those themes that resonate with Africans, however, are largely foreign to the people of Europe and North America, who have no experience with animal sacrifices. Moreover, the cosmology of Hebrews, with its overtones from Jewish apocalyptic thought and Middle Platonism, are remote for the modern reader. Thus the sustained argument over obscure themes makes Hebrews a particular challenge for many modern readers.

Hebrews is not likely to resonate with readers who, like older interpreters, regard the book as a theological polemic against Judaism. However, readers who observe the pastoral and rhetorical dimensions of the homily may recognize the continuity between the original audience and many communities today and discover that "Hebrews is our epistle" as well. The author's invitation to "bear with this word of exhortation" (13:22), despite the extended argument that is "hard to explain" (5:11), is also an invitation to contemporary readers to hear this homily just as the author invited his original listeners to hear the words of scripture once more.

If the point of contact for the African reader is the claim that the sacrifice of Jesus ends all sacrifices, the point of contact for other readers may be continuity between the situation of ancient and modern readers. Hebrews speaks to communities experiencing marginalization from the larger society, declining numbers, and cognitive dissonance between their Christian confession and the reality of actual experience. Those who face the problems of church renewal in a changing world may find in Hebrews a model for addressing these challenges.

The theological sections of Hebrews invite readers to see beyond the immediate context of suffering and marginalization and to recognize their place within the reality that is not limited by time and space. In his use of Platonic language to describe the tabernacle, the author challenges his readers to envision a world that is unchanging, which will be an anchor for those who live in insecurity. The author also invites readers to inhabit the world of scripture and to recognize their place in a larger narrative that begins with creation and ends with the fulfillment of God's promises. The community is the culmination of a long line of witnesses who confronted insecurity and homelessness by finding their security in another world (11:40). By locating the readers within an alternative world, the author motivates readers to remain faithful.

In acknowledging that "we do not see everything in subjection to him" (2:8), the author offers a distinctive understanding of faith, acknowledging that faithfulness involves living between the claims about the alternative world and the reality of experience. He offers no gospel of success complete with constant assurances of the benefits of believing, but depicts faith as the equivalent of endurance (10:36–39) in the midst of difficult tests. Indeed, only the author of Hebrews offers a Christology that portrays Jesus in unmistakable terms as the model of faith in the midst of testing (2:10–18). To have faith, therefore, is to endure for an indefinite period of time, even when one does not see the fulfillment of the promises (cf. 11:39). The imagery of Jesus as the leader through the wilderness on the way to the promised land (2:10; 3:7–4:11) indicates that faith involves enduring the tests that accompany the Christian community's marginalized existence, joining the predecessors who accepted this insecurity because they found their security in "things not seen."

Undoubtedly, the reason that an anonymous homily of the first century was preserved, despite the mystery surrounding it, is that it continued to address the needs of Christians in changing circumstances. Käsemann wrote the first draft of *The Wandering People of God* from a German prison in 1937. At a time when Christian leaders who challenged the policies of the Third Reich were persecuted, Käsemann found in the image of Christians wandering without a homeland an appropriate description of their place in a world hostile to Christian faith. He wrote this important book not only to break new ground in the interpretation of Hebrews but also to challenge Christians who had made peace with the policies of the Third Reich to recognize that authentic discipleship involves following Jesus through the path of suffering toward the goal: "By describing the church as the new people of God on its wandering through the wilderness, following the Pioneer and Perfecter of faith, I of course had in mind the radical Confessing Church which resisted the tyranny in Germany, and which had to be summoned to patience so that it could continue its way through endless wastes" (Käsemann 1982, 1:17, as cited in Käsemann 1984, 13). As the Christian church becomes a minority voice in Europe and North America, this homily offers encouragement to those whose faith has made them strangers in their own land.

PART 1

Hebrews 1:1–4:13

Hearing God's Word with Faithful Endurance

With the *inclusio* that binds together the first major section of Hebrews, the author focuses the attention on God's word. "God . . . has spoken in a Son" (1:2); God's word is "living and active, sharper than any two edged sword" (4:12). To say that God has spoken through a Son who is above the cosmos (1:3–4) is to recognize that this message is no ordinary word. It is the offer of a "great salvation" (2:2–3) and the promise (4:1) that the people of God will reach the ultimate place of rest (4:9). The author maintains the theme of God's speech throughout the homily, finally reminding the community of the blood "that speaks better than the blood of Abel" (12:24).

As the author begins this "word of exhortation" (13:22), the audience has not yet reached the promised land. Like their predecessors in ancient Israel they wander through the wilderness, and the promise appears more distant than ever. Consequently, their destiny rests on their willingness to "pay attention" (2:1), recognizing that they have reached the urgent moment when God speaks to them, "Today, if you hear his voice, do not harden your hearts" (3:7–8a). As ancient Israel learned, God's promise of salvation is also the oath that declares, "They shall never enter my rest" (3:11), to those who refuse to listen. Thus God's word is both the promise of salvation and the two-edged sword of judgment (März 1991, 263). Because "God has spoken to us in a Son" (1:2), "we must give an account" (literally "to whom is our word," 4:13). Only those who listen and demonstrate faithful endurance through the unpleasant conditions of the wilderness will enter the promised land.

Part 1 of Hebrews sets the stage for the rest of the homily. The author maintains the wilderness setting, describing his listeners as the people on the move toward the promised land. He introduces the theme of Jesus as the pioneer (2:10) who leads the way and consistently invites readers to follow where Jesus has gone (4:14–16; 10:19–23; 12:1–2). He insists that readers endure faithfully, even when they have not received the promises (3:1–4:13; 10:32–12:13). Thus the urgent situation demands that the people hear the voice of the God who has spoken.

Hebrews 1:1–4

Encountering God's Ultimate Word

Introductory Matters

Hebrews begins with an elegant style that is without parallel in the NT. Although it has an epistolary ending (cf. 13:18–25), it begins not with the traditional epistolary form but with a carefully structured combination of clauses in 1:1–4 (one sentence in Greek) that ancient writers called a period (*periodos*), literally a "way around" (*peri + hodos*), that organizes several clauses into a well-rounded unity. This elegant style, which is rare in the NT but common in Hebrews (cf. 2:2–4; 4:12–13; 7:1–3, 26–28; 12:18–24), reflects the author's gift for language. The literary quality of the book is evident also in the use of alliteration, with five words in verse 1 beginning with the letter *p* (*polymerōs kai polytropōs palai ... patrasin ... prophētais*).

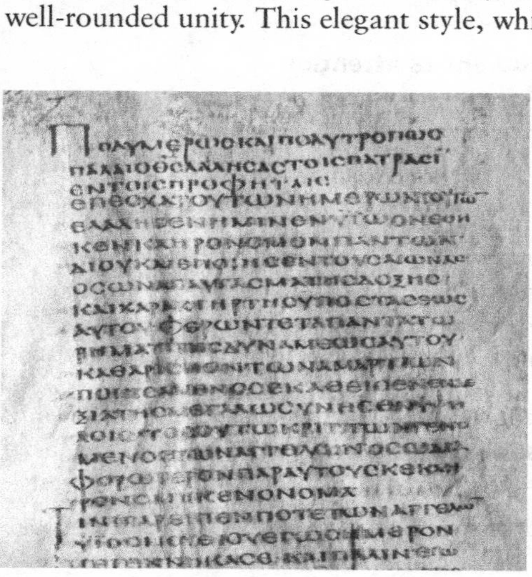

Figure 1. The Opening of Hebrews in an Ancient Manuscript.

Codex Alexandrinus is a fifth-century manuscript of the Greek Bible. The photograph shows the beginning of Hebrews at the top of the second column of folio 139 recto.

www.csntm.org

31

Alliteration, especially using the letter *p*, was also a common device at the beginning of a speech or literary work (cf. Homer, *Od.* 1.1–4, *polytropon . . . polla . . . pollōn*; Luke 1:1, *polloi . . . peri . . . peplērophorēmenōn . . . pragmatōn*).

Like ancient orators, the author has artfully developed the opening words of his sermon, knowing that the beginning of the speech, known as the *exordium*, is the most critical part of the message (cf. Berger 1977, 19). Hebrews 1:1–4 conforms to the classical understanding of the exordium, establishing the expectations of the readers and preparing the way for the message that follows. The author crafts an artful periodic sentence in place of the customary epistolary introduction in order to prepare the audience for the distinctive form of address that will follow. The opening words in 1:1–2a introduce the theme of God's speech, which the author later develops (cf. 4:12–13; 5:11; 12:24–25). The "purification for sins" in 1:3c anticipates the theme that the author develops in 9:1–10:18 (cf. 9:14, 22, 23; 10:2), indicating that the Levitical sacrifices provide the lens for the interpretation of the death of Christ. According to Exod 30:10, the Day of Atonement effected purification: "Aaron shall make atonement once a year upon its horns (of the altar); from the blood of the purification for sins of atonement he shall purify it once a year." According to Lev 16:30, the sacrifice of the Day of Atonement purifies the people from sins.

The claim that the Son has been exalted to God's right hand is a pervasive theme in Hebrews (cf. 1:13; 8:1; 10:12). The declaration that God has spoken in the past and "in these last days" anticipates the homily's consistent references to God's speech in the past and in the present (cf. 2:1–4; 4:12–13; 12:25–29).

Capturing the Audience's Attention

Ancient rhetoricians taught that the opening words of an address should introduce the topic and make the audience favorably disposed and attentive. According to the anonymous *Rhetorica ad Herennium*:

> *"We shall have attentive hearers by promising to discuss something important, new and unusual matters, or such as appertain to the commonwealth, or to the hearers themselves, or to the worship of the immortal gods; . . . and by enumerating the points we are going to discuss." (1.4.7, trans. Caplan 1954)*

In terms of style, the periodic sentence was a favorite way to begin a speech (Quintilian, *Inst.* 9.4.128; Lausberg 1998, 947), for it was an appropriate means to demonstrate that the subject matter was of global importance (Lausberg 1998, 270) and awaken the interest of an audience that was either indifferent to the topic or distracted by other issues.

The note of continuity and discontinuity between God's speech to the fathers and in a Son (1:1–2a) anticipates the comparison between the institutions of the old and the new covenant throughout the homily. Thus the author follows common rhetorical practice by providing a table of contents in the opening words of the homily.

The rhythmic praise of the Son has suggested to numerous scholars that 1:1–4 contains a hymn, in whole or in part. Indeed, comparison with other NT passages that are widely recognized as hymns reveals numerous parallels with 1:1–4. Like Heb 1:1–4, NT hymns have a christological focus, commonly describing the Son's role in creating and sustaining the universe (cf. Col 1:16–17), descent to earth, ascent to heaven, and adoration by heavenly beings (cf. Phil 2:6–11; 1 Tim 3:16; also 1 Pet 3:22). The titles describing the Son's eternal nature (i.e., "radiance of his glory," "exact representation of his being") resemble early Christian hymns, which describe Christ as the "form" (Phil 2:6) or "image" (Col 1:15) of God. The fact that these titles are used nowhere else in Hebrews has also suggested that the author is citing the words of a hymn. In addition, the parallelism and the relative clauses introduced by "who(m)" are also common features of NT hymns that are found in Hebrews. Consequently, Günther Bornkamm (1963, 198) has suggested that the prologue of Hebrews is a hymn. His view is widely accepted among scholars (e.g., Deichgräber 1967, 367; Hengel 1983, 84; Hofius 1991, 80).

These elements are not, however, sufficient evidence that the author is quoting a hymn. Indeed, most of the writers who identify the prologue of Hebrews as a hymn have difficulty demarcating the hymnic material from the surrounding prose. The introduction of major themes in 1:1–2a and 1:3b–4 indicates that the exordium is deeply rooted in the author's own message. The author's use of the periodic sentence at critical transition points throughout the homily suggests that he is not quoting a hymn (cf. 2:1–4; 4:12–13; 7:26–28). Indeed, the correspondence between the periodic sentence here and the one in 12:18–24 suggests that he has crafted this introduction to move the audience toward his goal.

Only in the present participial phrases "[being] the radiance of his glory and exact representation of his being" and "bearing all things with his powerful word" (1:3a–b) is the language noticeably different from the author's description of the Son and reminiscent of NT hymns. Although these descriptions are parallel in content to the NT hymns, the author's terminology has no parallel in the NT, which nowhere else describes the Son as the "radiance of God's glory" or the "exact representation of his being." The author of Hebrews could have appropriated these terms from wisdom literature and Philo, where they are widely used.

Whereas 1:1–2a and 1:3b–4 summarize God's revelation of the Son within history ("in these last days," "having made purification for sins"), 1:2b–3a describes the Son's relationship to the cosmos in a series of relative clauses,

---

Wisdom Literature

Wisdom literature is a genre of literature common in the ancient Near East typified by praise of God, often in poetic form, and sayings of wisdom intended to instruct about God and wise living (e. g., Psalms and Proverbs) or to reflect on the mysteries of life and death (Job and Ecclesiastes). In the apocryphal or deuterocanonical books, it designates Sirach and the Wisdom of Solomon. In this literature, wisdom is often depicted anthropomorphically: Wisdom "speaks" to the readers, pleading for them to live wisely. The designation "wisdom literature" is based on the fact that more than half of the references to wisdom are found in Proverbs, Ecclesiastes, and Job. The Greek word *sophia* appears more than one hundred times in Sirach and the Wisdom of Solomon. Occasionally, personified Wisdom is depicted as God's agent in creating and governing the world (Prov 8). The portrayals of Christ in John 1:1–14; Col 1:15–20; and Heb 1:1–4 resonate with images drawn from personified Wisdom.

---

all in the present tense, that echo Hellenistic reflection about Wisdom and the *logos* as mediators between God and the world. "All things" is a common designation for the totality of the universe (cf. John 1:3; Rom 11:36; 1 Cor 8:6; Heb 2:10) in Hellenistic philosophy that was adopted in the literature of Hellenistic Judaism (cf. Philo, *Spec. Laws* 1.208; *Heir* 36). God made his firstborn Son (cf. 1:6) "heir" of all things, fulfilling the promise to David that he would receive the nations as an "inheritance" (Ps 2:8; Koester 2001, 178). "Through whom he made the worlds" echoes NT affirmations about the Son's role in creation (cf. John 1:1–3; 1 Cor 8:6) and is reminiscent of the claims in Hellenistic Judaism of the role of Wisdom and *logos* in the creation of the world (cf. Prov 8:22; Wis 7:22). "Worlds" (*aiōnes*), which is parallel to "all things," can be used either temporally to mean "ages" (cf. 1:8; 6:5, 20) or spatially to mean "worlds" (cf. 11:3). The parallel to "all things" suggests that the author is speaking in spatial terms to describe the cosmos, probably including both the heavenly and the earthly world that will be the subject of the later discussion in the homily. In subsequent comments about the creation, the author does not mention the Son's role, but describes God as the one who created all things (2:10) by his word (11:3).

In 1:3a–b, the author employs the present tense to describe the Son's relationship to God and to the creation in language that Hellenistic Jewish writers, especially Philo of Alexandria, employed to describe Wisdom (*sophia*) and the word (*logos*). The "reflection of his glory and exact representation of his being" are parallel phrases that employ separate metaphors to describe the relation of the Son to God. "Reflection" (*apaugasma*) and "exact representation" (*charaktēr*) are parallel, just as "glory" (*doxa*) is parallel to "being" (*hypostasis*). "Glory" suggests the image of a shining light reminiscent of OT theophanies where the glory of God appeared (Weiss 1991, 145; Spicq 1994, 1:366; cf. Exod 16:10; 24:16; 33:18; 40:34–35; Lev 9:6, 23; Num 14:10; 16:19; 17:7 LXX [16:42 NRSV]; 20:6); thus it denotes the reality of God. *Apaugasma*, which can have either the active sense of "radiance," the view held by most of the church fathers (BDAG, 99), or the passive sense of "reflection," probably has the latter meaning here, as the parallel with *charaktēr* suggests. One may compare the description of Wisdom as the "reflection of eternal light," a "spotless mirror of the working of God," and the "image of his goodness" (Wis 7:26). Similarly, Philo's use of *apaugasma* as a synonym for "copy" (*Creation* 146; *Planting* 50) suggests that the author's focus is the likeness of the Son to the Father. The parallel metaphor is drawn from the reproduction of images to produce an "exact representation" (*charaktēr*). *Hypostasis*, rendered here as "being," has a wide variety of meanings, including *actual being, essence, reality, plan, confidence, undertaking,* or *situation* (BDAG, 1041; cf. 2 Cor 9:4; 11:17). In philosophical literature it described the reality behind all appearances. The term is used elsewhere in Hebrews at 3:14; 11:1. The parallel with "glory" and the image of the "exact representation" (*charaktēr*) suggests that the term refers to God's actual "being" that lies behind the image. "Exact representation" (*charaktēr*) evokes the image of the impression made on a seal or coin. *Charaktēr* was used for the likeness on a coin or trademark (BDAG) and was used metaphorically for a child as the likeness of the parent (4 Macc 15:4) or humankind as the likeness of God. Philo employs the term more than fifty times, most often as a metaphor drawn from the image on a coin. In numerous instances, he uses the term to describe the tabernacle as the likeness of the divine archetype (cf. *Alleg. Interp.* 3.102–104; *Drunkenness* 133) and the first man who was created in the likeness of God (*Creation* 69; *Alleg. Interp.* 3.95, 97; *Planting* 18). Thus Philo employs both *apaugasma* and *charaktēr* as synonyms for "image" (*eikōn*). The author's description of the Son as the "reflection of his glory and exact representation of his being" is, therefore, the equivalent of Paul's claim that Christ is the image of God (2 Cor 4:4; cf. Phil 2:6). These images indicate the Son's likeness to God in language that is indebted to the Wisdom literature and Philo.

The claim that the Son "bears all things by his powerful word" recalls ancient concerns about the potential dissolution of "all things" and the discussion of the power that holds the world together (cf. ps.-Aristotle, *Mund.* 6 [397b]). Hellenistic Jewish writers attributed this power to God's spirit (Wis 1:7), to Wisdom (Wis 7:27), or to God's word (Sir 43:26). In some instances Philo describes God as the one who sustains the world (cf. *Creation* 46; *Spec. Laws* 1.224; *Dreams* 1.157; *Decalogue* 155), while in other instances the *logos*, or "word," is the power appointed by God (cf. *Migration* 6) to sustain the world (cf. *Planting* 8; *Flight* 112; *Heir* 188). Colossians 1:17, like Heb 1:3, attributes to Christ a role not only in creating but also in sustaining the universe. Thus the claim that he bears all things would have been intelligible to readers who were educated in the literature of Hellenistic Judaism.

In the claim that the Son is "superior to the angels," the author introduces the first of a series of comparisons that pervade the homily. He often employs the term *kreittōn* (or *kreissōn*), commonly rendered "better" or "superior" (cf. 6:9; 7:7, 19, 22; 8:6; 9:23; 10:34; 11:16, 35, 40; 12:24), or other comparative forms (cf. 3:3; 7:26) to express the superiority of the Christian revelation to the people and institutions of the OT. Earlier scholars concluded from the author's frequent comparisons that his purpose was to demonstrate the superiority of Christianity to Judaism. Comparison (Greek *synkrisis*) was, however, a common rhetorical device designed, not for polemical purposes, but to demonstrate the greatness of the speaker's subject (Aristotle, *Rhet.* 1.9.39). Exercises in *synkrisis* were a common feature in rhetorical education. Thus the author's comparisons reflect not a polemic against Judaism but his desire to demonstrate the greatness of the Christian revelation.

The author may be citing or adapting the confessional tradition that the community already knows. If so, he is not introducing claims that are unfamiliar to the readers but is building his case on the basis of the community's common confession.

Tracing the Train of Thought

If the introduction of a speech is important for persuading the audience, it is especially critical for a community that has become "dull of hearing" (cf. 5:11). The opening words of Hebrews must be seen in the context of the lethargy that has overcome this second-generation community, for the author faces the formidable task of restoring the spiritual vitality that his wavering readers experienced in earlier days. Like the orators of his time, he gives special attention to the crafting of the opening words, speaking with poetic language because normal prose is inadequate for communicating the message. Thus the words come in waves, reflecting the author's own personal engagement with the topic and his desire to evoke the same response from the weary listeners.

1:1–2a. Inasmuch as the opening of a speech is no occasion to argue a new point but an opportunity for finding common ground with the listeners, the author reminds the community of the confession that it heard and accepted long ago. In 1:1–2a, he introduces the contrast between God's revelation in the past and God's

---

Hebrews 1:1–4 in the Rhetorical Flow

Hearing God's word with faithful endurance (1:1–4:13)

▶ *Exordium*: Encountering God's ultimate word (1:1–4)

God's word in a Son (1:1–2a)

The Son and the cosmos (1:2b–4)

Table 2.
God Has Spoken: Revelation Past and Present

Past	Present
In many and various ways	In these last days
to the prophets	in a Son
in the past	in these last days

revelation in a Son, anticipating the argument of the book. (See table 2.) As the main clause indicates, the central focus is God's speaking, which becomes a major theme of the book (cf. 2:1–4; 4:12–13; 6:13–20; 12:25–28). Indeed, the author places the entire narrative of God's people under the heading of God's speech in the past and present. The focus is not on *what* God has said but on the fact that **God has spoken to us** (1:1b), breaking the silence (Grässer 1990, 1:50). Indeed, the contrasts indicate the qualitative greatness of God's word "in a Son." Anticipating the series of comparisons throughout the homily, the author reassures the wavering community with the reaffirmation of its basic confession. **In many and various ways in the past** (1:1a) introduces the contrast to the revelation **in these last days** (1:2a), suggesting the incompleteness of the former and the finality of the latter and introducing a consistent theme, according to which the "many" (priests, 7:23; sacrifices, 9:25; 10:11–14) reflect incompleteness in contrast to the finality of the work of the Son and exalted high priest. The contrast between **the prophets** (1:1c) and **a Son** (1:2a) also indicates the superiority of the one over the many. Inasmuch as the author mentions "the prophets" elsewhere only in 11:32 ("David and Samuel and the prophets"), he probably uses the designation as a reference to all the agents of God's revelation, including the angels (2:1–4), Moses (3:1–6; cf. 8:5), and the Levitical system (Johnson 2006, 65). Indeed, the absence of the definite article in reference to the Son (a nuance that is omitted in the NIV's "his son"; cf. "a Son" in the NRSV) indicates the qualitative distinction between God's speaking through "a Son" and through "the prophets." God's speech to the prophets is preliminary rather than ultimate. The contrast between "the past" and "these last days" also anticipates the argument of the book, for Hebrews is a series of comparisons between the institutions of the old covenant and the work of Christ in which the latter is superior to the former (cf. 4:8; 7:11; 8:13). Thus in the focus on the finality of God's word, the author hopes to reinvigorate a sense of wonder in the community, offering certainty to a disoriented people in the fact that "God has spoken" the ultimate word.

The author, like other NT writers (Acts 2:17; 2 Tim 3:1; 1 Pet 1:5, 20; cf. Heb 9:26), identifies the era inaugurated with Christ as the "last days" described by the prophets. This contrast suggests both continuity and discontinuity in God's revelation. Continuity is suggested by the identification of the recipients of the OT revelation as **fathers** (2:16) and by the author's appropriation of

---

The Power of God's Word

The author follows OT writers in declaring that events are God's words, through which God is active as creator and redeemer.

According to Ps 33:6, "By the word of the Lord, the heavens were made." The psalmist adds, "For he spoke, and it came to be" (33:9).

According to Deutero-Isaiah, "The former things I declared long ago, they went out from my mouth and I made them known; then suddenly I did them and they came to pass" (Isa 48:3 NRSV). This word will not come away empty but will accomplish what God intends (Isa 55:11).

Just as this word acts in creation, it also actively punishes and judges those who are disobedient (Jer 23:29; see Lohse 1973, 11–12).

OT categories and scripture for interpreting the work of Christ. The reference to the "last days" also indicates the urgency of the moment, anticipating the claim that God has established a new "today" (3:7, 13–15) for the community to hear the divine voice. The constant insistence on the imperfection of the older institutions and the perfection of the work of Christ indicates the discontinuity in God's revelation. However, the author's acknowledgment that "God has spoken in the prophets" indicates that his purpose is not to denigrate the old covenant but to declare to his wavering readers that they have received God's ultimate revelation. Thus they have an incomparable privilege as well as the responsibility to listen to God's word (cf. 2:1).

The periodic sentence comes in two waves. God is the subject of the main clause, "God has spoken" (1:1–2a), and of the two dependent clauses that follow, "whom he made heir of all things" (1:2b) and "through whom he made the worlds" (1:2c). The Son is the subject of the clauses in 1:3–4. Together these two waves indicate the close relationship between the Father and the Son and narrate the cosmic drama of Christ as God's ultimate speech in a sequence that is carefully arranged to set the stage for the message that follows. The clauses, "whom he made heir of all things" (1:2b), "through whom he made the worlds" (1:2c), "having made purification for sins" (1:3c), and "he sat down at the right hand of the majesty in the highest" (1:3d), with all aorist verbs, elaborate on how "God has spoken . . . in a Son." "His coming to earth and exaltation, his word and his way are God's speech to us" (Michel 1966, 95; cf. Wider 1997, 38).

1:2b–4. The series in 1:2b–4 has an *inclusio* that declares the singular status of the one through whom "God has spoken," beginning with the reference to the Son as **heir of all things** (1:2b) and concluding with the claim that he inherited a new name (1:4). This claim reflects the close relationship between sonship and inheritance in the biblical tradition (cf. Ps 2:8). Jesus is the "heir" whose work enables his followers to become heirs of the promise (cf 6:12, 17; 11:7; cf. 9:15). The occasion for the inheritance is the exaltation of Christ, the event in the cosmic drama when the author begins and ends his description of the Son. This sequence is central to the author's message, for the exaltation of Christ is the focal point of the author's description of Jesus as Son and high priest (cf. 8:1; 9:11–14; 10:12–14). The author's affirmation is a response to the community's crisis, for he acknowledges that they "do not see all things in subjection" to the Son (2:8), although that claim has been central to their Christian identity. Thus the author's first affirmation in the series is a restatement of the conviction that the Son is "heir of all things."

Between the first and last clauses in 1:2b–4, which celebrate the exaltation of the Son, the author arranges statements about the Son in a careful sequence, first moving back from the exaltation to the first of three stages in the drama and indicating the relationship between creation and redemption. Although the author later refers only to God as the creator (cf. 2:10; 11:3), here he joins other early Christian writers in his claim that the one who is now exalted is the one **through whom he created the worlds** (1:2c; cf. John 1:3; 1 Cor 8:6; Col 1:16). This cosmological claim, like the previous one, is an assurance to a disoriented community that "God has spoken" in a Son who stands above the creation (on the author's use of *aiōnes* = "worlds," see Introductory Matters).

In 1:3a–b, the author moves from the first stage in the cosmic drama to describe the continuing relationship of the Son to God and to the world, as the series of present participles indicates. The present participial phrase **being the reflection of his glory and exact representation of his being** (1:3a) describes not an event in the story of the Son but a timeless relationship to God prior to the events described in 1:3c–4. With the images drawn from the "reflection" of light and the "exact representation" on a coin, the author emphasizes that the Son is dependent on God while sharing in God's very nature. With the present participial phrase **bearing all things by his powerful word** (1:3b), the author describes a permanent state after the creation (Meier 1985, 188) in a way that is analogous to the claim in Colossians that the whole world holds together in him.

In 1:3c–4, the author turns from the present to the aorist tense, describing the second and third stages as the culmination of the drama. Both the syntax and the subsequent argument indicate the inseparability of the events when **he made purification for sins and sat down at the right hand of the majesty on high** (1:3c) at the crucifixion and exaltation. The joining of the aorist participial phrase (lit. "having made" purification for sins) with the finite verb "he sat down" indicates the unity of Jesus' sacrificial offering and his exaltation. This inseparability is apparent elsewhere in the homily. The author's claim in 10:12 ("Having offered a sacrifice . . . he sat down") and 12:2

("endured the cross, having despised the shame, and is seated at the right hand of God") also indicates the unity of crucifixion and exaltation. Indeed, the "purification for sins" and exaltation "to God's right hand" become the focus of the argument in the central section of the homily (cf. 4:14–10:31). As 7:1–10:18 indicates, Christ was the high priest at God's right hand in the heavenly sanctuary (cf. 8:1; 10:12). He offered his own blood, not in an earthly sanctuary, but in the tabernacle that is not of this creation (9:11), and purified the human conscience (9:13). By uniting the crucifixion with the exaltation, the author has indicated that the one who has "made purification for sins" is also the triumphant one. By indicating the inseparability of the sacrificial work of Christ with the exaltation, the author anticipates the later argument that Christ is both a priest and a royal figure.

The exaltation is the event when the Son became **superior to the angels** (1:4a), a theme that the author will develop in 1:5–2:18. The saving work of Christ takes place when he enters the heavenly sanctuary. Although some interpreters have argued that the comparison of the Son with the angels is a response to a heresy involving angels, the author's comparison can best be understood when we consider the role of comparison in Hebrews and in ancient rhetoric. The fact that comparison (Greek *synkrisis*; see above, pp. 13, 36) is a common rhetorical device suggests that the author, like the rhetoricians of his time, employs comparison to praise his subject, not to denigrate the object of comparison.

With its consistent use of comparison, Hebrews associates the exaltation with the fact that Christ is greater than all objects of comparison. When **he inherited a more excellent name** (1:4b), Christ surpassed the angels, who do not share his exaltation or exalted name. This statement is analogous to claims elsewhere that the exaltation of Christ places him above cosmic powers or angels (1 Pet 3:18–22).

The author not only makes the listeners favorably disposed but also introduces the major themes of the book. The role of Jesus as Son is a dominant motif in the first four chapters. At the exaltation, Jesus was appointed God's Son (cf. 1:4; 5:5). The author never explains how the one who was declared Son at the exaltation was already Son from the beginning. Nor does he explicitly mention the descent of the preexistent one, although the reference to the "purification for sins" (1:3) at the crucifixion implies this stage in the drama. The subsequent reference to the "little while" (2:9) and the "days of his flesh" (5:7) also imply the significance of the incarnation. Thus the exaltation was the affirmation of the sonship of Jesus.

Like other NT writers, the author describes the exaltation with the language of Ps 110:1 (cf. Matt 22:44; 26:64; Acts 2:34; Rom 8:34; 1 Cor 15:25; Eph 1:20; Col 3:1). Indeed, Ps 110:1 plays a decisive role in a homily that focuses consistently on the exaltation (cf. Heb 1:13; 8:1; 10:12). The exaltation is the event when Christ received a new name and was designated Son and High Priest

The Significance of the Name

The "name" in the Bible is often synonymous with the character or identity of the person. The name of God is synonymous with God's own being and is the object of worship (Heb 13:15) and fear (Rev 11:18). A change of status is often accompanied by a change of name (Matt 16:17–18). According to Phil 2:9–11, Jesus at his exaltation received a new name that is "above every other name." As a result, every tongue will confess that "Jesus Christ is Lord."

Whereas the context of Philippians indicates that the name is "Lord," the equivalent of the divine name Yahweh, the argument of Hebrews indicates that the "name" is "Son."

(cf. 5:5–6; 6:20). The carefully arranged periodic sentence explores the full dimensions of the fact that "God has spoken," indicating that the incarnation, death, and exaltation are nothing less than God's ultimate word. This word is an offer of salvation that speaks to the church "today" (cf. 3:13), offering God's promise of the future (cf. 6:16–20) and providing certainty for an insecure community (März 1991, 263). Indeed, it is an offer of salvation spoken "to us," indicating the special place of the community as hearers of God's word. As the author indicates throughout the homily, this word also requires the community to "pay attention" (2:1), for it not only offers assurance but also holds the listeners accountable for their response. Thus the author invites the listeners to hold firmly to this promise (4:14; 6:18) rather than "refuse the one who is speaking" (12:25).

Theological Issues

In confronting the issue of church renewal with the poetic restatement of the community's faith, the author uses language that sets in motion questions that would be debated for several centuries. For the church fathers, the opening words of Hebrews provided the answer to the questions facing the church and a weapon in the trinitarian controversies, for the opening chapter's discussion of God, Christ, and the angels played an important role in the affirmation that the Son was "truly God." The claim that the Son participated in the creation indicated that he was also coeternal with the Father (cf. Theodoret, PG 82:680 on Heb 1:2). The affirmation that the Son was the "reflection of his glory" indicated the equality and inseparability of Father and Son (cf. Theodore of Mopsuestia's comments as cited in Heen and Krey 2005, 10). The church fathers appealed to Heb 1 and to the prologue to John to refute the Arian claim that there was "a time when the Son was not" (cf. texts in Heen and Krey 2005,

Arianism

Arius (ca. AD 260–336), presbyter and theologian at Alexandria, rejected the belief in the equal eternity of the Father and Son. At a synod of bishops in 318 or 319, he and his closest followers were excluded from communion. Because of the division caused by the rejection of the Arians, Constantine, the new ruler of the Roman empire, convened the Council of Nicea in AD 325, which confirmed the condemnation of Arius and his teachings. The phrases "true God from true God" and "one in substance with the Father" were included in the Nicene Creed to ensure the rejection of Arianism.

14–15). Thus the opening words of Hebrews have a firm place in Christian tradition, affirming the equality of the Father and the Son.

Hebrews 1:1–2:4 also presents a strong doctrine of revelation, as the church fathers noted in a few instances. Indeed, the author's theology of revelation provides the frame for the christological reflections, for the main clause of 1:1–4 is "God has spoken to us in a Son," and the warning in 2:1–4 is to pay attention to "what we have heard" that was "spoken by the Lord." The theme of God's word permeates the homily, reminding that God's word is both a promise of the future (6:16–18) and a warning "not to refuse the one who is speaking." With his emphasis on the God who speaks "from heaven" (12:25), the author expresses a fundamental conviction held by Christians of all ages: that the community of faith responds to a voice other than its own. In the liturgy of many churches, the reader ends the scripture lesson with the affirmation "The word of the Lord," to which the community responds "Thanks be to God," acknowledging that it stands under a word it did not invent and indicating its willingness to order its life around the revelation of God. Familiarity with the Bible may lead Christians to take the word for granted, as the author suggests (2:1–4). As he demonstrates throughout the homily, God's gracious word should not be turned into cheap grace but is always a voice that summons the people to obedience. Although the word of God is not limited to the actual words of scripture, God continues to speak in the present through the words of the past.

Just as the opening chapter of Hebrews addresses issues in the ancient church, it addresses issues in the contemporary church. The claim that "God has spoken in the past" and "has spoken in these last days by a Son" raises the question of the relationship between the testaments and, implicitly, the relation of Christianity to Judaism, an issue that dominates the entire homily. Indeed, recent literature has suggested that Hebrews is a primary source of anti-Semitism (see C. Williamson 2003, 266–67). Contrary to many interpreters throughout the centuries, the author is not engaged in a polemic against

Judaism but is a pastor reaffirming his community's commitment to its confession. Thus he denigrates neither the OT nor Judaism; nor does he speak of Jews or Gentiles. He affirms that God has spoken, and he cites the words of scripture as the voice of God. Indeed, the OT provides the narrative for the community's existence. He claims Abraham and the Israelites as the ancestors of his community, challenging the community to recognize their place as the heirs of the long history of faithfulness (11:40).

With his restatement of the community's own confession, the author indicates that the path to renewal for a weary church is the recapturing of the message that evoked its intense commitment at the beginning. The poetic language appeals to the emotions, evoking a sense of awe and suggesting the author's own passion for the confession of faith and desire to evoke the same response from the community. Thus the author's strategy for church renewal is an important model for Christians in Europe and North America who struggle with this issue. His introductory words indicate that only a passion for the Christian confession will sustain the community in a time of crisis.

Hebrews 1:5–2:4

Paying Attention to God's Word

Introductory Matters

As the connecting "for" indicates in 1:5, the series of citations in 1:5–14 is the scriptural confirmation for the christological claims of 1:1–4, and the introductory comments to the citations continue the theme of God's speaking (cf. "did he say?" 1:5, and "he says" in 1:6, 7). The author is the heir of early Christian hermeneutics of scripture, according to which the OT scriptures testify to the death and resurrection of Christ. Indeed, earlier interpreters had applied the royal Psalms 2:7 and 110:1 to the resurrection and exaltation of Christ (cf. Ps 2:7 in Acts 13:33; Ps 110:1 in Acts 2:34; Rom 8:34), as the author does throughout Hebrews (1:3, 5, 13; 5:5; 8:1; 10:12; 12:2). Moreover, this exegetical tradition combined passages. First Corinthians 15:25–27 and Eph 1:20–22 link Ps 110:1 and 8:6 to describe the exaltation of Christ (cf. Heb 2:5–9).

With the catena (Latin for "chain" or "series") of scriptures in 1:5–14, the author follows established practice in Jewish literature. Indeed, this passage has points of similarity with several documents of the Dead Sea Scrolls, including the use of brief introductory formulae (e. g., "it is written" or "he said") introducing the passages cited (Bateman 1997, 153). Hebrews 1:5–14 most closely resembles the text Florilegium from Qumran Cave 4, which gives messianic interpretations of 2 Sam 7; Exod 15:17–18; Deut 23:3–4; and Amos 9:11. The author also offers a messianic interpretation of the passages in 1:5–14 and even shares with 4Q Florilegium the messianic interpretation of 2 Sam 7 and Ps 2 (Heb 1:5). Hebrews does not, however, use the formula "it is written" here or elsewhere, but consistently introduces passages with "he says" (1:5–7) or "he said" (1:13; lit. "did he say?"). With this introductory formula, the author presents the catena as the voice of God to the Son and to the angels (1:7). According to 2:12–13, the Son responds to the voice of God. This mode of citation is one of the distinctive features of the homily, as the author cites scripture either with "the Holy Spirit says" (3:7) or "the Holy Spirit bears witness" (10:15), but most frequently cites scripture with the introduction "he said" (1:5, 13; 4:4–5; 5:5; 6:14; 10:30; 12:26; 13:5) or "he says" (cf. 1:6, 7; 5:6; 8:8).

The introductory formulae reflect the author's hermeneutic of scripture as he develops his initial claim that God has spoken "in the past" and "in these last days" (1:1) and anticipates the homily's constant interaction with the OT. In this "word of exhortation" (13:22), which is a series of expositions of OT texts, the author wants his readers to hear God's voice as it addresses their new situation. His task is to demonstrate that the OT, despite its incompleteness, remains a word that is "living and active" (cf. 4:12) for his own community (cf. G. Hughes 1979, 28). He never says that the words of the OT are fulfilled in Jesus Christ. Instead, he claims that the full meaning of the OT can be understood only in light of God's ultimate word in Jesus Christ. His christological convictions dominate his hermeneutical approach (Isaacs 1992, 69). The words of scripture are not locked in the past but continue to address the community.

Scholars in a previous generation argued that the chain of scripture references belonged to a testimonia list. Although the author of Hebrews probably inherited the combination of scriptural passages mentioned above from earlier exegetical traditions, a previously formed testimony list for Hebrews is unlikely, for the scriptures cited express themes that are interwoven into the message of Hebrews. Indeed, major themes of Hebrews are mentioned here for

4Q Testimonia

One of the most completely preserved manuscripts from Qumran is 4Q Testimonia, discovered in 1952. This manuscript, like 4Q Florilegium, is a collection of quotations linked together without transitions or comment. The quotations are messianic, and many scholars interpret them as referring to three different eschatological figures. Although this document was not written by Christians, it provides important context for the debate over whether early Christians used collections of prooftexts. Before the discovery of the Dead Sea Scrolls, the early Christian collection of prooftexts came from the third century AD. The discovery of *4Q Testimonia* has supported the hypothesis that first-century Christians also employed collections of prooftexts. The fact that early Christian writers combined texts around a theme and relied on the same passages may suggest that they were drawing from a common collection of prooftexts.

Figure 2. A Testimonia Collection at Qumran.
One of the scrolls found in Cave 4 at Qumran, called by scholars 4Q175 or 4Q Testimonia, contains a collection of Old Testament texts that the community saw as having messianic significance.

the first time. For example, Ps 110:1 provides the frame for the catena in 1:3, 13. The citation of Ps 2:7 in Heb 1:5 announces the theme of sonship, which will dominate the first four chapters, and anticipates the citation of the same passage in 5:5. The contrast between the unstable and transitory creation and the eternal being of the Son anticipates the final argument in 12:25–29.

The author quotes from the LXX in the seven citations, although in some instances he departs from it, either because he follows an alternate textual tradition or because he adapts the text for his own theological purposes. In the first (1:5a), second (1:5b), and seventh citations (1:13), he gives an exact rendering of the LXX text. In citations four to six (1:7–12; see table 3), Hebrews has only minor variations from the LXX, as table 3 indicates. The most significant variation from the LXX appears in 1:6, "let all his angels worship him," which has no precise equivalent in the LXX or the Hebrew Bible. The citation in Hebrews is either a conflation of Deut 32:43 LXX ("let all the sons of God worship him") and Ps 96:7 LXX ("worship him, all his angels") or a quotation of Deut 32:43 based on the LXX that was available to the author. Indeed, an excerpt of Deuteronomy that appears in a collection of liturgical texts printed after the Psalms in printed editions of the LXX, has the words, "let all his angels worship him" (Ode 2:43), as in Hebrews (Koester 2001, 193; Bateman 1997, 143).

Table 3.
Seven Old Testament Citations in Hebrews 1:5–13

Hebrews 1	OT Citations
5 For to what angel did God ever say, "Thou art my Son, today I have begotten thee"?	He said to me, "You are my son, today I have begotten you."—Ps 2:7
Or again, "I will be to him a father, and he shall be to me a son"?	I will be his father, and he shall be my son. When he commits iniquity, I will chasten him with the rod of men, with the stripes of the sons of men.—2 Sam 7:14
6 And again, when he brings the firstborn into the world, he says, "Let all God's angels worship him."	Let all the sons of God worship him.—Deut 32:43 LXX All gods bow down before him.—Ps 97:7 Worship him, all his angels.—Ps 96:7 LXX
7 Of the angels he says, "Who makes his angels winds, and his servants flames of fire."	who makes the winds your messengers, fire and flame your ministers.—Ps 104:4 (103:4 LXX)
8 But of the Son he says, "Your throne, O God, is for ever and ever, the righteous scepter is the scepter of your kingdom. 9 You loved righteousness and hated lawlessness; therefore God, thy God, has anointed you with the oil of gladness beyond your comrades."	Your divine throne endures for ever and ever. Your royal scepter is a scepter of equity; you love righteousness and hate wickedness. Therefore God, your God, has anointed you with the oil of gladness above your comrades.—Ps 45:6–7 (44:7–8 LXX)
10 And, "You, Lord, founded the earth in the beginning, and the heavens are the work of your hands; 11 they will perish, but you remain; they will all grow old like a garment, 12 like a mantle you will roll them up, and they will be changed. But you are the same, and your years will never end."	You laid the foundation of the earth, and the heavens are the work of your hands. They will perish, but you endure; they will all wear out like a garment. You change them like raiment, and they pass away; but you are the same, and your years never end.—Ps 102:25–27 (101:26–28 LXX)
13 But to what angel has he ever said, "Sit at my right hand, till I make thy enemies a stool for thy feet"?	The Lᴏʀᴅ says to my lord: "Sit at my right hand, till I make your enemies your footstool."—Ps 110:1

Septuagint

The Septuagint, the Greek translation of the OT, probably originated from the need of Greek-speaking Jewish communities in Alexandria to have the Bible in their language. It derives its name from the legend, recounted in the *Epistle of Aristeas*, that seventy scholars (hence the name *Septuaginta* [Greek for "seventy"] and the designation LXX; some sources say seventy-two) sent by the high priest in Jerusalem to Alexandria at the request of King Ptolemy II Philadelphus, translated the scripture. The word originally referred to the first five books of the Bible. Eventually, Greek translations of the other books of the Hebrew Bible were added. Since LXX manuscripts also included additional works (called "apocrypha" by Protestants and "deuterocanonical" by Catholics), printed copies of the LXX include those works. The LXX was the Bible of the author of Hebrews and other early Christian writers. It influenced the grammar and vocabulary of early Christians, providing terms such as *ekklēsia* (church), *diathēkē* (covenant), and *hagios* (holy one, saint). Most citations in the NT are from the Septuagint.

In order to demonstrate that the Son is "superior to the angels," the author weaves together royal psalms addressed to the king and citations that refer to Yahweh, both of which he recontextualizes to speak of the Son. Psalm 110:1, which is cited in 1:3, 13, is a royal psalm in which Yahweh assures the king, God's vice-regent, that he will triumph over all enemies. The NT regularly applies this passage to the exalted Christ (see above). Psalm 2:7, cited in 1:5, comes from a royal psalm announcing that the king enjoys a special status as God's son and will vanquish Israel's enemies. As a royal psalm, this passage came to be associated with the Messiah in Jewish thought (Schröger 1968, 37). In the NT, it appears with reference to Jesus' baptism (Mark 1:11 par.), transfiguration (Mark 9:7), and resurrection (Acts 13:33). Second Samuel 7:14, also cited in 1:5, was originally a promise to David about the permanence of his dynasty; it became a familiar messianic text in Jewish literature. Psalm 45:6–7 (44:7–8 LXX), cited in 1:8–9, was also a royal psalm praising the Davidic king for his virtues and indicating the reward that he receives.

The remaining citations refer originally to God. The citations from Deut 32:43 (Heb 1:6); Ps 104:4 (Heb 1:7); and Ps 102:25–27 (Heb 1:10–12) were addressed to God but are now given a christological interpretation. Psalm 104 praises God for his divine mastery over nature. In Ps 104:4, the emphasis is not on angels but on God's power to turn the winds into messengers and the fire and flame into servants. Similarly, Ps 102:25–27 is part of a larger hymn celebrating God's power over nature. As in the exordium in 1:1–4, the author focuses on the likeness of the Son to God as he adapts OT passages praising God to the praise of the Son. Thus the Son is "superior to angels" because

---

Hillel and Rabbinic Hermeneutics

Hillel, an early rabbinic authority, came to Palestine from Babylonia around 3 BC. He is remembered as an expositor of scripture and a founder of the midrashic method of scripture interpretation. Numerous stories about Hillel circulated in rabbinic literature, including his response to the would-be proselyte who asked him to explain the law while the inquirer stood on one foot: "What is detestable to you do not inflict upon your fellow man," a midrash of "Love your neighbor as yourself" (Lev 19:18). He was modest and tolerant and, unlike other teachers, prepared to teach the inquirer in simple terms. He is credited with establishing seven rules of hermeneutics (*middot*), two of which appear in Hebrews. The argument from the light to the heavy (*qal wachomer*) appears in Heb 2:1–4 and 10:26–31. *Gezera shewa* (two passages containing the same word interpret each other) appears in Heb 4:3–4 and 5:5–6. Hillel is also remembered for his differences with Shammai. In the disputes between the houses of Hillel and Shammai, Hillel is known for adapting the law to prevailing circumstances, while Shammai and his school are remembered as applying the law strictly.

---

he is inseparable from God. What the Torah says of God, the author says of Christ.

The warning in 2:1–4 is parallel to the climactic address to the community in 12:25–29. In both instances, the author describes the consequences of refusing the one who speaks, indicating that one does not escape the voice that speaks from heaven (2:3; 12:25; cf. 1:1–2a). In both instances the author argues from the lesser to the greater—from the giving of the law to the voice of the exalted one—to demonstrate the greatness of the Christian message and the consequence of refusing it. The same argument appears also in 10:26–31, where the author compares the consequences of disobeying the law to the consequence of showing contempt for the cross of Christ. The argument from the lesser to the greater (Hebrew *qal wachomer*), which was one of the hermeneutical rules of Rabbi Hillel, is common in the letters of Paul (cf. Rom 5:12–21; 2 Cor 3:7–11) and a favorite rhetorical device in Hebrews (cf. 10:26–31). It is consistent with the author's pervasive use of comparison (*synkrisis*).

The practical consequences of the author's claim that Christ is greater than angels become evident in 2:1–4, as "therefore, it is necessary" indicates. This transition from theological exposition to exhortation, which is characteristic of the author (cf. 3:7–4:11; 5:11–6:11; 10:19–25), indicates that theological exposition serves his pastoral purpose. In contrast to the letters of Paul, the exhortations of Hebrews, except 13:1–6, are addressed not to specific conduct but to the crisis facing the community. He is concerned that his community will "drift away" and "neglect" the "great salvation" (2:3)—that it will, like

Israel, fail to hear God's voice (cf. 3:7; 4:2, 7). The author introduces a nautical image with his concern that they might "drift away" (*pararreō*), evoking the image of a boat that runs off course. He returns to nautical imagery in 6:19 when he affirms that listeners have an anchor of the soul. Subsequent warnings elaborate on this danger facing the community (cf. 3:12; 6:4–6; 10:26–31), suggesting that to "drift away" and "neglect the great salvation" is the equivalent of falling away (3:12), falling (6:6), and sinning deliberately (10:26). The author never indicates what alternative the community is considering as it faces its crisis of faith, for his primary concern is with their "drooping hands and weak knees" (12:12) as their endurance is tested (cf. 10:36).

The author and the community belong to the second generation, having learned the Christian message "from those who heard him," the community's original leaders who taught them the word of God (13:7) but are now dead. The other references to the lapse of time (cf. 5:12; 6:10; 10:32) indicate the temporal distance between the founding of the community and its current situation. With this passage of time has come the decline of communal commitment and solidarity.

The "word spoken through angels" is the law. The OT does not mention the presence of angels at the giving of the law in Exod 19 and 20. However Deut 33:2 LXX adds: "angels were with him at his right hand." This tradition became commonplace in Jewish literature (cf. *Jub.* 1.27; 2.1, 26–27) and continues in the NT. Both Jewish writings and Paul (Gal 3:19) use this tradition in a positive way, while the author follows the less positive depiction of Acts (7:53). The context of 1:5–14 suggests the significance of this comment. The author's task is not to deny that God spoke through the law (cf. 1:1), for he affirms that the law was "valid." Instead, he continues the comparison from chapter 1. Having affirmed that the Son is greater than the angels (1:4), he now extends the comparison between the provisional and the ultimate word of God.

The author employs legal and rhetorical language to persuade his audience. English translations rarely communicate the nuance of the author's comparison between the word that was "valid" (*bebaios*) and the message spoken by the Son that "has been validated" (*ebebaiōthē*). Forms of *bebaios* are particularly important in Hebrews to demonstrate the certainty of the Christian possession (6:19) and the necessity that the community hold firmly to its possession (cf. 3:6, 14; 13:9). Here the contrast suggests a legal metaphor (cf. 9:17) for a law that is "in force" (BDAG). The legal metaphor continues in 2:3 with the claim that the message given by the Lord was "validated" by those who heard him and that God "testified at the same time" (*synepimartyrountos*). One may also note the legal language in 9:15–22 whereby the author describes the necessary conditions for a testament to be valid. The greater validity of the word spoken "through the Lord" demands that the community recognize the consequences of disobedience.

In the contrast between the word delivered through angels and the message given through the Lord, the precise meaning of "the Lord" is a matter of debate since the title (*kyrios*) may refer either to God or to Jesus. The author uses *kyrios* for God in most instances (7:21; 8:2, 11; 10:30; 12:5–6, 14; 13:6), but refers to Jesus as *kyrios* also (cf. 1:10; 7:14). According to 1:1–2, God has spoken in a Son, while in 12:25 the exalted Christ speaks to the community. In view of the parallel with 12:25 and the author's reference to "those who heard," he is most likely referring to the exalted Lord.

The "signs and wonders and powers" by which God testified evoke the memory of the exodus (Exod 7:3; Deut 4:34; 6:22; Ps 78:43) and signs of the new age. "Signs and wonders" (or "wonders and signs") is a common phrase in the NT (Matt 24:24; John 4:48; Acts 2:22, 43; 4:30; 6:8; 7:36; 15:12; Rom 15:19). The threefold "signs and wonders and powers" appears also in 2 Cor 12:12. The author describes the community's earlier experience of receiving the powers of the coming age (6:5). The author's statement that these are "distributions by the Holy Spirit" is a rare reference to the Holy Spirit in Hebrews. Elsewhere the author describes the Holy Spirit as the author of biblical texts (3:7; 9:8; 10:15) and as the possession of the Christian community (6:4).

Tracing the Train of Thought

The Victorious Christological Claim (1:5–14)

Just as ancient orators recognized that the citation of a recognized authority provides support for an argument, the author appeals to scripture to support the christological claim that the Son is "superior to the angels" (1:4), as "for" (1:5) indicates. In the catena that follows, the author continues the focus on God's word, introducing the citations as the words of God, who speaks first to the Son (1:5–6) and then to the angels (1:7) before speaking again to the Son (1:8–13). This unit reinforces the author's emphasis on the surpassing greatness of God's word in a Son.

Since the confirmation of the christological claims in 1:1–4 is composed primarily of actual quotations from scripture in 1:5–13 with little comment, neither the relationship between the scriptural proof and the preceding affirmation nor the author's train of thought is immediately apparent. However, two features of these quotations indicate the place of the citations in the argument of Hebrews.

In the first place, John Meier has observed that the seven quotations in 1:5–13 correlate with the seven claims made about the Son in 1:1–4 (Meier 1985, 176). (Table 4 shows these correlations.) The catena of scripture quotations also contains the same general plot of the preexistence, incarnation, and exaltation of Christ. In both instances the movement of thought begins with the exaltation of the Son (1:2b; 1:5–6) and then moves back to the Son's role in creation (1:2c;

Table 4.
Scripture Citations Correlated with Christological Claims in Hebrews 1

1:1–4	1:5–13
whom he made heir of all things (1:2b)	You are my Son, today I have begotten you (1:5 = Ps 2:7; cf. Ps 2:8, Ask of me, and I will make the nations your inheritance)
through whom he made the worlds (1:2c)	You are from the beginning, you laid the foundation of the earth (1:10 = Ps 102:26)
who is the radiance of his glory and image of his nature (1:3a)	Your throne, O God (1:8 = Ps 45:6)
Having made purification for sins (1:3b)	Having loved righteousness and hated lawlessness, therefore God has anointed you (1:9 = Ps 45:7)
he sat down at the right hand of the majesty in heaven (1:3c)	Sit at my right hand (1:13 = Ps 110:1)
becoming so much greater than the angels that he inherited a greater name (1:4)	the oil of gladness beyond your companions (1:9 = Ps 45:7)

1:10) before concluding with the exaltation of the Son and the quotation of Ps 110:1. Thus the author's primary focus is the exaltation. The arrangement of the citations, therefore, forms a carefully crafted argument that introduces the major themes of the homily. The author moves from the announcement of the identity of Christ (1:5–6) to the basis of the Son's superiority (1:7–13) before drawing the pastoral implications in 1:14.

In the second place, the author's introductory comments to the citations provide a guide to the train of thought, indicating that he has carefully arranged the citations in order to make his argument. He presents a dialogue between God and the Son, according to which God speaks to the exalted Son in chapter 1 and the Son responds in 2:12–13. The framework is provided by Ps 110:1, to which the author alludes in 1:3 and quotes in 1:13. Thus the author has arranged the passages in a very skillful way to introduce themes of the book.

Hebrews 1:5–2:4 in the Rhetorical Flow

Hearing God's word with faithful endurance (1:1–4:13)

Exordium: **Encountering God's ultimate word (1:1–4)**

Narratio: **Hearing God's word with faithful endurance (1:5–4:13)**

▶ Paying attention to God's word (1:5–2:4)

The victorious christological claim (1:5–14)

Coronation of the Son (1:5–6)

The transience of angels (1:7–9)

The eternity of the Son (1:10–13)

The listeners as heirs of salvation (1:14)

The severe consequences of rejecting God's word (2:1–4)

The necessity of paying attention (2:1)

God's judgment in the past and present (2:2–3a)

The testimony of God (2:3b–4)

The important place given to Ps 110:1 suggests that the catena is to be understood as a reflection on the exaltation. Since angels play an important role in Jewish tradition as heavenly beings, they provide an appropriate object of comparison as the author elaborates on the exaltation (cf. Eph 1:20–23; Phil 2:9–11; 1 Tim 3:16; 1 Pet 3:22). Despite the fact that angels are sometimes called "sons of God" in the OT, the citations in 1:5–13 indicate that the new "name" mentioned in 1:4 is "Son" and that this name distinguishes the Son from the angels.

1:5–6. The author introduces the first and last citations with a rhetorical question, a favorite device in the homily (cf. 3:13–18), to gain the assent of the audience. The introductory comments indicate that the citations in 1:5 address the Son, while 1:6 addresses the angels. **To what angel did he ever say** (1:5a) appeals to the silence of scripture, indicating that God spoke the following words only to the Son. In the citation of Ps 2:7, **You are my Son; today I have begotten you** (1:5b), the words of scripture that were once addressed to the Davidic king at his coronation are now God's word to the Son at his exaltation, for God has continued to speak "in these last days" through the words of the OT. This claim anticipates 5:5–6, according to which God declared Jesus to be both Son and high priest at the exaltation (cf. 5:10; 6:20), citing the words of Ps 2:7 once more alongside Ps 110. Thus "today" in the citation refers to "these last days" when God "has spoken in a Son" (1:2). This event offers the listeners a new "today" (cf. 3:7, 13, 15; 4:7) to obey God's voice. "I

Jewish Angelology

The OT records many narratives of divine messengers who both convey God's instructions and promises (Gen 16:11; 31:11) and intervene at special events (Gen 22:11; 48:16; Exod 23:20–23; 33:2; 1 Kgs 19:5; 2 Kgs 19:35; Isa 37:36). In addition, the later poetical books describe a wider class of celestial beings possessing the same characteristics as angels. They are called "sons of God" (Gen 6:2, 4; Job 38:7; Ps 29:1), "holy ones" (Deut 33:2; Job 14:15; Ps 89:5, 7), "holy myriads" (Deut 33:12), and "sons of the Most High" (Ps 82:6). The apocalyptic literature witnesses to a major change in the understanding of angels. Angels become intercessors in some instances (Tob. 12:1; *1 En.* 9.10; 15.2; 40.9; 47.2; 99.3, 16) and an army in others (*2 Bar.* 51.11; 70.7). In later writings they are increasingly given specific names and functions. According to *1 En.* 40.32:

"The first one is the merciful and forbearing Michael; the second one, who is set over all disease and every wound of the children of the people, is Raphael; the third, who is set over all the powers, is Gabriel; and the fourth, who is set over all actions of repentance unto the hope of those who would inherit eternal life, is Phanuel by name." (Trans. E. Isaac in Charlesworth 1983)

have begotten you" in the context of Hebrews refers to the Son's exaltation to a new status. Similarly, the words **I will be his Father and he will be my Son** (1:5c), taken from a classic messianic text (2 Sam 7:14), serve here to indicate the appointment of the Son to a unique status before God.

In 1:6 the author develops the theme of the superiority of Christ to the angels with the contrasting citation concerning angels. Although one can read the introductory phrase "but when he again brings the firstborn into the world," the context suggests that the more appropriate reading is **again, but when he brings the firstborn into the world, he says** (1:6a; cf. the use of "again" to introduce scripture citations 1:5; 2:13; 4:5; 10:30). The "world" (*oikoumenē*), therefore, is the transcendent world of the exaltation (cf. "coming world" [*oikoumenē*] in 2:5), the promised land to which God "brings" (*eisagagē*) "the firstborn son" in anticipation of the time when God will "lead many sons to glory" (2:10; cf. Exod 3:8; Deut 6:10; 11:29; 30:5; God "brings" [*eisagagē*] Israel into the promised land; Weiss 1991, 63). The "firstborn" refers to the exalted Son's new status, echoing the reference in Ps 9:27 to the messianic king. The image of "firstborn," taken from the privileges of the firstborn son in Israel, indicates the special relationship of the Messiah to God. Christ is described as "firstborn of all creation" (Col 1:15), "firstborn from the dead" (Col 1:18), and "firstborn among many brothers" (Rom 8:29). The words **Let all of his angels worship him** (1:6b; for the problem of the citation, see Introductory Matters) further demonstrate the exalted status of the Son as the author follows early Christian tradition in declaring the homage of angelic beings to the exalted Lord (cf. Phil 2:10–11; 1 Tim 3:16). This argument carries special force in Hebrews, for it is axiomatic to the author that the inferior renders homage to the superior (cf. 7:4–8; Thompson 1982, 132).

1:7–9. Having declared the superior dignity of the exalted status of Christ in 1:5–6, the author provides the basis for the argument that the Son is superior to the angels in 7–13, as God speaks to the angels in 1:7 before speaking to the Son in the series of quotations in 1:8–13. Hebrews employs a text that was often quoted in rabbinic literature to accent the transcendence of God or the might of the angels (Thompson 1982, 133) to demonstrate the inferiority of angels. In the parallel expressions, **He makes his angels winds and his servants a flaming fire** (1:7), quoted with only minor variation from Ps 104:4 (the LXX has "flaming fire" [*pyr phlegon*] rather than "flame of fire" [*pyros phloga*]), the author emphasizes that the angels do not have a unique relationship to God, for angels are at God's disposal.

The contrast between the Son and the angels is evident in 1:8, as the introductory phrase, **but to the Son** (1:8a), indicates. Citing Ps 45:6, he says, **Your throne, O God, is forever** (1:8b). Whereas angels are changeable (1:7), the Son is eternal (1:8). Undoubtedly, one reason for the author's choice of Ps 45:6 is the address to God (*theos*), a title the author applies to Christ. However, a major purpose of the citation is to press "forever" (*eis ton aiōna tou aiōnos*) as a contrast between the eternity of the Son and the mutability of the angels. The exalted one is thus unchangeable. The phrase *eis ton aiōna* is of major importance to Hebrews and is frequently used in reflections on Ps 110:4 (cf. 5:6; 6:20; 7:17, 21, 24, 28). As 6:19–20; 7:3, 16–17 make clear, the heavenly existence of Christ makes possible the unlimited duration of his existence, setting him apart from the created world (Thompson 1982, 135).

In contrast to earlier citations, the author cites Ps 45:6–7 (44:7–8 LXX) fully in 1:8–9. The **righteous scepter of your kingdom** (1:8c) belongs to the exalted Lord. As in 1:2–3, the author moves from the exaltation to the prior events, indicated by **having loved righteousness and hated lawlessness** (1:9a) and **therefore God anointed you** (1:9b). The context of Hebrews suggests that these phrases refer to Jesus' earthly life, death, and appointment to a new status at the exaltation. In the phrase **the oil of gladness above your companions** (1:9c), the author refers to the place of the exalted Christ above the angels.

1:10–13. In the lengthy citation of Ps 102:25–27 in Heb 1:10–12, the author recapitulates and interprets the claim about Jesus Christ from 1:1–4. The phrases **You are from the beginning, you laid the foundation of the earth** (1:10a), and **the works of your hands are the heavens** (1:10b) recapitulate the claim of 1:2b about the Son's role in creation. **They will be destroyed, but you remain** (1:11a; cf. the psalm's "you will remain") indicates the transitoriness of the creation and the abiding quality of the Son, introducing a major theme of Hebrews. The author reinforces the theme of the transitoriness of the creation in the parallel phrases **they will grow old as a cloak** (1:11b), **you will roll them up like a mantel**, and **they will be changed** (1:12a–b). With the claim that **you remain** (1:11a) and **you are the same** (1:12c), the author contrasts the eternity of the Son with the impermanence of the creation and introduces a major theme of the book. Forms of *menein* appear regularly throughout the book (cf. 7:3, 24; 10:34; 12:27; 13:14) to describe the eternity of the Son and high priest and the Christian possession in contrast to the transitoriness of everything that belongs to this creation.

The claim in 1:11–12 corresponds to the concluding section 12:26–27. In the latter passage, the author appropriates apocalyptic traditions to describe the removal of this creation at the end. Only those things that cannot be shaken remain. This contrast between the material creation and the abiding reality reflects the author's indebtedness to the Platonic tradition, according to which the transcendent world is eternal, while the material creation is subject to change (Thompson 1982, 51).

The author's argument in 1:5–13 confirms the affirmation of 1:1–4 and indicates the basis for the claim of the superiority of Christ, introducing the central argument of the homily. God's ultimate word (1:1–2) in the Son surpasses all alternatives. The subsequent argument will demonstrate that the Son is superior to Moses (3:1–6) and the cultic institutions inaugurated by Moses (8:1–10:18) insofar as the Son stands over creation. Thus Christians place their trust not in things that can be seen (11:1) but in the unseen world that transcends our experience.

The argument that only the transcendent Son "remains" and is "the same" (1:11–12) would have been intelligible to people in the ancient world who distinguished between two levels of reality, the transcendent world that is beyond our senses and the perceptible world that we see and touch. The Middle Platonists of the first century, most notably Philo of Alexandria and Plutarch, distinguished between the two levels of reality, the eternal world of being and the transitory world of becoming, locating God at the highest level of being. In contrast to a world that is constantly undergoing change, only God is "the same" (Philo, *Posterity* 19). Thus the wise person will leave behind the things of this creation and share in the existence of the transcendent God (*Dreams* 2.237).

The repetition of Ps 110:1 in 1:13 restates the claim made at the beginning of the argument (1:3–4), anticipating the homily's consistent appeal to this psalm and constant reflection on the exaltation of Christ throughout the homily. Only the exalted Son stands above this creation. Despite the fact that the community does not see the world in subjection (2:8), the author reaffirms this basic claim.

1:14. In the rhetorical question of 1:14, the author reaches the pastoral goal of his christological argument, indicating that the issue under consideration is not only the relationship between the Son and the angels but the place of this struggling house church in the world. Drawing on the earlier comment that the angels are mere "servants" (1:7; *leitourgoi*), he now concludes that they are **ministering spirits** (*leitourgika pneumata*) **sent for the sake of those who are about to inherit salvation.** Thus the author reassures the community of its place in God's plan, indicating that their relationship to the exalted Son places them above the angels, who exist to serve them. The community is "about to inherit (*klēronomein*) salvation" because it will participate in the triumph of the one who is "heir (*klēronomos*) of all things" (1:2). However, as the author insists throughout the homily, the community lives between the saving events described in 1:1–13 and the ultimate inheritance, undoubtedly facing a crisis of faith because they have not yet experienced the promised inheritance. He responds to the crisis, reassuring them of their special place in the divine plan, hoping to reestablish their confidence as he prepares the way for the exhortation that follows in 2:1–4.

The Severe Consequences of Rejecting God's Word (2:1–4)

2:1. Having compared God's word in the past with God's word in these last days (1:1–2a), the author now turns in 2:1–4 to the community's response to what it has heard. Indeed, **what we have heard** resumes the direct address to the community from the initial claim that God "has spoken *to us* in a Son" (1:2a), which the community received from its past leaders (cf. 13:7). "What we have heard," therefore, refers not only to the words of chapter 1 but to the entire Christian message that has shaped this community. Thus after the intervening description of the surpassing greatness of the Son through whom God speaks and of the salvation that the community receives through him (1:2b–14), the author draws the logical conclusion for the listeners, as the phrase **therefore it is necessary** indicates. The God who speaks demands that the people **pay attention** to what they have heard. As the author points out in the subsequent argument, those who "heard" God's voice in the past did not respond with faithfulness (cf. 3:16; 4:2). Consequently, in this "word of exhortation" (13:22), the author challenges his readers to "hear his voice" (3:7, 15; 4:7) rather than to "refuse the one who is speaking" (12:25). Indeed, the community that has received God's ultimate word in a Son must give special "attention" to what it has "heard," for the alternative is to **drift away** like a ship that goes off course and fails to reach its goal (note the nautical imagery discussed in Introductory Matters). The listeners stand, therefore, in a privileged position as the recipients of God's ultimate word, the "great salvation" (2:3). This privileged position is indicated in the contrast of 2:1–4 between a word spoken through angels (2:2)—the equivalent of God's word in the past (1:1)—and the ultimate word (cf. 1:2) spoken through the Lord (2:3). The author knows no other alternative responses to God's word. His constant warnings (3:12–19; 10:32–39; 12:25–29) indicate the dangers that he perceives in the community. At the present, the community that is "dull of hearing" (5:11) must "pay special attention" to the greatness of its salvation.

2:2–3a. Having stated the logical connection between the declaration in chapter 1 and the exhortation in 2:1, the author argues the case in 2:2–4 as to why the community must now "pay attention." The argument continues the contrast between God's word in the past and in these last days (1:1–2a) by elaborating on the appropriate response to the word spoken through angels (2:2) and the word spoken through the Lord (2:3). Just as the author argues consistently throughout the homily that the new revelation corresponds to God's word in the past but is qualitatively superior (1:4), the argument here is based on that distinction, as the parallels in 2:2–3 indicate:

> word spoken by angels // spoken by the Lord
> every transgression // if we neglect the great salvation
> was valid // was validated
> just recompense // how shall we escape such a great salvation?

The author begins the contrast between the two revelations in 2:2 with a premise that his listeners would accept. Rather than denigrate the old revelation, he indicates that it was **valid** (2:2a; *bebaios*). Although it was delivered **through angels**, this word from Mount Sinai was ultimately from God. The legal metaphor "valid" emphasizes the certainty and reliability of God's word (see Introductory Matters). The validity of the law is evident in the fact that the refusal to heed God's word had consequences: **every transgression and disobedience received a just penalty** (2:2b). Although the author is recalling the consequences of refusal to obey the commandments at Sinai (cf. Deut 17:6 = Heb 10:28; Grässer 1990, 1:103), he also anticipates the subsequent reminders of the certainty of God's promise of consequences for failure to heed the word that was spoken. When God swore that Israel would not enter God's rest (3:11), the words were irrevocable.

The premise in 2:2 is the basis for the comparison in 2:3–4 as the author argues, from the lesser to the greater (see above), that to **neglect a great salvation** (2:3a)—the "salvation" that the community inherits through Christ (1:14)—has greater consequences than the transgression of the word given to Israel. The rhetorical question suggests that the community that rejects God's ultimate word will not **escape** God's judgment (cf. 12:25). The author introduces the first in a series of warnings about the judgment that awaits those who reject God's word (cf. 3:12–19; 6:4–6; 10:26–31).

2:3b–4. The author indicates the greatness of this offer of salvation by giving three reasons it should be taken seriously in 2:3b–4. In the first place, the fact that it **was spoken by the Lord** (2:3b) rather than by angels indicates that the community has heard from the highest authority, for angels do not share in the exalted status of the Lord. As the author says later, the community has heard a word from heaven, not a word that comes from earth (cf. 12:25). In the second place, it was **validated by those who heard him** (2:3c). Although neither the author nor the readers belong to the first generation of Christians, they are the beneficiaries of predecessors who heard him (cf. 13:7), signifying that it was not only the word to Moses that was "valid" (*bebaios*), for the word spoken by the Lord was "validated" (*ebebaiōthē*) by the listeners of the first generation. The legal metaphor indicates the *guarantee* of the gift of salvation (Spicq 1994, 1:280). In the third place, the community has received additional testimony: **God bearing witness with signs and wonders and various powers of the Holy Spirit distributed according to his will** (2:4). The author extends the legal metaphor from the validation by the predecessors to be "witnesses" given by God, the ultimate confirmation. Just as "signs and wonders" accompanied God's revelation in the past (cf. Exod 7:3; Deut 4:34; 6:22), they have attested God's revelation to the community through the Holy Spirit, which the community has received (6:4).

Theological Issues

The catena of scripture quotations presupposes the author's role as the interpreter of scripture. The use of the present tense introducing the citations (cf. 1:6) indicates that God continues to speak through scripture. Because the author does not interpret the passages within their original setting but applies to Jesus Christ passages spoken to the king long ago, his interpretation is likely to appear fanciful to anyone who insists on reading passages within their historical context. According to the historical-critical reading of scripture that has reigned for more than two centuries, the study of the text yields a single meaning, and the task of the interpreter is to recover the way the passage was understood by the original audience. Consequently, many who observe the method of interpretation in Hebrews inquire about the validity of the author's method of interpretation (Motyer 1999, 3–5). Friederich Schröger concludes his study of the citations in 1:5–13 by maintaining that the author's claim "cannot be a proof in the sense determined by historical-critical exegesis; for the psalm says nothing about Christ" (1968, 71). Readers have also asked if the author's conclusions can be valid if the method of interpretation is not. Since Hebrews is composed primarily of expositions of scriptural texts, these questions are critical for engaging the message of the homily.

The historical-critical reading of scripture has been an invaluable instrument for the reading of the Bible, for its insistence on discovering the meaning of a passage in its original context often prevents arbitrary readings and provides a common method for interpreters from a variety of religious traditions to examine the same texts. While few today question the validity of historical-critical exegesis, many interpreters now challenge the view that a text has only one meaning, insisting that the meaning of a text depends on the questions we ask. Interpreters increasingly recognize that the meaning of a text is not exhausted by our attempts to hear the word in its original context. Early Christians maintained that what had occurred in the life, death, and resurrection of Jesus was of such importance that it transformed their entire biblical story, becoming a lens for reading all of scripture. The author of Hebrews read scripture through his knowledge of the plot of the entire narrative. Thus the meaning of the text was not frozen with the original readers but took on additional meaning when interpreters read it in light of the entire plot. With the faith that Jesus was the Messiah, the ultimate king, the author gave a messianic interpretation to the royal psalms. Because of his faith that the exalted Christ was equal to God, he read passages praising God as references to the one at God's right hand. The author neither claimed to interpret the passages in their original context nor spoke of them as predictions fulfilled in Christ. As a preacher, he read scripture on behalf of the community in order to find a word for his own time. He anticipated the later church as it interpreted scripture on the basis of the church's faith in Jesus Christ. Thus the author's method of interpreting scripture through the eyes of faith is not a practice to be jettisoned but a model for interpretation within a community that asks not only what scripture once meant but also what it means for those who seek its guidance in the present.

Hebrews 2:5–18

The Community's Present Suffering

Introductory Matters

In 2:5, the introductory "for it is not to angels that he subjected the coming world" suggests a continuation of the citations in 1:5–14 (cf. 1:5, 13). Here, however, the author introduces the extended quotation of Ps 8:4–6, which he will develop in 2:5–18. Psalm 8 is a hymn praising God for the glory and power that God has granted to humankind. After praising God for the wonder of creation (8:1–2), the psalmist expresses awe at the place of humankind above the creation.

The continuity with 1:5–14 implies the christological interpretation of the psalm. The author interprets the psalm as the celebration, not of the place of humankind over creation, but of the place of the Son over "the coming world" (*tēn oikoumenēn tēn mellousan*). "Son" in 1:5–14 is the equivalent of the "man" and "son of man" in the psalm (8:6; cf. Ps 8:4). Whereas the psalmist employs "man" and "son of man" in synonymous parallelism to refer to humankind, the author maintains the parallelism to equate the terms with the Son of God. Although "Son of Man" is the most frequent self-designation of Jesus in the Synoptic Gospels, the author does not reflect an interest in pursuing that title.

Oikoumenē (cf. 1:6) does not have its usual meaning of the inhabited world (cf. Luke 2:1; 4:5; 21:26; Acts 17:6, 31; Rom 10:18) but refers to the world that includes both humanity and transcendent beings (BDAG), including the angels (cf. 1:5–14), and is the equivalent of the "coming age" (6:5), the "good things to come" (9:11), and the city to come (13:14). To say that he subjected

Son of Man

In the OT, "son of man" is commonly used as a synonym for "man" (cf. Ezek 2:1), often in parallel with the latter (Num 23:19; Job 35:8; Ps 80:17). Daniel 7:13 describes the heavenly being called the Son of Man, who comes with the clouds at the end. This description is expanded in *1 En.* 46–48; 62–71. In some instances in the Gospels, the Son of Man is identified with the earthly Jesus (Matt 8:20 par. Luke 9:58; Matt 11:19 par. Luke 7:34; Mark 2:28; 8:31; 9:31; 10:33–34), while numerous passages identify the exalted Christ with the Son of Man who comes from heaven at the end (Mark 13:26; 14:62; cf. Matt 24:27 par. Luke 17:24).

the coming world to the Son is to restate that the Son is "greater than the angels" (1:4).

The phrase "he bore witness somewhere" (2:6a) indicates that it is God who speaks in scripture. "He bore witness" (*diemartyrato*) continues the legal metaphor in 2:3–4, suggesting that the scripture citation that follows is God's oath. God bears "witness" not only in signs and wonders (2:4) but also in scripture. The author frequently cites scripture without mentioning the human author (cf. 2:12–13; 3:7; 8:8). The indefinite "somewhere" was commonly used to introduce scripture citations (cf. Philo, *Drunkenness* 61; *Planting* 90) and reflects the author's conviction that all scripture is from God.

The author follows early Christian tradition in connecting Ps 110:1 with Ps 8 as christological statements celebrating the exalted status of Christ, who has put all things under his feet (Ps 8:6; 110:1; cf. 1 Cor 15:25–27; Eph 1:21–22). By

The Masoretic Text of the Hebrew Bible

The Masoretic Text (MT), the Bible recognized in Judaism and the basis for most translations of the OT into other languages, derives its name from *masora*, the Hebrew word for tradition. The term was used in Judaism for the extensive marginal notes (cross-references, word counts, alternative readings) included in many medieval Bibles. The scholars who compiled these notes were called masoretes. The standard edition of the Hebrew Bible is based on the only complete masoretic manuscript, the ben Asher text of Codex Leningradensis, written around AD 1010. The LXX was made from Hebrew manuscripts a millennium older, and fragments of the Hebrew Bible found among the Dead Sea Scrolls sometimes agree with the LXX against the MT, so scholars believe that in some cases the LXX represents an earlier reading than the MT. Other witnesses to the OT include the Samaritan Pentateuch and translations into other languages.

following the LXX with "lower than the angels" (2:7) instead of "lower than God" as in the Masoretic Text, the author fits the passage to his comparison of the Son with the angels. In the extended citation in 2:6–8 the author follows the LXX but omits Ps 8:6a, "You have given him dominion over the works of your hands," before continuing the interpretation of the psalm in 2:8b–16. In the words "he subjected" (2:5), "subject all things" (2:8b), and "a little while lower than the angels" (2:9), the author takes words from the psalm as the basis for the christological interpretation.

The major point in the exposition is derived from the LXX wording, "little while lower than the angels," in place of the MT's "little lower than God." Although *brachy ti* can refer either to "a little" (John 6:7) or to a "little while" (Isa 57:17), the author's argument depends on the temporal understanding of the term. By rendering the phrase "a little while," the author can find in the psalm a reference to Jesus' earthly life as the interim period between his preexistence and the "glory and honor" of the exaltation. Thus the author's interpretation of the psalm becomes an elaboration on the story of Christ in the prologue (1:1–4), which proclaims the preexistence, death, and exaltation of Christ. The author's elaboration focuses on the middle stage in the cosmic drama in 2:6–16: the human existence and death of the Son.

The description of the Son as "pioneer" (*archēgos*) is a distinctive contribution of Hebrews. The term appears elsewhere in the NT only in Acts 3:15 and 5:31. It can refer to a ruler or prince, to the first in a series, or to a founder or originator (BDAG), and was often used for the one who founded a city and gave it its name. In the LXX, the term is often used for leaders of the people (cf. Num 13:2–3; 16:2). Jephthah was asked to become *archēgos* over the inhabitants of Gilead in order to deliver them from the Ammonites (Judg 11:6 LXXB). He agreed on condition that the position be made permanent. The elders consented, and he was made head and commander (*kephalē* and

Heracles the Pioneer

Heracles (Latin *Hercules*) was the most prominent and widely worshiped hero in Greek and Roman myth. Stories of Heracles existed prior to Homer (ca. eighth century BC). Most of the stories about Heracles involve his twelve labors, in which he battled monstrous animals and other terrifying beings at Hera's command. A major theme is Heracles' victory over Hades in battle (Homer, *Il.* 5.395–398). Hellenistic philosophers allegorized the stories of Heracles, interpreting his battles with wild beasts as the struggle with vices. He overcame death through virtue, and he became a savior insofar as he showed others how they could overcome the tyrants that undermine moral improvement. He was a model for others, demonstrating how they could find the path to moral improvement in their own struggles. He was called *archēgos* because he led the way for others to follow.

Figure 3. Reincarnating Hercules.

The hero Hercules was honored at cult sites throughout the Hellenistic world and figured prominently in the popular imagination before and after the time of the letter to the Hebrews. This late-second-century sculpture at Rome, now housed in the Capitoline Museum, depicts the emperor Commodus (161–192), who presented himself as a reincarnation of the popular demigod. Here he carries Hercules' club and wears the pelt of the Nemean lion.

archēgos, Judg 11:11 LXXB; Scott 1986, 52) even before the battle. Other OT leaders during the time of the judges were also occasionally called *archēgos* by the LXX translators (e.g., Judg 5:2, 15b). In Greek literature *archēgos* was used for the originator or founder of a nation or a city. He served as a guide and pathfinder who cleared the way through the thick jungle and knew how to avoid sandpits and find oases in the desert (Klauck 2006, 425) as he took his followers to the destination. Cynic and Stoic philosophers depicted Heracles as *archēgos* (cf. Dio Chrysostom, *Or.* 33).

The significance of the word in Hebrews becomes evident in the author's usage. In 12:2, its combination with "perfecter" suggests that the term means "originator." Similarly, the term "forerunner" (6:20; *prodromos*) and the phrase "source of salvation" (5:9) are synonymous with *archēgos*. Christ is thus the one who opens the way for others to follow (cf. 10:19–20). The language allows the author to exploit both the solidarity of the Son with his people and the Son as the one who opens the way. The cosmic drama of preexistence, descent, exaltation, and new name resembles the plot of the hymn in Phil 2:6–11 but has the additional dimension of the solidarity of the Son with the "sons." The Son is the pioneer who "brings many sons to glory" by sharing in "the suffering of death." His solidarity with the sons is evident in the fact that he is "of one origin" with them and calls them "brothers." In his death

Gnostic Redeemer Myth

At the beginning of the twentieth century, the history-of-religions school, under the leadership of Richard Reitzenstein, argued that gnosticism (see the sidebar on p. 85) predated Christianity and provided the background for Christian views of redemption. Although the elements of the gnostic redeemer myth may vary, the basic components are as follows: Because the earth has fallen under the control of demonic forces, a heavenly being comes into the world from the realm of light to liberate the sparks of light that originated in the world of light but have been compelled to live in human bodies. This emissary takes a human form and carries out the works entrusted to him by the Father. He reveals himself in his utterances (e. g., "I am the shepherd"), and his own respond to him as he awakes in them the memory of their home of light. Thus he redeems them from the world in which they are imprisoned. Twentieth-century scholars, most notably Rudolf Bultmann, held that early Christian descriptions of the coming of Christ were based on the gnostic redeemer myth. Since evidence for this myth in pre-Christian times is nonexistent, few scholars hold to this view today.

he defeated the devil, the one who has the power of death (2:14), rescuing all who live in the fear of death.

The background of the author's description of the cosmic drama has been a matter of considerable debate. In *The Wandering People of God*, Ernst Käsemann noted the similarity of Heb 2:10–18 to Phil 2:6–11 and Col 1:15–20 and argued that these passages shared a common plot that included the pre-existence, descent to earth, heavenly enthronement, and a new name (cf. Heb 1:4; Phil 2:11) of the redeemer. This plot, according to Käsemann, was derived from a gnostic redeemer myth, according to which a supernatural being descended to earth to rescue humanity from its imprisonment in the fallen world. The redeemer, who shared a common origin and fate with humanity, led the redeemed out of earthly imprisonment and into the transcendent bliss of redemption. Käsemann observed the motif of the people on the way toward the promise in Hebrews (cf. 3:7–4:11; 10:19; 12:12), following behind their "pioneer" (*archēgos*, 2:10; 12:2) and "forerunner" (6:20), and argued that the motif of the redeemer as *archēgos* is a common theme in gnosticism. He maintained also that the theme of the solidarity of the Son with the sons (Heb 2:10–16) as people "of one origin" (2:11) is also rooted in the gnostic redeemer myth. Although Käsemann correctly noted the constant theme of the people on the way behind their "pioneer" in Hebrews, his view of the gnostic origins of this theme have been rejected by most scholars (Käsemann 1984, 127–32).

The author's depiction of the cosmic drama evokes images that ancient readers would associate with a common mythological plot in which the hero descends to the underworld to defeat the power of death and to lead death's captives back to life (Euripides, *Alc.* 837–1142; Diodorus Siculus, *Bib.* 4.25–26; Plutarch, *Thes.* 35, 46; Attridge 1989, 79). The oldest tradition that has been preserved of Heracles associates him with the conquest of Death (Homer, *Il.* 5.394–400; cf. Pindar, *Olymp.* 9.33; Lane 1991a, 61). In the classic legend, he rescues Alcestis by wrestling with Death (Apollodorus Mythographus, *Bibl.* 1.106). According to Seneca's tragedies, suffering is the path to his glorification (*Herc. Oet.* 1434–1440, 1557–1559, 1940–1988). In Seneca's *Hercules Furens* (585–592), the chorus sings of the liberation from the fear of death after hearing of Heracles's descent to the underworld and conquest of Death (Attridge 1989, 80). Like Jewish writers before him, the author of Hebrews evokes these images to reassure his readers of the triumph beyond death.

The claim in 2:10 that Jesus became "perfect through suffering" introduces a topic that is central to the argument of Hebrews but rare in other NT writings. The author applies the terminology of perfection both to Jesus and to those who follow him. Jesus became "perfect" (2:10; 5:9; 7:28); in contrast to the Levitical system, which was incapable of bringing about perfection (7:11, 19) or of perfecting the conscience of the worshipers (9:9; 10:1), the work of Christ has "perfected forever those who are being sanctified" (10:14; cf. 11:40). The verb *teleioō* (to perfect) and the noun *teleiōsis* have a range of meanings, of which the primary one is "to bring to completion" (BDAG, 996). When the word is employed for Christ in Hebrews, in each instance it involves the completion of the course that includes both his suffering and his exaltation (2:10; 5:8–9; 7:28). Thus the author implies not moral perfection but the entire course of events that culminated in Jesus' entry into the heavenly world. "That perfecting involved a whole sequence of events: his proving in suffering, his redemptive death to fulfill the divine requirements for the perfect expiation of sins, and his exaltation to glory and honor" (Peterson 1982, 73). It was the qualification for his service as eternal high priest (5:9–10; 7:28). The perfection

Seneca

Lucius Annaeus Seneca (ca. 4 BC–AD 65), brother of Gallio the proconsul (Acts 18:12), was the tutor of the emperor Nero. He was born into a wealthy Italian family and was a successful orator and senator. His philosophical writings are contained in ten ethical treatises known as *Dialogues*. He also wrote 124 *Moral Epistles* in which he employed Stoic philosophy in his care of souls. Christian writers admired his moral teachings, which had numerous parallels in thought and language to Christian instruction, prompting an unknown writer to produce an apocryphal correspondence between Paul and Seneca.

of believers is made possible by the perfection of Jesus, for he has "perfected forever those who are being sanctified" (10:14). The perfection of believers is the access to God that is possible only because the heavenly high priest has purified and sanctified them (Peterson 1982, 32, 166).

Because the terminology of perfection is used in a wide variety of literature with a range of meanings, the background of this category in Hebrews has been a matter of debate. In the LXX, the word can be used for a wholehearted relationship to God (2 Kgs 22:26 LXX; cf. 1 Kgs 8:61; 11:4; 15:3, 14), for the completion of the work on the wall of Jerusalem (2 Esd 16:15–16), and for the death of the martyrs (4 Macc 7:13–15). Philo uses *teleios* (perfect) more than four hundred times with a range of meanings. Lala K. K. Dey (1975, 32–81) has shown that Philo employs this language in numerous instances to describe the two levels of reality as realms of perfection and imperfection. The goal of human existence, according to Philo, is to rise above the imperfection of this world to the immediate access to God (*Alleg. Interp.* 3.44–45). Philo's leading heroes were models of perfection insofar as they cut all ties with the world, drew near to God, and lived the virtuous life on earth as strangers (Thompson 1982, 21). The use of perfection in Hebrews probably reflects both the Jewish martyr tradition, with its view of death as perfection, and Philo, who understood perfection as the transcendent world to which the believer may ascend.

In 2:17–18, the author recapitulates the argument of 2:5–16 and makes the transition to the central section of the book. "For this reason he had to be" (*hothen ōpheilen*) is typical of the author's appeal to logical necessity (cf. "it is necessary" in 2:1; "it is fitting" in 2:10). To be "made like his brothers (*tois adelphoi homoiōthēnai*) in every respect" summarizes the focus on family solidarity described in 2:10–16. The author follows early Christian tradition in emphasizing the full likeness of Jesus to humankind. Paul declares that God sent his son in the "likeness (*homoiōmati*) of sinful flesh" (Rom 8:3), and the Philippian hymn celebrates the one who "emptied himself and became in the likeness (*homoiōmati*) of humankind" (Phil 2:7). The context in Hebrews indicates the full extent of Jesus' likeness to humanity, for the author is referring specifically to the earlier statements that Jesus shared in the same way in the human condition with its slavery to the fear of death (cf. 2:14). Just as the author says later (4:15) that Jesus was tempted in quite the same way (*kath' homoiotēta*) "in every respect," here he says that he was like his brothers in "every respect." As the purpose clause indicates in 2:17b, his full humanity is the prerequisite for his becoming a "merciful and faithful high priest." Not only is Jesus the Son, as the first two chapters assert; he becomes the high priest. As the author indicates in 5:5–10, the Son "becomes" the high priest at the exaltation. Just as he had argued in 2:9–10 that the suffering of the Son is the prelude to glory, he now concludes that his full humanity is the foundation for his role as high priest.

Although the author introduces Christ as high priest for the first time in 2:17b, anticipating the theme of the central section of this homily (4:14–10:31), he has prepared the reader for this subject already by introducing sacrificial terminology into the argument. Christ "made purification for sins" (1:3) and is the one who sanctifies (2:11). The fact that the author introduces the topic without explanation in 2:17 and then speaks in 3:1 of the "high priest of our confession" suggests that the community is already familiar with this title for Jesus. Indeed, the author's description of the high priest as "merciful" and "faithful" suggests that his task is not to introduce Jesus as high priest but to define the nature of his high priesthood. The author has prepared the way for this interpretation in 2:5–16.

Inasmuch as Hebrews is the only book of the NT to describe Jesus as high priest, interpreters have been puzzled as to why this title plays such an important role in the homily. In one sense, this christological title is the natural result of early Christian reflection on the sacrificial meaning of the death of Jesus. Early Christians had already described the death of Jesus as the means of atonement (*hilastērion*, Rom 3:25). Paul's claim that Christ is exalted to God's right hand and intercedes for us (Rom 8:34) anticipates the presentation of Christ as the heavenly high priest who intercedes (cf. Heb 7:25). Paul also employs the language of the sacrificial system to describe his own work in priestly and sacrificial terms (Rom 15:16; cf. Phil 2:17). He describes the church as God's temple (1 Cor 3:16; cf. 6:19) and the ethical activity of Christians as a "living sacrifice" (Rom 12:1). Indeed, the Christian claim that Christ died "for our sins" (1 Cor 15:3) implied that the death of Christ replaced the traditional means of atonement.

The author's use of this terminology is also deeply rooted in Jewish reflection on the high priest developed from the Pentateuchal descriptions, according to which the priest was distinguished from others by his holiness (cf. Exod 28:36; Deut 10:8; 1 Sam 7:1) and appointed for a variety of tasks (cf. Deut 33:8–10), including instruction in the law, the giving of blessings, and the performance of sacrificial duties. In the intertestamental period, Jewish literature expressed fascination with the functions of the high priest. Sirach includes Aaron among the "famous men" (Sir 44:1), to whom he devotes extensive praise (Sir 45:6–22) for his work in the temple. In *T. Levi* 18.1–14, the high priest is a heavenly messianic figure who will defeat the evil one and provide "rest" for the righteous (*T. Levi* 18.9; cf. Heb 4:11; Attridge 1989, 99). In *1 Enoch*, the angel Michael is a heavenly high priest who intercedes for the people (*1 En.* 40.9; 68.2). Indeed, angels commonly play an intercessory role in the apocalyptic literature (cf. *1 En.* 9.1–11; 15.2; 40.6; 47.2; 99.3; 104.1; Attridge 1989, 99).

Philo's allegorical treatment of the ministry of the high priest in the tabernacle is also a possible background for the focus on the sacrificial work of the high priest in Hebrews. Philo repeatedly describes the symbolic significance of the high priest's ministry in the tabernacle. The high priest is often a symbol for the *logos*, or Word, understood either as a cosmic principle or as God's word in the soul (cf. Attridge 1989, 100). Of the sacrifices required of the high priests, the sacrifice of Yom Kippur (Lev 16) was the most important (cf. Philo, *Spec. Laws* 1.72; *Dreams* 1.215–216; 2.231; *Embassy* 306; *Giants* 52; *Drunkenness* 136). Whenever the high priest enters into the most holy place, he is not only a man but the divine *logos* (*Heir* 84), who is "less than God, superior to man" (*Dreams* 2.188; 2.231; cf. *Spec. Laws* 1.116). This high priest is at the same time merciful (*Spec. Laws* 1.97), perfect (*Dreams* 2.234), and sinless (*Flight* 109, 117).

While the author of Hebrews shares the interest in the heavenly high priest with intertestamental writers and Philo, his roots in the Christian tradition provide a dimension that makes his interpretation distinctive. Only in Hebrews does a historical figure become the heavenly high priest. No other writer depicts a high priest who sacrifices himself as a prelude to his enthronement. Nevertheless, the author shares with Philo the interest in the Day of Atonement (Heb 9) and the focus on the perfection and sinlessness of the high priest, which he incorporates into the narrative of the earthly Jesus.

Although the OT lists numerous tasks of the high priest (cf. Deut 33:8–11), the only task mentioned in Hebrews is to "make expiation for" (*hilaskesthai*) the sins of the people. *Hilaskesthai* is the translation of the Hebrew *kpr*, which can mean "wipe out" or "eliminate." In the LXX, the term (like the related *exilaskesthai*) is used for the sacrifices that atone for sins and take away the impediment to a relationship with God (BDAG; cf. Lev 4:20, 26, 31; 5:10; 16:16, 32–34). The term is used elsewhere in the NT only in Luke 18:13 for the prayer of the tax collector, "God be merciful to me a sinner." To make expiation for sins is the equivalent of "make purification for sins" in the opening words of Hebrews (1:3). The author's special emphasis on the sacrifice of the Day of Atonement in 9:1–10:18 suggests that "make expiation" refers to that sacrifice (Lev 16).

In 2:18, the author reaches the conclusion of his treatment of the humanity of the Son. Having emphasized already that the "suffering of death" was the path to the Son's ultimate glory (2:9–10; cf. 5:8; 9:26; 13:12), the author concludes in 2:18 that Jesus' suffering to the point of death (2:9, 14) was a test. *Peirazein* can mean either "tempt" or "test." The author's focus is not on the synoptic story of the temptation of Jesus (cf. Matt 4:1–11) but on Jesus' solidarity with "those who are being tested" by suffering (cf. 10:32) and hopelessness. Indeed, the one who "was made like his brothers in every respect" (2:17) also shared the same test that now confronts the community. Thus the author is not offering a general statement about temptation but is reassuring the wavering community that the "pioneer" (*archēgos*, 2:10) survived the test of suffering and is now able to "help those who are tested."

Tracing the Train of Thought

2:5–8a. In both the introductory formula in 2:5 and the interpretation that follows in 2:8a, the author focuses on the subjection of the world to the Son, reiterating the thought of 1:5–14. The verbal link between Ps 110:1 ("you have placed all things under his feet") and Ps 8:6 ("you have subjected all things under his feet") is the basis for the author's interpretation. However, as the exhortation in 2:1–4 indicates, the listeners stand in danger of drifting away (2:1) and neglecting the "great salvation" (2:3) because they experience dissonance between the christological claim and their own situation. Thus the transitional **for** (2:5) indicates the relationship between the exhortation in 2:1–4 and the christological reflection in 2:5–18. Although the listeners are about to share in the inheritance of the Son (1:2, 4, 14), they are in danger of neglecting the "great salvation" (2:3). Despite the claim of the psalm that God has "put all things in subjection under his feet" (Ps 8:6; Heb 2:8a), the community "does not see all things in subjection to him" (2:8b). That is, the reality of the readers' lives is a severe test for the community's claims. As inhabitants of a hostile world who have faced imprisonment and the confiscation of their property (cf. 10:32–34), they "do not see" the ultimate triumph of God described in chapter 1. Because the promises remain unfulfilled, the community faces the severe crisis of faith that the author hopes to alleviate in the exposition that follows. They face the cognitive dissonance between the faith claim that is stated in chapter 1 and the reality of discouragement and defeat that they experience, for they continue to experience suffering and the fear of death (cf. 2:15). Thus their most basic question is "How does one claim the sovereignty of Christ over the world in the midst of suffering?" (Söding 1991, 40).

The exposition of Ps 8 in 2:8–16 is the author's answer to that crisis as he brings the readers into the great narrative. The

---

Hebrews 2:5–18 in the Rhetorical Flow

Hearing God's word with faithful endurance (1:1–4:13)

Exordium: Encountering God's ultimate word (1:1–4)

Narratio: Hearing God's word with faithful endurance (1:5–4:13)

Paying attention to God's word (1:5–2:4)

▶ The community's present suffering (2:5–18)

He subjected all things (2:5–8a)

Crowned because of the suffering of death (2:8b–9)

Jesus the pioneer (2:10)

Jesus and his brothers and sisters (2:11–13)

Rescue from the fear of death (2:14–16)

A merciful and faithful high priest (2:17–18)

inclusio in 2:5, 16 ("for not to angels . . . for it is not with angels that he is concerned") indicates that the triumphant one also cares for them. The midrash on Ps 8 is both exhortation and christological reflection as the author responds to the community's crisis with an assurance that their suffering is the prelude to glory.

2:8b–9. In chapter 11, the author provides one answer to the dilemma posed by the community's struggle to "see" the world in subjection: when faithful people place their trust in "things not seen" (11:1) and "see the invisible one" (11:27), they are able to endure suffering. Here he responds to the community's dilemma by contrasting what **we do not** (2:8b) **see** with what we see. The thesis statement for the entire unit is 2:9, in which the author reorients the perspective of the listeners by offering a new perspective. He offers an alternative solution in his reading of the psalm, interpreting it in light of his Christian confession and the community's struggle. Following his christological reading of the LXX, the author finds a reference to Jesus' earthly existence in the **little while lower than the angels** (2:9a). Since *brachy ti* in the LXX can be read either in spatial terms as "a little lower than the angels" or in temporal terms as "a little while lower than the angels," the author finds a reference to Jesus' earthly existence prior to the time that he was crowned with "glory and honor" at the moment when he sat down at God's right hand (1:3, 13). That is, Jesus' triumph came only after a period of testing.

With this reading of the "little while" of the psalm, the author discovers both the humiliation and the exaltation of Christ. For the first time in the homily, the author speaks of Jesus. Indeed, **we see Jesus** (2:9a) anticipates the later exhortation "looking to Jesus" (12:2). In referring to Jesus rather than the title Son, the author refers to the human side of Jesus' existence and the time before the exaltation, when he received an appointment as Son and high priest (cf. 5:5–6). The earthly life of Jesus is critical for the homily (cf. 5:7–10), for the author now presents Jesus as one who met the same crisis of

The Use of Examples in Rhetoric

"These common proofs are of two kinds, paradigm and enthymeme." He continues, "Let us then first speak of the example. . . . There are two kinds of examples, namely, one which consists in relating things that have happened before, and another in inventing them oneself." (Aristotle, Rhet. 2.20.1–2 [1393A], trans. Freese 1939, 273)

"The most important of proofs of this class is that which is called example, that is to say the adducing of some past action real or assumed which may serve to persuade the audience of the truth of the point which we are trying to make." (Quintilian, Inst. 5.11.6, trans. Butler 1920)

A Textual Variant

Although the reading "by the grace of God" in Heb 2:9 is supported by manuscripts in both East and West, many Western and Eastern church fathers and a few Greek manuscripts and early versions have the reading "apart from God" (*chōris theou*). Some of the church fathers interpreted *chōris theou* to mean "in his human nature, to the exclusion of the divine" (Ellingworth 1993, 156). The reading *chōris theou* may be the result of the copyist's memory of Jesus' cry from the cross, "My God, my God, why have you forsaken me?" Thus the reading "by the grace of God" is attested by the dominant manuscript traditions in both East and West.

---

faith that the community now experiences. In a homily that offers numerous examples of both unfaithfulness (3:7–4:11; 12:15–17) and faithfulness (chap. 11), Jesus is the ultimate example of the latter (cf. 12:1–2). Like ancient orators, the author knows the persuasive power of examples. He invites the suffering community (cf. 10:32–34) to "see" the earthly Jesus as the ultimate example of faithfulness in his suffering that led to death. In speaking not only of Jesus' death but also of his suffering (cf. 2:10; 5:7–8; 13:12), the author connects the experience of Jesus with that of the community. His triumph with **glory and honor** (2:9c) came only **on account of the suffering of death** (2:9b). Thus as the opening words of Hebrews indicate, the death of Jesus precedes his triumph (1:3–4). To "see Jesus" is to discover that faith is manifest in suffering that leads to triumph.

Interpreters have recognized that the final clause in 2:9, **so that by the grace of God he might taste death for everyone** (2:9d), follows most naturally "on account of the suffering of death" (2:9b) rather than "crowned with glory and honor" (2:9c), suggesting that the sentence would be more logical if 2:9b were omitted or transposed with 2:9c. To "taste" is a common image signifying the full knowledge or experience of something. The readers have "tasted the heavenly gift" (6:4). To taste death is a common idiom in the Bible (Matt 16:28; Mark 9:1; cf. Matt 20:22; 26:27, 29). The present sequence suggests that the exaltation is the basis for the saving significance of Jesus' death. Because of the exaltation, his death has saving significance for all. Whereas the community has not yet experienced death (12:4), he "tasted death for all by the grace of God." Here the "grace of God" is the gift of Jesus' sacrifice (9:1–10:18), the means by which the community may now approach the "throne of grace" (4:16) and strengthen the heart (13:9).

2:10. As the conjunction **for** (*gar*) in 2:10 suggests, the author now elaborates on the "grace of God" and the "suffering of death." He begins with two axiomatic statements in 2:10–11 before applying them to Christ in 2:11b–16.

71

Argument from What Is Fitting

The categories of the necessary, the fitting, and the possible play an important role in the discussions of appropriate argumentation in the rhetorical handbooks. According to Hermogenes, "The fundamental questions are divided according to the so-called final main arguments, the just, the useful, the possible, the appropriate [or fitting]" (*Prog.* 11). Hebrews consistently appeals to three of the categories: the necessary, the appropriate (fitting), and the possible. In 2:10 and 7:26, the author appeals to what is fitting. He argues on the basis of the necessary in 7:12, 27; 8:3; 9:16, 23, and on the basis of the impossible in 6:4, 18; 10:4.

In the first axiomatic statement, he appeals to what is **fitting for him** (2:10a; i.e., God), using a rhetorical argument that was common in the Greco-Roman world. Greeks commonly described what was "fitting" for the deity (cf. Plutarch, *Is. Os.* 381e), frequently arguing that the Homeric stories about gods who engaged in stealing, adultery, and betrayal were not fitting (cf. Plato, *Rep.* 381c; 383a; 388b; Thompson 1998, 307). Although the phrase "fitting for him" (God) was well known to the Greeks, the author's depiction of what was fitting would have been totally unacceptable to them. He introduces the topic by identifying God as the one **because of whom are all things and through whom are all things** (2:10b; cf. 1:1–3), indicating God's role in creation (cf. 11:1–3). While the author indicates earlier that the exalted Christ is heir of "all things" (1:2) and that God has put "all things" under his feet, here he speaks of God's role in creating "all things," using the common term for the entire universe. The interchangeable language for the role of God and the Son in the universe suggests the unity of God and the Son. The author's focus is not, however, on the role of the Father and the Son in creation, for the primary focus is on the claim that, in **leading many sons to glory, he made the pioneer of their**

Sons (and Daughters)

The NRSV renders *huioi* (lit. "sons") as "children" in 2:10 and 12:5 and "my son" (12:5) as "my child." It also renders *adelphoi* (lit. "brothers") as "brothers and sisters" (2:11, 17). This rendering is appropriate, because ancient Greek regularly employs masculine plurals in regard to groups composed of both men and women. The author's use of the parallel "children" (2:13–14) confirms that he does not wish to be gender specific here. I have given the literal reading "sons," however, in order to maintain the author's link between the sons and the Son.

salvation perfect through suffering (2:10c). That is, God stands as creator and redeemer at both the beginning and the end. God's ultimate purpose to "lead many sons to glory" is achieved when they share in the glory of the Son (2:7) and reach the land of promise.

When the author speaks of one **leading many sons to glory** (2:10c), the syntax is not clear as to whether the one who leads is God or Christ, the "pioneer." Grammatically, "leading" could refer to either. Most translations assume that the subject is God, while some interpreters render the clause "God makes the pioneer of their salvation, the one leading many sons to glory, perfect through suffering." Inasmuch as God is the subject throughout 2:5–9, the author most likely refers to God's role as leader. Indeed, an important theme in the OT is that God leads the people out of Egypt and through the wilderness (Lev 26:13; Deut 8:2, 15; 32:12; Josh 24:8; Ps 78:52). Nevertheless, God's servants Moses and Joshua also lead (Deut 29:5) the Israelites toward the promised land. In using the verb *agein*, which was associated with the leadership of God and Moses through the wilderness, the author anticipates the portrayal of the community on its way to the promised land (3:7–4:11). Thus as God "leads many sons to glory," Jesus himself is the pioneer who opens the way to the promised land, the heir (1:2, 4) who has made it possible for the listeners to inherit eternal salvation (1:14). The "glory" is the equivalent of the inheritance mentioned in 1:14 and the promise that the author consistently holds before the community (4:1; 6:12–15; 8:6; 9:15; 10:36; 11:9, 13, 17, 33).

Although **pioneer** (2:10c; *archēgos*) is used only twice in Hebrews (cf. 12:2), the concept of the pioneer who opens the way for others to follow is central to the thought of Hebrews. It belongs to the same complex of themes as Christ the "source" of eternal salvation (5:9) and the "forerunner" (6:20) who entered into the heavenly world and opened the way for others to follow (10:19–20). The pioneer reached that ultimate goal only through suffering. The means by which God accomplishes the ultimate goal would have been abhorrent to Greek thought. Inasmuch as perfection for the author includes both the death and the exaltation of Christ (see Introductory Matters), the author indicates that only through suffering was the Son "crowned with glory and honor" (cf. 2:9). For a community that is now being put to the test, the theme of the pioneer who proceeded from suffering to glory is an encouragement to endure alienation. It communicates the concept of the solidarity of the pioneer with his people in suffering and glory (Weiss 1991, 209).

To be **perfect through suffering** (2:10c) is equivalent to "on account of the suffering of death crowned with glory and honor" in verse 9. Similarly, in 5:7–9 the author describes the suffering of Jesus before concluding, "Having been made perfect, he became the source of eternal salvation." The author employs the language of perfection frequently to describe the completion of the course in the presence of God (cf. 7:11, 28; 9:9; 10:1, 14; 11:40), indicating that the community's present suffering is a stage in their progress toward

Holy and Common

The OT distinguishes between what is holy (*hagios*) and what is common (*koinos*; cf. Heb 9:13; 10:29). To sanctify something is to make it holy. Thus the people are sanctified when they become holy as God is holy (Lev 19:2; cf. Exod 31:13; Lev 20:8; 21:15; 22:9, 16; cf. Koester 2001, 229).

the promised land. Those who face the crisis of faith caused by suffering can change their perspective, knowing that they follow the one whose suffering ended in glory.

2:11–13. The second axiomatic statement develops the first one, as **for** (2:11; *gar*) indicates. "It was fitting" for God to "make the pioneer perfect through suffering" (2:10) because **the one who sanctifies and those who are being sanctified are of one** (2:11). Although one cannot be certain why this statement is axiomatic for the listeners, the author appeals to it as the foundation for the argument that follows. In describing "the one who sanctifies," the author anticipates the description of the sacrificial work of Christ, which he describes in the language of sanctification (cf. 9:13; 10:10, 29; 13:12). "Those who are being sanctified" are the members of the community, the sons who are being brought to glory. The identity of "the one who sanctifies" and the designation of "one" is a matter of debate. Most ancient and modern readers interpret "the one who sanctifies" as a reference to God inasmuch as it is God who leads many sons to glory (2:10; cf. Attridge 1989, 89; Laub 1980, 77). However, God commissions servants with the special task of sanctifying others. In this instance God has commissioned the task to Jesus, who has sanctified the people by his blood (13:12). Thus the community that struggles with suffering is experiencing solidarity with the Savior.

The author applies the axiom in 2:11b–13, indicating that "of one" implies a family relationship, using this metaphor to emphasize the solidarity of the Son to the sons. He introduces citations of scripture to indicate that in the passages that follow, the Son is speaking through the words of scripture and calling the suffering community his **brothers** (2:11b). Whereas God is the speaker in the preceding citations, the Son is the speaker in 2:12–13. In the parallel phrases of 2:12 (cf. Ps 22:22; 21:23 LXX), the **brothers** (2:12a; NRSV "brothers and sisters") and the **congregation** (2:12b) are identical. The author then cites Isa 8:17–18 in 2:13 as the words of the Son, dividing two parts of the scripture by **and again** in order to make two claims. With the phrase **I will put my trust in him** (2:13a), the Son is expressing solidarity with the community that is challenged to trust in God when it cannot see God's triumph. Indeed, as the author will indicate later (12:2), Jesus is not the object of faith but the great example of faith in the midst of suffering. In the second phrase drawn from Isa 8:17–18, the Son's declaration, **Behold I and the children that God has given to me** (2:13b), continues the theme of family solidarity. Thus the author reorients the community's perception of its struggle by indicating that the exalted Lord is also the brother who has shared their suffering on his path to "glory and honor."

2:14–16. The author concludes his pastoral description of community solidarity in verses 14–16, providing the answer to the dilemma mentioned in 2:8b and elaborating on verse 9. Referring to the "children" (2:13), the author makes the general statement that **children share** (*kekoinōnēken*) **flesh and blood** (2:14a), an indication of their human frailty and limitations (cf. 1 Cor 15:50), and then applies the generalization to Jesus, **who shared with them** (*meteschen*) **in just the same way** (*paraplēsiōs*) (2:14b) as one would expect in any family relationship. Although he uses two different words for "share," he apparently does not distinguish between them. The author does not say how far the similarity extends (BAGD), but the context in 2:17–18 suggests that the author refers to the solidarity of temptation (2:18) and the fear of death in which "he became like his brothers in every respect" (2:17).

In the purpose clause of 2:14–15a, the author describes the consequence of this total solidarity and indicates the full meaning of the Son's role as "pioneer" (2:10). The claim that he **destroyed the one who has the power of death, that is, the devil** (2:14c), is reminiscent both of Paul's declaration that Christ, at his resurrection, destroyed death (1 Cor 15:26, 54–55; cf. 2 Tim 1:10) and of ancient apocalyptic portrayals of the Messiah's victory over demonic forces (cf. *As. Mos.* 10.1; *T. Levi* 18.2; *T. Dan* 5.10; *T. Jud.* 25.3; Attridge 1989, 92). Jesus' victory over "the one who has the power of death" is an elaboration of the claim that the world is in subjection to the Son of God (2:5, 8). The enthronement as victory over the powers is common in early Christian literature (cf. 1 Cor 15:25–27; Phil 2:9–11). The result of this victory was that he rescued those who lived constantly in the **slavery of the fear of death** (2:15). The author refers to the human condition that has confronted people in all ages. Ancient writers described the slavery of the fear of death, and the author alludes to Jesus' own fear of death in 5:7. As pioneer, Jesus shared humanity's fear of death and triumphed over it, opening the way for the community to follow. As the listeners struggle with dissonance because they have not seen everything in subjection to the Son, the author reminds them that they have been rescued by the triumphant Son.

In the conclusion in the next verse the author moves from the event of the death of Jesus to a generalization based on that event. The purpose of this section is to declare that **it is not with angels that he is concerned, but the seed of Abraham** (2:16), who are the sons and the children described in 2:10–14. As the author will consistently demonstrate, the community lives in continuity with the people of Israel. The allusion to Isa 41:8 LXX suggests that the author is indicating that, just as God cared for the seed of Abraham in the past, he continues to care for them.

2:17–18. In 2:17–18, the author summarizes the case that he has made in 2:1–16 and introduces the argument that he will develop in the rest of the homily. In the comment that **he had to be made like his brothers in every respect** (2:17a), he summarizes the focus on the solidarity of the Son with the community. In 2:18, as in 2:8b, he indicates the situation that is driving the argument. The Son's solidarity with the people is solidarity in temptation. The author affirms that although the community is now being tested (2:18) by its inability to see God's triumph (2:8b), its suffering (2:18), and its weariness, it does not stand alone. Jesus is not only the exalted Son; he is also the pioneer (2:10), whose path to glory involved suffering and the same temptations now faced by the community. He became high priest only after being tested.

The emphasis is not only on the high priesthood of Christ but on his significance as the answer to the crisis facing the people. In declaring that he is **merciful and faithful** (2:17b), the author introduces the subjects that follow. He will describe the faithfulness of the Son in 3:1–6 and challenge the community to respond with faithfulness in 3:7–4:13. He will elaborate on the theme of the merciful high priest in 4:14–5:10 before developing the theme of the exalted high priest in 7:1–10:18. Thus he responds to the community that is being tested (cf. 3:7–4:11) by affirming that the exalted Son and high priest has also faced the same test and consequently **is able to help** (2:18).

Theological Issues

Just as Heb 1 was a valued resource for the church's claim that the Son was equal to God, Heb 2:5–18 provided the most explicit claim in the NT for the full humanity of Jesus, which the author reiterates in 4:14–5:10. Despite the Platonic language about the transcendence of the exalted Son (1:10–12), the claim that the Son was tempted in every way as we are (2:17–18; cf. 4:15) and was "made perfect through sufferings" indicates that the Greek language

Docetism

Several early Christian writings reject the view that the humanity of Jesus was only an appearance, a view known as docetism (from the Greek *dokēsis*). Some docetists held that the spiritual Christ entered the human Jesus at his baptism and left at his crucifixion. The letters of Ignatius (beginning of the second century) engage in polemic against the docetists. Docetic views may also have provoked the polemic in 1 and 2 John (1 John 4:2; 2 John 7).

of the impassibility of the transcendent deity is not an appropriate way to describe the transcendent Christ, whose suffering preceded the glory described in chapter 1. Consequently, the church fathers appealed to Heb 2 to affirm the reality of the incarnation and insist on the full humanity of Jesus. John Chrysostom cited Heb 2, for example, to refute any denial of the full humanity of Jesus: "Let all the heretics be ashamed, let those hide their faces who say that he came in appearance and not in reality" (*Hom. Heb.* 4.5; NPNF[1] 14:385).

Although the author of Hebrews gave the ancient church a rich vocabulary for facing the trinitarian and christological controversies, his claim that Jesus was "tempted in every way" was intended not to settle christological disputes, but to address a community that faced the temptations caused by the dissonance between the christological claims of chapter 1 and the reality of their lives. Thus despite the triumphant claims of chapter 1, the author offers no gospel of success, for Christians of all ages have shared the anguish of saying, "We do not see all things in subjection to him" (2:8).

The author's christological portrait offers a new way for disoriented Christians to see the world. In portraying Jesus as the "pioneer" (*archēgos*), the author has provided an image that will interpret the community's own suffering, for this image indicates that, before the Son was triumphant, he suffered the same anguish that the community now suffers. He followed a path from suffering to glory, opening the way for others to follow. In the assurance that "he was like his brothers" (2:17) and was tempted (2:18), the author does not speculate on the range of temptations suffered by Jesus but portrays him as suffering the temptations that the discouraged community now suffers. Thus the author shows that the anguish of suffering Christians is the necessary prelude to the glory described in chapter 1. He indicates to Christians that anguish and disorientation are necessary parts of Christian existence and a prelude to reaching the ultimate goal.

Unlike Paul, the author of Hebrews never speaks of the community's faith in Jesus but portrays Jesus as the exemplar of faith who says, in solidarity with his people, "I will put my trust in him" (2:13; cf. 12:2). As the example of faithfulness, Jesus demonstrates that faith involves enduring suffering, even when one does not "see everything in subjection to him." With the language of kinship in 2:10–18, the author indicates that the community follows the path of suffering behind its pioneer and brother, knowing that the Son has reached the ultimate goal. The church is, therefore, the community that confesses faith in the victorious Son in the midst of its own suffering, knowing that its present suffering is the path to the inherited promise.

Hebrews 3:1–4:13

Hearing God's Voice Today

Introductory Matters

After addressing the community's disorientation with the claim that the exalted Son is also its pioneer through the path from suffering to glory, the author now elaborates on the urgency of the community's response (cf. 2:1–4) in 3:1–4:13. The central focus is the community's response to God's word.

The Faithfulness of Jesus

In the *synkrisis* of 3:1–6, the Son is greater than Moses, Israel's greatest revealer. This comparison amplifies the earlier contrast between the word spoken by angels (2:2) and the word spoken by the Lord (2:3). In the midrash

---

Midrash

Midrash, a term derived from the Hebrew verb *darash* (seek, inquire), is both an activity and a form of literature involving the interpretation of authoritative texts. Rabbis engaged in the activity in the schools as they attempted to make the text applicable to the age in which they lived. As a form of literature, the midrash consisted of citations of sacred texts followed by commentary. Expositional *midrashim* (plural of *midrash*) were running commentaries, while homiletical *midrashim* were independent units based on specific topics or holy days. Paul employs the midrashic form in Rom 4:1–23; 2 Cor 3:7–18; Gal 3:6–29.

---

on Ps 95:7–11 in 3:7–4:11, the author focuses on God's oath that continues to address the community (cf. 3:11; 4:3). The summary reflection on the word of God in 4:12–13 is the conclusion to the midrash on Ps 95:7–11, reinforcing the author's claim for the urgency of responding to the word that God "swore" (3:11; 4:3). These words form an *inclusio* with 1:1–2, reflecting the author's focus on God's ultimate word "in a Son."

The author employs the rhetorical argument by means of amplification (Olbricht 1993), a common mode of argument among orators. Amplification, a broad term covering various means of promoting or denigrating any given matter, is often used where orators reiterate what has already been demonstrated. Here the author reiterates the argument of chapters 1 and 2. In each case, the author compares the Son with a servant (1:14; 3:5) and concludes that the ultimate word spoken by the Son gives special urgency to those who hear (2:1–4; 3:7–4:11). However, this unit also prepares the way for the central section on the high priestly work of Christ in 4:14–10:25. Having announced for the first time that Jesus has become "the merciful and faithful high priest" in 2:17, the author calls on the community to "consider the high priest of our confession" in 3:1 but does not develop this theme until 4:14. Indeed, "consider the high priest of our confession" (3:1) forms an *inclusio* with "having a high priest . . . let us hold fast the confession" (4:14). Thus 3:1–4:13 is a hortatory interlude in the author's presentation of Jesus as the "high priest of our confession" appropriate to the author's description of his work as a "word of exhortation."

The purpose for this interlude is evident in the theme that the author pursues in 3:1–4:13. Having announced that Jesus is a "faithful (*pistos*) high priest" in 2:17, the author demonstrates in 3:1–4:13 that the "faithful" Son (3:2, 6) demands the faithful response of his people. The one who "leads many sons to glory" (2:10) has demonstrated what faith is and now requires a faithful response. Thus the author indicates that the Israelites did not enter the promised land because of their lack of faith (3:12, 19; 4:2), while God's promise is still available to those who have faith (4:3). With its memory of the church's predecessors and its call for faithfulness in 3:1–4:13, the passage corresponds to the unit that follows the central cultic section in 10:32–12:11. The call for the community's faithfulness both before and after the central section indicates that Jesus' sacrifice of his own blood (9:11–14) was the supreme act of faithfulness that now evokes the community's faithful response.

For the first time, the author refers to the community's "confession" (cf. 4:14; 10:23; cf. 13:15), to which he will challenge them to hold fast (4:14; 10:23). As in the Pauline epistles, the community's "confession" is a christological claim (cf. Rom 10:9; Phil 2:11). The precise content of the confession in Hebrews has been a matter of debate. The exhortation in 4:14 suggests that the community confesses that Jesus is the Son of God, while in 3:1 Jesus is the high priest of our confession. The reference to "our" confession indicates that the community is familiar with its content, which may include some or all of the introduction in 1:1–4. The confession may be the baptismal creed of the church, which the community recalls regularly in its assemblies (Weiss 1991, 244). The fact that the author challenges the community to "hold fast to the confession" at the beginning and end of the central section (4:14; 10:23) suggests that the exposition is an elaboration on this article of faith.

The place of Moses in Jewish literature also indicates why he is the natural object of comparison. In the OT, he is the giver of the law, a member of the tribe of Levi (Exod 2:1–4), and a priest (Ps 99:6) who serves at the altar (Exod 24:4–8). He is especially glorified in the intertestamental age. The many legends about Moses in such literature as the *Assumption of Moses* indicate his unique place in Jewish memory. According to Sirach, Moses was "equal in glory to the holy ones" (45:2), the only one who was allowed to hear God's voice and speak with God face to face (45:5). In *Ezekiel the Tragedian*, Moses is shown in a dream that God will place him on a heavenly throne and invest him with a crown and scepter, the symbols of his unique authority. According

Alinari / Art Resource, NY

Figure 4. Moses with the Tablets of the Law.

This painting by Guido Reni (1575–1642) depicts Moses returning from the mountain to find the unfaithful Israelites worshiping a golden calf.

to one rabbinic tradition, Moses ascended to heaven, prompting the "ministering angels" (cf. Heb 1:14) to ask, "What business has one born of woman among us?" When God tells the angels that Moses came to heaven to receive the Torah, the angels exclaim, "Thou desirest to give to flesh and blood! What is man, that thou art mindful of him. And the son of man that thou visitest him?" (*b. Sabb.* 88b–89a and *Pesiq. Rab.* 20.4, cited in Moffitt 2007). Thus the author's transition from "ministering angels" (1:14) to the christological interpretation of Ps 8 and the comparison of Jesus to Moses may be indebted to traditions in rabbinic literature. Philo calls Moses a "high priest" (*Heir* 182; *Sacrifices* 130; *Moses* 1.334) and God (*Moses* 1.158; *Dreams* 2.189; cf. Ellingworth 1993, 194).

For the development of the *synkrisis*, the author alludes to Num 12:7 in 3:2, 5. This passage was a logical place to begin, for it was the classic text in describing Moses as revealer par excellence. In the original context, Aaron and Miriam complain about Moses' leading role, asking, "Has the Lord spoken only through Moses?" (Num 12:2). The Lord responds to the question by indicating that Moses is unique among God's revealers: "If there is a prophet among you, I will make myself known in a dream or vision, but not so with my servant Moses. He is faithful in all my house. With him I will speak mouth to mouth, in a form and not through enigmas, and he saw my glory" (Num 12:6–8). The role of Moses as "servant" is an honorific description, indicating that he holds a special place before God.

This text played an important role in Jewish literature. Philo, for example, reflects on this passage on several occasions. He compares Moses to sense perception, personified in Miriam, who found fault with Moses and declares that the one who was "faithful in all God's house" (*Alleg. Interp.* 2.67) is worthy of praise. Moses is the model of the mind that looks beyond created things in order to apprehend the uncreated One (*Alleg. Interp.* 3.100). Moses' capacity to see beyond the created order is evident in the fact that he made the tabernacle in accordance with the heavenly archetype. Philo emphasizes Moses' special status as the one to whom God manifests himself openly because "Moses was faithful in all his house." As a result, God will speak to him "mouth to mouth in manifest form and not through dark speeches" (cf. Num 12:6–8). Philo also appeals to Num 12:7 to indicate that Moses is the model of the faithful one who trusts not in his own reasonings but in God (*Alleg. Interp.* 3.228). The fact that Philo connects Num 12:7 with Moses' role as the one to whom the archetype of the heavenly tabernacle was revealed (cf. Exod 25:40) is significant for the interpretation of Hebrews, for the story line of Hebrews moves from Moses as the one who "was faithful in all his house" to his role in the making of the tabernacle (Heb 8:1–5).

Unlike Philo, the author does not focus on Moses as the one with whom God spoke face to face. He cites only the phrase, "he was faithful to the one who made him as Moses was faithful in all his house." The reference echoes Num

12:7, to which the author will also allude in 3:5. Here he adapts the passage in two ways. He adds to Num 12:7 the phrase "to the one who made him," clarifying the relationship between the Son and the Father. He also changes the first person "my house" to "his house," changing the oracle to a third-person reference. Whereas the LXX has "not so my servant Moses," the author has "Moses was faithful as a servant." Thus the passage at one level recapitulates chapters 1 and 2 by comparing the Son and the "servant." Like chapter 2, it employs the language of an OT text to describe Jesus in midrashic form.

The point of comparison between the Son and Moses is that both Christ and Moses were "faithful in all God's house." Three words in Num 12:7 are important for the comparison. First, both Moses and Jesus are "faithful." Having affirmed that Jesus is the faithful high priest (2:17), the author pursues this theme in order to contrast the faithfulness of the Son (3:1–6a) with the unfaithfulness of Israel (3:12, 19).

When the author cites Num 12:7 in 3:5–6a, he introduces the second term from the Numbers passage that he will develop. The Numbers passage describes Moses as servant, which the author contrasts with the Son, setting up a comparison similar to that involving Christ and the angels (cf. 1:14). Both angels and Moses are servants (1:14; 3:5) whose status is inferior to that of the Son. The author's interest is not to engage in polemic against the angels or Moses, but in each case he uses the familiar *synkrisis* to declare the greatness of Christ.

The author's reference to the "house" involves the third term from the Numbers passage. This reference leads the author to describe Christ as the builder of the house. Although both Moses and Jesus are "faithful," the author maintains that Christ was "counted of greater honor than Moses" (3:3) because the "builder has greater honor than the house." Although the reference to Moses as "faithful in all God's house" comes from Num 12:7, the elaboration concerning the builder in 3:3–4 does not derive from this passage; the author introduces other passages to develop his argument. He alludes to the oracle of Nathan in 1 Chron 17:14, "I will establish (*pistōsō*) him in my house and in my kingdom forever." In Jewish tradition, the oracle of Nathan was already linked with the oracle to Eli in 1 Sam 2:35, "I will raise up for myself a faithful priest, . . . and I will build him a faithful house." Other passages in the OT describe God's role as the builder of the house of David (cf. 2 Sam 7:13; 1 Chron 17:12). The texts of 1 Chron 17:14 and 1 Sam 2:35 had been combined in the Jewish tradition to describe both a faithful priest and a faithful Davidic king (D'Angelo 1979, 79). David is also described as "faithful" in the house of Saul (1 Sam 22:14) and in the house of Jessie (2 Sam 23:1–2 LXX).

The "house," according to Numbers, is the people of Israel. The term had other associations. It could be used for an extended family or dynasty (cf. Gen 7:1). The house was the term for the sanctuary (cf. Gen 28:17; 1 Kgs 6:1c, 14a; *TDNT* 5:120). To "found a dynasty" is to "build a house" (cf. 2 Sam 7:11;

1 Kgs 2:24; *oikon oikodomein*). This idiom is the background to the author's use of the additional metaphor of the building. In his adaptation of the passage, to be his "house" is to live in continuity with Israel.

The Unfaithfulness of the Ancestors

In 3:7–4:11, the author elaborates on the warning in 3:6, which has expressed uncertainty about the listeners finishing the course. "Therefore" indicates that the following passage will support the author's claim. He moves from the portrayal of Moses to the reflection on the wilderness generation from Ps 95:7–11, which is the basis for the comments that follow. This introduction also continues the consistent use of *synkrisis* typical of the author's rhetorical style.

Psalm 95 is a song of thanksgiving that invites the people of Israel to worship. It celebrates the kingship of God (95:3–5) and calls the community to worship (95:6–7) and celebrate their status as the children of God. After the call to worship (95:1–7a), the psalmist indicates the urgency of responding to God's invitation by recalling the scene in Exod 17:7, where the people complained to Moses and Moses struck the rock and called the place Massah and Meribah because the people had tested him. According to Num 14:20–23, God responds to Israel's complaints with the declaration that none of the people who had seen his glory would enter the promised land. In recalling that scene, the psalmist urges the listeners not to repeat the mistakes of their ancestors.

The experience of the wilderness generation became an example for others in the prophetic tradition and in the period of the NT. Some OT passages recall the period of the wilderness wanderings as a time when Israel enjoyed a harmonious relationship with God (cf. Jer 2:2–3; Amos 2:10), while others recall this period as a time of rebellion (Ezek 20:13–31; cf. Ps 78:15–19; 106:7, 13–33). One may note Paul's use of the same story to show that the wilderness generation was a prototype of the Christian community (1 Cor 10:1–11). Like the author of Hebrews, Paul emphasizes the disastrous consequences of Israel's disobedience and uses the story as a warning to the church. Like the author of Hebrews, Paul recalls the story as the narrative of disobedience.

The author of Hebrews introduces the psalm with "therefore the Holy Spirit says," using "therefore" to connect the citation with the implied warning in 3:6b. Whereas the author has introduced previous citations as words of God (cf. 1:5–13) or Jesus (2:12–13), here the source is the Holy Spirit, to whom the author also attributes scripture citations in 9:8 and 10:15. The author employs the present tense (cf. 8:8; 12:5), indicating that the words from the psalm are a divine oracle that now speaks to the community. The author cites the LXX version of Ps 95:7–11 (94:7–11 LXX) with minor variations. The most significant change is the addition of "therefore" in 3:10, which allows him to make a shift in the citation. The LXX has "Where your fathers tested, they tried and saw my works. I was angry with that generation for forty years," a reading similar to the MT. With the addition of "therefore," the text in

Hebrews reads, "They saw my works forty years. Therefore I was angry with that generation." That the author is familiar with the LXX reading that God was angry forty years is evident in the allusion in Heb 3:17. Thus the author of Hebrews interprets the forty years not as a time of God's wrath but as a time of God's mighty works. The author's shift probably reflects his desire to speak to the church, which is now in the wilderness and looking toward the promised land (cf. Enns 1997, 353–54).

The author also renders an etymological translation of the place names Meribah and Massah (cf. Exod 17:7), rendering them as in "the rebellion" (3:8) and "with scrutiny" (3:9). This reading may reflect the Septuagintal text cited by the author or it may be the author's own adaptation.

The psalm speaks a stern warning about entering God's rest. Neither the psalmist nor Hebrews acknowledges that the Israelites entered the promised land under the leadership of Joshua. In keeping with the author's focus on Moses in 3:1–6, he recalls only God's declaration that Israel will not enter the rest. Thus according to the midrash that follows the author's citation in 3:12–4:11, Israel did not enter the rest, which is now available to the people of God. The church is the people of the wilderness looking over the Jordan and awaiting the promised rest. Therefore, the rest in Hebrews is the promise of the transcendent reality that awaits those who have a heavenly calling.

Because "rest" can have a variety of meanings, one of the major debates of the twentieth century involved the intellectual background of the author's reflections on rest. The OT reflects the polyvalence of the word. In Exod 33:14, God promises Moses, "I will go before you and I will give you rest" (*katapausō*). In OT passages, Joshua, Caleb, and the succeeding generation of Israelites entered the "rest" in the land of Canaan (Deut 12:10; 25:19; Josh 1:13, 15; 21:44; 22:4; 23:1). The word was also used for the temple as a place of God's rest, for the God who has given Israel rest now rests in Jerusalem (1 Chron 23:25; Thompson 1982, 82). In Num 10:33, the ark goes before Israel, seeking a place to rest for the nation. According to Isa 66:1, the Lord says, "Heaven is my throne and the earth my footstool. What is the house that you have built for me, or what is the place of my rest?" The "rest" of the psalm is no longer the earthly Canaan. Indeed, the psalm opens the way for the metaphorical use of the term (Rad 1958, 101–8).

Ernst Käsemann argued that the theme of the wilderness wanderings of the church toward the promised rest behind its pioneer (2:10; *archēgos*) was the central motif of Hebrews. He asserted that the author did not merely derive this theme from his reading of Ps 95 but that he was dependent on gnostic views of the redeemer who delivered the people from their bondage in this world into the transcendent rest (1984, 74–75). Using the gnostic texts that were available at that time, Käsemann observed that rest (*anapausis*) was frequently identified with the highest aeon, the place from which the individual came and to which the gnostic will return. The term was also used for God,

Gnosticism

Derived from the Greek *gnōsis* (knowledge), the term *gnosticism* covers a variety of religious movements that flourished from the second to the fifth centuries AD. Gnostics claimed a knowledge that was revealed only to those who had received the secret teachings of a heavenly revealer. Many gnostics held to an elaborate mythology explaining how the material world, dominated by a demonic god, came into being. The most common characteristics of gnosticism included a radical dualism between the material world and the divine realm and a belief in the soul's longing to escape this world by returning to the divine. Before the discovery of the gnostic documents near Nag Hammadi in upper Egypt in 1945, information about gnostics came primarily from church fathers who were engaged in debate with them.

who is sometimes addressed in prayer as rest and the "one who rests" (*Gos. Truth* 42.22; cf. *Unknown Gnostic Work* 22; Thompson 1982, 89). Since the discovery of the gnostic library of Nag Hammadi, other texts have revealed the gnostic fascination with rest. Judith Wray has examined the use of rest in the Nag Hammadi writings, concluding that the pervasiveness of the theme in gnostic literature indicates that it was a major theological metaphor among the gnostics. It was used with a variety of meanings, including both the present state and the eschatological goal of the believer (Wray 1998, 140). In her study of the relationship between the concept of rest in Hebrews and the *Gospel of Truth*, she concludes that the latter is dependent on Hebrews.

Since the gnostic literature is indebted to a variety of sources, including the Bible and philosophical literature of that period, the gnostic references to rest do not indicate that this category originated in gnostic sources. Indeed, since gnosticism was indebted to Middle Platonism for its cosmology, the references to rest in that literature probably reflect the use of biblical references to rest and the concepts of Middle Platonism. Among Middle Platonists, rest belongs to the highest realm of being, in contrast to the material world, which is constantly changing. Philo of Alexandria, in his integration of Judaism and Middle Platonism, described God as the one who rests: "Rest belongs in the fullest sense to God and to him alone" (*Cherubim* 90). Philo often identifies God's rest with the Sabbath. Both are symbols of transcendence (Thompson 1982, 85). Philo argued that the Sabbath rest is available to mortals who rest in God (Thompson 1982, 86; *Flight* 174; cf. *Posterity* 28). Clement of Alexandria, who was indebted to Philo, shared the view that rest belongs to the highest world.

Otfried Hofius (1970b) challenged Käsemann's interpretation, observing that eschatological rest is a major theme in apocalyptic texts. The collection of texts cited by Hofius is also a challenge to the proposed Philonic background of rest as a theological metaphor. In apocalyptic texts the concept of rest was commonly identified with a restored paradise. According to *4 Ezra* 8.52, "Because it is for you that Paradise is opened, the tree of life is planted, the age to come is prepared, plenty is provided, a city is built, rest is appointed, goodness is established and wisdom perfected beforehand" (trans. Metzger, *OTP*). The author warns that "we shall not enter" into the paradise because "we have lived in unseemly places" (7.123). Hofius appeals to a wide range of other passages to demonstrate that rest is a common theological metaphor for the hope of the righteous in Jewish apocalyptic literature, maintaining that these texts provide the most likely background to the metaphor of rest in Hebrews.

Other Jewish writings also knew the metaphorical use of rest. In the Hellenistic Jewish writing *Joseph and Aseneth*, God is addressed: "Bless this virgin . . . and let her enter into your rest forever" (8.10–11). The passage echoes Ps 95 and suggests that it comes from the same milieu as the interpretation in Hebrews (Weiss 1991, 272). Rabbinic texts interpret the rest of Ps 95 as the coming aeon and interpret the Sabbath as the foreshadowing of the coming kingdom (Weiss 1991, 272).

Since rest was a common image throughout ancient literature, a choice between these alternative backgrounds is unnecessary, for Judaism and Hellenism intersected in many ways. The author is probably aware of the rich associations evoked by his appeal to his congregation to learn from Israel's failure to enter into God's rest. Thus the author's appeal to enter the transcendent rest would have been intelligible to a wide audience in the first century. This rest (*katapausis*) is the author's equivalent to his numerous images for the heavenly world. It is the "city with foundations whose maker and builder is God" (11:10; cf. 11:16; 13:14), "homeland" (11:14), and "heavenly Jerusalem" (12:22).

Confronted by the Word of God

In the reflection on the "word of God" in 4:12–13, the author concludes the first major section of the homily. The stylistic change from 3:7–4:11 is noteworthy. The author now speaks in an extended periodic sentence composed of two balanced clauses, each with rich images. In the Greek text, the author employs an *inclusio* marked by the use of *logos* ("word" in 4:12; "account" in 4:13). Because of the distinctive style of 4:12–13, scholars have suggested that the author is citing either a traditional saying (cf. Michel 1966, 201) or a hymn (Nauck 1960, 205). However, the author's frequent rhetorical flourishes (cf. 1:1–4; 5:7–10; 12:18–24) suggest his own capacity for poetic speech. Thus the beginning (1:1–4) and the end (4:12–13) of the first unit are distinguished by poetic reflections on the word of God. These reflections anticipate the final appeal in 12:25 not to "refuse the one who is speaking."

The "word of God" has many possible associations for the readers. The passage recalls prophetic statements about the power of God's word. The "word of the Lord came to" occurs 123 times in the OT. The prophets describe the power of God's word to overwhelm them and call them to ministry. Amos says, "The Lord roars from Zion, and utters his voice from Jerusalem" (1:2 NRSV). Jeremiah reports God's words, "I am now making my words in your mouth like fire" (5:14 NRSV) and "like a hammer which breaks a rock in pieces" (23:29). According to Isa 55:11, God's word "will not return empty" because it will accomplish God's purpose.

"Living and active" (*zōn kai energēs*) are both attributes for God that are used with reference to God's activity in the world as creator and judge. God is the "living God" (cf. 3:12; 9:14; 10:31), who is "active" (*energēs*) insofar as the divine *energeia* (NRSV "power") is at work in the cosmos (Eph 1:19; 3:7) and in the church (Eph 1:11; 3:20; Phil 2:13). The author's use of divine attributes to describe the word of God indicates that "word of God" is an expression of God's activity in the world. Just as the "living God" in Hebrews regularly relates to God's activity as judge, the word of God is also "living and active" as God's power both to save and to judge.

The "two-edged sword" is an instrument for battle (cf. Judg 3:16) that was used metaphorically in a variety of contexts (cf. Ps 149:6; Prov 5:4; Rev 1:16). The sword is a common metaphor for God's judgment in the Bible and Jewish literature (Deut 32:41; Ps 17:13; Isa 27:1; 34:5; 66:16; Matt 10:34; Eph 6:17). According to apocalyptic literature, God comes with the sword of judgment (*1 En.* 88.2; Rev 1:16; 2:16; 19:15, 21). The claim that no creature is hidden before the eyes of God is also a commonplace (cf. Job 34:21–22; Ps 44:21; 139:1–6; cf. Williamson 1970, 400).

The closest parallels to the author's description of the word of God appear in the Wisdom literature and in Philo of Alexandria. According to Wis 7:23, Wisdom is "overseeing all, penetrating all things." According to Wis 18:15–16, "[God's] all-powerful word leaped from heaven, from the royal throne, into the midst of the land that was doomed, a stern warrior carrying the sharp sword of [God's] authentic command, and stood and filled all things with death, and touched heaven while standing on the earth" (NRSV). The statement in Sir 39:19 that "the works of all are before him, and nothing can be hidden from his eyes" (NRSV) recalls Heb 4:13.

Philo refers to the *logos* as "the fiery sword" (*Cherubim* 28), and often describes it as sharp and capable of severing all things. "That severing Word whetted to an edge of utmost sharpness never ceases to divide" (*Heir* 130). Philo asserts that the *logos* severed all creation into different species as well as severing male from female (*Heir* 130–140) and divided the soul into two parts (*Heir* 132). Although Philo, unlike the author of Hebrews, is speaking of the cosmic functions of God's word, his language suggests that the imagery associated with the word of God in Heb 4:12–13 is indebted to Hellenistic Judaism as represented by the Wisdom literature and Philo.

The metaphor changes in 4:13, for the subject now is God, before whom "no creature is hidden" (*aphanēs*) and every creature is naked (*gymna*) and laid bare (*tetrachēlismena*). The nakedness recalls Gen 3. In focusing on "the eyes of the one to whom we give an account," the author changes the image, indicating that the reader is exposed not only to the word but to God's own eyes. God who sees and judges is the one to whom our account must finally be rendered.

Tracing the Train of Thought

The Faithfulness of Jesus Christ (3:1–6)

Here the author sets out the faithfulness of Jesus as a model for the community. Just as the comparison between Christ and the angels (1:4–14) is the basis for the exhortation not to drift away (2:1–4), the comparison between Christ and Moses (3:1–6) is the basis for the exhortation in 3:7–4:13 not to fail because of unbelief. In both units, the response to God's word is the controlling theme (cf. 3:7, 15). The comparison has shifted from the word spoken through angels at Sinai to Moses, the one who spoke for God. Everything depends on the response to God's word, for the greatness of salvation is accompanied by great consequences for those who hear.

Moses is a natural object of comparison in Hebrews, for the events surrounding God's speech in the past (1:1–2) have focused on the wilderness generation. Thus the author proceeds from the giving of the law through angels (2:2) to Moses, God's supreme spokesman. Indeed, the comparison between Jesus and Moses follows naturally from the description of Jesus as pioneer (2:10–18), for it was already implicit in the description of God, who leads the people to glory through the pioneer. The wilderness setting continues throughout the homily. In the exhortation that follows (3:7–4:11), the author compares the church to the wilderness generation. In the comparison between the heavenly and earthly sanctuaries (8:1–9:28), his object of comparison is not the Jerusalem temple but the tabernacle that was built by Moses (8:5). Similarly, in 12:18–24, he compares the church's approach to the heavenly Zion to Israel's approach to the earthly Mount Sinai. Thus throughout the homily, the author envisions the community as the wandering people on the way to the promised land.

3:1–2. For the first time, the author speaks directly to the listeners in 3:1 (cf. 3:12), recapitulating what has been said and turning to a new stage in the argument. **Holy brothers, participants in a heavenly calling** (3:1a), focuses on what has been said and emphasizes the special status of the listeners. Although the NT nowhere else calls Christians "holy brothers," the identification here recalls Paul's address to members of the community as "called to be saints" (Rom 1:7; 1 Cor 1:2). "Participants in a heavenly" calling resembles both Paul's reference to the "upward calling" (Phil 3:14) and to his readers as "called"

(1 Cor 1:24–26; 7:20; cf. Eph 1:18; 4:1, 4). They are "holy brothers" insofar as they are the sons (2:10) who are being made holy (2:11), and they are "participants (*metochoi*) in a heavenly calling" because their brother (cf. 2:12–13) has participated (*meteschen*, 2:14) with them in the anguish of human existence and is the pioneer who will take them to glory (cf. 2:10). With this reminder of their status (cf. 1:14), the author now reinforces his attempt to guide the people to see beyond the earthly realities of a world that has raised doubts in their mind and to recall their confession of the high priest who has triumphed over death.

In encouraging the readers to **consider Jesus** as the **apostle and high priest of our confession** (3:1b), the author employs a verb drawn from the visual sphere (Grässer 1985; *katanoein* means to "look at in a reflective manner" or "contemplate," BDAG, 522), a term that he employs later when he encourages the readers to "consider one another" (10:24). The encouragement to consider Jesus, an echo of the earlier claim that "we see Jesus" (2:9), focuses on the entire path of the earthly Jesus from suffering to glory,

> ### Hebrews 3:1–4:13 in the Rhetorical Flow
>
> **Hearing God's word with faithful endurance (1:1–4:13)**
>
> *Exordium*: Encountering God's ultimate word (1:1–4)
>
> *Narratio*: Hearing God's word with faithful endurance (1:5–4:13)
>
> Paying attention to God's word (1:5–2:4)
>
> The community's present suffering (2:5–18)
>
> ►Hearing God's voice today (3:1–4:13)
>
> The faithfulness of Jesus Christ (3:1–6)
>
> Faithful in all his house (3:1–2)
>
> Greater glory than Moses (3:3–4)
>
> Faithful as a son (3:5–6)
>
> The unfaithfulness of the ancestors (3:7–4:11)
>
> Confronted by the word of God (4:12–13)

in which he proved to be faithful (2:17; 3:2). The introduction of Jesus as "apostle" has no parallel in the NT. Here the term is used in the more general sense of one who is sent to bring the message of salvation. Paul uses the verb form *exapostellein* ("to send," Gal 4:4) to describe God's sending of Jesus. Erich Grässer suggests that "apostle" refers to Jesus as the one sent to speak the word of salvation (1:1–2:4), while "high priest" refers to the new status of the Son as suggested by 2:5–18 (Grässer 1990, 1:161).

The author expands on the community's "confession" with a new turn in the argument, echoing and adapting Num 12:7 with the claim that Jesus was **faithful to the one who made him as Moses was faithful in all his house** (3:2). Just as the author's task in chapters 1 and 2 was not to engage in polemic against angels, here his task is not to denigrate Moses but to introduce one who was faithful as a point of comparison to the Son. This claim continues the author's affirmation that Jesus is a faithful high priest (2:17) and introduces the topic that is the central focus of 3:1–4:13 and to which the author will return in 10:32–12:13. As 2:10–18 has indicated, Jesus demonstrated his faithfulness through "suffering of death" (2:9). Unlike the latter section, in which the author recalls the faithfulness of the fathers, here he contrasts the faithfulness of the Son to the unfaithfulness of the wilderness generation (3:12, 19; 4:2) in order to urge the community to respond appropriately to its heavenly calling. As the continued discussion in 3:1–6 indicates, the "house" is the family of God, continuing the familial imagery of 2:10–18.

The literal reading that he "was faithful to the one who made him" reinforces the comparison to Moses and continues the image of the people on the way (cf. 2:10) behind the pioneer. Inasmuch as the language echoes Samuel's statement that God "made" (NRSV "appointed") Moses and Aaron to lead the people out of Egypt (1 Sam 12:6), he is evidently continuing the theme of the pioneer, which he introduced in 2:10 (*anagagōn*, "leading," appears in both 1 Sam 12:6 and Heb 2:10). As chapters 1 and 2 indicate, God appointed him at the exaltation.

3:3–4. Although Moses and Jesus are both faithful (3:2), they are not equivalent. The claim that the Son **was counted of greater glory than Moses** (3:3a), like the previous affirmation that the Son is greater than the angels (1:4), is intended to reinforce the struggling community's appreciation of its confession by maintaining the focus on God's word. Although Moses was Israel's greatest spokesman, the community contemplates someone even greater. While Num 12:7–8 indicated that only Moses would be the recipient of God's direct revelation, the Son is even greater.

Although 3:1–6 appears to be a midrash on Num 12:7 comparable to the midrash on Ps 8 in the previous chapter, the author introduces this passage in 3:2 and does not return to it until 3:5. In 3:3b–4, he offers confirmation that the Son excels Israel's greatest revealer, indicating that he is greater because the **builder of the house** has **greater honor than the house** (3:3b). The argument appears to be an appeal to common sense and a claim that the Son is the builder of the house. The author clarifies, however, that **the builder of all things is God** (3:4). The close relationship between the Father and the Son recalls 1:2, "through whom he made the worlds," and the reminder of God as the one "through whom are all things and to whom are all things" and the one who led many sons to glory through the one Son (2:10). Thus the Father and the Son are united in creation.

Undoubtedly the "house" in Num 12:7 evoked other associations to which the author will appeal. The reference to the faithful high priest in 2:17 was an echo of 1 Sam 2:35 and the divine promise, "I will raise up for myself a faithful priest." The promise continues: "I will build for him a faithful house." According to the promise to Nathan, God will "establish David's descendant in his house" (1 Chron 17:14). Thus the "house" of Num 12:7 has led to reflections about the superiority of the builder of the house. These free associations are made possible by the variety of meanings of "house" in the Bible. At one level, the house is the family, the basic unit of society. At another level, the house is God's temple (cf. 2 Sam 7:1–11). At still another level, the house is a term for David and his descendants. Thus the author's claim that Jesus is faithful over God's house has evoked further associations related to God's house. The parenthetic statement in 3:4, like the other *synkriseis* in Hebrews, is not a criticism of Moses or the law but an opportunity to reinforce the greatness of the community's confession.

3:5–6. The author concludes the argument in 3:5–6 declaring that, while both Moses and Jesus are faithful in God's house, Jesus is the Son in the household while Moses is a servant. The reference to the house continues the theme of family solidarity from chapter 2. Here the comparison appears to be based on Num 12:7. The distinction between a servant and a son in a household was evident. Just as the author has compared the Son with the ministering angels in 1:14, he contrasts the Son with Moses the servant, deriving the term "servant" from the text of Num 12:7. Indeed, as a servant Moses is a **witness of the things that will be spoken later** (3:5b). That is, just as the author says later that Moses bore the "abuse of Christ" (11:26), he declares here that Moses announced the ultimate revelation in the Son in advance (cf. 1:1–2; Grässer 1985, 304). As the author indicates throughout the homily, the entire OT is a "witness" to Christ (cf. 1:5–13).

Thus it is the creator God who distinguishes the Son from the servant. The author rebuilds the community's symbolic world in the bold affirmation, **We are his house** (3:6b). They are the "children" whom God is bringing to glory (cf. 2:10–18). The center of gravity moves to the community, which is commonly described as God's house in the NT (1 Cor 3:9, 11; Eph 2:19–22; 1 Tim 3:15; 1 Pet 2:4–10). Just as the author moves from the description of the cosmic work of Christ to the community that receives the great salvation in 1:14, he moves here to the first person plural to reaffirm their place in God's plan as he did in the parallel phrase, "participants in a heavenly calling" in 3:1. Having demonstrated the special place of the Son in a house that includes not only the small house church but all of creation as well, the author attempts to restore the community's place in the world by showing them their special status within the household. Such a status is so great that the community will not want to abandon it.

This status is, however, conditional, as the warnings have already indicated (cf. 2:1–4). The reassuring claim, "we are his house," is followed by the conditional sentence, **if we hold firm to the confidence and pride in our hope** (3:6b). That is, the community must ensure that it maintains the heavenly calling (3:1). The "confidence" (*parrēsia*) that the author describes is not confidence in the community's own resources but the right of full access to God (cf. 10:19), which allows Christians to draw near to God's throne (cf. 4:16). Thus it is a gift that the community dares not throw away (10:35). The "pride in our hope" is also the gift of God, for hope has been made possible by the entry of Christ into the heavenly sanctuary (6:18; 7:19; cf. 10:23). Such extraordinary gifts can remain the community's possession only if they "hold firm" to what God has given rather than neglect the great salvation (cf. 2:3). The community, therefore, faces a choice in its response to God's gracious gift. It can either "fall away" (3:12; cf. 6:4; 10:26) or "hold firm" to its possession (cf. 3:14; 10:23). The author's frequent use of this verb (*katechein* in 3:6, 14; 10:23; cf. the synonym *kratein*, "hold firm" in 4:14; 6:18) indicates that it is synonymous with "being patient" (6:15), enduring (10:36; 12:1–2), being faithful (10:36–39). This conditional clause provides the transition to the depiction of the unfaithful Israelites in 3:7–4:11.

The Unfaithfulness of the Ancestors (3:7–4:11)

In 3:7–4:11, the author cites the unfaithfulness of the ancestors as a warning for the community.

3:7–19. The author follows the affirmation that the community's status as God's "house" is conditional with the citation of Ps 95:7–11, which offers ancient Israel as the example of those who did not hold firm to its hope. The citation is another reminder that the God who has spoken in the past (1:1) now speaks to the church inasmuch as it begins with a call to **hear God's voice** (3:7) and concludes with God's oath to Israel (3:11). These were not, however, merely words for the ancient audience, for the author contemporizes this stern warning for the benefit of the wavering people who hear his voice. **Beware, brothers** (3:12a), indicates that the psalm's warning speaks to the church, and the "today" of the psalm (3:7) is the "today" of the church (3:13). The church, God's house (3:6), lives in continuity with Israel, and it also stands at the entrance to the promised land. Just as the author later presents his church as the successors of Israel in 11:39, he now instructs his community to hear God's voice, which once spoke to the ancestors.

The psalm addresses the church as both warning and promise. The warning tells of the consequences of not listening to God's voice in 3:12–19, where unfaithfulness forms an *inclusio* that frames the exhortation. Although the author uses a variety of words in this midrash to describe Israel's failure— they rebelled (3:16), sinned (3:17), and disobeyed (3:18)—he summarizes their experience in the *inclusio* as unfaithfulness (cf. 4:2). He uses the unfaithfulness (3:19) of Israel as a warning against the church's unfaithfulness, indicating the tragic consequences of the church's failure to heed God's voice. He paints with a broad brush, leaving no place for exceptions in this dismal categorization of Israel. Only later (chapter 11) does the author describe Israel's history in another way—as the story of faithful men and women who endured when they were tempted to abandon the faith.

Assuming that words that were addressed to Israel now speak to the church as it, like Israel, moves through the wilderness to the promised land, the author speaks directly to the community (3:12–14), warning them against following Israel's example (3:12) and offering a means to maintain their faithfulness (3:13) before reminding the community that it holds a possession worth holding on to with all of their strength (3:14). The warning to beware **lest there be in any one of you an evil heart of unfaithfulness** (3:12b) echoes the psalmist's **harden not your heart** (3:8) and summarizes the bitterness and rebellion as unfaithfulness.

As with other NT writers, the author places great significance on faith (*pistis*). However, for the author of Hebrews, *pistis* is described never as faith in Christ but as the faithfulness of one who holds firm or is reliable. Not only does he describe Moses and Jesus (2:17; 3:2, 5) as faithful;

> **An Outline of Hebrews 3:7–4:11**
>
> The unfaithfulness of the ancestors (3:7–4:11)
>
> Ancestors who did not enter the rest (3:7–19)
>
> Those who believe may enter (4:1–5)
>
> Let us enter his rest (4:6–11)

he also describes God as faithful in keeping promises (10:23). Thus faithfulness is the appropriate response to the promises of God. *Pistis* is the equivalent of patience (6:12) and endurance (10:36–38) in holding firm until the end. Thus the unfaithfulness against which the author warns is the equivalent of **falling away from the living God** (3:12c), and the prime example is Israel in the wilderness. To "fall away" is also the equivalent of neglecting the great salvation (2:3).

Only by corporate solidarity will the church maintain its faithfulness. Indeed, the author is concerned not only that the community not fall away but also that unfaithfulness not be present in **any one of you** (3:12b). The author repeats this focus on "any" later in this homily (cf. 12:15–16), indicating his concern for the solidarity of the whole community. Thus it can retain its fidelity as members **encourage one another each day** (3:13). The author asks for the same kind of solidarity that the members demonstrated at the beginning of their Christian experience, when they cared for each other in times of distress (cf. 6:10; 10:32–34). One of the ways they encourage each other is by being present in their assemblies (10:25). The community will find encouragement in the reading of scripture and exhortation (cf. 12:5). Indeed, the fact that the "today" of the psalm is also the "today" of the church gives a special urgency to the church's response.

The reason for the community's endurance is that they **are partakers of Christ** (3:14a). The claim recalls the author's statement that they are participants (*metochoi*) in a heavenly calling (3:1) and that they are his "house" (3:6). That is, the community has been caught up in the narrative of the one who triumphed over death and is now in heaven. Because such an extraordinary possession must be maintained, the author indicates once more the conditional nature of this possession. Just as he appended the "if" clause to the affirmation in 3:6, here he adds, **if we hold the beginning of the reality** (BDAG, "original commitment") **firm until the end** (3:14b). The community had begun well (6:9–12; 10:32–34), but now their task is to hold firm (*katechein*; cf. 3:6; 10:23). What the community needs, therefore, is to hold on in the midst of disappointment.

93

In 3:15–19 the author returns to scripture to recall the wilderness generation and to address his audience with rhetorical questions, presenting Israel as the example of those who heard the word but did not "hold firm" and of the consequences of such failure. The sequence follows the citation of the psalm as the author asks about those who **rebelled** (3:16) and **sinned** (3:17b), and with whom God **was angry** (3:17a). This response to God's voice had devastating consequences, for God swore that they would never enter his rest (3:18), and the bodies were left in the wilderness (3:17; cf. Num 14:29, 32). The author does not mention that Israelites actually did enter the promised land because his focus is on the absoluteness of the consequences of refusing God's voice. Although the psalm does not speak of unfaithfulness, the author sums up Israel's rebellion and disobedience in that word. Israel demonstrates the consequences of not listening to God's word. Having shown that Jesus was faithful, the author declares that the appropriate response to him is to be faithful.

This warning is analogous to frequent other warnings in Hebrews (cf. 2:1–4; 6:4–6; 10:26–31; 12:25–29), indicating the consequences of rejecting God's voice. The warning suggests the irrevocability of the community's choice. Just as God's decision was final for Israel, God's response will be ultimate for the community that fails to hold firm to its commitment.

4:1–5. The citation from the psalm introduces a promise to the church in 4:1–11. The hortatory subjunctives **Let us fear lest any . . . fail to enter his rest** (4:1) and "Let us then strive to enter his rest" (4:11) frame the discussion as the author holds out the hope that those who hold firm will receive the promise that Israel never received (4:1, 11). Thus God's oath is not only a stern warning; it is also a promise to those who have faith. The author speaks with warnings and with hope that the listeners have not yet forfeited God's promise (4:1–11), as the *inclusio* in 4:1, 11 indicates. Unlike Paul, who speaks of promises to Israel that have been fulfilled in Jesus Christ (cf. 2 Cor 1:20; Gal 3:15–19), the author holds before the community a promise that **remains open** (4:1). Just as the ancestors wandered without a homeland but lived to obtain the promise (cf. 11:9, 13, 17, 33; cf. 6:12), the new community also lives in hope of a homeland. Having indicated that Israel failed to enter God's rest (3:12–19), at the beginning and end of this section the author urges his readers to enter into the rest in the land of promise that Israel forfeited.

The continuity of salvation history is that God has spoken both in the past and in these last days (cf. 1:1–2; 2:2–3). Thus both the church and Israel **received the good news** (4:2a). However, God's speech requires a response (cf. 2:1–4), and Israel did not meet the conditions for entering God's rest, for the message **was not mixed with faith** (4:2b). These conditions are still open to the author's community inasmuch as **we who have faith enter that rest** (4:3a). Thus the church stands poised before the promised land with the opportunity to enter into God's rest if the wavering listeners are faithful. Their faithfulness is not only an assent to the facts of the gospel but also their patient endurance and commitment to God's promise despite the alienation and weariness that tests their capacity to endure.

Although the author has assumed throughout the midrash that the "today" of the psalm is addressing his own church (3:13) and that the rest "remains open" for his church (4:1), he does not explain how the church centuries later could participate in and complete the ancient story by entering into God's rest until 4:4–8. Using the rabbinic hermeneutical principle *gezera shewa*, according to which the same word in two different passages means the same, the author quotes Gen 2:2, **God rested (*katepausen*) on the seventh day from all his labors** (4:4), alongside **They shall never enter my rest (*katapausis*)** (4:5) and concludes that the rest described by the psalm is God's Sabbath rest in Genesis. Indeed, the psalm prepared the way for this interpretation with the reference to "my rest" (cf. Heb 3:11). The rest, therefore, is the transcendent rest that belongs to God.

4:6–11. In 4:6–7, the author explains why this rest remains open to the community. Because the earlier generation **did not enter** (4:6), the "today" of the psalm is a new day. The announcement of "today" in the psalm indicates that Joshua never gave the earlier generation rest in the promised land. Indeed, he concludes that, because the psalmist wrote after the time of the conquest, the "today" of the psalm is actually speaking of a new day that is available to the church. Unlike Paul, who interprets the story as a prototype for the church, the author of Hebrews demonstrates the continuity of the church with ancient Israel. As Israel's descendants, the community still stands overlooking the promised land, and God has announced a new opportunity to enter. Thus in the ancient scripture the God who has spoken to us in a Son (1:2) now speaks to the church, challenging the people to recognize the urgency of the moment.

With the argument that the announcement of the new day indicates that Joshua did not give Israel rest, the author introduces a hermeneutical principle that will play an important role throughout the argument of the homily. Instead of the time-honored hermeneutical principle that the more ancient passage is the basis for interpreting a later passage, the author consistently uses the Psalms and Prophets to demonstrate that mandates of the Torah have been superseded by something greater (cf. 7:11; 8:13; 10:9). The church has a new opportunity because God has established a new day.

With the assurance that **there remains a Sabbath rest for the people of God** (4:9), the author is reaffirming the earlier claim that "we who believe enter God's rest," alluding to the argument that the rest that believers enter is God's Sabbath rest. This assurance is the basis for the exhortation in 4:11 not to follow the example of Israel's disobedience. The solidarity of the community remains in view in the exhortation that not any fall.

The author consistently speaks of the Christian experience of a people on the move, and he has a special emphasis on verbs for entering and drawing near. The goal of the pilgrimage is the transcendent God. The exalted Lord is the guarantor that the pilgrimage leads to the goal. He is the pioneer (2:10; *archēgos*) of the exodus to heaven (cf. 12:2) and our forerunner. According to 6:19–20, Jesus is the forerunner who entered behind the curtain of the heavenly sanctuary. He entered a sanctuary not made with hands to offer a sacrifice (9:12, 24) and opened the way for others to follow (10:19–23). Thus to enter into God's rest is to follow Jesus into the heavenly world. "Rest" in Hebrews is the equivalent of other terms describing the hope of the believer. Elsewhere the author speaks of the hope for a homeland (11:14), a city (11:10, 16; 12:22; 13:14), and an unshakable kingdom (12:28).

The author's appeal to the community anticipates the appeal to faithfulness in chapter 11. In chapters 3–4, Israel is the example of unfaithfulness whose failure left the heavenly rest available to the community, while in chapter 11 the Israelites are the examples of faithfulness. In both instances, the land of promise stands before the faithful, who are wandering without a home. In chapter 4, the faithful look to enter the rest, which is an alternative term for the city and the homeland.

Confronted by the Word of God (4:12–13)

In 4:12–13 the author reminds his readers of the implications of being confronted by the word of God. Although the poetic statement here appears to be an isolated aphorism, the significance of the author's statement becomes evident when we notice the role of the word of God in Hebrews, for the history of salvation can be described in terms of God's speech and the human response. As the opening words of Hebrews indicate, God has spoken both to ancient Israel and the Christian community. Ancient Israel received a "word" spoken through angels (2:2), while the Christian community heard the "word" spoken by the Lord (2:3). Near the end of Hebrews, the author recalls that ancient Israel heard a "word" at Sinai that shook the earth (12:19, 26), but the church has heard a voice from heaven that will shake both heaven and earth. The author introduces citations from scripture as words of God (1:5–13), Christ (2:12–13), or the Holy Spirit (3:7). The reflection on the word of God in 4:12–13 is an appropriate summary of the first major section of the homily, as the *inclusio* with 1:1–2 suggests. Thus God has spoken in the event of the death and exaltation of Christ, and the church hears the divine voice through the medium of scripture.

The author's reflection on the word of God is not only a summary of the first major section of Hebrews; it forms the appropriate conclusion to 3:7–4:11, which focuses on God's oath to Israel. The author cites Ps 95:7–11 as God's oracle recorded in scripture (see above, p. 83), concluding with the divine words, "As I swore in my wrath, they shall never enter my rest" (3:11).

4:12. The author's warning to the community not to "fall away from the living God" (3:12) and his insistence that God's oath was irrevocable provide the background for the statement that **the word of God is living and active** (4:12a), for it is the power that determines salvation or punishment, as the oath to Israel indicates (3:12–19). God's oath prohibiting Israel from entering God's rest is an indication of the irrevocability of God's word. God's word to Israel indicates the consequences of refusing that word. This living and active word that addressed Israel (cf. 4:2) now speaks to the church.

The imagery of the sword dominates the author's reflections, indicating the role of the word of God as the instrument of judgment. The focus of 4:12 is the surgical capacity of the word, which is **sharper than any two-edged sword** (4:12b). In **penetrating between the division of soul and spirit, joints and marrow** (4:12c), the word pierces the innermost part of the person. The imagery points not to a distinction between "soul and spirit" or between soul and body but to the whole person (Wider 1997, 76; Attridge 1989, 135). The function of the word in "penetrating" the whole person is illuminated by the parallel phrase **judging the thoughts and intentions of the heart** (4:12d), for the "heart" also stands for the whole person. The warning to the community to avoid "an evil, unbelieving heart" (3:12) is the background for the author's reflection. Thus the penetrating function of the word is its activity of judging the heart. As God's oath to Israel indicates, those who hear God's voice mediated in scripture are confronted with the God who is "judge of all" (12:23).

4:13. In 4:13, the perspective shifts to that of the **creature** when confronted with the two-edged sword. The penetrating and judging function of the word of God determines the perspective of every creature (i.e., every human), whose situation the author describes with three parallel terms: in the presence of God's word they are not **hidden** (*aphanēs*); they are **naked** (*gymna*) and **laid bare** (*tetrachēlismena*) (4:13a). The penetrating sword exposes the innermost parts of the human being (cf. Braun 1984, 121). *Tetrachēlismena* (laid bare) is derived from *trachēlos* (neck) and means literally "grab by the neck" in order to shake or drag away (Grässer 1990, 1:238). Philo uses the word metaphorically for the calamities that "prostrate" (*Cherubim* 78) people or place someone "in the grip" of another (*Moses* 1.297). Thus in 4:13 the sharp word of God uncovers and judges the listeners, leaving them defenseless and prostrate before the eyes of the one **to whom we give an account** (4:13b). The author anticipates the later comment that "it is a fearful thing to fall into the hands of the living God" (10:31).

This judgment takes place not only at the end, for it occurs in the present as the community is confronted by the word of God. The church has a new opportunity to respond appropriately to God's word, and it knows the consequences of failing to listen to God's voice.

The irrevocable oath of God to Israel is not only a word from the past, for it now stands as a word that judges the hearts of listeners who are tempted to ignore God's summons. Because the church has a new opportunity to hear the voice of God, the ancient words continue to be "sharper than any double-edged sword." The surgical capabilities of the word now confront the community that is faced with a decision about its response.

Theological Issues

While the first two chapters of Hebrews offer the marginalized community one of the most extended interpretations of the nature of Christ in the NT, in 3:1–4:13 the author demonstrates the inseparability of Christ and the church. Having described the community of faith as the brothers and sisters of Christ in 2:10–18, the author expands on the imagery of family in 3:1–6, affirming that they are God's "house" (3:6). This claim is a ringing assurance to marginalized people whose Christian faith has left them wondering if they have a place to belong and a reminder that their place in God's household is an extraordinary gift. He invites the people to see beyond the realities of the house church to recognize that they are the house of the exalted Son. Thus the church, despite the anguish and disappointments, is still his "house," and the members are "partners in a heavenly calling" (3:1). The listeners have found a new family in the community of believers. This image suggests that the house church assumed many of the responsibilities that ancient families provided. They gathered regularly, shared meals, provided intimacy, and functioned as the social safety net for members. Thus Christian faith was no private matter, and members could not sustain their allegiance to Jesus in isolation.

The visible manifestation of the church has varied throughout the centuries, and the diversity of churches is especially evident today with the expansion of the church to the global South. As denominational loyalties erode in the modern era, new forms of church are emerging. Hebrews offers a reminder of essential elements in the nature of the church. The image of family, the most persistent symbol in the NT for the community of faith, is no empty metaphor. Whatever forms of church life emerge, the Christian faith will be sustained only with a vital community life that provides a place of caring and account- ability. Philip Jenkins's book *The Next Christendom* (2002) has shown that Christianity in Europe and North America is in a period of decline that will result in the marginalization of Christians in the traditional Christian lands. The contemporary church can recognize in Hebrews the importance of the community of faith. Megachurches discover that their vitality depends on the capacity to grow smaller through the intimacy of small groups. To say "whose house are we" is to recognize that we find our identity only within the family of God, which extends beyond the local community of faith.

Our place in God's house is conditional, as the author's repeated "if we hold fast" indicates (3:6, 14). The Son who was "faithful in his house" sum- mons the community to be faithful (3:12, 19; 4:2–3). The author explores this theme by describing in greater detail the nature of the church.

In the first place, the church is a community of hope. By transforming God's promise for a land of rest, one of the central symbols of Israel's identity, into a metaphor for the transcendent hope of ultimate salvation, the author has provided an evocative image that has shaped Christian thought for centuries. The image of the church looking from Mount Pisgah to the promised land has been the focus of countless hymns and sermons. The "rest that remains open" (4:1) for the community is the transcendent place where the exalted Son has gone (1:3, 13), not the earthly Canaan. Similarly, the place of Abraham's inheritance was not the land of Canaan but "the city that has foundations, whose maker and builder is God" (Heb 11:10). Thus the promised rest is the equivalent of the heavenly city (11:10, 16) and homeland (11:14). More than any book of the NT, Hebrews refers to the promise (cf. 4:1; 6:12–13, 15, 17; 7:6; 8:6; 9:15; 10:23, 36; 11:9, 13, 17; 12:26), the inclusive term for all the images of ultimate salvation.

Unlike other NT writers, the author never indicates that the promises have been fulfilled in Christ (cf. 2 Cor 1:20), for the people of God continue to await the fulfillment of the promise. Eschatological hope is thus a central feature of the exhortation, placing all other hopes in perspective. Those who orient themselves toward the ultimate hope recognize the provisional nature of human expectations. The hope for the land pales in significance in contrast to the heavenly promise. Indeed, the hope for the heavenly place of rest is the author's alternative to all false hopes. If the hope for the land is only provisional, the hopes for nationalistic, political, or materialistic redemption are also illusory. No other author of the NT demonstrates as effectively as the author of Hebrews that this hope is a foundation for Christian existence (cf. Backhaus 2001, 187).

At the same time, a community of hope offers an alternative not only to the false hopes that human society holds but also to the despair of the present culture. The author invites the church to see beyond apocalyptic images of economic or ecological chaos to a vision of hope. This vision of hope is the motivation for Christians neither to deny the threats to human society nor to withdraw from engaging these problems, for hope provides the stimulus to meet the challenges that face society.

In the second place, the church is a community on the way. Believers wait quietly in hope, for they cannot enter the promised land without first going through the wilderness (Käsemann 1984; Grässer 1986, 161). Indeed, the wilderness setting is the focal image for the entire homily, for the author not only envisions his readers as a wilderness community in 3:7–4:11 but also draws the tabernacle imagery of 8:1–10:18 from the wilderness experience and returns to the events at Mount Sinai (12:18–29) in his climactic appeal. He consistently employs imagery of movement to describe believers as on the way behind Jesus, the pioneer (2:10) and forerunner (6:20), who opened the "new and living way" into the heavenly world (10:20). Thus believers "draw near" to the way that the exalted Christ has opened (4:16; 10:22) and "go out to him" outside the camp (13:13). Their models for faith are their ancestors, who were "strangers and pilgrims on earth" (11:13). As Ernst Käsemann (1984) noted, the underlying theme of the homily is the people on the way (see pp. 27–28 above).

Unlike Philo, who described the soul's path toward the divine, the author speaks not of individual pilgrimage but of a corporate path through the wilderness in which the people encourage each other (3:13) to maintain their identity, rejecting the values of the dominant society. Thus the author offers an important insight for the self-definition of the church as the community living between two worlds. This view of the church was the inspiration for other ancient thinkers. It found classic expression in the anonymous second-century apology known as the *Epistle to Diognetus*:

> They live in their own countries, but only as nonresidents; they participate in everything as citizens, and endure everything as foreigners. Every foreign country is their fatherland, and every fatherland is foreign. They marry like everyone else, and have children, but they do not expose their offspring. They share their food but not their wives. . . . They live on earth, but their citizenship is in heaven. (5.5–9; 6.1, trans. Holmes 2006)

More than two centuries later John Chrysostom proclaimed, "Do you not know that life here is a journey? . . . You are wanderers! . . . You are not citizens, but wanderers and travelers! Do not say, 'I have this or that city!' No one has a city, for the city is above. The present is a pathway" (*Capt. Eutrop.* 5, PG 52.401, cited in Backhaus 2001).

In the third place, the church is a community confronted by God's word, understanding its place only as it hears the word of God. Scripture is not a word locked in the past but a voice that addresses the community in the present, saying, "Today, if you hear his voice, harden not your hearts" (3:7–8). While scripture offers assurance of hope, it also invites the readers to see themselves in the unfaithfulness of the ancestors. This scripture is "sharper than any two-edged sword" (4:12) because of its capacity to perform surgery on the readers and confront them with their own unfaithfulness. Those who hear scripture will encounter the God "to whom we give an account" (4:13) and will experience God's claim on their lives. Thus Hebrews offers a model of hermeneutics in which the church hears in scripture the voice of the God who continues to speak a word of promise and judgment as the community journeys through the wilderness toward the goal.

P A R T   2

Hebrews 4:14–10:31

Discovering Certainty and Confidence
in the Word for the Mature

In part 2, the author develops the theme of the high priestly work of Christ, which he mentions only briefly in part 1 (2:17–18; 3:1) and to which he returns with the brief exhortation in part 3 (13:10–13). The words "having . . . a great high priest. . . let us hold fast the confession . . . let us draw near" in 4:14–16 form an *inclusio* with 10:19–23, demarcating the central section of the homily. Within this outer frame, the author gives a lengthy description of the sacrifice of the high priest in the heavenly sanctuary (7:1–10:18). Parts 1 and 3, however, have a remarkable symmetry in which the author announces that "God has spoken" (1:1–2; cf. 2:1–4; 12:24) and now summons the community to listen (2:1–4; 12:25) and endure faithfully on a pilgrimage, even when the destination is far away (3:1–4:13; 10:32–12:13). Near the beginning and the end of the homily, the author presents Jesus as the model of faithful endurance and the pioneer (2:10–18; 12:1–3) who leads the way. This change of topic in part 2 raises the question of the relationship between the lengthy description of the high priestly work of Christ and the themes of parts 1 and 3.

Despite the differences in content, the central section is interwoven with parts 1 and 3 in numerous ways. Indeed, the author's perspective remains consistent throughout the homily, for his treatment of the tabernacle in 8:1–10:18

101

maintains the wilderness setting of parts 1 and 3 (cf. 2:1–4; 3:7–4:11; 12:18–29). When Jesus enters into the heavenly sanctuary (9:11–14) and opens the way for his people to "draw near" (4:16; 10:22), he is the pioneer (cf. 2:10) who leads his people into the promised rest (3:7–4:11). Thus part 2 is not a change of topic but an elaboration of the word that "God has spoken" (1:2) in a Son. Inasmuch as God's speech "in a Son" included the cross and exaltation (1:1–4), the central section interprets these events with images drawn from Israel's sacrificial system.

The author describes this section as the "word" that is "hard to explain" (5:11), indicating that he has not abandoned his emphasis on the word of God. This elaboration on the confessional statement in 1:1–4 suggests the importance of the community's continued advancement in the hearing of the divine voice. Despite the difficulty of the topic for those who were "dull of hearing," the elaboration of this theme indicates the necessity of hearing a word for the mature if the church is to maintain its vitality. As Graham Hughes has suggested, the word of God, which unfortunately has become a "word that is *logos dysermēneutos* ('word that is hard to explain') is a recalling in newer and deeper ways of those verities wherein we hear God's call: the life, death, and exaltation of Jesus" (G. Hughes 1979, 49). Thus the answer to the community's crisis of faith is the theological foundation that comes only from hearing the profound significance of God's word.

The theme that most unites part 2 with the other sections of Hebrews is the reflection on the promise of God. According to parts 1 and 3, faith involves waiting patiently on promises that have not been fulfilled (4:1; 6:12, 15, 17; 10:36; 11:9, 13, 17, 33). In part 2, the author assures the community that the death and exaltation of Jesus is the oath of God that confirms the promise (6:16–20). The entry of Jesus behind the curtain provides the hope that is the steadfast anchor of the soul (6:19; cf. 7:19). As a result, Jesus is the "guarantor" of the better covenant (7:22), and those who are called receive the promise of an eternal inheritance (9:15). Thus, although the community cannot see the goal, the sacrifice of Christ is the guarantee of the future, providing the "full assurance of faith" (10:22) as the basis for their endurance as they wander through the wilderness. Although the people have not yet received the promise, they may now follow the pioneer into the sanctuary, drawing near to God in worship. Thus, as the outer frame of this section indicates, the purpose of 4:14–10:31 is to provide the community with the stable reality to which they may "hold firmly" (März 1991, 275).

Hebrews 4:14–10:31 in Context

Hearing God's word with faithful endurance (1:1–4:13)

▶ *Probatio*: Discovering certainty and confidence in the word for the mature (4:14–10:31)

Peroratio: On not refusing the one who is speaking (10:32–13:25)

Hebrews 4:14–5:10

Drawing Near and Holding Firmly

Introductory Matters

The distinctive feature of Hebrews as a word of exhortation is the close connection between "we have/having" and the hortatory subjunctive "let us,"
which appears for the first time in 4:14–16 (cf. 10:19–23; 12:1–2; 13:13–15;
cf. also "have" for the community's possession in Christ in 6:9, 18–19; 8:1;
10:34 and "let us" in 4:11; 6:1). Between the opening and closing words of the
central section (4:14–10:31), the author develops the theme of the heavenly
priesthood of Christ (7:1–10:18) as the basis for his exhortation to the community. Here the author describes what we "have" (4:14–15; 10:19) as the basis
for the exhortation to the wavering community to be faithful to its original
confession and "draw near."

The concentric structure of Hebrews offers an insight into the pastoral
concerns that the author addresses in the central section. As the units immediately before (3:1–4:13) and after (10:32–12:13) the central section indicate,
the author deals with a crisis of faithfulness in the community; he reminds
the readers that only those who are faithful enter into the promised land (4:3).
After twice using the conditional clause "if we hold fast" (3:6, 14) to describe
the community's precarious situation in part 1, the central section begins and
ends with the exhortation, "let us hold fast to the confession" (4:14; 10:23),
which is the appropriate alternative to the temptation to "drift away" (2:1) or
"fall away from the living God" (3:12). Thus the central section offers a basis
and motivation for the community to "hold fast," knowing that the saving
work of Christ is the anchor to which they may hold (cf. 6:18–19).

103

The author's pastoral purpose is evident in the interweaving of christologi-cal reflection and exhortation in 4:14–5:10, the turning point of the argument of Hebrews and the foundation for the central section. In the affirmations in 4:14–16, "having a great high priest who has passed through the heavens" and "we do not have a high priest who cannot sympathize with our weaknesses," the author reiterates the focus on Jesus as both transcendent and human (cf. 2:5–18). As he has already indicated in 2:8, the fact that the community does not see the world in subjection to the Son creates cognitive dissonance for read-ers who can see only suffering and death and tempts them to abandon their confession. Thus the exalted Christ appears to be remote from the realities on earth. The author has addressed that concern in 2:5–18, declaring that Jesus is the Son who descended for a "little while" (2:9) into the world and shared the sufferings and temptation that now face the community (2:10–16) before his exaltation, and that his solidarity with humans was the basis for his work as a merciful and faithful high priest. In the same way, 4:14–5:10 speaks of the "days of his flesh" when he suffered before he was appointed Son and high priest at the exaltation (5:5–6, 10). Thus 4:14–5:10 assures the community that Jesus is not only the eternal high priest at God's right hand; he is also the sympathetic one whose triumph was preceded by suffering and tempta-tion. If the community's struggle is rooted in its distance from the heavenly world, the author reassures them that they follow the suffering one to glory. Therefore 4:14–5:10 moves from the anguish of suffering to the community's access to God's throne. In 5:1–10, the author elaborates on these two dimen-sions. These claims become the basis for the exhortations, "let us hold fast to the confession" and "let us draw near."

As "having therefore a great high priest" indicates, the author builds on the previous argument, in which he established that Jesus became a merciful and faithful high priest at the exaltation (2:17; 3:1). Having introduced Jesus as the "high priest of our confession" (3:1), the author now makes the transition from the portrayal of Jesus as Son (1:1–4:13; cf. esp. 1:2–14; 2:10–13; 3:1–6) to his role as the great high priest, which he develops in 4:14–10:31.

Although the author never states the precise content of the "confession," it is central to his concern, as the exhortations in 4:14 and 10:23 indicate. Like other confessions in the NT (cf. Rom 10:9–10; 1 Tim 6:12; 1 John 2:23; 4:2; 2 John 7), it is undoubtedly a christological claim, which the community has shared from the beginning of its existence. The focus on Jesus as Son of God in 1:1–4:13 suggests that the community confesses Jesus as Son and high priest. The author now elaborates on the confession in 4:14–10:18.

The claim that the community has "a high priest who has passed through the heavens" anticipates the subsequent contrast between the heavenly high priest and the Aaronic priesthood that ministers on earth (7:11–19). Although "the heavens" can refer to the sphere above the earth (cf. 1:10; 7:26; 12:26), "has passed through (*dielēlythota*) the heavens" is here the equivalent of "Jesus

... entered (*eiselthen*)" (6:20; cf. 9:12–14, 24) into heaven and is "at the right hand of the majesty in the heavens" (1:4, 13; 8:1). This claim establishes the parallel between the high priests on earth (cf. 8:1–6; 9:1–10) and Christ as the heavenly high priest who offered his own blood in the heavenly sanctuary to cleanse the people (9:11–14).

The fact that Jesus overcame human temptation and "passed through the heavens" is the basis for the exhortation, "let us draw near with boldness to the throne of grace." "Draw near" (*proserchesthai*) in the LXX depicts the priestly approach to God (Lev 9:7–8; 21:17–24; 22:3) or the approach of the people for worship (Exod 16:9; Lev 9:5; Num 18:4; Scholer 1991, 94). In the LXX, ordinary priests are never characterized as drawing near to the "mercy seat" within the holy of holies. According to Num 4:19–20 LXX Aaron and his sons "draw near" to the holy of holies but do not enter it, because this entry is reserved only for the high priest (Scholer 1991, 93). Verbs of movement play an important role in Hebrews. The author employs *eiserchesthai* ("enter," 6:19–20; 9:12, 24) for the entry of Christ into the heavenly sanctuary at the exaltation; in 4:11 he urges listeners to enter (*eiselthein*) into God's heavenly rest where Christ has gone. He uses *proserchesthai* for Christians who "draw near" (7:25; 10:22; 12:18). In 4:16 and the parallel passage in 10:19–22, Christians "draw near" to the heavenly throne because Christ the high priest has entered the sanctuary, opening the way (10:19–20) for them to enter the sanctuary as well. In 12:18, 22, the author employs the perfect tense, declaring that the listeners have "drawn near." Although the fulfillment of the promise appears remote, Christians may nevertheless "draw near" to God in worship and prayer (cf. Jer 7:16; Scholer 1991, 108). The author employs both cultic and royal images in describing a sanctuary where Christ sits on a throne (cf. 8:1; 12:2).

The "boldness" (*parresia*) with which Christians draw near is not a subjective experience but the right of access to God. In the political sphere the term meant freedom of speech or the candor to speak the truth to power. In the LXX and Jewish literature, it is a gift of God. According to 10:19 it is the access to God granted to Christians through the high priestly work of Christ. In 10:35, the author challenges the readers not to cast aside their "boldness." In Job 22:26–27 and 27:9–10, the verb form (*parresiazomai*) is used in the context of prayer. For Philo of Alexandria, *parresia* distinguishes the friend of God who speaks to God with "boldness." *Parresia* is the quality of those who speak openly with their superiors. It was exemplified by Joseph, who was not awed by the high dignity of royalty (*Joseph* 107; cf. 222). Faithful people speak frankly with the Master of the Universe when they are "pure from sin" and free from the judgments of the conscience (*Heir* 5–7). "Boldness" characterizes the friends of God who, like Moses, fearlessly bring their complaints before God (*Heir* 19–20). This background suggests that boldness here is the right to stand before God in prayer made possible by the Christ event. As a people tested by its failure to see the world in subjection to God

(2:8a), it experiences its "time of need." With his challenge to "draw near," the author invites his readers to come into the heavenly world in worship and prayer, where they will "receive mercy and find grace" to overcome the current difficulties. "Mercy" and "grace" are indistinguishable in meaning and are often used in connection with each other (cf. 1 Tim 1:2; 1:13–14; 2 Tim 1:2; Wis 3:9; 4:15; Philo, *Unchangeable* 74–76). With this assurance, the author demonstrates how Jesus is the merciful high priest (2:17).

The reference to "every high priest" (5:1) establishes the basis for comparison (Greek *synkrisis*) that the author employs throughout the homily (cf. "every [high] priest" in 8:3; 10:11) to establish that Jesus both corresponds to and exceeds Levitical high priests. As in 2:17, the author mentions only one of the functions associated with the office of high priest in the OT: to offer sacrifices for sins. He maintains this focus throughout the central section of the homily (4:14–10:18). Although the law prescribes a variety of "gifts and sacrifices" (cf. Exod 29:38–42; Lev 6:12–16; Num 28:3), the author uses the terms synonymously for the sacrifices "for sins." The distinction between "those who do wrong unintentionally" and those who "go astray" echoes the Levitical distinction between sins that were committed in ignorance (Lev 5:17–18) and those committed "with a high hand" (Num 15:30–31).

Of the qualifications for the high priesthood, the author chooses only two for comparison. In the first place, the *inclusio* in 5:1, 4 indicates that the high priest does not choose the honor himself but "is chosen" (5:1), "appointed" (5:1), and "called" (5:4). Levitical regulations require the proper appointment (Exod 28:1; Lev 8:1–2; Num 3:10; 17:5; 18:1) and investiture (Exod 28:2 LXX) of the high priest and condemn those who act as priests but have no right to do so (Num 3:10; 16:40). In the second place, priests were able to "deal gently with those who do wrong unintentionally and those who go astray."

While the first of the qualifications for the high priesthood is based on the OT requirement that the high priest be called, the law has no requirement for the second qualification: that the high priest be able to "deal gently" (*metriopathein*) with sinners. The claim that the high priest is "beset (*perikeitai*, lit. "clothed") with weakness" (cf. 7:28) is also not specifically mentioned in the Levitical regulations but is probably an inference based on the fact that the high priest offers sacrifices "for himself" (5:3; cf. Lev 9:7). Thus the author did not determine the qualifications for the high priest directly from the OT but began with the Christian confession of the solidarity of Jesus as high priest before deriving these qualifications from the Levitical regulations.

Metriopathein means "to moderate one's feelings." It was often used of one who did not display excessive anger. It does not appear anywhere else in the Bible, but it appears in philosophical discussions for the golden mean between passion (*pathos*) and apathy (*apatheia*). According to Plutarch, the true sage must not be too easily moved (*pathētikos*) or unfeeling (*apathēs*) but should be *metriopathēs* (*Virt. mor.* 12; *Cohib. ira* 458c; *Frat. amor.* 489c; Spicq 1994,

2:486). Philo of Alexandria uses this term on frequent occasions, indicating that a special virtue of the sage is moderation in the emotions (*Abraham* 257). Although Philo follows the Stoic ideal in regarding the absence of emotions (*apatheia*) as the highest ideal, he also had a high regard for moderation in the emotions (*metriopathein*; cf. *Alleg. Interp.* 3.129) as the characteristic of those who are making progress toward the goal. According to Philo, Joseph responds to the evils that have confronted him, "Many desperate calamities I have seen and heard: thousands of them have I experienced myself, but trained to moderate my feelings at such I remain unmoved" (*Joseph* 26). Aaron also moderated his emotions (*Alleg. Interp.* 3.132). This interpretation of Aaron is consistent with Philo's description of the laws on high priests. Philo maintains that the law prohibited priests from all outward mourning. In order to remain undefiled, the priest "ought to be estranged from all the ties of birth and not be overcome by the affection to parents or children." The priest will "have his feeling of pity under control and continue free of sorrow" because the law prescribes that he "be endued with a nature higher than the merely human and to approximate the divine, on the borderline, that one may have a mediator through whom they may propitiate" (*Spec. Laws* 1.112–114, trans. Colson and Whitaker 1929).

Philo and the author of Hebrews agree that the Levitical high priest moderates the emotions and that the true high priest is sinless (cf. Philo, *Virtues* 176–177; *Spec. Laws* 1.230; 3.134–135; *Flight* 108–109; *Dreams* 2.185) and "higher than the merely human" (cf. Heb 7:26–28), although these qualities are not mentioned in the OT. The distinctive feature of Hebrews is the contrast between the Levitical priest, who is able to "deal gently" (*metriopathein*) with sinners, and Jesus, who is able to "sympathize" (*sympathein*) with the believers (4:15) because of his total solidarity with his people. Unlike the Levitical high priest, who "moderates the emotions" toward sinners, Jesus has total solidarity with the temptations that face the community. As the one who had once shared the temptations that accompany human existence and is now exalted, he continues to have "pathos" for his brothers and sisters in the realm of flesh and blood (Dey 1975, 226). A community that experiences the weakness of the flesh may trust in the high priest, who had been "beset by weakness."

The term *sympatheō* is used elsewhere in the NT only in Heb 10:34, where it describes the care that the more fortunate members of the community extended to prisoners. The term is closely related to the mercy ascribed to the high priest in 2:17. The term means participating in the pain of another, and it is "tinged with pity" (Spicq 1994, 3:320; cf. Philo, *Embassy* 273). It was used in antiquity for God's sympathy for humans (4 Macc 5:25), mothers for their children (4 Macc 14:13–14, 18, 20), and brother for brother (4 Macc 13:23). The author's double negative "we do not have . . . not able" suggests that the one who expresses sympathy also has the resources to help (Spicq 1994, 3:320).

Jesus was tested, and now the community is tested (2:18). The sympathy of the high priest is based on his being "tested in every respect."

After establishing the qualifications for the high priesthood in 5:1–4, the author demonstrates how Jesus meets and exceeds them. In 5:5–6, he indicates how Jesus meets the first qualification. He did not glorify himself but was called by God, who spoke to him with the words of Ps 2:7 ("you are my son") and 110:4 ("you are a priest forever after the order of Melchizedek"), both of which are royal psalms addressed by God to the king declaring his special status. In connecting the two passages that begin "you are," the author is following the rabbinic hermeneutical principle of *gezera shewa*, according to which passages with similar words or phrases are interpreted in light of each other. He has already described the exaltation as the occasion when God "spoke" to the Son with the words of Ps 2:7 (cf. 1:5) and Ps 110:1 (cf. 1:3, 13). The new dimension in 5:6 is the citation of Ps 110:4, declaring that the Son is also the "priest after the order of Melchizedek," the theme that the author will pursue at length in chapter 7 (see below for the discussion of Melchizedek). As in chapter 1, the author focuses on the fact that God has "spoken" in a Son (1:2) through the OT scriptures (1:5–13; cf. 2:6–8a). This acclamation is reminiscent of the expectation of a royal and priestly messianic figure in intertestamental Judaism. The Dead Sea Scrolls describe a priestly and royal messiah. In the *Testaments of the Twelve Patriarchs*, the eschatological redeemer is a priestly figure (*T. Levi* 5.1–2; 18.2). Following the Maccabean revolt, the Hasmonean family apparently appealed to Ps 110:4 to justify its rule over Israel, declaring that Simon, the ruler, was "high priest forever" (1 Macc 14:41). These citations mark a transition in the argument of Hebrews, as the author now moves from the description of Jesus as Son to the exploration of his role as "high priest after the order of Melchizedek."

In 5:7–8, the author demonstrates that Christ meets the second qualification for the high priesthood, exceeding the requirement that the high

The Maccabean Revolt

The prohibition of Jewish practices (circumcision, keeping of the Sabbath, and observance of food laws) by Antiochus IV Epiphanes (168 or 167 BC) provoked the revolt led by the priest Mattathias and his sons. Judas, the eldest son, led the movement after the death of his father. He bore the nickname "the Maccabee" (the "hammerer"), a name that was then extended to his brothers. They founded the Hasmonean dynasty, which ruled Israel until the Romans took over in 63 BC. The story of their struggle for liberation is contained in four books (1–4 Maccabees), the first two of which are included in Orthodox and Catholic Bibles; the third and fourth are printed in some Orthodox Bibles. The NRSV includes all four in its "apocryphal/deuterocanonical" section.

priest "deal gently" (i.e., "moderate the passions," *metriopathein*, 5:2) by being fully sympathetic (*sympathein*, cf. 4:15). In Greek, verses 7–10 are one complicated sentence that, like the opening words of the homily (1:1–4), summarizes the Christ event in terms of Jesus' incarnation, death, and exaltation. "In the days of his flesh," like the "little while" of 2:9, marks the time between the Son's entry into the world and his exaltation (the phrase is used in the LXX of Gen 6:3; 9:29; 10:25; 35:28; Deut 30:20). The combination of participles and verbs in this indicates the stages in the existence of the Son and high priest. In the two main verbs, "he learned" (5:8; *emathen*) and "he became" (5:9; *egeneto*), the author describes the stages in the Son's role and status. The subordinate participles clarify the author's narrative, indicating events prior to the death and exaltation. Thus, according to a literal translation of the author's description of the first stage, "having offered prayers and supplications . . . and having been heard, . . . although he was a Son, he learned obedience from what he suffered." In this stage, therefore, the "prayers and supplications" and God's response ("having been heard") precede the moment when he "learned obedience." The author expands on the sympathy of the Son in his humanity that took him all the way to death. According to a literal translation of the second stage, "having been made perfect (*teleiōtheis*) and having been designated (*prosagoreutheis*) high priest after the order of Melchizedek, he became the source of eternal salvation to those who obey him." Thus, just as he "was made perfect through sufferings" in order "to lead many sons to glory" in 2:10, he was "made perfect" and "designated high priest" through his death and exaltation. In 2:10 and 5:9, to be "made perfect" is both to suffer and to be exalted to God's presence. The central focus of this complicated sentence is the claim in 5:8 that "he learned obedience from what he suffered,"

Figure 5. A Hasmonean High Priest.
This Judean coin from the late second century BC bears the Hebrew inscription "Yehohanan the High Priest and the Council of the Jews." The reference is to John Hyrcanus I, son of Simon Maccabeus and nephew of Judas Maccabeus, king and high priest over the Hasmonean realm from 134 BC until his death in 104 BC.

CNG Coins (http://www.cngcoins.com)

for it expresses the author's thesis that Jesus became the "source of salvation" only through the path of suffering.

While the focus on the solidarity of Jesus with his people is evident in 5:7–10, the passage raises problems for interpretation. In the first place, several scholars (e.g., Friedrich 1962; Schille 1955) have argued that the combination of participial phrases and the three-stage Christology of preexistence, incarnation, and exaltation (cf. 1:1–4) are the marks of a hymn comparable to Phil 2:6–11. The author's frequent poetic sentences (cf. 1:1–4; 7:26–28; 12:18–14), however, indicate that he is capable of such compositions without quoting hymnic material. In the second place, the author's description of the human Jesus is a problem for interpretation.

Although the "prayers and supplications to the one who could save him from death with loud cries and tears" vaguely recalls Jesus' prayer in Gethsemane, the Gospel narratives do not use this language. The description is heavily indebted to the portrayals of prayers offered in deep distress in Jewish literature. When the psalmist was surrounded by the snares of death (Ps 116:3 [114:3 LXX]), God heard his supplications (*deēsōn*) and saved his soul from death (116:8 [114:8 LXX]). Indeed, a common theme in the Psalms is "supplications" accompanied by "tears" (cf. Ps 31:22 [30:23 LXX]; 39:12 [38:13 LXX]). "Prayers and supplications" (*deēseis kai hiketēria*), which occur together elsewhere only in Job 40:27 LXX, refer to the intense entreaty of one who calls for help. Although the words are nearly synonymous, *hiketēria* is the more intense word for an imploring entreaty (Grässer 1990, 1:299). The two words signify the intensity of Jesus' petition to God. "Loud cries and tears" (*krauge ischyra kai dakryōn*) are also signs of prayer in deep distress (cf. Exod 3:7, 9; Num 12:13; Judg 3:9, 15; 4:3; 6:7; 10:10; 3 Macc 5:7), indicating the intensity of Jesus' "prayers and supplications" and suggesting that his situation was like that in Job 34:28 and Ps 5:2 (Kurianal 1999, 71). Philo describes Moses as the ideal man of prayer who is "bold not only to speak and cry aloud, but actually to make an outcry of reproach, wrung from him by real conviction, and expressing true emotion" (*Heir* 19). Here the combination of *parrēsia* to describe Moses' "boldness" with the reference to his outcry is a significant parallel to Hebrews. Thus the description of Jesus' anguish is not limited to the Gethsemane narrative but is a summary of Jesus' response to suffering based primarily on the author's reading of the Psalms. It encompasses all the "prayers and supplications" of Jesus that culminated in his death (Kurianal 1999, 68).

A third problem for interpretation is the statement that the Son addressed his prayers "to the one who could save him from death," and that "he was heard because of his reverence." "The one who could save him from death" is a periphrasis for God, and the passive voice of "he was heard" indicates that God answered Jesus' prayer. Some have interpreted Jesus' prayer in light of Jesus' petition in Gethsemane, "Let this cup pass from me" (Matt 26:39). If Jesus' petition, according to Hebrews, is a request to avoid death, the phrase "he was heard" becomes problematic. Adolf Harnack (1929, 248) suggested that the original reading was "he was not heard." Since no manuscript evidence supports Harnack's solution, one must look to the context of Hebrews to find a solution to the problem.

The reference to "the one who could save him from death" specifies the object but not the content of Jesus' prayer; the author does not say that Jesus prayed to avoid death. In Jewish literature, to be "saved from death" can mean either "to prevent from being killed" (Prov 15:24; Jas 5:20) or "to rescue one by raising him out of death" (cf. Wis 14:4; John 12:27; Kurianal 1999, 69). According to Heb 13:20, God is the one "who brought back [Jesus] from the dead." Since, according to Hebrews, Jesus entered death's domain and conquered the one who had the power of death (2:14–15), the author is not referring to a petition that Jesus might avoid death. The context suggests that Jesus "was heard" insofar as he became victorious over death at the exaltation. He prayed for the power to remain faithful in the midst of the temptation to fall away. The prayer echoes the author's earlier description of humanity's fear of death and Jesus' descent into death's domain (2:15) to rescue those who lived in fear of death.

The author's statement that he "was heard because of his reverence" (5:7; *apo tēs eulabeias*) is also a subject of scholarly debate because an alternative translation is "He was heard *from his anxiety*." *Eulabeia* can mean either "fear" or "reverence," and *apo* is most often rendered "from." Thus, because the context describes the anguish of Jesus in prayer, some translate, "he was heard from his anxiety." Since *eulabeia* (and the verb *eulabeomai*) refers to "reverence" elsewhere in the homily (cf. 11:7; 12:28), the most suitable reading is "He was heard because of his reverence."

In 5:9–10, the author reiterates the earlier claim that Jesus' human solidarity was the path to his glory (cf. 2:10–18; 4:14–16). The two Greek participles indicate the sequence with which Jesus became the "source of eternal salvation to those who obey him." He was first "made perfect" at the exaltation (cf. 7:28), the event when he "passed through the heavens" (cf. 4:14) and sat down at the right hand of God (1:3, 13), overcoming the suffering described in 5:7–8. As a result, he was "designated high priest after the order of Melchizedek" at the exaltation, fulfilling the qualification that the high priest be called (5:4–5). As the one who "learned obedience" through suffering, he became the model of obedience for the community, becoming "the source of eternal salvation for those who obey him." The term "source" (*aitios*) is the equivalent of "pioneer" in 2:10. The term "designated" (*prosagoreutheis*) indicates that he was appointed by another, fulfilling the requirement that the high priest be called (5:4). The author emphasizes here that he was designated by God in the words of Ps 110:4, "You are a priest forever according to the order of Melchizedek." Just as the Son is the pioneer who brings his brothers and sisters to glory through his sufferings (2:10), he is the "source of salvation" who enters the heavenly sanctuary and opens the way for others to follow (6:19). The author has indicated earlier that Jesus became a heavenly high priest at the exaltation (cf. 2:17) but first identifies him with the order of Melchizedek in 5:5–10 as a prelude to the extensive treatment of the theme in 7:1–10:18.

Tracing the Train of Thought

As the preceding section (3:1–4:13) indicates, the author faces the challenge of persuading his readers to hold fast to their confession of faith "until the end" (3:14) when they suffer alienation from the surrounding society and cannot see a reason to remain faithful. The claim that the exalted Son is at God's right hand now seems remote to a community that does not "see all things in subjection to him" (cf. 2:8b).

Jesus, Transcendent and Human (4:14–16)

As the "let us" clauses indicate, the author's appeal to the community to "hold fast to the confession" (4:14) and "draw near with boldness to the throne of grace" (4:16) elaborates on his earlier exhortation to faithfulness, suggesting that to "hold fast" is equivalent to remaining faithful. However, these exhortations to the weary community are ineffective unless the author rebuilds their symbolic world and restores their confidence in their Christian confession. Thus he builds the "let us" clauses on the foundation of what the community has in 4:14–16 and elaborates on this theme in 5:1–10. What the community has is a gift from God, so the exhortations to hold fast and to draw near are the community's response to God's saving work. Thus, in 4:14, the author provides the foundation for the exhortations.

**Hebrews 4:14–5:10
in the Rhetorical Flow**

Hearing God's word with faithful endurance (1:1–4:13)

Exordium: **Encountering God's ultimate word (1:1–4)**

Narratio: **Hearing God's word with faithful endurance (1:5–4:13)**

Probatio: Discovering certainty and confidence in the word for the mature (4:14–10:31)

▶ **Drawing near and holding firmly: following the path of Jesus from suffering to triumph (4:14–5:10)**

  Jesus, transcendent and human (4:14–16)

    The transcendent priest (4:14)

    Human yet sinless (4:15)

    Boldness in worship (4:16)

  Jesus qualified as high priest (5:1–10)

    Priestly qualifications (5:1–6)

    Solidarity with the people (5:7–8)

    Designated high priest (5:9–10)

4:14. In the words, **having therefore a great high priest who has passed through the heavens** (4:14a), the author looks back to his earlier reminder that we have a "merciful and faithful high priest" (2:17) and forward to the recurring theme that the high priest of the community's confession (3:1) is no ordinary high priest who serves in an earthly sanctuary (cf. 8:1–5; 9:1–5), but one who sits at God's right hand (8:1). This affirmation is a constant theme of Hebrews (cf. 1:3–14; 6:19–20; 8:1; 9:11–14), reminding a community that suffers alienation from the surrounding society that its situation is not the full story, for the readers are "partakers in a heavenly calling" (3:1). The fact that Christ is the priest who "has passed through the heavens" assures the community of the reality beyond their own experience of suffering. Despite their current sufferings, the fact that the high priest has overcome death reassures the community that they have a possession to which they can **hold fast** (4:14b), even in times when they appear to be losing their grip. Such a claim rebuilds the community's symbolic world and provides the basis for their endurance.

4:15. This assurance is only part of the answer to the community's crisis, for even if the high priest is the transcendent one, he may be remote from the struggles of the community. The author answers this question by declaring that the transcendent one can "sympathize" with the community in its suffering. The double negative **We do not have a high priest who is unable to sympathize with our weaknesses** (4:15a) indicates that the community in fact has a high priest who sympathizes with human weaknesses (2:8–10). This sympathy is not only a subjective feeling but is the capacity to share the pain of another. He is not remote from the suffering and alienation that the community now experiences. The one who became like his brothers in every respect (2:17) also shares their temptations. Now the author recalls Jesus was also tested (*pepeirasmenon kata panta*) with the same struggles that confront the community. Just as the community's present suffering now tempts it to abandon the path toward the goal, the exalted high priest was tempted to abandon his mission. This sympathy is evident in the fact that the heavenly high priest was first **tempted in every respect** (4:15b). The author thus returns to the theme of the solidarity of the Son with his people first introduced in 2:10–18. Whereas the author says that "he was like us in every respect" (2:17) and that he was "tested" (2:18), here he expands on the theme of the testing of the human Jesus. The author is not making an abstract claim about the variety of temptations that every individual experiences but is addressing the specific temptations that now face the community, declaring that the heavenly high priest is not remote but that he bears the marks of his testing even in his exaltation. Before he was the exalted high priest, he experienced the temptation to fall away and abandon his mission.

Although the author shares with early Christian tradition that Jesus was **without sin** (4:15c; cf. Matt 4:1–11; 2 Cor 5:21; 1 Pet 2:22), his focus here is on the specific sin that now tempts this community (cf. 3:12). As in 2:10–18, he recalls that Jesus shared the temptations now facing the listeners and that he did not surrender to the temptation to abandon his faithfulness to God. Jesus faced the same temptation to fall away that the community now experiences and went to his death in the ultimate act of solidarity with the people before he "passed through the heavens." Thus Jesus' path of suffering was the ultimate demonstration of the faithfulness that he desires from the readers.

4:16. As **therefore** indicates, the fact that Jesus has been tested and has passed through the heavens is the basis for the exhortation, **let us draw near with boldness to the throne of grace** (4:16). Even now, while the community can see only suffering and alienation, it has access to the "throne of grace," for it can "draw near" because the one who was tempted opened up the way (cf. 10:19) when he entered the heavenly world (cf. 6:19–20). The community is able to "draw near" in worship and prayer because it follows the path of the one who proceeded from suffering to glory (cf. 2:10–18). The community's worship is the occasion when they see beyond the sufferings of the moment and anticipate their entry into the promised land (cf. 4:3–11). Jesus expresses solidarity with the community not only in suffering but also in opening the way for his people to follow him into the heavens.

Jesus Qualified as High Priest (5:1–10)

In 5:1–10, the author provides the supporting argument for the exhortation in 4:14–16, demonstrating that Jesus meets the qualifications for the high priesthood. The author's focus becomes evident in the structure of the comments:

A The human high priest chosen from among men (5:1)
  B The solidarity of the high priest with the people (5:2–3)
    C The appointment of the Levitical high priest (5:4)
    C′ The appointment of Christ as high priest (5:5–6)
  B′ The solidarity of Christ with the people (5:7–8)
A′ The exalted high priest designated by God (5:9–10)

5:1–6. The author mentions only two qualifications for the high priesthood: that the high priest be called (5:4–6) and that he demonstrate solidarity with the people (5:2, 7–8). In the chiastic structure noted above, Jesus meets the qualification that he be "called" when he **did not glorify himself to become high priest** (5:5a). Having already established in 1:5 that God said, "You are my son" at the exaltation, the author now reiterates in 5:5b that God "spoke" those words from Ps 2:7, fulfilling the requirement that the high priest be "called." This event was also the occasion when God said, **You are the priest after the order of Melchizedek** (5:6), which the author reiterates in 5:10, describing the occasion when the high priest was designated to this office. This heavenly priesthood becomes the subject of 7:1–10:18. Thus the one who "passed through the heavens" (4:14) was called to a new order of priesthood. Unlike the earthly high priest, who offered **gifts and sacrifices for sins** (5:1) that were not

Table 5.
The High Priest in the Old Testament and in Hebrews

	Old Testament	Hebrews
Qualifications	Appointed by God (Exod 28:1; Lev 8:1–2) Separated from the people (Exod 29; Lev 28) Free from physical defects (Lev 21:16–23)	Appointed by God (5:1, 4) Has solidarity with the people (4:15; 5:7–8)
Functions	Offers sacrifices (Lev 16; Num 18:5, 7) Gives instruction (Deut 33:10; Mal 2:6) Receives oracles (Deut 33:8; Exod 28:30) Protects physical health of community (Lev 13–15) Administers justice (Deut 17:8–9; 21:5)	Offers sacrifices (2:17; 5:3)

ultimately effective (10:1–4), the "high priest after the order of Melchizedek" (5:10) belongs to the heavenly world, where he will offer the ultimate sacrifice (cf. 10:1–18).

5:7–8. Between the two declarations of the Son's status as the heavenly high priest (5:5–6, 9–10), the author demonstrates that Christ met the second qualification for the priesthood. The **days of his flesh** (5:7a), like the "little while" in 2:9, refer to the period between the Son's preexistence and his appointment to office at the exaltation. Just as Paul indicates that the one who was in the form of God "emptied himself" of his divine status (Phil 2:6–8), the author describes Jesus' earthly life as "the days of his flesh," emphasizing the Son's solidarity in suffering with those who "share flesh and blood" and live in fear of death (2:14–15).

The requirement for solidarity is nowhere mentioned in the OT. The author is apparently familiar with Philo's claim that the Levitical high priest moderates the emotions but keeps his feelings under control (see Introductory Matters). However, he indicates that Jesus not only meets these qualifications but exceeds the qualification of showing moderate feelings (5:2), for he is able to show full sympathy by entering into the sufferings and temptations of the people. Beginning with their weakness and temptation, he develops the theme of the sympathetic high priest to assure them that they are not alone in their suffering.

The full extent of the sympathy of Christ as the new high priest is evident in the recapitulation and expansion of the theme of solidarity first introduced in 2:5–18. The summary of the Christ event in 5:7–10 is not only the memory of the death and exaltation of Jesus but is also a description of the community's present experience. Indeed, the interpretative difficulties with the passage mentioned under Introductory Matters become intelligible when one recognizes that the author is merging the experience of Jesus with the community's own situation, demonstrating that Jesus is their pioneer who has entered into their experience. In the statement that he **offered** (*prosenenkas*, from *prospherō*) **prayers and supplications** (5:7b), the author may be contrasting the human Jesus with the Levitical high priest who "offers" (*prospherei*) gifts and sacrifices, but he is also signifying that Jesus has joined the vulnerable community in crying out to God. The "prayers and supplications" indicate that Jesus sympathizes with the community's helplessness as it calls on God in prayer. The **cries and tears** that he offered reflect the full extent of his solidarity and the intensity of his prayers, for those who live in desperation cry to the Lord in prayer (cf. Job 34:28; Ps 5:2). Although the description may remind the reader of Jesus' prayer in Gethsemane, the author does not limit his description to that one event. Instead, his focus is on the fact that Jesus shared the same anguish that the community has faced.

The author echoes familiar Jewish appellations for God when he speaks of Jesus' prayer to **the one who was able to save him from death** (5:7b). This term for God does not suggest that Jesus prayed that he might avoid death.

Indeed, as the author has said earlier, through death Jesus destroyed the one who had the power of death (2:14). The passage suggests the solidarity of Jesus with the community in the fear of death (2:15). The affirmation that **he was heard because of his reverence** (5:7c) also indicates that Jesus did not pray to escape death, although he shared the human fear of death (2:14). Instead, he "was heard" when he defeated the one who had the power of death (2:15), becoming victorious at the exaltation. In his "reverence" (*eulabeia*) before God, he displayed the same qualities that now distinguish the community in its worship (cf. 12:28, "let us worship with reverence [*eulabeia*] and awe"). In his sympathy, therefore, Christ is the one who has cried out to God in anguish, just as the community now does. As the pioneer (2:10) who goes before the community to heaven, he first shared the community's suffering. He thus exceeds the requirement that the high priest "deal gently" (*metriopathein*) with sinners by demonstrating genuine sympathy (*sympathein*) for his people in their time of testing.

At the center of the author's description of Jesus' humanity is the claim that, **although he was a Son, he learned obedience from what he suffered** (5:8). Here the author employs a well-known Greek wordplay (*emathen aph' hōn epathen*) that is common in Jewish and Greek literature (Aeschylus, *Ag.* 177; Herodotus, *Hist.* 1.207; Philo, *Heir* 73; *Flight* 138; *Spec. Laws* 4.29; *Dreams* 2.107; *Moses* 2.280) to express the idea that humans learn through suffering. The opening phrase, "although he was a Son," suggests that, while ordinary sons learn through suffering (cf. 12:4–11), Jesus is no ordinary Son (Attridge 1989, 152). Nevertheless, he followed the path of sons in a normal family as he "learned obedience from what he suffered." This problematic passage anticipates the subsequent discussion of the community's own suffering in 12:4–11, which the author describes as a learning experience. Addressing a community in the midst of suffering, the author describes their experience as "the discipline (*paideia*, 'education') of the Lord." The author's wordplay must be seen in the context of his earlier reflections on Jesus' suffering. He "became perfect through suffering" (2:10), and he "was tested by what he suffered" (2:18). Thus he "learned obedience" at the cross as he experienced the full cost of doing God's will without falling away (Grässer 1990, 1:308), and he completed the journey which is still unfinished for the community. As the author indicates in 10:5–10, Jesus exemplified obedience by coming to do God's will, offering his body as a sacrifice to God.

5:9–10. Obedience and faithfulness cannot be separated in the author's mind. According to 4:6, Israel did not enter the promised land because of disobedience. According to 11:8, "By faith Abraham . . . obeyed to go out . . . to his inheritance." Similarly, the author speaks of those **who obey** (5:9b) the one who was first obedient. However, as 5:9–10 indicates, they do not obey an ordinary person. In the sequence of verbs and participles in 5:9–10, the author indicates the outcome of Jesus' obedience in suffering: **having been**

made perfect, he became (5:9a) . . . having been designated (5:10a). That is, two events precede the occasion when he became **the source of eternal salvation** (5:9b). In the first place, he was "made perfect" after he "learned obedience." This claim recalls the earlier affirmation that he "became perfect through suffering" (2:10) and anticipates the later statement that the exalted high priest was "perfected forever" (7:28). The author is referring not to moral perfection but to the completion of Jesus' work, when the outcome of his suffering was exaltation. He was "made perfect," therefore, at the cross and exaltation, when he "passed through the heavens" (4:14). In the second place, he was **designated high priest after the order of Melchizedek** (5:10) at the exaltation, fulfilling the requirement that the high priest be called (5:4). The final result of the path from suffering to exaltation, as the main verb indicates, is that he "became the source of eternal salvation," just as he "became" a merciful and faithful high priest after his incarnation (2:17). His role as "source" (*aitios*) of eternal salvation is parallel to his role as "pioneer" (*archēgos*, 2:10; 12:2) and "forerunner" (*prodromos*, 6:20). Thus, as the author will maintain in the later argument, he provided what the earthly priests could not provide, for only his sacrificial work was "once for all" (7:27; 9:12; 10:10). The sacrifices of the earthly tabernacle were unable to "perfect those who drew near" (10:1; cf. 7:11). In passing "through the heavens" (4:14) to sit at God's right hand, Jesus was able to do what the "gifts and sacrifices" (cf. 5:1) of the earthly high priests could not do. Because he had entered the heavenly sanctuary, he enabled his community to "draw near" to God.

Theological Issues

Because Heb 4:14–5:10 introduces the major themes of the central section, it has a density of theological claims that is incomparable to any other part of the homily. These claims, which are also accompanied by a variety of exegetical difficulties, have been the basis for theological debate for centuries. Most of these issues concern the author's elaboration on the solidarity of the sympathetic high priest with the people. Phrases like "tempted in every way as we are," "he was heard" in his prayer to "the one who could save him from death," and "he learned obedience from what he suffered" evoke major discussion of the author's Christology.

Only by looking at the pastoral dimension and the rhetorical impact of the entire passage can one see the author's distinctive theological contribution. His purpose is not to engage in theology as an abstraction but to retell the basic narrative of the Christ event (cf. 1:1–4) with vocabulary that will speak to the experience of the listeners. Thus the whole of this unit is greater than the sum of its parts as the author blends pastoral care with theological reflection. If the christological claims are problematic, the primary reason is that the author has merged the story of the community with the story of Jesus, indicating that they participate in a larger narrative that includes the temptation to abandon the faith (cf. 4:15) and the prayer to God in their fear of death. Indeed, as the author indicates in 12:4–11, they are learning through suffering. The author makes sense of their own suffering by indicating that it is one stage along the journey.

In placing the community's story within the larger narrative, the author has provided an important model for both theological reflection and pastoral care. His narrative theology not only reassures the community by connecting their story to the Christ event but also invites them to continue to share the narrative of Jesus in which the path of suffering precedes triumph. Just as this narrative was the alternative to competing narratives of antiquity, it undoubtedly remains an alternative to competing narratives. The author's exhortations indicate that those who recognize that they belong to a larger story are empowered to "hold fast" and "draw near."

In 4:16, the author introduces the cultic image of drawing near for the first time (cf. 7:25; 10:1, 22; 12:18, 22), indicating that the community may now enter where others could not go because the pioneer has opened the way. Although the author may include the totality of the people's response to God, the imagery suggests that worship is the occasion when the community reaffirms the confession (4:14) and draws near to the throne of grace. Worship is not limited to private prayer but includes the communal assemblies (10:25) when the people on the way encounter the exalted Christ. Only by participating in corporate worship can the people reach the destination.

The description of worship provides insight for contemporary communities of faith about the nature of worship. Only through worship can the community resist the temptation to fall away, for worship provides the opportunity for the discouraged community to envision the end of the journey. Thus worship is an expression of Christian hope and an anticipation of ultimate salvation. To draw near to the throne of grace in the present is to visualize another world in the midst of the community's anguish.

Although the worship may include private prayer, the author undoubtedly envisions the gathering of the community in the house church as a source of renewal for the journey. The insistence that worship is a privilege initiated by God shows that the focus of worship is on God and not the worshiper. Thus worshipers do not come as consumers into the assembly but in response to the gracious act of God. The invitation to come "with boldness" is a reminder of the transcendence of God, and that only through Christ does one have the right to approach God. God is, as the author indicates, "the one to whom we give an account" (4:13) and the "consuming fire" (12:29). Thus the opportunity to come before God is not a thing to be taken for granted but is a gift from the exalted Christ (10:19).

Hebrews 5:11–6:20

Preparing to Hear the Word
That Is Hard to Explain

Introductory Matters

After declaring that Jesus was "designated high priest after the order of Melchizedek" (5:10), the author does not return to the theme until 6:20, when he speaks, in almost identical language of Jesus' "becoming high priest after the order of Melchizedek," a topic that he explores in Heb 7. Because the claim in 5:10 introduces the topic that the author begins to explore in chapter 7, E. Riggenbach has suggested that the intervening section in 5:11–6:19 could have been removed without being missed (Riggenbach 1922, 139; cf. Grässer 1990, 1:317). This section is, however, a lengthy exhortation that prepares the community to grasp the instruction on Melchizedek in chapter 7. The section conforms to the ancient rhetorical practice of including a digression in order "that the ears of the jury may be more ready to take in" the point to follow (Quintilian, *Inst.* 4.3.10). The author prepares the way for this theme by testing the readiness of the listeners to hear and awakening them to the importance of the topic (Grässer 1990, 1:317). The author signals the end of the digression by returning to the theme of the high priest after the order of Melchizedek in 6:20 (Koester 2001, 307).

Two sections in 5:11–6:20 reflect the two dimensions of the exhortation. In the first section in 5:11–6:12, the *inclusio* signaled by *nōthroi* (sluggish) encloses an indictment ("you have become sluggish" [*nōthroi*]) and a severe warning against apostasy (5:11–6:8) with the exhortation to remain faithful (6:9–12; cf. 6:12, "that you may not be sluggish" [*nōthroi*]), while in the second section in 6:13–20 the author provides the scriptural basis for the community's faithfulness. The description of the oath to Abraham (6:13–14) prepares the way for the discussion of God's oath to the high priest according to the order of Melchizedek (cf. 7:20–21).

Within this "word of exhortation" (13:22; *logos tēs paraklēseōs*), the author prepares for a word (*logos*) that is both long (*polys*) and hard to explain (*dysermēneutos*). The phrase "much to say" (*polys ho logos*) was commonly used for a long speech (BDAG, 848; cf. Acts 15:32; 20:2). *Dysermēneutos* is derived from *hermēneuō*, which means interpret, explain, or translate from one language to another (cf. Matt 1:23; John 1:38; Acts 4:36; 9:36; Heb 7:2). In classical Greek literature, Hermes was the messenger and interpreter of the gods (cf. Plato, *Crat.* 407). The related word *diermēneuō* is used for the interpretation of the scriptures (Luke 24:27). Philo uses *dysermēneutos* for a teaching "which no words can express" (*Dreams* 1.188), and Origen uses the word to describe the sublimity of the Christian message. In his commentary on John 1:21, Origen says that "the theory of the soul is vast and difficult" (Thompson 1982, 31). He speaks elsewhere of the doctrine of the resurrection and of the Sabbath rest of God as *dysermēneutos* (*Cels.* 5.59; 7.32). Thus the author describes a hermeneutical problem of communicating the sublime message of 7:1–10:18 because of the incapacity of the listeners to understand the divine message.

The author's analysis of the readers' situation is heavily indebted to Greek educational theory, which Philo had adapted into the Jewish tradition. "Sluggish in hearing" (*nōthros tais akoais*) was a common expression for mental obtuseness (Thompson 1982, 29). The author's distinction between two levels of education is unique in the NT but common in Greek philosophy. Although the illustration contrasting children who drink milk with adults who eat solid food resembles the imagery of 1 Cor 3:1–3, the author has taken the images in a new direction. The metaphors of "children" nourished by "milk" and the "mature" who eat "solid food" also belong to ancient discussions of educational development. The athletic metaphors of "practice" and "training" were commonly used to communicate the discipline of those who were properly nourished as they exercised the mind and developed toward maturity. In Greek educational theory, the basic subjects (*enkyklios paideia* in Greek; *liberales artes* in Latin) learned in childhood included grammar, rhetoric, dialectic, music, geometry, arithmetic, and astronomy (cf. Thompson 1982, 18). These subjects prepared the way for the study of matters of ultimate importance (Plato, *Rep.* 7.536e). According to Epictetus, people begin their study as children (*nēpioi*) but progress to the higher subject of philosophy. Those who receive the education are the true athletes in training, as they exercise themselves in the subject of philosophy (*Diss.* 2.18.27).

Philo's major heroes exemplify the progress from the childhood of the lower subjects to the maturity of those who can see beyond the material world.

The initial learner is the child (*nēpios*) who is unacquainted (*apeiros*) with the higher knowledge (*Migration* 29; *Agriculture* 9, 160). Philo describes the lower education as "the simple and milky foods of infancy" (*Prelim. Studies* 19), and he depicts the soul's advancement from the milk of early instruction to the meat of philosophy (*Good Person* 160; *Agriculture* 9).

Philo frequently employs athletic imagery to describe the exercise that accompanies good intellectual nutrition. He speaks of those who are perfect (*teleios*) through practice (*Confusion* 181; *Prelim. Studies* 35; *Names* 85; *Abraham* 53), indicating that "continued exercise makes solid knowledge" (*Sacrifices* 85–86). He describes those who are "drilled in the gymnastics of the soul" (*Names* 81; cf. *Worse* 41). Philo assumes, with his contemporaries, that the instruction received must be "trained" and "practiced" before one reaches perfection (Thompson 1982, 25).

Like Philo, the author uses language commonly associated with athletes who recognized the need for the "faculties" (*aisthētēria*, literally "sense organs") to be "trained" (*gegymnasmena*) before they could enter into a contest. Rigorous training resulted in the proper "condition" (*hexis*) of the body (Kiley 1980, 501–3). *Hexis* was commonly used for the condition of the body as the result of food (cf. Dan 1:15 LXX) or exercise (Aristotle, *Pol.* 1335b.6–12; Plato, *Rep.* 404a) or of the mind that had been trained. Shepherds have the "condition" to live in the open because of their training (Aristotle, *Pol.* 1319a.20–24), and athletes have the proper "condition" because of their exercise. According to Epictetus, "Every character [*hexis*] is maintained by the corresponding activities, that of walking by walking, that of running by running" (*Diss.* 2.18.1). Philo uses the word to refer to the "character" or "fixed state" of the person as a result of past practices (*Alleg. Interp.* 3.210), and Albinus uses *hexis* to describe the one who has so developed his skills as no longer to be a

Education (*Paideia*) in the Greco-Roman World

The goal of *paideia* (education, discipline) in antiquity was the formation of the whole person. Until the age of six or seven, the Greek child was cared for primarily by its mother (Plato, *Prot.* 325c; Spicq 1994, 3:1). At that age, it was entrusted to a *paidagōgos* (cf. 1 Cor 4:15; Gal 3:24) who watched over the children and ensured that they completed their studies. At a later period, the *paidagōgos* was also the teacher. In most schools, a single teacher was responsible for the education of the youth. Prior to Plato, the Greeks had developed a basic curriculum that included grammar, rhetoric, dialectic, music, geometry, arithmetic, and astronomy. This curriculum was later designated by the term *enkyklios paideia*. The lower education is the foundation for higher education in the "more difficult matters" (Epictetus, *Diss.* 1.26.3) of philosophy, the knowledge of ultimate reality. Only through exercise of the mind (Epictetus, *Diss.* 2.18.27) can the person advance to maturity.

121

grammarian or a flute player. The one who has acquired that skill (*hexis*) will be able to act on the basis of past training (Albinus, *Didask.* 26; Kiley 1980, 501–2). The author, like Philo and other philosophers, uses the metaphor of athletic training (on athletic metaphors, see also 10:32–34; 12:1–2) to describe the condition of the mind that follows rigorous training, encouraging his readers to make progress toward intellectual maturity.

The author's claim that only rigorous training of the mind equips the listeners to "distinguish between good and evil" also echoes ancient conversations about the goal of education. The physician Galen complains about those who have not trained the mind to make logical distinctions (Galen, *Adv. Lyc.* 7.21–22), and he insists that one needs to "train the faculties" in order to distinguish truth from error (Galen, *Temp.* 2.2; cf. Strecker and Schnelle 1996, 1110). According to Stoic theory, the purpose of the study of ethics is to distinguish between the good, the evil, and the indifferent (cf. Sextus Empiricus, *Pyrr. hyp.* 3.168). Hebrews omits the third category in the moral development of the person but agrees with the ancient philosophers that the goal of knowledge is to lead to ethical maturity. Indeed, the structure of the homily indicates the close relationship between knowledge and appropriate behavior, for the author proceeds from the word that is hard to explain (7:1–10:18) to the ethical implications of the theological section (10:19–39).

Like the author of Hebrews (6:7–9), Philo employs the image of agriculture to describe intellectual advancement. This imagery is the basis for the tractate *On Agriculture*, which is based on the account of Noah's work as a husbandman in Gen 9:20–21. Here he describes how one progresses from *nēpios* to *teleios* and from "milk" to "solid food." Those who produce only weeds or who produce nothing at all are cut down (*Agriculture* 12, 17). Good soul husbandry determines the outcome of the individual who has received the good seed (Thompson 1982, 25).

In the warning that "it is impossible again to restore to repentance," the author makes the first of four references to the impossible (cf. 6:18; 10:4; 11:6). Together with the author's consistent appeal to the "necessary" (*anankē*, 7:12, 27; 9:16, 23; cf. *anankaion*, 8:3) and the *fitting* (2:10), this terminology is a distinctive aspect of his argument, reflecting his appeal to reason and logic that is unparalleled in the NT (Thompson 1998, 303). Ancient rhetorical theorists discussed the importance of the possible, the necessary, and the appropriate in deliberative argument. According to Hermogenes (*Prog.* 11), "The fundamental questions are divided according to the so-called final and main arguments, the just, the useful, the possible, the appropriate" (Löhr 2005, 206). Aristotle suggested that the orator include propositions concerning the possible and the impossible (*Rhet.* 1.3.8 [1359a]). This terminology is also widely used in philosophical literature to describe what is fitting for the deity and was frequently used by Philo to describe what is "necessary" or "impossible" because of the structure of reality (*Spec. Laws* 1.8; *Planting* 126;

Alleg. Interp. 2.16; Thompson 1998, 309–11). Although the author employs the categories that were common in philosophical literature, his claims about the impossible and the necessary do not always correspond to the ancient use of those categories, for the author appeals to a logic that grows out of his Christian convictions.

The author's claim that "it is impossible to renew to repentance" those who "fall away" has perplexed interpreters for centuries. In the ancient church, Heb 6:4–6 played a role in discussions of church discipline. The sternness of the passage has made it especially troublesome to post-Reformation interpreters who have attempted to harmonize the passage with their understanding of salvation by grace. The path to progress in understanding this passage entails not fitting it into a prearranged doctrinal system but placing it within the conventions of the author's world.

Interpreters have sought to understand the passage by searching for the background of the author's claim in OT and Jewish texts that distinguish between kinds of sins and reflect on the irrevocable punishment of those who persist in disobedience to God (cf. Braun 1984, 171). Those who sin with a "high hand" (Num 15:30–32) will be cut off from God's people. Some scholars have pointed to the blessings and curses of Deuteronomy as the background to the author's warning (cf. Deut 11:26–28; 27:15–28:6). The apocalyptic literature offers abundant examples of stern warnings that functioned to evoke fear among the readers (Nongbri 2003, 273). According to *4 Ezra*, an apocalypse written around AD 100 in response to the sufferings of the Jewish people after the destruction of Jerusalem in AD 70, God rejected the Israelites who did not keep the law "because they did not keep what was sown in them" (9.29–36). The ground in which God sows the seed is destroyed if it rejects the

Forgiveness after Falling Away?

The possibility of repentance and restoration for Christians who lapse was hotly disputed for centuries. *The Shepherd of Hermas* is a Christian apocalypse written in Greek in stages between around AD 90 and AD 150. A later source claims that its author (Hermas) was the brother of Pius, who was bishop of Rome in the mid-second century. His book holds out the possibility of repenting only once for grievous sin committed after baptism. Relevant passages include 6.4; 30.2–31.7; 61–64; 103.6.

Later, Montanists and Novatianists appealed to Heb 6 when arguing against allowing Christians who apostatized under persecution to repent and return. Montanism was an ecstatic prophetic movement centered in Asia Minor in the late second and early third centuries. For an example of Montanist teaching, see Tertullian, *Modesty* 20. Novatian was the leader of a rigorist faction in the church at Rome in the middle of the third century.

law, God's seed (Nongbri 2003, 273). The agricultural image is similar to Heb 6:7–8, which compares apostates to land that does not produce.

Philo offers a significant parallel to the stern warning of Hebrews. In his comments on the expulsion of Adam and Eve from the garden, he concludes, "He who is cast forth by God is subject to eternal banishment. . . . To him that is weighed down and enslaved by [wickedness], the horrors of the future must be undying and eternal" (*Cherubim* 2, trans. Colson and Whitaker 1929). Similarly, he says of the banishment of Cain, "The soul that has once been dismissed from hearth and home as irreconcilable, has been expelled for all eternity and can never return to her ancient abode" (*Worse* 149). Lot's wife is an example of those who have "desired to repent and not been permitted by God to do so" (*Alleg. Interp.* 3.213; cf. Braun 1984, 171).

While the author's stern warning may resonate with Jewish traditions about the impossibility of repentance, the situation of the readers and the logic of his argument determine the meaning of the passage. As the frequent warnings in Hebrews indicate (cf. 2:1–4; 3:7–4:11; 10:26–31), the concern of Hebrews is neither with church discipline nor with a theoretical discussion of the fate of apostates, for his readers have not yet fallen away. As with the warning that "they shall never enter my rest" (cf. 3:11), the author's primary concern is to awaken the listeners to the danger of abandoning God's gift. The comment is most likely an example of what rhetoricians called a *deinōsis*, the attempt to shock the audience (cf. Nissilä 1979, 254–55; Lausberg 1998, §257.3c; Quintilian, *Inst.* 6.2.24) into listening to the speaker's message. Aristotle discusses the appeal to fear in *Rhet.* 2.5.1 (cited in Nongbri 2003, 275):

> Let fear be defined as a painful or troubled feeling caused by the impression of an imminent evil that causes destruction or pain; for men do not fear all evils, for instance, becoming unjust or slow-witted [*bradys*], but only such as involve great pain or destruction [*phortikou ē lypērou*]. (Trans. Freese 1939)

The move from stern warning in 6:4–8 to the expression of the author's confidence in the community in 6:9–12 also reflects rhetorical practice. Rhetorical theorists advised that harsh words should be followed with words of assurance to avoid rendering the exhortation useless. Several ancient writers express this principle. For example, according to the *Rhetorica ad Herennium*:

> If frank speech of this sort seems too pungent, there will be many means of palliation, for one may immediately thereafter add something of this sort: "I here appeal to your virtue, I call on your wisdom, I bespeak your old habit," so that praise may quiet the feelings aroused by the frankness. (*Rhet. Her.* 4.37.49, cited in DeSilva 2000, 244–45)

Plutarch compares the orator to the physician who, after surgery, provides soothing lotions (*Adul. amic.* 74d; Nongbri 2003, 276–77).

The author makes the transition from the exhortation to the subject of Melchizedek, first introduced in 5:5, 10, by recalling the story of Abraham, the one who met Melchizedek (cf. 7:4–10) in Genesis. As "for" (*gar*) indicates, Abraham is the specific example of those "who through faith and patient endurance inherit the promises" (6:12). Having established that the readers are the "seed of Abraham" (2:16), the author sets him forth as the model for the community. He will return to the same theme in 11:8–20. In this instance the author cites the words "surely I will bless you and surely I will multiply you" (Gen 22:17), God's promise to Abraham after the binding of Isaac (Gen 22:1–16). He introduces the citation with God's words from Gen 22:16, "I have sworn by myself," which he changes to the third person, "he swore by himself." He also omits the specific reference to the binding of Isaac ("because you have done this, and have not withheld your beloved son because of me," Gen 22:16), but adds, "since he had no one greater by whom to swear." This adaptation from the Genesis texts reflects the author's specific focus.

Scarcely any story in the Jewish tradition gripped the imagination as much as the binding of Isaac. In the history of interpretation prior to the author of Hebrews, two emphases were dominant: (1) the divine oath and its validity became the subject of discussion; and (2) Abraham became the paradigm for trust in God (Koester 2001; Moxnes 1980, 184). The latter concern is evident in 6:13–15, where the focus is Abraham's response to God's promise. Unlike the wilderness generation (cf. 3:7–4:11), Abraham, "having patiently endured, inherited the promise." Although Genesis repeatedly refers to two separate promises to Abraham (the promise of land and of offspring), the author does not describe the nature of the promise. According to 8:8–16, Abraham was looking for a homeland (11:14) and a celestial city (11:16), which he did not receive in his lifetime.

The divine oath was also a major concern to ancient interpreters. Philo indicates his concern in several passages (*Alleg. Interp.* 3.203–208; *Sacrifices* 91–96; and *Abraham* 273). Acknowledging ancient questions about the appropriateness of swearing by the deity (*Sacrifices* 91), Philo maintains that this oath was one that was "befitting God" (*Alleg. Interp.* 3.203–204). He adds, in words similar to those of Hebrews, "God swears not by some other things, for nothing is higher than He, but by himself" (*Alleg. Interp.* 3.204). When the author of Hebrews explains that an oath is "for confirmation" (*eis bebaiōsin*), he also echoes the language of Philo, who indicates that God confirmed his promise with an oath (*Abraham* 273; *Alleg. Interp.* 3.203–204; *Sacrifices* 93). The similarities in terminology between Philo and Hebrews probably suggest that the author's treatment of Abraham is based on conversations and exegetical traditions within Hellenistic Judaism (Moxnes 1980, 141). In each of Philo's references to the promise to Abraham, he maintains that the oath is "for confirmation."

Having affirmed the general principle that an oath is for confirmation (6:16), the author elaborates on the principle in 6:17–18, appealing to the OT to demonstrate the reliability of God's promise. The claim that "it is impossible for God to lie" (6:18) echoes Num 23:19:

> God is not a human being, that he should lie,
> or a mortal, that he should change his mind.
> Has he promised, and will he not do it?
> Has he spoken, and will he not fulfill it? (NRSV)

The validity of God's promise in maintaining his oath with Israel was a familiar theme in the OT (cf. 2 Sam 7:28; Ezek 12:28; Isa 40:8; 55:10–11; Ps 89:26–28). As in Hebrews, the claim that it is "impossible for God to lie" was associated in rabbinic literature with the promise that Abraham would have many descendants (Hofius 1973, 142), suggesting that the author is drawing on a common tradition about the trustworthiness of God.

Although the author appeals to OT passages involving God's fidelity, his language is filled with the terminology of the law courts (Grässer 1990, 1:380). Contracts and treaties were pronounced "unchangeable" (*ametathetos*; cf. Braun 1984, 188) when "guaranteed" (*emesiteusen*) by an oath. Thus the author indicates that the Christians are the heirs to whom God has guaranteed his covenant with an oath.

In 6:19, the author mentions the curtain separating heaven and earth for the first time, anticipating the claims in 9:12–14 and 10:19–23. Against Ernst Käsemann's claim that the theme of the cosmic curtain is rooted in gnosticism (1984, 224–25), Otfried Hofius (1972) has demonstrated that this curtain was a common theme in rabbinic literature. *Targum on Job* 26:9 speaks of the curtain around God's throne, which separates God from the angels. Although angels cannot see God, they sometimes overhear what happens inside the curtain. According to *Targum Pseudo-Jonathan* on Gen 37:17, Gabriel tells Joseph that he has heard "from behind the curtain" on which day the slavery in Egypt

Targums

As knowledge of biblical Hebrew declined, interpreters of the Torah in the synagogue began the practice of offering a paraphrase in Aramaic known as a *targum*. The *targumim* (targums) provide an important witness to Jewish interpretation in the two centuries before and after Christ as interpreters not only paraphrased but also clarified and expanded on the text. Targums survive on all of the books of the Old Testament except for Ezra-Nehemiah and Daniel. *Targum Onqelos* and *Targum Pseudo-Jonathan* are well-known targums on the Pentateuch. *Targum Jonathan* is the primary targum on the prophets.

Metatron

Metatron is an archangel in Jewish apocalyptic texts and in later mystical literature. *Third Enoch* describes him as "lesser Yahweh" in contrast to God himself, the "greater Yahweh," who withdraws from the world, leaving Metatron in charge. Metatron is called "Prince of the World" and presides over the heavenly law court composed of the princes of the kingdoms, the angelic representatives of the nations of the earth. In some passages he is identical with the archangel Michael. He also functions as the heavenly scribe and high priest in the heavenly tabernacle. According to *3 Enoch*, he spent part of his existence on earth as the patriarch Enoch.

---

begins. In *Midrash Tanḥuma* on Deut 3:23–28 (*Wa-ethannan* 6), Moses hears the announcement of his death from Metatron and pleads for him to appeal to God to lengthen his life. Metatron answers: he has learned "from behind the curtain" that his appeal will not be heard. According to Hofius, the curtain before the throne of God marks the deep distance and inapproachability that existed between God and his heavenly servants (Hofius 1972, 8). Thus in the entry inside the curtain by the exalted Christ, the author portrays the access to the God who had previously been inaccessible.

Consistent with the author's frequent allusions to the community as a people on the way, he describes them in 6:18 as those "who have fled," suggesting the precarious nature of their existence as refugees. They find their stability as they grasp "the hope set before them" at the exaltation, just as they grasp their confession (4:14). As the verb suggests, the author speaks of a stable reality which the insecure readers may grasp. Indeed, he introduces a nautical image of people who can be rescued only if they grasp the hope that has been set before them (cf. 12:2, "the joy set before him"), which he identifies as an "anchor."

The image of hope as an anchor of the soul appears nowhere else in the Bible but has numerous analogies in Greek literature. As the reports in Acts indicate (27:29, 30, 40), the anchor was a weight connected to a ship by a rope in order to prevent drifting. Consequently, it became a common metaphor for stability and hope. Philo uses the image to describe the soul's security in relation to God (*Sacrifices* 90; *Cherubim* 13). Aelius Aristides (born ca. AD 129) defends Themistocles, who was criticized for his leadership in war, recalling that the people "left temple, graves and earth behind" and "held to his word as to a holy anchor" (*Or.* 3.252). According to Heliodorus (third century AD), when the hero Theagenes and his beloved were captives of a Persian satrap, Theagenes said, "Every anchor of hope has been destroyed" (*Aeth.* 7.25.4). The anthologist Stobaeus (fifth century AD) reports that Socrates said, "Basing your hope on a false conviction is like tying your boat to a weak anchor" (*Ecl.* 3.2.45).

With confusing metaphors, the author indicates that the anchor "enters" the heavenly world behind the curtain and that Christ is the forerunner who "enters" into the heavenly sanctuary. The author employs this mixture of metaphors to indicate that the listeners will find stability only when they see beyond the realities of their current experience and "grasp" the heavenly reality. This perspective is probably indebted to Philo, who contrasted the stability of God with the instability of the creation (*Confusion* 96; *Names* 175; *Dreams* 2.219–220). Thus only the one who stands by God's side can be unwavering (*Giants* 49).

Nowhere else in the NT is Jesus described as the "forerunner" (*prodromos*), a term that in Greek literature was used for the advanced units of an army (Polybius, *Hist.* 12.20.7; Herodotus, *Hist.* 4.121; 7.203; cf. Johnson 2006, 173) or a reconnaissance ship that pointed the way for the other ships to follow (Grässer 1965, 116). It corresponds in Hebrews to the role of Jesus as "pioneer" (2:10; 12:2). In the context of 6:20, it suggests that those who "have fled" follow the one who leads the way toward a secure place of refuge.

Tracing the Train of Thought

Before the author explores the full dimensions of the high priesthood of Melchizedek (7:1–10:18), introduced in 5:5, 10, he pauses to prepare his readers with the exhortation in 5:11–6:20.

That You May Not Be Sluggish (5:11–6:12)

5:11–12. About whom (5:11a), referring to Melchizedek, marks the transition to the "word" that is "hard to explain," which is the elaboration of the "word of hearing" (4:2) that the community has heard already (cf. 2:1) and the unfolding of the implications of the Christ event described in 1:1–4. These introductory words continue the earlier focus on God's word (1:2; 2:1; 4:2) and the community's responsibility for hearing (2:1; 3:7; 4:7). In this instance, however, the author indicates the community's continued need for hearing the full implications of God's speech "in a Son" (1:2). Just as he has previously challenged the readers to "hear his voice" (3:7), he now indicts them for their inability to hear the profound significance of the Christ event.

The *inclusio* formed by "sluggish" (*nōthroi*) in 5:11 and the same word in 6:12 suggests a tension in the author's outlook, for he begins the unit with the indictment **you have become sluggish in hearing** (5:11b) and concludes with the exhortation "that you may not be sluggish" (6:12). A similar tension exists between the author's indictment **you need for someone to teach you the elementary principles** (5:12b) and the exhortation to go on to perfection, "not again laying a foundation" (6:1). The author also includes a severe warning against falling away (6:4–6) but expresses the assurance that the readers will not, like Israel (3:7–4:11), fail to inherit the promises of God (6:9–12). Thus the tension reflects the author's rhetorical plight and his attempt to motivate the readers to come out of their sluggishness and renew their obedience. In the final reflection on Abraham in 6:13–20, the author offers an example of faithfulness from the past as a contrast to the examples of unfaithfulness in 3:7–4:11.

The pause in the presentation of the high priesthood of Melchizedek in 5:11–6:20 suggests the author's severe hermeneutical dilemma. The combination of a long speech, indicated by **there is much to say that is hard to explain** (5:11a), with listeners who are "sluggish in hearing" will make the author's presentation on the high priesthood of Melchizedek unintelligible unless this problem can be overcome. In this instance, the author indicates that the primary problem is not with the subject

---

Hebrews 5:11–6:20 in the Rhetorical Flow

Hearing God's word with faithful endurance (1:1–4:13)

Probatio: Discovering certainty and confidence in the word for the mature (4:14–10:31)

  Drawing near and holding firmly: following the path of Jesus from suffering to triumph (4:14–5:10)

▶ Preparing to hear the word that is hard to explain (5:11–6:20)

  That you may not be sluggish (5:11–6:12)

    Milk and solid food (5:11–12)

    Training and nutrition (5:13–14)

    Let us go on to perfection (6:1–3)

    Impossibility of repentance (6:4–6)

    A lesson from agriculture (6:7–8)

    Imitators of the faithful (6:9–12)

  God's irrevocable oath (6:13–20)

---

matter but with the hearing capacity of the listeners. With the phrase "sluggish in hearing," which was commonly associated with those who were intellectually lazy or slow to learn, the author introduces educational imagery into the argument, suggesting that the community's capacity to remain faithful depends on its intellectual development in Christian instruction.

The author begins this interlude with an indictment of the readers. His indictment is similar to the complaint of Philo about those for whom "the inward uproar makes it impossible for them to listen to the speaker, who discourses as in an audience not of human beings, but of lifeless statues who have ears, but no hearing in those ears" (*Heir* 13). Philo also speaks of the saying that "is not for all to hear," for there are "few whose ears are opened and pricked up to receive these holy words" (*Names* 138). Similarly, Epictetus complains: "Why are we still indolent and easy-going and sluggish, seeking excuses whereby we may avoid toiling or even late hours, as we try to perfect our own reason?" (*Diss.* 1.7.30).

The indictment that listeners **ought to be teachers** but **need someone to teach you** (5:12a) does not refer to an official office in the church but suggests a contrast between people in two stages of learning: teachers and those who are being taught. The author presupposes the ancient pattern of education, according to which the teacher dictated to the students, who copied the basic subjects onto a clay tablet (Koester 2001, 308). Children from the ages of seven to fourteen learned the basic lessons of grammar, language, and mathematics (see Introductory Matters) from their teachers.

The author elaborates on the indictment in the rest of 5:12, describing what they need in two parallel phrases. In the first place, they need someone to teach them **the elementary principles** (5:12b; *stoicheia tēs archēs*). *Stoicheia*, which means "basic components" of something (BDAG, 946), was also used for the letters of the alphabet (cf. Philo, *Prelim. Studies* 150; cf. Xenophon, *Mem.* 2.1.1; Plato, *Crat.* 434a). The readers do not fit the ancient ideal of educational progress from elementary education to the higher education in philosophy and virtue (cf. Seneca, *Ep.* 88.20). This indictment is especially severe, as the author suggests in the phrase **because of the time** (5:12a), for the readers have been Christians long enough to progress to the higher learning. The reference to "the former days" (10:32) and the repeated references to an earlier time in the community's experience indicates that they belong to the second generation (cf. 2:1–4; 6:9–12; 13:7). Thus listeners who have been Christians long enough to have progressed to higher education are still pupils in the elementary school.

The "elementary principles" that the readers have not yet mastered have to do with **the oracles of God** (5:12b; *tōn logiōn tou theou*). *Logia* is a term used in antiquity for the oracles of the gods (cf. Grässer 1990, 1:327, citing Wettstein 1962). In the OT, the term refers to the scriptures (cf. Num 24:16; Ps 107:11 [106:11 LXX]; cf. Acts 7:38; Rom 3:2; 1 Pet 4:11; Attridge 1989, 159). Here, however, the "oracles of God" refer not only to the OT but to the Christian revelation and to the Christian interpretation of the OT. As the author demonstrates with the "word" that is "hard to explain" in 7:1–10:18, the "oracles of God" include a full range of learning that begins with the elementary principles and extends to the advanced instruction.

In the second place the community needs **milk not solid food** (5:12c). Since the basic education was commonly associated with milk, the metaphor moves naturally from elementary principles to milk to describe the basic instruction in the oracles of God. Unlike Paul, who employs the image of milk and solid food to distinguish between childish and adult behavior (1 Cor 3:1–5), the author employs these images for the levels of education, using the language of Greek *paideia*. In Hebrews, however, the "elementary principles" and "milk" are not the basic studies in Greek education (*enkyklios paideia*; see Introductory Matters) but the basic catechetical instruction (the "foundation") that he describes in 6:1–2. At their conversion, the readers learned the "elementary principles," but like children who have not mastered the basic subjects, the readers have made no progress.

Education and Catechesis in Early Christianity

Early Christianity inherited the emphasis on education from both the Greek and Jewish traditions. Just as Greek education prepared pupils for a life of virtue, Jewish education prepared them for a life of obedience to God. Jewish education emphasized the transmission of the history of God's covenant with Israel and the ethical requirements of the Torah (Deut 6:20–25). In early Christianity, converts received extensive catechetical instruction, which included the basic memory of the saving events (1 Cor 15:3; cf. 1 Cor 11:23–26) and the ethical expectations of the community. Paul frequently alludes to previous catechetical instruction (Rom 6:3; 1 Cor 6:2–3, 9; Gal 5:21; 1 Thess 3:4; 4:2, 11; 5:2). Lists of vices and virtues (1 Cor 6:9–11; Gal 5:19–23) probably served as instruction for new converts. Like his contemporaries in both Jewish and Greek cultures, Paul was a model for his new converts, providing both instruction and an example (Phil 4:9). In the Pastoral Epistles, instruction consists primarily of ethical instruction (1 Tim 4:11; 6:2; Titus 2:1). The education of children, which is mentioned only in Eph 6:4 and Titus 2:4, is ethical instruction given by the parents.

5:13–14. In 5:13–14, the author elaborates on the community's situation by offering a theory of education that was well known in Greco-Roman antiquity. Like Philo, he moves easily from the metaphor of nutrition to the metaphor of athletics to describe the exercise that necessarily accompanies the solid food of education. Philo compares the nourishment of the soul to the nourishment of the athlete (*Alleg. Interp.* 1.98). According to *On the Sacrifices of Cain and Abel*, those who eat and drink the food of the soul must also exercise in order to receive the full nourishment (85). Thus Philo and other philosophers would have agreed with the author's assessment that the one who lives on the milk of the lower education is inexperienced (*apeiros*) in intellectual growth. Indeed, Philo compares human progress from the beginning stage to perfection with the wrestler who is inexperienced (*apeiros*) and incapable of confronting sophistic arguments without training comparable to that of the athlete (*Worse* 41). Similarly, the author of Hebrews describes Christians who have not proceeded to solid food as inexperienced. However, for the author of Hebrews, **those who live on milk are inexperienced in the word of righteousness** (5:13), which is the solid food that is hard to explain.

The goal of the believer is to progress from being a **child** (5:13; *nēpios*) nourished by milk to becoming a **mature** (5:14a; *teleios*) person nourished on solid food. Philo, who frequently describes the basic education as milk, agrees that solid food is for the mature when he speaks of the "solid food of philosophy" (*Good Person* 160). The author's term for "mature" (*teleios*) is the common term for an adult (BDAG, 995) in contrast to a child (*nēpios*; cf.

1 Cor 2:16). In Hebrews, the term and its cognates are also employed for the perfection that Christ, the one who was "made perfect" (5:9) as a result of his sufferings (2:10), grants to believers (cf. 9:9; 10:1, 14). The author speaks not of moral perfection but of the right of access to God. Here, however, the author employs the Greek language of pedagogy, envisioning Christian experience as a path from being a child (*nēpios*) to being a mature person (*teleios*).

This path involves not only good nutrition but rigorous exercise of the mind, for the mature are those who **because of their condition, have the faculties trained to discern good from evil** (5:14b). For the author, however, the goal of eating solid food is "to be able to distinguish between good and evil." Thus the knowledge of the word that is hard to explain has practical consequences. Although this word involves knowledge of the heavenly work of Christ, the ultimate result of this instruction is to provide the basis for the ethical conduct that the author encourages. Those who grow to maturity learn to be involved in the work, service to the saints, and acts of love (6:9–12). When they have grasped the "solid food," they will be able to hold firm (10:23) and express communal solidarity (10:32–34).

With this indictment of the readers and the theory of education, the author indicates the close relationship between spiritual and intellectual lethargy, indicating that only a healthy diet and rigorous training of the mind will provide the community with the means to overcome its present lethargy. Just as the Greeks taught that the teaching of philosophy is the path to virtue, the author argues that intellectual development in scriptural interpretation provides the basis for the community's health. Only through this conditioning can the community sustain itself in the midst of the temptation to abandon the faith.

6:1–3. Having described the characteristics of the "mature" (5:14), the author returns to his audience in 6:1–3, encouraging them to adopt these qualities, **leaving the elementary teaching of Christ** (*ton tēs archēs tou Christou logon*) (6:1a). This elementary teaching, like the foundation, is equivalent to the milk and the elementary principles (*stoicheia*) mentioned in 5:12. **Maturity** is the spiritual receptivity and response to the truth that the author will explore in 7:1–10:18. In this instance, however, the author says not that the community needs for someone to teach them the elementary principles but that the community should **move on** to maturity and **not lay a foundation again** (6:1b). This tension with the earlier claim that the community needs milk and the elementary principles suggests that the author first spoke in hyperbole before he urged the community to "move on to maturity."

Unlike the ancient writers who described the basic education in grammar and mathematics as the foundation for learning, the author lists six components of the foundation that the listeners had received, arranged in three groups of two. Inasmuch as this list contains no reference to Christ, one must conclude that the list is not comprehensive. The "foundation" is most likely the catechetical instruction given to new converts. The fact that the items listed were at home in the Jewish synagogue suggests that early Christian catechesis employed the basic instruction commonly used in Jewish missionary preaching (Weiss 1991, 337). **Repentance from dead works and faith in God** (6:1c), marking the first stage in the experience of the convert, were themes in Jewish missionary preaching (cf. Wis 11:23; 12:2 for the combination of repentance and faith) adopted into Christian preaching (cf. repentance in Acts 2:38; 17:30–31; 26:20; 1 Thess 1:9–10). The "dead works" are not the Jewish works of the law but the works associated with idolatry, which lead to death (cf. the references to death as the characteristic of the pre-Christian existence in Eph 2:5; Col 2:13). The second stage in Christian existence included a **teaching of baptisms and the laying on of hands** (6:2a), two practices that were sometimes associated in early Christian initiation (Acts 8:16–17; 19:5–7) with roots in the Jewish tradition (cf. Gen 48:14; Num 27:15–23; Deut 34:9). The plural "baptisms" may suggest that the catechetical instruction distinguished Christian baptism from the various baptisms (cf. 9:10) and washings practiced in antiquity (Weiss 1991, 339). **Resurrection of the dead** and **eternal judgment** (6:2b) were also themes of Jewish tradition (cf. Dan 12:2; 2 Macc 7:14; 12:43–44; cf. *1 En.* 91.15), that were adopted into the Christian tradition (cf. 1 Thess 1:9–10).

6:4–6. The recollection of the list of items in the catechetical instruction in 6:1–2 leads the author to reflect further on that foundational experience with a new list of items indicating the significance of the event in 6:4–6. As **for** (6:4a) suggests, the author now indicates the alternative to the movement toward "maturity." **It is impossible** is used frequently in Hebrews to state a general principle that the author applies to his audience (cf. 6:18; 10:4; 11:6). Before the author completes the sentence in 6:6b, describing what is impossible, he reflects on the initial experience of the readers in 6:4b–5 and the possibility that they will fall in 6:6a. Here, as elsewhere (cf. 6:9–12; 10:32–34), the author reflects positively on the community's beginning. In the series of aorist participles in 6:4–6a, the author describes a singular event in the lives of the readers. At the head of the list is the memory that they were **once enlightened**. Here, for the first time in this homily, the author emphasizes the singularity of the event by the use of "once" (*hapax*), a theme that will be central to the argument (9:7, 26, 27, 28; 10:2; 12:26; cf. *ephapax*, 7:27; 9:12; 10:10). Just as the saving significance of Jesus' death is "once for all," so also believers have been "once enlightened" at their conversion (cf. 10:32 for conversion as enlightenment). This claim heads the list of other experiences that are all associated with the community's conversion, as the author lists items in two pairs. In the twofold use of "tasted" at the beginning of each pair, the author employs a metaphor that was commonly used to mean "experience" (2:9, "taste death"; Matt 16:28; Mark 9:1; 1 Pet 2:3) and here signifies their full experience of extraordinary gifts from God. To **taste the heavenly gift** (6:4b) is to become "partakers in a heavenly calling" (3:1) and gain access to God's throne. To become **partakers in the Holy Spirit** (6:4c; cf. 3:14, "partakers of Christ") is to receive the heavenly power of the new age. To taste the **good word of God** (6:5a) is to be the recipients of the divine word that has spoken in Jesus Christ (1:1–2). Just as Jesus has already subjected the "coming world" (2:5), the listeners have experienced **the powers of the coming age** (6:5b). The cumulative effect of this list is to recall the enormity of the conversion experience for the listeners, for it marked their participation in an unrepeatable event in which they became participants in the victory of Christ.

In 6:6, the author raises the prospect that those who have received these extraordinary gifts might **fall away** (6:6a). Just the series of images for the new existence in Christ recalls a decisive moment of turning from darkness to light, the aorist participle "fall away" (*parapesontas*) points to a decisive moment of abandonment of the extraordinary gifts that the author has enumerated. The word does not refer to an ethical lapse or to theological error in this context. Those who have "once been enlightened" would annul all the gifts of the new age and return to darkness. This warning expresses the concern that pervades the entire homily: that the readers will "neglect the great salvation" (2:3), "fall away from the living God" (3:12), or "sin deliberately" (10:26).

The enormity of abandoning the heavenly gifts enumerated by the author is evident in the consequences: it is impossible **to renew to repentance again** (6:4a) those "who fall away." The author's argument in the larger context indicates why this renewal is impossible. In the argument that follows, the author insists that the sacrifice of Jesus was "once for all" (*hapax, ephapax*). Christ offered himself "once" (7:27; 9:28), entering into the heavenly sanctuary "once" (9:12). As a result, believers are sanctified "once for all" (*ephapax*; 10:10). In 6:4–6, the contrast between "once" (6:4) and "again" (6:6) indicates why "it is impossible to renew" apostates to repentance. That is, as "once" suggests, the experience of being "enlightened" and of tasting "the heavenly gift" is unrepeatable. Thus to renew to repentance again is impossible because the decisive moment of conversion cannot be repeated. According to the parallel passage in 10:26–31 (cf. 12:15–17), "there no longer remains a sacrifice for sin" for those who sin deliberately. A great salvation has equally great consequences for those who reject it.

The author explains why it is impossible to repeat the saving event in the participial phrase **crucifying** (*anastarountes*) **for themselves the Son of God and holding him up for public contempt** (*paradeigmatizontas*) (6:6b). With the two participles, the author recalls the public contempt associated with the crucifixion and the role of those who crucified Jesus. In changing from aorist to present participles, the author describes the devastating and continuing impact of the apostasy of those who have "once been enlightened." They place themselves on the side of those who crucified the Son of God and join in publicly humiliating him. In the parallel passage in 10:29, the author speaks in graphic terms of the dreadful effects of apostasy. Those who "sin deliberately" (10:26) "trample the Son of God under foot and profane the blood of the covenant" (10:29).

6:7–8. The author reinforces the warning with an illustration from nature, using an image that is deeply rooted in the OT (cf. Deut 11:11; Isa 5:1–7). The land that **drinks the rain that comes frequently** (6:7a) is an image for those who received the heavenly gifts enumerated in 6:4–5. Just as this land **produces useful vegetation** and **receives a blessing from God** (6:7b), converts who remain faithful to their confession continue to receive the heavenly gift. In the image of the land that bears only **thorns and thistles** (6:8), the author points to those who "fall away," whose fate will be like that of the unproductive land that is at the point of being cursed and in the end will be burned.

If the author meant for this passage to disturb his readers, he managed to disturb interpreters throughout the centuries even more, for this passage has been the center of controversy more than any in Hebrews (see Introductory Matters). The missing dimension in the history of interpretation is the recognition that the passage fits the logic of the author's argument and his relationship to the readers. This passage is one of a series of warnings to the community about the danger that they face (cf. 2:1–4; 3:7–19). The author is neither addressing questions of church discipline nor answering questions about receiving into the community those who lapsed during times of persecution nor addressing post-Reformation questions about the security of the believer. Indeed, the author speaks only to those who have not fallen away. Since this apostasy has not occurred, the author's words remain hypothetical. His words are intended to shock the readers into recognizing the cost of abandoning God's heavenly gift.

6:9–12. The author's concern for rhetorical effect becomes clear in the abrupt change of tone in 6:9–12, as he moves from the impersonal warning in 6:4–6 to an intimate familial tone in which he attempts to create a bond with his readers. Addressing the audience for the first time as **beloved** (6:9), he moves from the appeal to fear to another form of the argument from pathos, indicating his affection for the readers. He enhances this emotional bond with the expression of assurance in the audience. In the words **although we speak in this way, we are confident of better things that belong to salvation in your case** (6:9), the author distinguishes his audience from those who "fall away." In the "better things that belong to salvation," the author reaffirms his repeated insistence that the Christian revelation is a "great salvation" (cf. 2:3) that is "better" *(kreittōn/kreissōn;* cf. 1:4; 7:19; 8:6; 11:16, 40; 12:24) than all alternatives. Despite the stern warnings of 6:4–6, the author is confident that the readers will not ultimately fail to reach the goal of inheriting the promises of God (cf. 6:12).

The author indicates the reason for his confidence in 6:10, recalling the principle that **God is not unjust** (6:10a), and assuming, with the psalmist, that God rewards people for their work (Ps 62:12). In addition to creating a bond with himself, the author describes the bond that has existed among the readers from the very beginning. They once demonstrated **work** and **love** by **serving the saints** (6:10b), and they continue to do so. According to 10:32–34, their work and love were evident when they shared the tribulations of others and observed sympathy for prisoners. As the author indicates in 13:1–6, a marginalized community can exist only when the people exhibit a strong sense of family solidarity.

As 6:11 indicates, the community now stands between the early days described in 6:10 and the end. As the earlier exhortations have indicated, the community's capacity to finish the course remains an open question (2:1–4; 3:6, 14), leading the author to plead for them to inherit the promise (cf. 4:11). Thus he hopes to maintain the emotional bond with the community, proceeding from the confidence he expressed in his "beloved" (6:9) to the passionate **desire** (6:11a) for the readers to complete what they have begun. The strong verb "desire" suggests both the author's longing and the urgency of the situation (Grässer 1990, 1:366). The author appeals not only to the community as a whole but to individual listeners—**each of you**—knowing that the response of the community depends on individual members. Just as the community demonstrated work and love in the past, he desires that they move beyond the earlier expression of communal solidarity to **demonstrate the same zeal for the full assurance of hope until the end** (6:11b), hoping that the "zeal" of the past will motivate the audience "until the end." With such zeal the community will not be sluggish (cf. 5:11).

The central problem facing the readers, as the series of warnings suggests, is the danger that the community will not survive "until the end," for it has been disoriented by the lack of visible evidence of the truth of its confession that "all things are in subjection" to the Son (2:18) and by the marginalization that it has experienced. In holding before the community the "full assurance of hope," the author alludes to the "assurance" (*plērophoria*) that provides the basis for the community's endurance. As the later phrase "full assurance of faith" (*plērophoria pisteōs*) suggests, faith and hope are indistinguishable in Hebrews (cf. Heb 11:1). The response to the cognitive dissonance that the community experiences is hope and faith, the unwillingness to concede that the visible reality is ultimate.

Having presented Israel already as the negative example (4:11) of those who, because of their lack of faith (3:12, 19; 4:2), failed to inherit the promises (4:1–2), the author encourages the community to **become imitators of those who through faith and patience inherit the promises** (6:12b), inasmuch as God's promise of heavenly rest remains available (4:1). Such models for imitation include the heroes of chapter 11 and the community's founders (13:7), who demonstrated faith to the end. "Faith and patience" function as a hendiadys, two words or phrases used to say the same thing. Here they illuminate the hope mentioned in 6:11 and give further definition to faith.

"Patience" (*makrothymia*) was evident in Abraham's response to the promise (cf. 6:15, *makrothymeō*). As the story of Abraham suggests, patience involves endless waiting for the promise. As the author demonstrates in chapter 11, faith is indistinguishable from perseverance (*hypomonē*, cf. 10:36–39; 12:1–3) as the response of those who undergo suffering, insecurity, and marginalization because they have the "full assurance" that the ultimate reality will be experienced only at "the end."

God's Irrevocable Oath (6:13–20)

As "for" in 6:13 indicates, the author's task in the exposition that follows is to provide the foundation that will enable the readers to maintain the "faith and patience" to inherit the promises and to overcome the lethargy that threatens to master them.

6:13–15. In 6:13–15, he offers Abraham as an example. Abraham is often cited to illustrate faithfulness in Jewish literature (Sir 44:19–21; 1 Macc 2:52) and the NT (Rom 4:3–22; Gal 3:7–28; Jas 2:23–24). The reference to Abraham as the example of faith in 6:13–15 anticipates the treatment of Abraham in 11:8–20, where the author indicates that he was "about to receive an inheritance" (11:8–10). However, the focus in 6:13–15 is less on Abraham than on the absolute reliability of God's promise. The opening statement that **God made a promise to Abraham** (6:13a) anticipates the later claim that "the one who promises is faithful" (10:23; 11:11). The use of the aorist participle (*epangeilamenos*) implies correctly that God had made the promise to Abraham twice before (Johnson 2006, 169): first in Gen 12:2–3, when God promised Abraham a new land, and again in 15:5, when God reiterated the promise. The author now cites the third report of the promise from Gen 22:16. In order to demonstrate the reliability of God, which is evident when God **swore by himself**, he adds, **since he had no one greater to swear by** (6:13b). The additional emphasis on God's oath is evident in the quotation of Gen 22:17, **Surely I will bless you and surely I will multiply you** (6:14). The author does not, however elaborate on the content of God's oath (cf. Gen 22:17–19) but focuses instead on its certainty.

This emphasis on God's oath is a consistent feature of the argument of Hebrews. In the reflection on the wilderness generation, the author has recalled that God swore, "They will never enter my rest" (Heb 3:11). In the discussion of Melchizedek that follows, the author cites the words of Ps 110:4, "The Lord has sworn and will not change his mind." Therefore, whether God speaks in a warning (Heb 3:11) or a promise (6:13–15), his word is reliable.

An Outline of Hebrews 6:13–20

The reliability of God's promise is evident in the fact that Abraham, **having waited patiently, obtained the promise** (6:15). This affirmation stands in tension with the subsequent observation that neither Abraham and his immediate descendants nor any of the heroes of faith "received the promise" (11:13, 39). This tension is not the result of an oversight by the author but is an indication of his purpose in each passage. In 11:13, 39, the author focuses on heroes who believed without seeing the ultimate fulfillment of God's promise until the day they died. In 6:15, the author's focus is on the trustworthiness of God. As **and thus** indicates, the emphasis is on the fact that God's promises come true. Thus, in the context of the community's own struggle with faith, the basis for its endurance is the certainty that God's promise provides.

God's promise came true only after Abraham "waited patiently" (*makrothymēsas*), becoming the model for others who live without seeing the triumph of God (cf. 2:8). Because Abraham lived in the certainty of God's promise in the midst of his many trials, he is the model for a Christian community under duress. This patient waiting is the equivalent of faith (cf. 6:12) and perseverance (10:36; *hypomonē*), which is lacking among the readers. Unlike the wilderness generation, Abraham did not fail to obtain the promise (6:15).

6:16–18. The author elaborates on the certainty of the oath by piling images for certainty drawn especially from the law court. That is, **people swear by something greater** (6:16a; cf. Matt 5:35–37; 23:16–18; Josh 2:12; 1 Sam 20:42; 2 Cor 1:18, 23; Gal 1:20; Phil 1:8; 1 Thess 2:5, 10), calling on God to ensure the reliability of the oath. As an indisputable fact that **puts an end to all dispute, the oath** is **for confirmation** (*eis bebaiōsin*) (6:16b), a principle acknowledged by the author's contemporaries (see Introductory Matters). Thus an oath has special significance in providing certainty for those who receive a promise, for it gives them the basis for persevering in the midst of their own suffering. The phrases "beyond dispute" (*antilogias peras*; cf. 7:7) and "for confirmation" (*eis bebaiōsin*) are technical terms in the law courts; the former refers to an objection in a trial, while the latter refers to the legally valid guarantee (Weiss 1991, 361).

The general principle in 6:16 is the basis for the author's application to the community in 6:17–20. If the oath in a human court provides "confirmation," God demonstrates the **unchangeability of his will even more** (*perissoteron*) for the author's own readers who, like Abraham, are the **heirs of the promise** (6:17; cf. 1:14; 9:15 for Christians as heirs). The community has received an oath that is even more reliable than the one God gave to Abraham (on *perissoteron* [even more], see also 2:1, where the author says that recipients of the new revelation should "especially" [*perissoterōs*] pay attention). Continuing the legal imagery, the author says that God "guaranteed" (*emesiteusen*) his promise, using the language that was commonly used for the one who was the guardian of oaths (Josephus, *Ant.* 4.133), deposits, and contracts (Spicq 1994, 2:467). This guarantee made the contract unchangeable. Thus the author

Legal Terminology in Hebrews

The author's consistent use of legal terminology is without parallel in the New Testament. Recognizing, with Quintilian (*Inst.* 5.11.32, 34), that comparisons from the law courts provide effective arguments, the author makes abundant use of legal terminology to describe the Christ event. With the frequent use of forms of *bebai-* ("firm," "valid," "guaranteed" in 2:2–3; 3:6; 6:16, 19; 9:17; 13:9), a term commonly used in the law courts for a binding promise (cf. 6:16), the author argues that the Christian message is legally valid and a guarantee of God's promise. The terms "guarantor" (*engyos*, 7:22), "unchangeable" (*ametathetos*, 6:18), and "guaranteed" (*mesiteuein*, 6:17) are technical legal terms. The consistent description of the Christian promise as an oath (Heb 3:18; 6:13, 16; 7:20–21, 28) and final testament (or will, 9:16) that is in force (9:17) through the death of Jesus and attested by God (2:3) demonstrates the certainty of the Christian confession.

refers to the "unchangeability" of God's will (6:17) and the **two unchangeable things** (6:18a) that ensure the reliability of the oath. The author employs the synonymous term "surety" (*engyos*) in 7:22.

The "two unchangeable things" in which **it is impossible for God to lie** (6:18b) are the promise and the oath that God gives to the heirs. This constant emphasis on certainty is the basis for the exhortation to the community, which the author now describes as **those who have taken refuge** (6:18c; *hoi kataphygontes*), knowing that those who are "refugees" live without certainty. The author's description of the community as those "who have taken refuge" is consistent with the repeated emphasis on the marginalization that tests those who do not see God's triumph. As the author has indicated with the imagery of a people on the way to the promised land, following their leader (2:10), insecurity characterizes their existence. Thus God's oath (6:17) provides the readers with a **hope** that is **set forth** (6:18c; *prokeimenēs elpidos*) for the community to **grasp** (*kratēsai*), providing the stability that refugees lack.

6:19–20. The author further emphasizes this certainty with the image of hope as **a stable and firm anchor of the soul** (6:19a). Having introduced the nautical image in the concern that the readers will "drift away" in 2:1, the author offers the solution to this temptation in the "anchor of the soul," an image that was common in Greek literature but unknown elsewhere in the Bible to depict certainty and hope. The adjectives "stable and firm" (*asphalē kai bebaian*), a common phrase in Greek (Wis 7:23; Philo, *Heir* 314; *Cherubim* 103), add to the emphasis on certainty. Indeed, the related words *bebaian/bebaiōsis* stand at the heart of the argument of Hebrews (2:2; 3:6 [in some manuscripts], 14; 6:16; 9:17), indicating the importance of certainty for a community whose faith is constantly tested.

Figure 6. Hope: Anchor of the Soul. Early Christian art uses symbols that would not have seemed unusual to outsiders but had special significance for believers. This third-century funerary epitaph of a woman named Licinia Famia bears two such images: the fish and the anchor. For Christians, the Greek word for fish (here used in the phrase "fish of the living") was an acrostic for "Jesus Christ, God's Son, Savior," and the anchor recalled Heb 6:19. Licinia's family anchored their souls in the hope that their departed loved one was among the living who were saved by God's Son, Jesus.

In an unusual mixture of metaphors, the author describes this hope as **entering inside the curtain** (6:19b) into the heavenly sanctuary (cf. 10:19). He then clarifies the image, describing Christ as the **forerunner** (6:20a; *prodromos*) who entered behind the curtain into the heavenly world. As the imagery suggests elsewhere (10:19–23), the exaltation of Christ was his entry into the heavenly world (9:24), when he opened up the way for his people to draw near. The image of the forerunner is parallel to the image of Christ as the pioneer (2:10; 12:2; *archēgos*) who leads others to glory. With the claim that the exaltation was the occasion when Jesus became **high priest after the order of Melchizedek** (6:20b), the author returns to the subject that he introduced in 5:5, 10. Having attempted to awaken those who were "sluggish in hearing" (5:11), the author proceeds in chapter 7 to develop the theme of the high priesthood of Melchizedek. As the exhortations immediately preceding and following the major section in 7:1–10:18 indicate, the author's task in this "word" that is "hard to explain" is to provide stability for wavering readers and an anchor that they may grasp.

Theological Issues

The fact that the subject of the high priest according to the order of Melchizedek is a "word" that is "hard to explain" (5:11) does not prevent the author from exploring it fully in chapter 7, even if the readers are "dull of hearing" (5:11). He prepares the readers to hear the message in 5:11–6:20 by shaming (5:11–14), warning (6:4–8), and encouraging the community to remain faithful to the promise (6:9–10). Despite the difficulty of the topic in 7:1–10:18, the author cannot dispense with it, for it is vital to the community's future. As he indicates in 5:11–14, the future of the community requires its progression from the milk of catechetical instruction to the solid food of advanced study—from being taught to being teachers of the faith. Ceslas Spicq (1977, 100) has shown that this passage, more than any other in the NT, indicates the importance of developing a "biblical culture" shaped by knowledge of the Christian faith.

In borrowing language from Greek education (*paideia*), the author indicates the importance of theological reflection for the community of faith. Theological reflection is the task not only of the community's leaders but of the whole church. Although the author envisions a progression from the alphabet to higher learning similar to what Greek educational theorists advocated, his concern is not with the basic subjects taught in the schools but with an alternative curriculum rooted in the interpretation of scripture. With his secular counterparts he recognizes the importance of education for maintaining the cultural memory and identity of the people. Evangelism involves not only initiation of new converts into the community but also catechesis that instructs members into the community's corporate memory. Because a culture needs more than fundamental instruction, however, the author challenges the readers to a continuing educational progress in the study of scripture.

Like ancient educational theorists, the author recognized that education is not the goal in itself but is meant to instill the capacity to "distinguish good from evil" (5:14). The author's metaphors indicate that progress requires good intellectual nutrition and exercise (5:14). The metaphor of athletic training also indicates that discipleship and growth require disciplined study of the scripture. As a place of theological reflection, the church offers opportunities for intellectual growth in the Christian faith. Preaching, Bible study groups, and youth programs contribute to the formation of Christian identity when they engage in rigorous interpretation of the scripture.

The transition from the focus on education (5:11–6:3) to the warning against falling away (6:4–8) suggests that the alternative to progress toward intellectual maturity is the abandonment of the rich gifts that have come in Christ. This severe warning is not the basis for a comprehensive theology of apostasy and renewal but an attempt to awaken the readers to the urgency of their situation. The author answers neither the questions of the church fathers who appealed to this passage for instruction regarding the return of those who lapsed during persecution nor those of modern readers who attempt to fit the passage into their view of eternal security. He writes to awaken the gratitude of the readers for their salvation and to make their apostasy unthinkable. Inasmuch as the entire homily is written with the concern that the readers might fail to finish the course (cf. 3:7–4:11), the author indicates the magnitude of the gift of Christ and the horror of rejecting it.

The alternative curriculum in scripture gives the community the resource for interpreting its own situation, as the author's appeal to Abraham in 6:13–20 suggests. Those who identify with Abraham discover that, although the church lives in hope, it does not reach its destination without waiting patiently on the promises (6:15). People of faith discover that the fulfillment of their hopes may seem endlessly deferred as they live with disappointment and suffering. As the ancient story of Abraham indicates (Gen 12–25), a major theme in scripture is that of promise delayed. To have faith is to wait patiently when one sees no signs of God's action in the world. Abraham's endless waiting is the model for the people of all ages who struggle with the dissonance between the reality they see and the hope that they confess. Christians live in hope because God's ultimate promise is the entry of the forerunner into the presence of God. In the meantime, the members of the community do not wait alone. They wait as a community, supporting one another with acts of love and service (6:9–10).

Hebrews 7

The Priesthood of Melchizedek as the Anchor of the Soul

Introductory Matters

Having contrasted "every high priest" (5:1; cf. 8:3) of the Levitical system with Christ, the high priest according to the order of Melchizedek (5:6, 10), the author returned to the topic in 6:20 after the preparatory digression in 5:11–6:19. He had already established that Christians confess a "high priest who has passed through the heavens" (4:14) after the "days of his flesh" (5:7), when he experienced the same sufferings that now face the readers. The author now develops the theme of the heavenly high priesthood in the "word" that is "long and hard to explain" (cf. 5:11) in 7:1–10:18. In the discussion of Melchizedek in chapter 7, he prepares the way for his "main point" (8:1) of the high priest who serves in the heavenly sanctuary, expanding on the theme of the order of Melchizedek and the high priest who has "passed through the heavens" (4:14).

Like other early Christian writers, the author appeals frequently to Ps 110:1 to describe the exalted status of Christ (1:3, 13; 8:1; 10:12; 12:2; cf. Matt 22:44; Acts 2:34–35; Rom 8:34; 1 Cor 15:25; Eph 1:20; Col 3:1). In declaring that the exalted one is also a heavenly high priest, the author expands on the psalm to include 110:4, "You are a priest forever after the order of Melchizedek" (5:6, 10; 6:20; 5:10 omits "forever"). The opening words of chapter 7, "for this Melchizedek," indicate that the author will now elaborate on Ps 110:4. He develops this theme by adding words from Gen 14:17–20, the only other OT passage that mentions Melchizedek. Chapter 7 is a midrash on these two passages in which the author offers a christological interpretation in order to develop the theme of a priesthood that is superior to that of Aaron.

Because Melchizedek is an obscure figure in the OT, the author's interest in him has puzzled interpreters for centuries. Melchizedek appears suddenly on the scene in a singular encounter with Abraham and then disappears as quickly as he appears (Gen 14:17–20). According to the Genesis narrative, he "brought out bread and wine" (14:18) and blessed Abraham, who "gave him a tenth of everything." He is identified as "king of Salem" and "priest of God Most High." According to Ps 110:1–4, the king who sits at God's right hand executes justice and is also a "priest forever after the order of Melchizedek." This appearance of a priest-king inevitably evoked interest in a tradition that required that kings and priests come from different tribes.

The extensive discussion about Melchizedek in Jewish literature is probably the background for the author's interest in the subject. Rabbinic interpreters identified Melchizedek with Shem, son of Noah (*Tg. Ps.-J.* on Gen 14:18). This argument derives from the statement in Gen 11:10 that Shem lived for five hundred years after the birth of his son, thus outliving Abraham by thirty-five years (Koester 2001, 338). One tradition claimed that Melchizedek transferred the priesthood to Abraham, creating a line of descent from Israel's patriarch to Aaron (*b. Ned.* 32b; *Lev. Rab.* 25.6). Josephus said that Melchizedek inaugurated temple worship in Jerusalem (*JW* 6.438; Koester 2001, 339).

Philo of Alexandria also expresses an interest in Melchizedek on three occasions. In one instance Philo recalls the story of Melchizedek to show the importance of tithing (*Prelim. Studies* 99). In *On the Life of Abraham*, he adds to the story of Abraham's encounter with Melchizedek that the latter was overjoyed at Abraham's victory, that he offered sacrifices, and that he and Abraham became friends from that moment on (*Abraham* 235). In his most extended treatment of Melchizedek, Philo, like the author of Hebrews, offers the etymology of Melchizedek's name as "king of righteousness" and "king of peace," gives an allegorical treatment of the bread and wine brought out by Melchizedek (cf. Gen 14:18) and concludes that Melchizedek was the divine *logos* (*Alleg. Interp.* 3.79–82).

In the apocalyptic literature of the first century, Melchizedek becomes a heavenly figure who executes justice on God's behalf. According to 11Q Melchizedek in the Dead Sea Scrolls, he is an eschatological redeemer who secures liberty for those held captive by the power of Belial and exacts the judgments of God against Belial and the evil spirits allied with him. Standing at the head of the good angels, the heavenly leader Melchizedek leads the forces of good against the forces of evil at the end of days (see Kobelski 1981, 3). The function of Melchizedek in 11Q Melchizedek is remarkably similar to the role of Michael in other apocalyptic texts, in which the primary role attributed to Michael in this final age is the defeat of Belial (1QM 17.5–8). Both Michael and Melchizedek act as God's principal agent in wreaking vengeance upon the

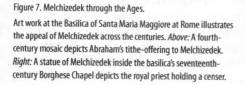

Figure 7. Melchizedek through the Ages.

Art work at the Basilica of Santa Maria Maggiore at Rome illustrates the appeal of Melchizedek across the centuries. *Above:* A fourth-century mosaic depicts Abraham's tithe-offering to Melchizedek. *Right:* A statue of Melchizedek inside the basilica's seventeenth-century Borghese Chapel depicts the royal priest holding a censer.

enemy, and both are at the head of the angelic forces (1QM 17.7; 11QMelch 2.14; cf. *3 Bar.* 11.4; *As. Mos.* 10.2). The outcome of the eschatological war in 1QM 17.5–8 is the establishment of the reign of Michael, while in 11Q Melchizedek it is the reign of Melchizedek announced by the herald, "Your God is king" (Kobelski 1981, 72).

The apocalyptic imagination about Melchizedek is nowhere more evident than in *2 Enoch*, a text that survives only in Old Slavonic. The treatment of Melchizedek appears in chapters 69–73, a section that appears to be an appendix to the first sixty-eight chapters (Gieschen 1997, 366). Because of the complicated textual history, scholars have been uncertain about the date of either *2 Enoch* or the appendix. Indeed, the earlier edition of *2 Enoch* in R. H. Charles's *Apocrypha and Pseudepigrapha of the Old Testament* did not include chapters 69–73. Nevertheless, the presence of themes that are common in the first century and the absence of a reference to the destruction of the Jerusalem temple suggest that the original text of *2 Enoch* may be as early as the first century AD.

The appendix in *2 En.* 69–73 develops a theme that pervades the entirety of the book: How can evil be defeated and purity restored (Gieschen 1997,

367–68). The concern of chapters 69–73 is the need for a priestly mediator to deliver the people from impurity. After Enoch was gone, Methusalam (i.e., Methuselah) asked God to raise up a priest (69:5). After God granted him the priesthood, the priestly office then passed to Nir, the brother of Noah. Sophonim, the wife of Nir, gave birth to a child in her old age on the day of her death. She conceived the child, "being sterile" and "without having slept with her husband," hiding herself during all the days of her pregnancy. When she died, Melchizedek was born from Sophonim's corpse. When Nir and Noah came in to bury Sophonim, they saw the child sitting beside the corpse and "having his clothing on him." They were terrified because "the child was fully developed physically." The child spoke and "blessed the Lord." The newborn child was marked by the sign of priesthood. The "badge of priesthood was on his chest, and it was glorious in appearance." In response to Nir's concerns about the destruction of the child along with the rest of the world, the Lord appeared to Nir in a vision and assured him that Melchizedek would be the head of priests for the future (71:29). Michael descended after Melchizedek's birth and took him away to the Paradise of Eden (72:9). Thus Melchizedek was the head of a new kind of priesthood that did not suffer destruction.

The fascination with Melchizedek in Jewish tradition, as reflected in a variety of texts, suggests that the author of Hebrews would expect this theme to resonate among many readers who had engaged in speculation about this individual. However, little point of contact exists between the author and the literature contemporary with him. Although the author and Philo are both interested in the etymology of Melchizedek's name, the two writers share little else. Nor does the author share the interpretation found in 11Q Melchizedek, where Melchizedek is the instrument of God's justice rather than a priest who offers sacrifices. Similarly, the author does not share the legendary details found in 2 Enoch. Nevertheless, the author shares with 2 Enoch the desire to establish the legitimacy of an alternative priesthood. Furthermore, he shares with both 11Q Melchizedek and 2 Enoch the focus on Melchizedek as a heavenly figure. Thus, while the author is not directly dependent on the secondary literature on Melchizedek, he is probably responding to conversations that were taking place in the first century AD. As a heavenly figure, Melchizedek provided a basis for comparison to the exalted Christ.

The author's citation from scripture indicates his particular emphasis on aspects of the story that are important for the argument. While the LXX says that the king of Sodom met Abraham, the author indicates that Melchizedek met the patriarch, a theme that the author develops in 7:4, 10. The author omits the reference to the bringing of bread and wine by Melchizedek (Gen 14:18). He indicates an interest in Melchizedek's identity and two actions that are important for the argument. Although "God Most High" is a name for a Canaanite deity, the author incorporates the title into the tradition of the worship of Yahweh, presenting Melchizedek as "priest of the most high

God" (cf. "most high" [*hypsistos*] in Acts 7:48; 16:17) who calls on the God of Abraham. The author's interest in the Hebrew etymology of Melchizedek's name also suggests an interest in his identity. In his statements that Abraham "apportioned a tenth of everything" and that Melchizedek "blessed" Abraham, the author introduces two actions that are important for the argument in 7:4–10.

After citing the Genesis narrative in Heb 7:1–3, the author refers to it again only in 7:4–10, maintaining his primary emphasis on Ps 110:4. Even in 7:3, he introduces elements that are not present in the Genesis narrative. The description in 7:3 is arranged in a poetic style of four lines that are similar in length. Gerd Theissen has noted such poetic elements as the absence of the definite article, the use of the participial style ("having . . . resembling"), alliteration (*apatōr, amētōr, agenealogētos,* "without father, without mother, without genealogy"), and assonance (the repetition of similar vowel sounds preceded and followed by different consonants; *aphōmoiōmenos . . . tō huiō,* "resembling the Son"). He concludes that these poetic qualities suggest the author's employment of a hymn (Theissen 1969, 21). However, the author's frequent use of poetic style (1:1–4; 2:1–4; 7:26–28) suggests that he has composed these lines to signify the central idea in his interpretation of the Melchizedek story.

Interpreters have frequently observed that the claim that Melchizedek was "without father, without mother, without genealogy" is an example of the author's use of a rabbinic interpretative principle that later interpreters called *quod non in Thora, non in mundo* (What is not in the Torah is not in the world), a common argument from the silence of scripture. However, the author's use of these terms reflects more than an appeal to the silence of scripture, for he employs this interpretation to develop a theme that is important for him. His focus becomes evident in 7:3d in the reference to "a priest forever," a phrase from Ps 110:4 that he has cited already (5:6; 6:20), and to which he adds "he remains" (*menei*). His substitution of *eis to diēnekes* for the LXX *eis ton aiōna* ("forever" or "without interruption"; cf. BDAG, 245) is probably only a stylistic alteration. This interest in the eternity of Melchizedek as one who "remains forever" is consistent with the earlier declaration that the exalted Son "remains" (*diameneis,* 1:11), while all that is earthly passes away. Thus, as the focus on the exaltation indicates in 1:3, 13, and 6:20, the author makes the consistent claim that only the one who is exalted to the heavenly world is eternal. Similarly, he claims that Christians have a heavenly possession that "remains" (10:34; 13:14). This theme becomes the major thread of the midrash in chapter 7 (cf. 7:23–24).

The description of Melchizedek in 7:3d is the foundation for the author's comments in the three lines that precede it. "Without father and without mother" do not only reflect the author's argument from silence. The terms are well known in the Hellenistic world, where they are used for deities (cf. Neyrey 1991, 439–55). Athena was without mother (*amētōr*), but not "without

147

a father" for she was the daughter of Zeus (Plato, *Symp.* 180d). Hephaistos was "without a father" but had a mother (cf. Windisch 1931, 60; Neyrey 1991, 446). Philo describes the number seven as the ideal number, a fitting symbol to describe the deity. Seven is the only one of the first ten numbers that has neither factor nor multiple within that set; thus it neither begets nor is begotten. Certain unnamed philosophers therefore say it is like the motherless and virgin Nike (i.e., Athena; Philo, *Creation* 100; cf. *Moses* 2.12: "motherless . . . unbegotten . . . abiding"). Although most texts use either "without father" or "without mother" but not both, J. H. Neyrey (1991) cites two passages that describe the deity in this way. Lactantius quotes an ancient oracle of Apollo that describes the deity as "self-produced, untaught, without a mother, unshaken." Since this cannot refer to Jupiter, who had a mother, Lactantius quotes Mercury to the effect that a true god must be without both mother and father: "Mercury, that thrice greatest . . . not only speaks of God as 'without a mother,' as Apollo does, but also as 'without a father,' because he has no origin from any other source but himself" (*Epit.* 1.7.1). A similar passage occurs in the *Apocalypse of Abraham*, which addresses God:

> Eternal One, Mighty One, Holy El, God autocrat
> self-originate, incorruptible, immaculate,
> unbegotten, spotless, immortal,
> self-perfected, self-devised,
> without mother, without father, ungenerated (*Apoc. Ab.* 17.8–11, trans.
> R. Rubinkiewicz in *OTP*, 1:697)

To be "without genealogy" would normally disqualify one from office in a tradition that placed high value on the proper genealogy (cf. Lev 21:7, 13, 15; Num 3:10, 15–16; Neh 7:63–64; Ezek 44:22). However, the author's comment is similar to that of Philo (*Abraham* 31), who says that Moses extols the sage by not giving his genealogy, for the sage has no family except virtuous actions (Dey 1975, 91).

The phrase "having neither beginning of days nor end of life" in 7:3b, which interprets the scripture cited in 7:3d, was also commonly attributed to the deity, for that which is without father and without mother is eternal (Thompson 1982, 119). This formulation is analogous to Plutarch's description of true Being as "not having been nor about to be, nor has it had a beginning nor is it destined to come to an end" (*E Delph.* 393b). Similarly, the *aiōn* inscription at Eleusis speaks of the *aiōn* as a deity who has no beginning or end (*SIG* 1125).

In describing Melchizedek as "resembling [*aphōmoiōmenos*] the Son of God," the author indicates that he is interested in Melchizedek not for his own sake but as a point of comparison to the Son of God. Whereas the reader might have expected the author to say that the Son was like Melchizedek, the author claims the opposite relationship. Having demonstrated that the Son of God is the exalted one, the author now describes Melchizedek as one who belongs to the same category. Thus this phrase incorporates the claims about Melchizedek in 7:3a–b, d, indicating that the Son of God is divine, transcendent, and eternal.

The combination of terms in 7:3 indicates the author's attempt to incorporate the categories of Hellenistic philosophy into his retelling of the biblical story. Although his primary allegiance is to the claim that God has acted "in these last days" (cf. 1:1–2) through the incarnation, death, and exaltation of the Son—an affirmation that would have been unacceptable to his philosophical contemporaries—he appeals to the language of Middle Platonism to explain his basic convictions, appropriating terms that Hellenistic philosophers employed to describe the deity to affirm the status of the ideal priesthood. For Middle Platonists, all reality is divided into the two realms of the intelligible and the perceptible world. The former is characterized by being, while the latter is characterized by becoming. True being in the intelligible world exists in timeless eternity (*aiōn*), while the perceptible world is subject to constant becoming (*genesis*). For Philo and Plutarch, the deity and the intelligible word remain (*menei*) forever (cf. Philo, *Dreams* 2.221; Plutarch, *Garr.* 507a), while all that belongs to the perceptible world is subject to death and decay (Plutarch, *E Delph.* 392b).

As a commentary on the two OT passages that mention Melchizedek, chapter 7 resembles the midrash homily (cf. Rom 4:1–22; Gal 3:6–29), and thus it forms a separate unit within the "word" that is "hard to explain." As in the exposition in 3:7–4:11, the psalm supersedes the law not only in chronology but also in metaphysical significance. In both instances, the psalm points to a transcendent reality in which the community participates. Indeed, in the entire midrash in chapter 7, the institutions of the OT belong to the inferior created order, while the order of Melchizedek belongs to the transcendent reality. The focus of the author's argument in chapter 7 is the comparison between the one heavenly priest who "remains forever" and the many "dying men" (7:8; cf. 7:23) of the Aaronic priesthood, who have become high priests through a "physical commandment" (7:16). This contrast between the one and the many also corresponds to the claims of the author's philosophical contemporaries, who distinguished the heavenly and eternal One from the many who belong to the material world and are subject to death. This comparison of two priesthoods, like the author's earlier use of *synkrisis*, is not intended as a polemic against Judaism or the temple but is a rhetorical device to demonstrate the greatness of Jesus Christ as high priest. Only a high priest who has entered the heavenly world can provide the wavering community with an anchor of the soul.

In the summation of the argument in 7:26–28, the author appeals once more to what is "fitting," using a term from Greek philosophy. Instead of saying that the saving event was "fitting for God," as in 2:10, he suggests his pastoral concern in 7:26, indicating that such a high priest was "fitting for us." The descriptive terms in 7:26 conclude the contrast to the Levitical high priests, who offered sacrifices for their own sins and were beset by weakness (5:1–3) and reiterate the emphasis on the sinlessness of Christ (4:15). The terms "holy" (*hosios*), "innocent" (*akakos*), and "undefiled" (*amiantos*) recall prescriptions for the ritual purity of the Levitical priests (Lev 10; 21:10–23). The author's addition of "separated from sinners" and "becoming higher than the heavens" indicates the relationship between the exaltation of Christ and the separation from sinners, signifying that only one who is separated from sinners can come to their aid. The description resembles Philo's portrayal of the perfect high priest. This high priest belongs to the highest order (*taxis*, Virtues 177; cf. Heb 7:3, 11), is "immune from sin" (*Spec. Laws* 1.230), innocent (*Spec. Laws* 3.134), and "blameless and perfect" (*Dreams* 2.185).

In the description of the sacrifice of the Levitical high priest, the author appears to have intermingled two different sacrifices. On the Day of Atonement, the high priest made a sacrifice "for his own sins" and for the "sins of the people" (7:27; cf. Lev 16:6, 11, 16), but not in the daily sacrifice (Exod 29:38–42; Lev 6:12–16; Num 28:3–8). The author's focus is not on the precise recollection of the sacrifices but on the contrast between "each day" and the exalted high priest's sacrifice of himself "once for all." This contrast continues the argument involving the one and the many in 7:23–25 and anticipates the distinction between the repeated annual sacrifices (9:1–10) and the final sacrifice of Christ (9:25; 10:11–14). The author concludes the contrast in 7:28, indicating that "once for all" (7:27) is the equivalent of "forever" (*eis ton aiōna*) in Ps 110:4. Appealing to the Platonic distinction of the "weakness" of the material world and eternity in the heavenly world, he concludes that Jesus became "perfected forever" at the exaltation.

Although the high priestly language echoes the influence of Philo and other Jewish writings, the affirmation that Jesus "offered himself" has no analogy in ancient literature. The author will elaborate on this claim in chapter 9.

Tracing the Train of Thought

With the words "this Melchizedek" (7:1), the author begins the extended treatment of the "word" that is "hard to explain" (cf. 5:11). The pastoral concerns of the author frame the discussion, for his task is to remind the wavering readers of the reality beyond the temptations that they presently experience (cf. 2:8–10). These "refugees" (6:18) can find their anchor (6:19; cf. 4:14; 10:23) in the fact that the Christ who shared their temptations has now become the "high priest according to the order of Melchizedek" at the exaltation. After exploring the high priesthood of Melchizedek, the author returns to the pastoral significance of this priesthood in the assurance that "he is able to save forever those who draw near to him, always living to intercede for them" (7:25). Thus the larger purpose of the argument is to provide certainty for a people on the way who have abandoned the security of home and country.

Having introduced the topic of Melchizedek in 5:6, 10 and having prepared the hearers for the extended exhortation in 5:11–6:20, the author now elaborates on the significance of this claim for the weary readers. Although he has already said that the listeners are "dull of hearing" (5:11) and need to learn the alphabet and be nourished on milk, he moves beyond these elementary teachings to the solid food (cf. 5:12) that will nourish them in the midst of their temptations. Only this "solid food" will provide the assurance that will equip the community with the patient endurance to inherit the promises (cf. 6:15).

Although Melchizedek is not mentioned after chapter 7, the author's description of this priesthood is a vital part of the "word" that is "hard to explain" (5:11) in 7:1–10:18. The discussion of the priesthood of Melchizedek in chapter 7 establishes the identity of the high priest, comparing the heavenly order of Melchizedek with the earthly order of Aaron (7:11). The comparison continues in 8:1–10:18 in the treatment of the work of the two priesthoods. The author introduces topics in chapter 7 before developing them in 8:1–10:18. The eternal high priest (7:3, 8, 16, 24) offers a sacrifice that is "once for all" (7:27; 9:12), securing an "eternal redemption" (9:12). He becomes the guarantor (7:22) and mediator (8:6; 9:15–22) of a better covenant. The one who has been "perfected forever" (7:28) has also "perfected those who are being sanctified forever" (10:14).

Melchizedek and Abraham (7:1–10)

7:1–3. In 7:1–3 the author lays the foundation of the argument that he develops in the remainder of the chapter, shifting the focus from Abraham as the model of patient endurance (6:13–15) to this Melchizedek . . . who met Abraham (7:1). With the *inclusio* describing the moment when Melchizedek "met" Abraham in 7:1, 10 (*synantēsas*, 7:1; *synēntēsen*, 7:10), the author initiates the comparison between Israel's greatest patriarch and this mysterious figure without mentioning that the LXX text indicates that actually the king of Sodom "met" Abraham. Drawing only on the parts of Gen 14:17–20 that advance his argument (see Introductory Matters),

---

Hebrews 7 in the Rhetorical Flow

Hearing God's word with faithful endurance (1:1–4:13)

Probatio: **Discovering certainty and confidence in the word for the mature (4:14–10:31)**

Drawing near and holding firmly: following the path of Jesus from suffering to triumph (4:14–5:10)

Preparing to hear the word that is hard to explain (5:11–6:20)

Grasping the anchor in the word for the mature: the sacrificial work of Christ as the assurance of God's promises (7:1–10:18)

▶ The priesthood of Melchizedek as the anchor of the soul (7:1–28)

Melchizedek and Abraham (7:1–10)

He abides a priest forever (7:1–3)

The greatness of Melchizedek (7:4–10)

A new order of priesthood (7:11–28)

The Argument from Etymology

The argument from etymology was a common technique in Hellenistic Judaism. It was derived from the practice of Stoic philosophers, who gave an etymological interpretation to the names of deities in the myths. Philo employs the argument in more than three hundred passages. Although he apparently did not know Hebrew, he usually took a Hebrew word, provided a Greek translation, and depicted the symbolic significance of the word. For example, Philo indicates that Noah means "rest" or "righteousness," and then concludes that the one who rests upon what is noble is righteous (*Alleg. Interp.* 3.77). The theoretical foundation for the etymological interpretation of names was the belief that names originated from a wise man's insight into the nature of things. Consequently, names were fundamental to the identity of persons.

the author recalls that Melchizedek **blessed** Abraham and that Abraham gave him a **tithe** (7:1–2a) but does not elaborate on the significance of these two acts until 7:4–10.

In 7:2b–3, the author moves away from describing the encounter of Melchizedek with Abraham by shifting the focus to the identity of Melchizedek. Holding to the popular view that the name actually signifies the identity of the person, he follows Philo (*Alleg. Interp.* 3.79) and Josephus (*JW* 6.438) in finding significance in the etymology of Melchizedek's name and location. **King of justice** (7:2b) reflects the ancient royal ideology of the king's role in preserving justice. Although Salem was commonly associated with Jerusalem (Josephus, *Ant.* 1.180, 438), the author indicates no interest in the location of the place but focuses on the defining characteristic of the **King of Salem** as **King of peace** (7:2c), which he discovers in the etymology of Salem (peace). Indeed, in Jewish literature justice and peace together are the gifts of the new age (cf. Isa 9:5–7; Jer 23:5–6; Dan 9:24; Mic 5:4). According to the *Testament of Judah*, the Messiah will be a "star of Jacob in peace" and the "sun of righteousness" (*T. Jud.* 24). Thus in the author's description of the "king of justice" and "king of peace," he describes Melchizedek in terms that were associated with the messianic age in Jewish literature (Schröger 1968, 135).

The author does not elaborate on the significance of the etymologies but shifts the focus in the poetic description in the four phrases in 7:3 from the Genesis narrative to Ps 110:4, the only other OT passage that mentions Melchizedek. Using the common interpretative principle that two passages containing the same word must be interpreted in light of each other (*gezera shewa*; cf. 4:3 and comments) and arguing from the silence of scripture (see Introductory Matters), the author concludes that Melchizedek has the qualities commonly associated with the deity. **Without father, without mother**

(7:3a) are not only conclusions based on the silence of the Genesis narrative; they associate Melchizedek with deities who belong to the ideal and invisible world (see Introductory Matters). As in Greek reflection, such a being is **without beginning of days or end of life** (7:3b) and **abides forever** (7:3d). **Without genealogy** (7:3a) recalls the demand that the Levitical priests have the appropriate genealogical origin from Aaron and suggests that one who is "without father" and "without mother" is above the need for genealogy. At the same time, "without genealogy" prepares the reader for the argument that Jesus, who was without Levitical genealogy, belongs to a greater order of priesthood (7:12–16).

This emphasis on the eternity of this priesthood is the controlling theme of the description of the high priesthood of Melchizedek in 7:4–28 (cf. 7:8, 16, 24–25). As the author demonstrated in chapter 1, the exalted Son is eternal (1:10–11). Thus the words **being like the Son of God** (7:3c) clarify the relationship between Melchizedek and the Son of God. As the subsequent argument will demonstrate, the author is not concerned with Melchizedek as a historical person. Thus he says not that the Son of God is like Melchizedek but that Melchizedek is like the Son of God. Indeed, Melchizedek drops out of the discussion as a person after 7:10. The author's focus is on the "order of Melchizedek" (cf. 6:20; 7:11), an ideal that he compares with the "order of Aaron" (7:11). The author's knowledge of the Son of God as one who is exalted and eternal is the basis for the description of the order of Melchizedek.

In the remainder of the midrash the author develops the argument by subordinating Gen 14:17–20 to Ps 110:4. Indeed, Gen 14:17–20 disappears from the story after 7:10. The structure of the argument is then determined by the wording of the psalm. In 7:11–19, the focus is the "order" (*taxis*) of Melchizedek in comparison to the "order" of Aaron. In 7:20–22, the psalmist's report that God "swore" becomes the focus of the discussion, while in 7:23–25 the focus is the content of the oath, "you are a priest forever." The focus on "forever" dominates the midrash, as the concluding words "a Son who is perfected forever" indicate (7:28).

7:4–10. In 7:4–10, the author develops the themes introduced in 7:1–3, indicating the significance of the two aspects of Abraham's encounter with Melchizedek mentioned in 7:1–2a: that **Abraham gave a tenth of the spoils** (7:4, 6) and that Melchizedek **blessed** Abraham. With the phrase **see how great he is** (7:4a), the author sets the stage for the comparison (*synkrisis*) that becomes explicit in the contrast between the lesser and the "greater" in 7:7. The comparison is not, however, between Melchizedek and the Son of God. Nor is it merely a contrast between Melchizedek and Aaron, for the author moves immediately to the contrast between the Levitical priesthood and the priesthood of Melchizedek, introducing the distinction between the one and the many that is developed later in the argument (7:23–25). In that encounter between the two men described in Gen 14:17–20, the author sees two priesthoods. Only in 7:9–10 does he offer the basis for the argument that the Levitical priesthood was present in that encounter. In his comment that Levi was **in the loins of the father** (7:10) when Abraham met Melchizedek, he appeals to the common Jewish tradition, according to which the fate of the one determines the fate of the people (cf. Rom 5:12–21; 1 Cor 15:22; 2 Cor 5:14).

Contrary to the traditional interpretation of Gen 14:17–20, the author argues that the encounter between Melchizedek and Abraham demonstrated the superiority of Melchizedek and his priesthood. In the first place, 7:5–6 contrasts those who are appointed to receive tithes according to the law (i.e., Num 18:21) based on their genealogy with the one who is "without a genealogy." As 7:3 indicates, to be "without genealogy" is a sign of greatness, indicating that this priesthood is above genealogical requirements. Thus Abraham, the **one who had the promise** (7:6) and who was the model of faithful perseverance (6:15), acknowledged this greater priesthood by paying tithes. In the second place, the fact that Melchizedek "blessed" Abraham indicated the superiority of the former to the latter. Although the principle that the **lesser is blessed by the greater** (7:7) did not always hold true (cf. 2 Sam 14:22; 1 Kgs 1:47; Job 31:20), the author assumes that it **is apart from all dispute** (*chōris de pasēs antilogias*) for his audience. Using the language of the law courts (cf. 6:16; cf. Attridge 1989, 180), he offers the rational argumentation that is typical throughout the homily (cf. 2:10, "it is fitting"; 2:17, "thus he ought"; 6:4, "it is impossible").

The fundamental difference between the two priesthoods is evident in the contrast between **dying men** (7:8a) who receive the tithes and the **one about whom it is testified that he lives** (7:8b). Using the language that often introduces a citation of scripture (*martyreō*, "testify"; cf. 7:17; 10:15; and *diamartyromai* in 2:6), the author now appeals to the statement of Ps 110:4 that "he remains a priest forever" (7:3d) and alludes to the earlier comment that Melchizedek is "without beginning of days or end of life" (7:3b). Thus only the exalted high priest is eternal, while the Levitical priesthood belongs to this world and is subject to death. Just as the author later distinguishes between the earthly and heavenly sanctuaries and the sacrifices of each (8:1–10:18), he distinguishes between a mortal and an eternal priesthood in 7:8.

A New Order of Priesthood (7:11–28)

7:11–13. In 7:11–19, the Genesis narrative of Melchizedek disappears from the account, and the author turns exclusively to reflections on Ps 110:4. This unit is marked by the *inclusio* "if there were perfection through the Levitical priesthood" (7:11) and "for the law made nothing perfect" (7:19), which continues the comparison introduced in 7:4–10. With the term "priesthood" (*hierōsynē*; also 7:12, 24), a word that is used nowhere else in the NT and only nine times in the LXX (Johnson 2006, 185), the argument moves from the encounter of the two men to a discussion of the author's central concern, the adequacy of the priestly system and the need for a new priesthood. As 7:11, 19 indicate, this issue cannot be separated from the status of the law, a subject that the author introduced first in 7:5 and develops throughout the remainder of the "word" that is "hard to explain" (7:12, 16, 19, 28; 8:4, 10; 9:19, 22; 10:1, 8, 28). According to 7:11, **the people received the law on the basis of it** (i.e., the priesthood), while 7:19 concludes, "the law made nothing perfect." This claim is consistent with the later comment that the gifts and sacrifices of the Levitical cultus were unable to "perfect the conscience of the worshiper" (9:9; cf. 10:1).

Within the context of Hebrews, "perfection" involves purification and access to God. Jesus was "made perfect" (5:9; cf. 2:10) and was "perfected forever" (7:28) at the exaltation, opening up the way for others to draw

> **An Outline of Hebrews 7:11–28**
>
> A new order of priesthood (7:11–28)
>
> A change of priesthood (7:11–13)
>
> According to the likeness of Melchizedek (7:14–17)
>
> Former commandment vs. better hope (7:18–19)
>
> Oath vs. no oath (7:20–22)
>
> The many vs. the one unchangeable forever (7:23–25)
>
> The greatness of the high priest (7:26)
>
> The two priesthoods (7:27–28)

near to God (cf. 7:19). When the author speaks of the "law" (7:12, 19), he does not use the term in the Pauline sense but refers exclusively to the Levitical priesthood. Similarly, the "commandment" (7:5, 16, 18; 9:19), which the author describes as weak and useless (7:18) for bringing the worshiper to God, refers only to the Levitical priesthood.

This negative evaluation of the Levitical priesthood can be understood only within the pastoral purpose of the author, who is not engaged in a polemic over the relative merits of Christianity and Judaism. As with the earlier *synkriseis* throughout the homily, the comparison of priesthoods serves to reaffirm the ultimacy of the Christian confession and provide an anchor of hope for Christian refugees (6:18–19). The focus for the comparison in 7:11–19 is the reference in the psalm to the order (*taxis*) of Melchizedek, which becomes the basis for the comparison to the order of Aaron. The rhetorical question, **if there was perfection through the Levitical priesthood, what need was there for another priest to arise according to the order of Melchizedek and not according to the order of Aaron** (7:11), is reminiscent of the earlier statement, "If Joshua had given them rest, he would not have spoken of another day" (4:8), and anticipates the subsequent argument, "If the first covenant were blameless, there would have been no need of a second one" (8:7). In each case, the author employs the contrary-to-fact conditional sentence to demonstrate the precedence of a later passage over an earlier one. Thus the reference to the high priest according to Melchizedek in Ps 110:4, coming after the institution of the Levitical system, indicates a change to a new order of priesthood. Because the later passage points to the finality of the eschatological blessings in

Christ, the author concludes that the experience under the law was provisional and temporary. Thus his negative statements about the law and the Levitical priesthood must be seen within the context of his rhetorical purpose. Since the psalm announces the ultimate high priesthood that brings access to God, any alternative is "weak and useless."

Again using the language of rational argumentation (cf. comments on 7:7) taken from the law courts, the author argues from a general principle in 7:12–13, which he applies to Jesus in 7:14–17. According to this principle, which the author derives from the psalm's announcement of an alternative priesthood (7:11) a logical **necessity** (cf. *anankē,* "necessity," in 7:27; 9:16, 23; *anankaios* in 8:3) of a **change in the law** (7:12), for the **priesthood** and the law are inextricably bound together. Extending this general principle, he indicates that this priest **belonged to another tribe, from which no one has ever served at the altar** (7:13). The author's later affirmation that "we have an altar" (13:10) suggests that the author here refers to the earthly altar as the place where the sacrifices were offered.

7:14–17. Having excluded the Levitical priests from this new order of priesthood, the author demonstrates in 7:14–17 that Jesus qualifies as the high priest according to the order of Melchizedek. In the first place, **it is evident** (*prodēlon*) according to common knowledge **that our Lord arose from Judah** (7:14a). Although "arose" (*anatetalken*) may echo passages from the OT (cf. Num 24:17; Isa 58:10; 60:1; Zech 3:8; 6:12) about the rise of the age of the Messiah, the author's emphasis is on the fact that Jesus came from the tribe **about which Moses said nothing about priests** (7:14b). Thus Jesus' origins from the tribe of Judah meets the negative qualification that he not come from the tribe of Levi. In the second place, whereas "it is evident (*prodēlon*) that our Lord arose from Judah," **it is especially evident** (*perissoteron . . . katadēlon*) that the change of priesthood should occur **if another priest arises according to the likeness of Melchizedek** (7:15). Echoing the words of the author's question in 7:11 ("what need is there for another priest according to the order of Melchizedek?"), the author now paraphrases the "order" of Melchizedek, rendering the phrase the "likeness" *(homoiotēta)* of Melchizedek. The word "likeness" recalls the claim in 7:3 that Melchizedek is "like the Son of God."

The author indicates in 7:16 that this "likeness" consists of the fact that both Melchizedek and Jesus are heavenly and eternal. Because the author knows that this priest has come, he moves to the past tense to say that he has **become** (*gegonen*; Greek perfect tense; note the author's frequent use of *ginomai* to indicate that Jesus became high priest at the exaltation [2:17; 5:5, 9; 6:20; cf. 1:4; 9:11]) high priest of this new order. He is qualified, not by a **law of a physical commandment** (7:16a, *nomos entolēs sarkinēs*; lit. "law of a fleshy commandment"), but by the **power of an indestructible life** (7:16b, *dynamin zōēs akatalytou*). This qualification recalls the description of Melchizedek as "without beginning of days or end of life" (7:3) and the author's earlier contrast between the "dying men" of the Levitical priesthood and "the one who lives" (7:8).

The priesthood according to the order of Melchizedek is superior not only because it is later in time; it is qualitatively and metaphysically superior. The Levitical priesthood belongs to the sphere of the flesh and of death (cf. 7:8), while the priesthood of Melchizedek belongs to the heavenly and unchangeable sphere. The "physical commandment" is the opposite of the "indestructible life" (*zōēs akatalytou*). As the citation in 7:17 indicates, the author draws this insight from Ps 110:4, **You are a priest forever according to the order of Melchizedek**, which he cites once more (cf. 7:3; 5:6). In this instance he focuses on the word "forever" (*eis ton aiōna*) in the psalm.

Just as the author distinguished earlier between the transitory angels and the eternal Son (1:5–13), he now distinguishes between the temporary and eternal priesthoods. Similarly, in the description of the ultimate sacrifice of Christ, he distinguishes between incomplete, temporary sacrifices and the eternal sacrifice of Christ. In each instance, he describes two levels of reality, indicating that eternity belongs only to the reality that is beyond the sphere of flesh and death. This argument is similar to Plato's distinction between the spheres of being and becoming. The reality of the world beyond the senses (true being) is eternal, while the reality of the senses is subject to death and decay (see Introductory Matters for the influence of Plato). The author undoubtedly employs this demarcation of the two levels of reality to encourage the community to withstand the temptation to live according to the reality that it sees around it and instead to look beyond the visible temptations and place their trust in the exalted high priest, who has entered into the heavenly world.

7:18–19. In 7:18–19, the author summarizes the previous argument and indicates the pastoral concern that underlies the discussion of Melchizedek in the first of three antitheses between the old and the new order that are marked by the Greek *men . . . de* (i.e., "on the one hand . . . on the other hand"; 7:18–19, 20–21, 23–25). The author indicates the qualitative distinction between the two (Backhaus 1996, 105):

[on the one hand]	[on the other hand]
annulment of the previous commandment	introduction of a better hope
weak and useless command/made nothing perfect	we draw near to God

Thus the **annulment** (*athetēsis*) of one system means the **introduction** (*epeisagōgē*) of the other. Corresponding to the **former commandment** is a **better hope** (*kreittonos elpidos*). An order that was **weak and useless** and **made nothing perfect** is replaced by a new order in which **we draw near to God**. These antitheses indicate the qualitative changes in the order of Melchizedek.

The author no longer speaks of the "change [*metathesis*] of the law," as in 7:12, but uses the stronger language of the "annulment" (*athetēsis*) **of the previous commandment,** using the common legal metaphor for the cancellation of an agreement (cf. 2 Macc 14:28) or law (see Braun 1984, 213, for relevant texts). In stating the reason for the annulment (the commandment was weak and useless), the author elaborates on the earlier statement that it was associated with a "fleshy commandment" (7:16) in the earthly sphere and anticipates the later claim that sacrifices in the earthly sanctuary were able to purify only the flesh, not the conscience (9:9–14; 10:1–4). "Weak and useless," therefore, characterizes the Levitical system that could not do what it was intended to do: open the way of access to God (Scholer 1991, 115). The parenthetical remark that the **law made nothing perfect** (7:19a), which forms the *inclusio* with 7:11, elaborates on the deficiencies of the Levitical cultus. As the author's frequent usage of the language of perfection indicates (cf. 2:10; 5:9; 10:1), perfection denotes access to God and entry into the heavenly world.

The author's pastoral emphasis is evident in the claim that the new priesthood offers a **better hope** (7:19b) to replace the "former commandment," for hopelessness is a major temptation to a community that now experiences suffering, social alienation, and the inability to see the ultimate victory (cf. 2:8). In the words "if we hold fast to the confidence and pride in our hope"

"Better" in Hebrews

The author of Hebrews consistently uses "better" (*kreittōn*) to show the superiority of heavenly realities to their earthly counterparts:

"[The exalted Son is] greater than the angels" (1:4).

"We are confident of better things . . . that belong to salvation" (6:9).

"The inferior is blessed by the greater" (7:7).

"There is . . . a better hope, through which we draw near to God" (7:19).

"He is the mediator of a better covenant" (8:6).

"It was necessary for the sketches of the heavenly things to be purified . . . with better sacrifices" (9:23).

". . . knowing that you have a better and abiding possession" (10:34).

"[You have come] . . . to Jesus, the mediator of a new covenant, whose blood speaks better than the blood of Abel" (12:24).

(3:6), the author has indicated the community's struggle with hopelessness. He has encouraged them to demonstrate "earnestness for the full assurance of hope until the end" (6:11), pointing to Abraham as the example of the patient endurance necessary for inheriting the promise (6:12–15). The exaltation of Christ offers the community the opportunity to "grasp the hope that is made available" (6:18). As the author indicates in 7:19, the community now has a "better hope" than that provided by the Levitical priesthood. His consistent use of "better" (*kreittōn*; cf. 1:4; 6:9; 7:7, 19; 8:6; 9:23; 11:16, 40; 12:24) to show the superiority of heavenly realities to their earthly counterparts gives the community assurance and a reason to persevere. This "better hope," therefore, is the "anchor of the soul" (6:19) that gives the wavering community a reason to persevere, knowing of the future that awaits them.

Although the community now perseveres, hoping for the future promise, it also experiences the present reality in which **we draw near to God** (7:19c) as the result of our forerunner's entry into the heavenly world (cf. 6:20; 10:19–20). The Levitical system, which did not provide access to God (i.e., "made nothing perfect"), is now replaced by the better hope through which "we draw near to God" (*engizomen tō theō*). In the first-person plural, the author indicates the relevance of his christological claims for the life of the community and indicates their participation in the approach to God. "Draw near" is frequently used for the cultic approach to God (Scholer 1991, 118; cf. Exod 3:5; 24:2; Lev 10:3) and is employed especially for the approach of priests to the altar in the sanctuary (Exod 19:22; Lev 21:21, 23; Ezek 40:46; 42:13; 43:19; 44:13; 45:4; cf. comments on 4:16). Thus the author says not only that the community now has a privilege formerly reserved for priests but also that the people, unlike the Levitical priests, "draw near" in a heavenly sanctuary, not in the earthly tabernacle. While they wait for God to fulfill the promises, seeing only the anguish of this world, they draw near to God in the heavenly world in prayer and worship (cf. 4:14–16; 10:19–23). *Engizein* in 7:19 and *proserchesthai* (4:16; 7:25; cf. 12:18, 22) are synonymous terms for the community's privilege of drawing near to God (cf. Scholer 1991, 118).

7:20–22. Just as 7:11–19 discovers in the wording of Ps 110:4 a reference to an "order" (*taxis*) of priesthood that replaces the previous order in 7:11–19, the antithesis of 7:20–22 focuses on another word from the psalm to indicate the superiority of the exalted high priest: the Lord "swore" an oath. The structure of 7:20–22 is determined by the correlative phrases in verses 20 and 22: **to the degree that . . . to the same degree** (*kath' hoson . . . kata tosouto*); thus 7:20b–21 becomes an extended interjection (Johnson 2006, 191) supporting the claim of the main clause. According to the main clause, the oath ensures that Christ is the guarantor of a better covenant, while the parenthesis demonstrates from Ps 110:4 that only the exalted Christ received the oath.

The author has indicated earlier in the homily the importance of God's oath, recalling that God swore to the wilderness generation, "They will never enter my rest" (3:11), and that he swore to Abraham that he would bless him, giving him the assurance that enabled him to persevere (6:12–15). The oath is "for confirmation" (6:16) and signifies the unchangeability of God's will. Immediately prior to the treatment of Melchizedek, the author indicated that the wavering community, like Abraham, has received the oath and the promise (see comments on 6:18) that allows them to grasp the hope that is now available when Christ became high priest according to the order of Melchizedek (6:18–10). In 7:20, 22, the author draws on the imagery of the law court to declare that, because of the oath, Jesus has become the **guarantor of a better covenant** (7:22).

In legal documents, the **guarantor** (*engyos*) supplied a security deposit and took the responsibility for another's debts. The guarantor was normally a relative or a friend who could be trusted. According to Sirach, "A good man serves as guarantor for his neighbor, but the one who has no shame will fail him" (29:14). Sirach then offers the advice, "Do not forget the gift of the guarantor (*engyos*), for he has offered his life for you." Philo and Josephus use the related word *engyētēs* for one who guarantees the promises of God. For Philo, Moses is the guarantor of God's words (cf. Philo, *Cherubim* 45). For Josephus (*Ant.* 6.21), Samuel is the guarantor of the promises of God (see further texts in Spicq 1994, 2:391). This image, like the earlier image of the anchor (6:19), indicates the stability and certainty of the promises of God. The community's perseverance through suffering is worthwhile because Jesus has become the guarantor of the future.

The **better covenant,** like the "better hope" (7:19) that accompanies the new order of priesthood, is better than the old order that was "fleshy" (7:16) and "weak and useless" (7:19), for this covenant belongs to the heavenly world in which the exalted high priest offers a sacrifice in the heavenly sanctuary (cf. 9:11–14). The covenant (*diathēkē*), of which this is the first mention in the homily, becomes a major theme in 8:6–10:18. Once again the author introduces a new subject (cf. 2:17; 5:6, 10) that he will develop only later in the homily. In Jewish literature and in other NT writings, the covenant refers to the full range of God's relationship to the people, but in Hebrews this theme relates to the priestly work of Christ. Indeed, the "better covenant" is based on the "better promise" (8:6) that ensures the ultimate outcome of the community's journey. In Christ's act of offering his blood, the community discovers the guarantee of the validity of God's promises.

In the antithesis of 7:20b–21, the author demonstrates from scripture that only the high priest according to the order of Melchizedek has received the oath that qualifies him to be the guarantor of the better covenant. Arguing from the silence of scripture, he concludes that the earlier priesthood was **without an oath** (7:20b), unlike the exalted high priest, who is **with an oath** (7:21; cf. "not without an oath" in 7:20a). He cites Ps 110:4 once more, introducing the quotation as the word of God to the exalted Christ (through the one [i.e.,

God] speaking to him [i.e., Christ]). Even the words **The Lord swore and will not change his mind** (7:21b) are quoted as the words of God. This emphasis reflects the author's focus on the irrevocability of God's promise.

7:23–25. As the antithesis of 7:23–25 indicates, the author is interested not only in the fact that God swore but also in the content of God's oath. As a summation of the focus on eternity throughout the treatment of the order of Melchizedek (7:8, 16), the author returns once more to the words *eis ton aiōna* (forever) in the psalm, comparing the many who become high priests but are forbidden from remaining because of death and the one who has the priesthood **because he remains forever unchangeable** (7:24, *dia to menein auton eis ton aiōna aparabaton*). As the author has indicated earlier, the Levitical priesthood belongs to the sphere of death (7:8, 16), while the priest of Melchizedek abides forever (7:3, *menei hierys eis to diēnekes*). This contrast is heightened by the distinction between the many and the one, which plays a role in the later argument (cf. 9:23–28; 10:1–18). In Hebrews, the many (including priests and sacrifices) belong to the physical world of earthly imperfection, while the one belongs to the transcendent world that abides forever (Grässer 1993, 2:58). Only the exalted one is "unchangeable" (*aparabatos*), a term that can mean "without a successor" or "permanent" (BDAG, 97). In Hebrews it fits within the dualistic distinction between the abiding and stable heavenly things and unstable earthly matters (cf. Grässer 1993, 2:61).

The author's insistence on the abiding and unchangeable priesthood has an intensely pastoral dimension, as **consequently** (7:25, *hothen*) indicates. Just as the author introduces the discussion of the order of Melchizedek with the assurance that the community has an anchor of stability, he concludes the discussion with the confirmation that the one who abides forever (7:3, 24) **is able to save forever** (*eis to panteles*) **those who draw near in worship, for he always** (*pantote*) **intercedes** for the community. As the author has indicated earlier in the homily, the community continues to struggle with the temptation (2:17–18; 4:15) that has resulted from its failure to see the fulfillment of the promises, and he has summoned the people to draw near (4:16). Now he assures them of what the eternality of the high priest according to Melchizedek means for them. This eternal high priest not only belongs to the past and the future but always intercedes for them in the present. The author follows Paul in the claim that the exalted one "intercedes" (*entynchanei*; cf. Rom 8:34; for other uses of the word, see Acts 25:24; Rom 8:27; 11:2) for the people. Although this word in most contexts refers to someone who makes a petition on behalf of another, within the context of Hebrews it refers to the one who has been tempted and "is able to help those who are being tempted" (2:18). Those who now suffer temptation do not only wait for future deliverance; in the present time they may draw near in worship and find the strength to continue their pilgrimage.

7:26. In 7:26–28, the author moves from argument to conclusion, speaking in poetic terms here as he did at the beginning of the midrash in 7:1–3 (cf. 1:1–4; 5:7–10), in order to move the community to a renewed commitment to their confession. He neither bases his comments on the wording of Ps 110:4 nor mentions Melchizedek but moves beyond the reflections on the psalm to indicate the high priest's greatness. In 7:26, he speaks only of the greatness of the high priest, piling up attributes that indicate the exalted status of the high priest.

With the affirmation that **it was fitting that we have such a high priest** (7:26a), the author once more demonstrates his pastoral concern by including the readers in the story, as he has on numerous occasions (cf. 7:14, 19). According to 1:2, "God has spoken to us in a Son." In other instances he affirms that "we have a high priest" (cf. 8:1; 10:21). Unlike 2:10, when the author says, "It is fitting," here he says that it was fitting for us. In the description of the high priest in 7:26, the author not only summarizes 7:1–25 but also establishes a strong contrast to the initial description of the earthly high priest in 5:1–4. Unlike the Levitical high priest, who is "beset by weakness" and offers sacrifice for his own sins (5:2–3), the community has a high priest who is **holy, innocent, undefiled, and separated from sinners** (cf. 4:15), **becoming higher than the heavens** (7:26b). These five characteristics indicate the extent to which the high priest is "fitting" for the community. Although the terms "holy" (*hosios*), "innocent" (*akakos*), and "undefiled" (*amiantos*) commonly referred to righteous or moral purity (cf. *hosios* in Ps 16:10; 1 Tim 2:8; Titus 1:8; *akakos* in Job 2:3; 8:20; Prov 1:4, 22; Rom 16:18; *amiantos* in Heb 13:4; 1 Pet 1:4), together they describe the cultic purity of the priests serving at the altar (Exod 30:19; Lev 16:4; 21:1; 11:24, 26). In the juxtaposition of "separated from sinners" (*kechōrismenos apo tōn hamartōlōn*) and "becoming higher than the heavens" (*hypsēloteros tōn ouranōn genomenos*), the author not only recalls the Levitical requirement for the separation of the priest from the people but redefines this separation with a reference to the exaltation. The one who was tempted but was without sin (4:15) is able to help those who are being tempted because of his separation from sinners at the right hand of God.

7:27–28. In 7:27–28, the author returns to the comparison of the two priesthoods to make two additional points, summarizing the argument of 5:1–7:28 and anticipating the claims that he will make in 10:1–18. In 7:27, he contrasts the two priesthoods (cf. Koester 2001, 373; parentheses below signify what is not explicitly stated but is inferred from the context):

Levitical priests	Christ the exalted high priest
daily sacrifices	once-for-all sacrifice
for his own sins	(sinless)
(offered animal sacrifices)	offered himself

He contrasts Levitical priests, who offer sacrifices **each day** (7:27a; cf. Exod 29:38–42; Num 28:3–8; Sir 45:14) for their own sin (cf. 5:3), with the exalted high priest, who offered himself **once for all** (7:27b; *ephapax*). This contrast between repetition of the Levitical sacrifices and the finality of the sacrifice of Christ corresponds to the distinction between the many and the one in 7:23–25 and anticipates the author's frequent contrast between the repetition of Levitical sacrifices and the work of Christ that was *ephapax* (cf. 9:12; 10:10; *hapax* in 9:7, 26–28; 10:2; 12:26–27), a term that signifies the finality of the sacrifice of Christ. Here the contrast is between the daily sacrifice, while chapter 9 contrasts the annual sacrifice of the Day of Atonement (*yom kippur*) with the ultimate sacrifice of Christ. Unlike the Levitical sacrifices, which were offered continually, only the sacrifice offered in the heavenly sanctuary is once for all. Thus repetition and incompleteness (i.e., the many) belong to the physical world, while completeness and perfection belong to the heavenly world that is unseen (11:1) and unshakable (12:27–28).

For the first time, the author indicates that Jesus is both priest and sacrifice, for he offered himself. The author will develop this claim in chapter 9 when he contrasts the sacrifice of animals in the earthly sanctuary with the sacrifice of the blood of Christ in the heavenly sanctuary (9:11–14) and the offer of Jesus' body, which put an end to the Levitical sacrifices (10:5–10).

In the second contrast in 7:28, the author summarizes the argument of 5:1–7:28, contrasting the effects of the law and the word of the oath (see Koester 2001, 373):

Ephapax and the One and the Many

The relationship between the one and the many is a major theme in Middle Platonism, according to which all of reality may be divided into the two realms of the intelligible and the perceptible world. According to this tradition, true being in the intelligible world exists in timeless eternity, while the perceptible world is subject to constant change. Corresponding to this distinction, Middle Platonists distinguish between the One, which transcends the universe, and the Indefinite Dyad, the principle of duality. The One belongs to the intelligible world, while the latter, as a basis for the many, exists in the material world. Middle Platonists identify the transcendent God with the One (Thompson 2007, 572). In distinguishing between the work of Christ, which is *(eph)apax* (7:27; 9:28) and "forever" (7:28; 10:12), and the many high priests (7:23–25) and sacrifices (9:25–10:4; 10:11–14) of the levitical cultus, the author of Hebrews reflects the Platonic distinction between the one and the many. The one belongs to the transcendent world, while the many belong to the material world.

The law establishes	The word of the oath establishes
high priests	a Son
who have weaknesses	who is perfected forever

Those who have weaknesses (cf. 5:3) belong to the physical world (cf. 7:8, 16), while the one who has been perfected forever now sits at the right hand of God. To be **perfected forever** (7:28) is to achieve what was impossible under a priesthood that failed to bring perfection (7:11, 18). "Forever" (*eis ton aiōna*), as the equivalent of "once for all" (7:27; *ephapax*), summarizes the theme of the midrash (7:3, 8, 16, 23–24), indicating that the exalted Christ has entered into eternity. The community can look to this assurance as their "anchor of the soul" as they face the temptations that now confront them.

Theological Issues

No part of Hebrews is as mysterious to the reader as the claim that Jesus Christ is the "high priest after the order of Melchizedek." Indeed, only the author of Hebrews among NT writers explores the topic of the high priesthood of Jesus. The author undoubtedly chose an image that resonated with those who were initiated in the Jewish scriptures and would understand that the role of the high priest was to "offer gifts and sacrifices for sins" (5:1). Kwame Bediako (2000) has indicated that the image of priesthood speaks to other cultures as well. Indeed, the comparison of the heavenly order of Melchizedek with the earthly order of Aaron indicates that Christians of all nations have access to the ultimate high priest, the only one who sits at God's right hand.

Beyond the obscure argumentation of Heb 7 is the author's attempt to provide a theological answer to a pastoral problem that is more global and enduring than the issues about the high priesthood. Indeed, the author's comparison is between two competing means of anchoring human existence—between the transient and the eternal. The image of the refugee searching for an anchor (6:18–19) communicates to Christians of the Western world as much as it did to their predecessors at the end of the first century. Indeed, the postmodern climate and the claim that we have reached the end of all certainties leave many people disoriented, intellectually homeless, reaching out to alternative means of stabilizing their lives. The author addresses the universal temptation to substitute human mediators for the ultimate high priest. Although the image of high priest may be remote for people in the Western world, the comparison between the transient and the eternal priesthoods calls into question all alternative mediators. The appeal of alternative and ephemeral "priesthoods" was not limited to the first century.

The distinctive feature of the high priest according to Melchizedek is that he abides forever (7:3, 16, 24–25). The author is not interested in mere metaphysical speculation, however. The eternal high priest provides the hope that is the "anchor of the soul," security for a vulnerable people (6:19–20). He offers God's guarantee (7:22), and he "always" intercedes (7:25) insofar as his sacrifice is final (7:27). Thus the knowledge that the high priest according to the order of Melchizedek is eternal provides the stability for a people whose world is shaken.

Hebrews 8

The Sacrificial Work of Christ as the Assurance of God's Promises

Introductory Matters

In order to elaborate on the basic confession that the Son "made purification for sins" (1:3; cf. 2:17) in the exordium, the author now comes to the "main point" (8:1), developing this theme with a lengthy interpretation of the sacrificial system in 8:1–10:18. He anticipated this theme in the description of the high priest's task of offering sacrifices for sins (5:3) and the discussion of the high priest according to the order of Melchizedek in chapter 7. The interpretation of the death of Jesus as the sacrificial offering of the high priest is without parallel in the NT. The lengthy section 8:1–10:18 is a series of reflections on OT passages through which the author interprets the work of Christ, using unique hermeneutical procedures that have been at the center of scholarly debate on the homily, raising questions about the author's intellectual heritage and the assumptions that underpin the argument in this extended section. The frame provided by the allusion to Ps 110:1 in 8:1 and 10:12 as a reference to the exaltation places the saving acts of Christ in heaven, while the subordinate passages interpret the cross in cultic terms.

The argument employs a series of antitheses, as table 6 indicates (cf. Attridge 1986, 1–9). In 8:1–6, the author contrasts the true tabernacle in heaven (8:2, 5; cf. 9:24) with the earthly shadow and copy (8:5; 9:24) and the minister of the former with the ministers of the latter. In 8:7–13, he contrasts the first and the second covenant. In 9:1–14, he contrasts the sacrifices in the earthly sanctuary with the sacrifice in the heavenly tabernacle, distinguishing between

Table 6.
Antitheses in Hebrews 8:1–10:18

true tent (8:2; 9:23)	antitype of true tent (9:24)
which the Lord made (8:2)	made by man, handmade (8:2; 9:11)
archetype (8:5)	copy and shadow (8:5; 9:23)
greater and more perfect tent (9:11)	earthly sanctuary (9:1)
most holy place (9:3)	holy place (9:2)
second covenant (8:7)	first covenant (8:7)
new covenant (8:13; 9:15)	old covenant (8:13)
better ministry (8:6)	serve in a copy (8:5)
once for all (9:27)	constantly/each year (10:1)
once (9:26; 10:10, 14)	many times (9:25–26; 10:11)
conscience (9:9, 14)	flesh (9:10, 13)
time of reformation (9:15)	present time (9:9)
his blood (9:12)	blood of bulls and goats (9:12; 10:4)

the cleansing of the flesh and the cleansing of the conscience (9:9–10). He also distinguishes between the present time (9:9) and the end of the ages (9:26) and contrasts the one and the many (9:26; 10:11–14). With these antitheses, the author affirms that the heavenly realities experienced by the listeners are superior to their earthly counterparts and that the new is better than the old, hoping to reassure his community with a barrage of comparisons (Greek *synkrisis*), using a favorite rhetorical device in antiquity to reassure his community of the reality beyond all appearances.

The author prepares the way for the argument for the saving work of Christ in 8:1–6. By subordinating Exod 25:40 to Ps 110:1, he proceeds from the royal image of the throne in 8:1 to the cultic setting of the "true tent," the scene of the action in 8:1–10:18. The author introduces the instruction to Moses, "you will make all things according to the archetype shown you on the mountain" (8:5), with "it was revealed." This word (*chrēmatizein*) has the connotation of an oracle (Philo, *Moses* 2.238; Josephus, *Ant.* 5.42), a revelation (cf. Matt 2:12, 22; Luke 2:26; Acts 10:22), and a warning (cf. 11:7; 12:25). Consistent with the author's focus on God's speaking to the ancestors (1:1–2; 2:1–4), he describes the instructions for the sacrificial system as a revelation (Johnson 2006, 201).

According to the Hebrew text, God instructs Moses to build the tabernacle according to the pattern (*tabnit*) that he saw on the mountain. The term *tabnit* has a range of meanings, including "structure," "pattern," or "image." Therefore, in the original Hebrew God instructs Moses to build a tabernacle like the one he saw on the mountain. According to this reading, the building of the tabernacle according to the divine pattern indicates the special divine character of the tabernacle. The reading of the LXX text is critical for ancient interpreters, including the author of Hebrews, for it renders *tabnît* as *typos* (archetype). Prior to this instruction, according to the LXX, God instructed Moses, "You will make for me everything that I show you on the mountain, the pattern (*paradeigma*) of the tent and the pattern (*paradeigma*) of its vessels" (Exod 25:9).

The Greek translation permits an inference that would resonate with readers in the Hellenistic world. The terms "archetype," "shadow," and "copy" echo Plato's distinction between the heavenly archetype and the earthly copy (*Rep.* 514–517), suggesting a vertical dualism throughout this extended section. Thus 8:1–6 is at the center of the debate over the intellectual world of the author of Hebrews. Many scholars assert that the language of the author's dualism between heavenly archetype and earthly shadow indicates his indebtedness to Platonism similar to that of Philo of Alexandria. Numerous others have argued, however, that the author is thoroughly indebted to the OT and Jewish apocalyptic literature. They observe that the author's distinction between "the present age" (9:9) and the end of the ages (9:26) as well as the contrast between the old and the new (8:13) reflect the horizontal dualism characteristic of apocalyptic literature (e.g., Mackie 2007, 83–104). Furthermore, Lincoln Hurst (1990) maintains that the author's statement that "the law is a shadow of the good things to come" (10:1) indicates that the shadow in 8:5 is actually a "foreshadowing" of the future rather than the Platonic shadow of the heavenly archetype.

The idea that the sanctuary is a copy of a heavenly original was common, not only among those influenced by Platonism but throughout the ancient world. The command that Moses build the tabernacle according to the heavenly archetype reflects the common idea in the ancient Near East, the OT, and Jewish literature that the sanctuary was a copy of the divine pattern (cf. Exod 25:9; 26:30; 27:8). The heavenly sanctuary is a major theme in rabbinic and apocalyptic literature (Ezek 40–48; Rev 11:1, 19; 15:5–8; 16:1; 21:22; *2 Bar.* 4.2–7; 6.9; 32.3–4; *Ascen. Isa.* 7.10). According to a common rabbinic tradition, on Mount Sinai Moses saw the temple, the table of shewbread, and the candlestick (see texts in Ego 1989, 27–34). The *Testament of Levi* refers to a heavenly temple (5.1) that contained the divine throne and the archangels who offer bloodless sacrifices. The *Apocalypse of Baruch* mentions the pattern of the tabernacle (*2 Bar.* 4.5). In apocalyptic literature, the heavenly sanctuary will be revealed at the end time.

Although the heavenly sanctuary is a common theme in the ancient world, the language of 8:1–5 contains such a dense combination of Platonic terms that the background in Greek philosophy is indisputable. The contrast between the "true tabernacle" (8:2) and the inferior earthly "copy" and the "shadow" (8:5) is indebted to the Platonic distinction between the reality of that which is true and eternal and the copy (*Laws* 1.643c), which is a mere shadow. Plato and Middle Platonists such as Philo used archetype (*typos*) to denote the idea and shadow to denote the material world (*Rep.* 514–517; Philo, *Alleg. Interp.* 3.99–103; *Posterity* 112–119; *Unchangeable* 177; *Planting*

23–27; *Dreams* 1.206; *Abraham* 119–120). Platonists also spoke of the *hypodeigma* (copy) but most often used the word for the idea rather than the earthly counterpart (Sterling 2001, 193).

The author's employment of Platonic categories does not indicate that he is a consistent Platonist. In a world where cultures collided, people adopted the dominant Greek heritage in a variety of ways. Thus the author is probably neither a consistent Platonist nor directly dependent on Philo of Alexandria but rather belongs to two worlds, adopting both the Jewish hope for a new age and the Platonic distinction between the two spheres of reality, integrating both of these worlds into his interpretation of the sacrifice of Christ. Indeed, his use of *hypodeigma* (copy) probably reflects the influence of Ezekiel's vision of the heavenly temple (Ezek 42:15) in which he "measured the temple all around" (NRSV; lit. "measured the outline [*hypodeigma*] of the house"). Because of his Christian confession, he parts company with both the apocalyptic and the philosophical traditions at significant points, using them for his own purposes. Nevertheless, the mysterious argument of 8:1–10:18 reflects the author's interaction with Hellenistic philosophical traditions.

The author has much in common with Philo in his interpretation of Exod 25:40. Indeed, both he and Philo (*Alleg. Interp.* 3.102) add the words "all things" to the citation of Exod 25:40, a reading that agrees neither with the MT or the LXX but may reflect the text in an Alexandrian tradition. Philo cites Exod 25:40 on several occasions as a foundation for his Platonic reading of the OT (*QE* 2.52; *Alleg. Interp.* 3.100–102; *Planting* 26–27; *Moses* 2.71–75). His primary interest in all of these passages is to demonstrate the greatness of Moses as the one who was "called up" (*Planting* 26) to see a vision that is unavailable to other mortals. Moses was a high priest (*Moses* 2.75) who saw the forms for all created things in the heavenly world. Because *typos* in Exod 25:40 LXX (here rendered "archetype") has a variety of meanings, including "image" or "statue," he rarely uses the word but prefers "pattern" (*paradeigma, Alleg. Interp.* 3.102) or "form" (*archetypos, Moses* 2.74; *idea, Alleg. Interp.* 3.101; *Moses* 2.74). He contrasts Moses, who saw the actual forms in the heavenly world, to Bezalel, who worked only with the "shadow" of the ideal tabernacle (*Planting* 27).

The claim that the tabernacle was a copy of a heavenly original resonated widely in the first century. Stephen cites Exod 25:40 when he recalls that Moses made the tabernacle according to the pattern that he saw on the mountain, contrasting the tabernacle with the temple (Acts 7:44–50). According to Wis 9:8, the temple is "a copy of the holy tent" that God prepared from the beginning. The church fathers read the passage from Exod 25:40 with the lenses of Platonism. Origen and Eusebius link Exod 25:40 with Plato's theory of ideas. Origen maintains that Exod 25:40 distinguished between the corporeal and spiritual worlds (*Hom. Exod.* 9.2). Eusebius quotes Exod 25:40 and 25:9

alongside Plato, *Rep.* 500d–501c, to demonstrate the agreement between Moses and Plato (*PE* 12.19.1–9).

The author's use of Exod 25:40 both intersects with and departs from Philo's interpretation. For both, the "true tabernacle" (cf. 9:24) is the archetype, which is superior to the copy and shadow. The claim that Levitical priests serve in a "copy and shadow of the heavenly one" is analogous to Philo's discussion of Bezalel, who worked with the shadow rather than the heavenly archetype. Nevertheless, the author departs from Philo at a significant point. While Philo's major purpose was to elevate Moses and to show that the tabernacle was a symbol for the cosmos (*Moses* 2.71–108), the author of Hebrews employs the language to demonstrate the superiority of the ministry of Christ to the inferior earthly copy.

The extended citation of Jer 31:31–34, which forms an *inclusio* framing the argument (8:7–13; 10:15–18), also reflects the author's conversation with other interpreters, for this passage played a central role in the NT and in the Dead Sea Scrolls. In its original context, Jer 31:31–34 (38:31–34 LXX) is a word of encouragement for a despairing community promising that God would restore the people with a covenant inscribed on their hearts. This promise was important for the Qumran community, which identified itself as the people of the new covenant (CD 6.19; 8.21; 19.33–34; 20.12; 1QpHab 2.3). It is also central to NT writers, becoming a part of the liturgy for the Lord's Supper (Matt 26:28; 1 Cor 11:25). Paul describes himself as a minister of the new covenant (2 Cor 3:6), comparing his role with that of Moses (2 Cor 3:7–18). His assurance that the covenant people are empowered by the Spirit to keep the demands of the law (Rom 8:4) also suggests Paul's conviction that the new covenant of Jeremiah has become a reality.

Like other writers of that period, the author of Hebrews interprets the new covenant as a current reality. In devoting the extended section in 8:1–10:18 to the topic, he develops this theme more than any writer of the NT. However, his interpretation goes in a new direction, for he interprets the new covenant strictly in terms of the Levitical cultus, as he indicates by introducing and concluding the description of the work of Christ in the sanctuary with the citation of Jer 31:31–34.

The extended citation of Jer 31:31–34 (the lengthiest in the NT) in 8:8–12 agrees with the LXX with only minor variations, none of which have major theological implications. The wording of the prophecy corresponds to themes that the author develops in 9:1–10:18. For him, "the days [that] are coming" in Jer 31:31 are "these last days" (1:1), the "today" (3:13) when he invites the people to hear God's voice. The promise of a covenant "on their hearts" (8:10) anticipates the focus in chapter 9 on the cleansing of the inner person (cf. 9:14). His primary interest, as the frame in 8:7, 13 indicates, is the replacement of the old and ineffective covenant (cf. 7:11, 19) and its earthly sanctuary with the new covenant and its heavenly sanctuary.

Tracing the Train of Thought

After demonstrating from scripture that Jesus is the exalted and eternal high priest in chapter 7, the author turns in the lengthy argument of 8:1–10:18 to the ministry (*leitourgia*) of the high priest. The assurance that "we have such a high priest" (8:1) continues the focus on the order of Melchizedek in chapter 7. The continuity of the exposition is suggested by the appeal to Ps 110 to elaborate on the person and work of Christ. Having based his claim in chapter 7 for the eternity of the ideal priest on Ps 110:4, he frames the discussion of the work of Christ with an appeal to Ps 110:1 in order to show that Jesus is "at God's right hand" (8:1; 10:11–12) and returns to Ps 110:4 to speak of his being "perfected forever" (10:14). With this emphasis on Jesus' exaltation to God's right hand, the author's entire argument involves the comparison between the person and work of the exalted high priest with the work of earthly high priests in his attempt to reassure the readers of the greatness of their possession.

The author crafts his argument carefully. In 8:1–6, he states the primary case to be argued. Reference to the "minister" (8:2) and the "ministry" (8:6) provides the frame for this thesis statement, indicating that the extended exposition will focus on the work of the exalted high priest. The comparison between the "minister . . . in the true tent" and "those who serve in a shadowy copy" (8:5) introduces the series of antitheses that will dominate 8:1–10:18. The dualistic distinction between the heavenly and the earthly realities continues this theme from chapter 7 (cf. 7:16) and sets the stage for the author's threefold claim in 8:6 that the Christian possession is "better" than all alternatives. The author employs comparison (*synkrisis*) to reassure the community of the greatness of its possession, knowing the ancient rhetorical practice of using *synkrisis* to exalt the person whom one wishes to praise.

The remainder of the argument provides support for the claim in 8:1–6. The argument is framed by the use of Ps 110:1, 4 (8:1; 10:11–14) as well as the citation of Jer 31:31–34 (8:7–13; 10:15–18). The author supports the thesis statement with the extended quotation in 8:7–13 and recapitulates the claim of chapter 8 in 10:1–18. Chapter 9 gives the detailed argument for the superiority of the heavenly ministry of the new covenant. The argument is a series of antitheses developing the central thesis in 8:1–6 (Backhaus 1996, 181).

A Exposition: old and new priestly ministry (chap. 8; cf. Ps 110:1; Jer 31:31–34)
  B The old covenant and sacrifice (9:1–10)
    C The sacrifice (9:11–14)
    C' The new covenant (9:15–22)
  B' The new covenant and sacrifice (9:23–28)
A' Summary: old and new priestly ministry (10:1–18; cf. Ps 110:1; Jer 31:33–34)

True Tabernacle, Earthly Copy (8:1–6)

8:1–2. Like many ancient orators, the author summarizes his **main point** (8:1a), using the term (*kephalaion*) for the main argument or fundamental question in a law case (Löhr 2005, 202). Indeed, the statement that **we have such a high priest** who is **seated at the right hand of the throne of the majesty** (8:1b) accurately summarizes the preceding argument, recalling the claim, based on Ps 110:1, that the exalted Christ is at God's right hand (1:3, 13; cf. 12:2) and has "passed through the heavens" (4:14) after experiencing the trials that the community now faces (4:15; 5:1–10). As the author has demonstrated in chapter 7, this high priest belongs to the order of Melchizedek, which is both final and superior to the priesthood of Aaron. "We have" (or "having"), a favorite expression of the author (4:14; 6:9, 19; 10:19, 34; 12:1; 13:10), points to a possession that the community has as a gift and indicates the author's pastoral concern to rebuild the community's shattered world. Thus the "main point" that we have a high priest who is "seated at the right hand of the throne of the majesty" in heaven looks back to the preceding argument, while the affirmation that this high priest is a **minister . . . in the true tabernacle** (8:2a) looks forward to the exposition of 8:1–10:18, which develops both the role ("minister") and the place ("the true tabernacle") of the eternal high priest. The initial claim in 8:1–6 is the thesis statement for the entire unit in 8:1–10:18. As the exhortations before and after this central section indicate (5:11–6:20; 10:19–25), this exposition is intended to reassure a community that has experienced only suffering and disappointment, pointing them beyond the world that they can see (cf. 2:8).

The thesis statement in 8:1–2 indicates that the primary issue is the superiority of the ministry of Christ, which the author establishes with the dualistic distinction between the heavenly and the earthly sanctuaries.

A The minister (*leitourgos*) in the true tent (8:2)
  B those who are on earth (8:4)
  B' Those who minister (*latreuousin*) in the shadowy copy (8:5)
A' The better ministry (*leitourgia*, 8:6)

With the introduction of Christ as a **minister** (*leitourgos*, 8:2a), the author introduces the major topic of 8:1–10:18. He also uses the related term *latreia/latreuō* (8:5; 9:1, 9, 14; cf. 13:10), which was also used for service in the sanctuary, for he wishes to demonstrate that the community has a better ministry (*leitourgia*, 8:6). "Minister" (*leitourgos*) and "ministry" (*leitourgia*) commonly appear in the LXX for priestly service in the temple (Isa 61:6; 2 Esd 20:40 [= Neh 10:40]); the verb "to minister" appears to describe the activity in the sanctuary (Exod 28:35; 29:30). Thus the fact that "we have . . . a minister" (8:1) initiates the comparison between the work of Christ and "every high priest" who stood "ministering" (*leitourgōn*) in the earthly tabernacle (10:11;

cf. 5:3). The nature of this ministry becomes evident in the extended description of the sacrifice of Christ in 9:1–10:18. Laying the foundation for the comparison between the earthly and heavenly sacrifices in 9:1–14, the author establishes that the task of the minister is to offer sacrifices (8:3; cf. 5:1). The high priest at the right hand of the throne of the majesty implies a contrast to the Levitical priests, who belong to the material world. As the author will demonstrate in chapter 9, the "true tent" implies a comparison to the tent made with hands (9:11).

As this thesis statement indicates, the author is interested not only in the fact that Christ is a minister but that his ministry takes place **in the sanctuary and true tabernacle** (8:2a). "The sanctuary" (*ta hagia*) is the most holy place behind the second curtain (1 Kgs 8:6; 2 Chron 4:22; 5:7; Heb 9:3; Philo, *Alleg. Interp.* 2.56). Hebrews uses the plural *ta hagia* (cf. 9:8, 12, 24–25; 10:19; 13:11) for the sanctuary rather than the singular form (*to hagion*), which is most often used in the LXX (Lev

> ## Hebrews 8
> ## in the Rhetorical Flow
>
> **Hearing God's word with faithful endurance (1:1–4:13)**
>
> *Probatio*: **Discovering certainty and confidence in the word for the mature (4:14–10:31)**
>
> Drawing near and holding firmly: following the path of Jesus from suffering to triumph (4:14–5:10)
>
> Preparing to hear the word that is "hard to explain" (5:11–6:20)
>
> Grasping the anchor in the word for the mature: the sacrificial work of Christ as the assurance of God's promises (7:1–10:18)
>
> The priesthood of Melchizedek as the anchor of the soul (7:1–28)
>
> ▶ The sacrificial work of Christ as the assurance of God's promises (8:1–13)
>
> True tabernacle, earthly copy (8:1–6)
>
> A minister in the true tent (8:1–2)
>
> A copy of the heavenly tent (8:3–5)
>
> Mediator of a better covenant (8:6)
>
> A better covenant (8:7–13)

16:2, 3, 16, 17). This place behind the curtain is the heavenly world, as the author has indicated already (6:19) and will describe further in chapter 9. The sanctuary is the innermost part of the "true tabernacle," which the author introduces explicitly for the first time and develops at length in 9:1–10:18. In keeping with the imagery of the wilderness (3:1–4:13; 12:18–24), the exposition consistently places the work of Christ in the tabernacle (8:5; 9:11; 13:10) rather than the temple. Indeed, the discussion of the building of the tabernacle by Moses resumes the contrast in 3:1–6 between Moses and Jesus.

Thus the author's focus in 8:1–10:18 is on the contrast between the earthly and the heavenly tabernacle. Just as the comparison between the two priesthoods in chapter 7 employs the dualistic distinction between the physical/transient and the heavenly/eternal realities, the comparison of the two tabernacles and two ministries also assumes the distinction between the earthly and the heavenly sphere. The exalted high priest serves in the tabernacle that **the Lord, and not humankind, set up** (8:2b). The verb (*pēgnymi*) evokes the language of the setting up of the tabernacle in the LXX (Exod 33:7; 38:26). "The tents that the Lord pitched" in Num 24:6 refers to the houses of Jacob rather than the sanctuary but also anticipates the claim in 9:11, 24 that Christ entered a sanctuary "not made with hands" and the statement that Abraham sought a city "whose maker and builder is God" (11:10).

8:3–5. Only because he is not **on the earth** (8:4) can he be a high priest (cf. 7:14–15 for a similar argument about the priesthood of Melchizedek). The author appeals to Exod 25:40 to support the contrast between heavenly and earthly tabernacles, introducing the citation with the statement that Moses **was warned** (*kechrēmatistai*; cf. 11:7; 12:25) **when he was about to erect the tent, "Make everything according to the archetype shown you on the mountain"** (8:5b). With the addition of "everything" (*panta*), the author has incorporated additional passages from the context (Exod 25:9; 26:30; 27:8) to indicate that both the tabernacle and the utensils were made according to the divine pattern. This citation indicates that the "archetype" is the same as the "true tent" (8:2). The author employs Platonic language (see Introductory Matters) not to engage in polemic against the Levitical system but to establish the metaphysical superiority of Christ to any alternative that might tempt the community. For listeners who worship in house churches and see only threatening forces around them, this vision of Christ ministering in the heavenly sanctuary points to realities beyond what they can see, indicating that they may now place their trust in someone who is above this creation. Christians have not placed their confidence in something in the material world but in the ministry that is abiding and unshakable. This is the anchor of the soul for the community.

8:6. The declaration that he has **attained a more excellent ministry** (8:6a; *diaphorōteras tetychen leitourgias*) resumes the claim in 8:2 that "we have . . . a minister" (*leitourgos*) and establishes a contrast to those who serve in the earthly sanctuary (8:4–5), anticipating the description of the heavenly work of Christ in chapter 9. The "more excellent ministry" takes place in heaven, as the contrast with 8:2–4 and the argument in chapter 9 indicate. This comparison (*men . . . de*) is a familiar means for the author to claim the metaphysical superiority of the exalted Christ over the earthly ministers (cf. 7:20–21, 23–24). In the three *synkriseis* of 8:6, the author indicates the close relationship between the "ministry," the "covenant," and the "promise," three of the major themes of the homily, all of which are introduced by the comparative "more excellent" (*diaphorōtera*) or "better" (*kreittōn*). The reference to the threefold ministry, covenant, and promise suggests the close relationship between these themes and the place of 8:1–10:18 within the homily. Throughout the homily the author defines Christian existence as faithfully waiting on the promise (4:1; 6:12–17; 10:36; 11:9, 13, 17, 33). The Christ event is God's oath and promise (6:16–20); the establishment of the covenant (9:15–22) guarantees the ultimate fulfillment of the promise. Thus the author demonstrates in 8:1–10:18 that the community, which continues to endure hardship, has received the guarantee that the promises will ultimately be fulfilled. The "more excellent ministry" (*diaphorōtera leitourgia*), as the author indicates in 9:1–14, is a present reality that guarantees the future.

The fact that he has attained a "more excellent ministry" insofar as he is the **mediator of a better covenant** (8:6b; *kreittonos diathēkēs mesitēs*) is reminiscent of the exordium of the homily (1:1–4), which says that Christ has become "greater than the angels" (*kreittōn angelōn*) insofar as he has inherited "a more excellent name" (*diaphorōteron onoma*). It also accords with the frequent use of *kreittōn* (6:9; 7:7, 19; 8:6; 11:16, 40; 12:24) to demonstrate the superiority of the community's possession over all alternatives. The claim that Christ is the "mediator of a better covenant" points back to the earlier statement that the exalted high priest is the "guarantor of a better covenant" (7:22) and anticipates the full development of that theme in 8:7–10:18 (especially 9:15). Although "mediator" (*mesitēs*) often means an arbitrator between two sides, here it is synonymous with "guarantor" (7:22). Inasmuch as the author has evoked the name of Moses in 8:5 (cf. 3:1–6) and recounts his role in instituting the covenant in 9:15–22, he probably implies a comparison to Israel's lawgiver, the mediator par excellence in the OT and Jewish tradition (*T. Moses* 1.14; Philo, *Moses* 2.166; cf. Gal 3:19–20). Through the death of Christ the "better covenant" is now in force (9:15; cf. 12:24). The covenant was **legally enacted on better promises** (8:6c, *epi kreittosin epangeliais nenomothetētai*). With the verb *nomothetein*, used also in 7:11 for the legal enactment of the priesthood on the basis of the law (7:11–12), the author speaks of the enactment of the "better promises." He indicates the relationship between the covenant and the promise in 9:15 when he says that the death of Jesus is the basis for the covenant, enabling the community to receive the promise of the eternal inheritance.

A Better Covenant (8:7–13)

In 8:7–13, the author offers scriptural support for his claim for a better ministry and better covenant in an extended citation from Jer 31:31–34 (38:31–34 LXX), the classic passage announcing the new covenant. The outer frame of the passage in 8:7, 13 offers his interpretation. Although the passage was commonly interpreted as a promise for a despairing people, the passage has a different function in Hebrews, as the introductory words **finding fault** (*memphomenos*) **with them, he says** (8:8a) indicates. Referring to the question of the "faultless" covenant in 8:7, he interprets the passage as a critique of the old covenant, suggesting that the limitations of the old covenant demonstrate that the community has a "better" covenant. Using the familiar argument that the later passage cancels the earlier one (cf. 4:8, "if Joshua had given them rest, he would not have spoken of another day"; 7:11, "if there were perfection under the Levitical priesthood, . . . what need is there for another"), the author concludes, **for if that first (covenant) were** faultless (*amemptos*), there would have been no occasion to seek a second one (8:7). A similar argument appears near the conclusion of this section in 10:1–10 (10:9, "He takes away the first in order to establish the second"). That is, just as the announcement of a high priest after the order of Melchizedek indicates the imperfection of the Levitical high priesthood (7:11–19), the announcement of a new covenant implies that the first covenant was not faultless. Although the passage that he cites in 8:8–12 speaks of the new covenant, implying a contrast to an old covenant, he speaks literally of the "first" and the "second" without actually using the word "covenant" (cf. 8:13; 9:1, 15, 18). Therefore, not only is the better covenant metaphysically superior; it also replaces the earlier one.

The author's interpretation of Jer 31:31–34 is especially evident in his introduction of the citation, for "finding fault with them, he says," implies that the passage is actually a critique. This introductory citation has been the source of debate, for 8:7 indicates that the fault is with the covenant rather than the people, while 8:8a indicates that he finds fault "with them." Moreover, the conclusion in 8:13 also focuses on the problem of the covenant rather than on the people. Some scholars have noted the textual variant, according to which "he found fault, saying to them," which is more consistent with the author's argument. Nevertheless, one cannot separate the people from the covenant. Indeed, the passage from Jeremiah recalls that the people did not remain in God's covenant (8:12). Thus the author envisions the citation as a critique of the Levitical system and a promise of a replacement.

The author probably cites the passage at length because it provided him with the opportunity to develop important themes for the argument. The announcement of a **new covenant** in **the days** that **are coming** (8:8b) provides scriptural support for the introduction of the theme of the better covenant, which the author will develop in 9:15–22, and for declaring that those days have already come in the sacrifice of Christ. The failure of the people to keep the covenant (8:9) is reminiscent of the earlier memory of Israel's failures (3:7–4:11) and the sinful condition that necessitates the new covenant. The author's primary focus is on the final phrase, **I will be merciful to their wrongdoing, and I will remember their sins no more** (8:12), which he will explain in the description of the atoning sacrifice of Christ in 9:1–10:18.

The conclusion that **in saying new (covenant), he made the first obsolete** (8:13), the author restates the interpretation in 8:7, indicating that the listeners share in God's ultimate covenant, not the one that God has replaced. In saying that what is **becoming obsolete and growing old is about to disappear**, he reiterates the contrast between the impermanence of everything that belongs to the created world and the eternity of the better covenant. Just as the exalted Christ remains eternal when everything else is transient (cf. 1:10–12; 7:3, 23–24), the more excellent ministry and the better covenant provide eternal salvation.

Theological Issues

As a skilled communicator, the author pauses in the middle of this advanced word for the mature to remind the reader of the "main point" of all that he has said. "We have a high priest, who sat down at the right hand of the throne of the majesty in the heavens" has a special significance for readers who have experienced only disappointment over an extended period of time. To a vulnerable community that lives in a small house church, that claim is a ringing assurance. Having described the transcendent high priest in chapter 7, the transition to what "we have" moves the conversation to the relevance of the work of Christ for the disoriented readers. Despite appearances, "we have" what appears to be remote from us. Indeed, the author's frequent references to what "we have" (cf. 4:14; 6:19; 10:19; 13:10) all describe a gift that we receive as a result of the saving work of Christ. While the people move through the difficult terrain in the wilderness toward the promised land, they already have a high priest in the heavens, and they already share in a divine liturgy led "by the minister in the true tent."

The contrast between "the minister in the true tent" and "those who serve in a copy and a shadow" is not a polemic against Judaism but a reassurance to the disoriented community of the extraordinary gift that it has received. That is, those who struggle with alienation are actually the privileged ones, for what "we have" transcends present circumstances. Although the people will be tempted to accept only the realities that they see, their ultimate hope lies in the unseen reality of the ministry of Christ in the heavenly sanctuary. Thus the "main point" for a discouraged community is the reassurance that God has offered a "better liturgy," and that Jesus is the "mediator of a better covenant" that is established on "better promises." In what "we have" already, we discover the certainty of the promise.

Readers who interpret Heb 8 apart from its original context easily lose sight of its theological and pastoral significance. For example, Origen frequently cited Heb 8:5 and 10:1 as demonstrating that the entire OT was a mere shadow of things to come (cited in Greer 1973, 9). Both ancient and modern commentaries have interpreted Heb 8 as a contrast between Christianity and Judaism. The author's purpose, however, is not to denigrate the OT or Judaism but to reassure his readers of the supreme value of the saving event of Christ, even if they cannot presently see the ultimate triumph.

Hebrews 9:1–10:18

The Ultimate Sacrifice in the Heavenly Sanctuary

Introductory Matters

In chapter 9, the description of the tabernacle also raises questions about the influences on the author's interpretation, for it is based not only on the OT but also on interpretations in his own time, as his description of the furnishings in the tabernacle (9:1–10) indicates. Although the placement of three items in the holy place corresponds to OT tradition (Exod 25:23–40; 1 Kgs 7:27–37), the actual items listed in 9:2–3 are not consistent with the OT description of the table and the presentation of the bread as one item (Exod 25:30). While the location of the altar of incense (*thymiatērion*) is not entirely clear in the OT, it appears to belong to the holy place (Exod 30:1–16) "in front of the curtain" (Exod 30:6) where Aaron is expected to burn incense "every day" (Exod 30:7; Attridge 1989, 234). Although Philo and Josephus also locate it in the holy place, Hebrews places it in the most holy place (9:4). Codex Vaticanus (B), one of the major manuscripts, corrects this reading by placing the altar of incense in the holy place. The author follows the OT in locating the ark of the covenant (Exod 25:10, 14, 16; 39:35; cf. 1 Kgs 8:6 on Solomon's temple), the ten commandments (Deut 10:3–5), and "the cherubim of glory overshadowing the mercy seat" within "the most holy place" (Heb 9:4), but adds details that do not derive from the OT. Although the Israelites preserved both the manna and Aaron's rod for generations (Exod 16:33; Num 17:2–9), only Hebrews locates it in the ark of the covenant.

The climax of the author's description of the tabernacle furnishings is the mercy seat. As the place where the priest made atonement for sins (Lev

Mercy Seat

The *hilastērion*, the translation of the Hebrew *kappōret* (commonly rendered "mercy seat" in English translations), was the most important object in the most holy place in the tabernacle and temple. It was a gold plate on top of the ark of the covenant. On both sides were the cherubim, whose wings covered the place of the invisible God. It was the place where the high priest made atonement for the sins of the people on the Day of Atonement. The priest sprinkled the blood of a bull on the front of the mercy seat (Lev 16:15). The instructions for the construction of the *hilastērion* appear in Exod 25:16–21. The term appears only twice in the New Testament. In addition to Heb 9:5, it also appears in Rom 3:25, where Paul, perhaps in dependence on earlier tradition, interprets the death of Jesus with the imagery of the Day of Atonement. The related term *hilasmos*, normally rendered "expiation," appears in 1 John 2:2; 4:10. The author of Hebrews used the verb form *hilaskesthai* in 2:17 to describe Jesus as the high priest who "made atonement for sins."

16:13–16) on *yom kippur*, the mercy seat (*hilastērion*) is of special importance to the author's presentation of the sacrifice of Christ as the ultimate Day of Atonement. According to Exod 25:17–22, the mercy seat was the most important object of the most holy place. It was a gold plate placed on the ark of the covenant. Above it were the cherubim, whose wings covered the dwelling of the invisible God.

The comment that the author cannot "speak in detail" (9:5), a common rhetorical maxim (cf. 2 Macc 2:28–32; Philo, *QE* 2.52; *Heir* 221), suggests his acquaintance with extended treatments of the significance of the tabernacle. Indeed, the inclusion of items within the tabernacle that are unknown in the OT and his comment that the ritual on the Day of Atonement is a symbol (9:8) suggest his familiarity with a symbolic reading of the ritual in the tabernacle. Both Philo and Josephus have lengthy symbolic interpretations of the tabernacle (Josephus, *Ant.* 3.123, 181–183; *JW* 5.213–218). For Philo the table, candlestick, tabernacle, curtains, and altar are symbols for the universe and the progress of the worshiper toward communion with God (*Moses* 2.74–160). Philo is especially interested in the symbolism of the distinction between the holy place and the most holy place. According to *Moses* 2.81–82, the five pillars separating the tabernacle's forecourt from the outer court symbolically distinguish the realms of mind and sense. In *Moses* 2.101–108, the furnishings of the outer court correspond to heaven, earth, and sea in the world of sense perception (Koester 1989, 61). Thus the holy place symbolizes the world of sense perception, while the most holy place represents the heavenly world (cf. Philo, *QE* 68; *Drunkenness* 134). This fascination with the tabernacle furnishings suggests that the author's description of the furniture is not only derived from his reading of the OT but is also a response to the symbolic interpretations that were current in the first century. Unlike the author of Hebrews, Philo speaks "in detail," giving the significance of all of the furnishings of the tabernacle. The author of Hebrews does not speak "in detail" because his interest lies not in the furnishings of the tabernacle but in the sacrifice of Christ.

The description of the furnishings in the tabernacle provides the setting for the interpretation of the death of Christ as the ultimate Day of Atonement. The instructions for the ritual in Lev 16 now become the subordinate text to Ps 110:1, which frames the discussion (8:1; 10:12). As with the furnishings, the author does not describe the Day of Atonement "in detail." His interest is only in the significance of the separation of the tabernacle into two compartments: the contrast between the daily sacrifice and the annual sacrifice on the Day of Atonement, and the inaccessibility of the most holy place for the people (9:8). The author omits major aspects of the Day of Atonement ritual, including the ritual involving the "scapegoat" sent into the wilderness to bear the sins of the people (Johnson 2006, 217). He also incorporates elements from other sacrifices, including the ashes of the red heifer (Num 19:1–10) and the ritual inaugurating the covenant (9:15–22; cf. Exod 24:3–8).

The entire argument in chapters 9:1–10:18 rests on a complex dualism that reflects the author's place on the boundary between two intellectual worlds. On the one hand, his roots in Jewish eschatology are clear in his insistence that the sacrifice of Christ occurred in a singular event that marks the dividing line between "the present time" (9:9) of the "shadow of good things to come" (10:1; cf. 9:11, "the good things to come") and the "end of the ages" (9:26). The Levitical sacrifice belongs to the first covenant (cf. "first" in 8:6; 9:1; 10:9; the author never refers to the "old covenant"), while the sacrifice of Christ inaugurates the new covenant (9:15; cf. 8:13). On the other hand, in addition to this "horizontal" frame of reference, the author also maintains a vertical perspective, distinguishing between the sanctuary that is "earthly" (9:1; *kosmikos*) and the one that is "not made with hands" and "not of this

The Day of Atonement

Leviticus 16 describes a complex ritual on the Day of Atonement. The high priest bathes before putting on the linen tunic and turban (Lev 16:3–4) and then takes from the people two male goats for a sin offering and one ram for a burnt offering (Lev 16:5). After offering the bull for a sin offering for himself, he casts lots over the two goats. One is presented to the Lord, and the other is sent into the wilderness (Lev 16:6–10). The high priest enters the most holy place, where he sprinkles the blood of the bull and the goat on the mercy seat (Lev 16:11–14). After completing the ritual, he washes his clothes and offers a sacrifice for himself and for the people (Lev 16:23–28).

creation" (9:11; cf. 9:24). The entry of the high priest into the most holy place is nothing less than an entry into the "archetype" that Moses saw on the mountain (8:5). Thus the events of the new age are not only new but are qualitatively different because they occur in the higher realm. Although the author's Christian conviction that Christ offered the ultimate sacrifice at a specific time separates him from the philosophical speculation of his own time, Platonic categories serve as a vehicle to express the grandeur of the Christian confession.

The author also employs philosophical categories to augment his critique of the Levitical system and demonstrate the qualitative greatness of the work of Christ. The interpretation of the death of Christ as the ultimate Day of Atonement (Heb 9:1–14) involves a sharp critique of the Levitical system that also reflects the author's familiarity with Hellenistic thought. The author brings a new dimension to the prophetic critiques of sacrificial practices (Isa 1:12–17; Hos 2:11; Amos 5:21; Mic 6:6–8) that were not accompanied by ethical conduct, maintaining that the sacrifices cleansed the flesh and not the conscience (9:9–10) and adding that these sacrifices were only a reminder of sins (10:3). This critique of the Levitical system, which would have been remarkable in the Jewish tradition, also reflects the discussions among Philo and other ancient authors on the efficacy of animal sacrifices and physical sanctuaries (Thompson 1982, 109–15). According to the pervasive philosophical critique, the deity does not need material sacrifices but should be approached only with the mind (Porphyry, *Abstin.* 2.34). According to Philo no earthly tabernacle is adequate for God, for "it is not possible genuinely to express our gratitude to God by means of buildings and oblations and sacrifices" (*Planting* 126; *Heir* 123). God has no need for sacrifice (*Decalogue* 41; *Spec. Laws* 1.294; QE 2.50), for God abhors external approaches (*Worse* 21, 107).

Just as the author of Hebrews distinguishes between the purification of the conscience and the cleansing of the flesh (9:9–10), Philo distinguishes between the higher and lower aspects of human existence. "A man may submit to sprinklings of holy water and to purifications, befouling his understanding while cleansing his body" (*Worse* 20). Philo also says that the sacrifices were not a remission but a reminder of sins (*Moses* 2.107). In the same way, the author offers a critique of animal sacrifices in the earthly sanctuary.

A consistent feature of the author's argument is the contrast between the "many" sacrifices offered under the Levitical system (9:25–26; 10:1–4) and the one sacrifice offered by the heavenly high priest (10:11–14), which is reminiscent of the contrast in chapter 7 between the many mortal high priests and the one exalted high priest (7:23–27). The "many" belong to the created world, while the "one" is exalted to God's right hand. This argument also becomes intelligible against the background of the Platonic distinction between the one and the many. In the Platonic tradition, the number one is the characteristic of the perfect heavenly world, while the many belong to the imperfect creation.

The author's reflection on the tabernacle suggests neither a date for the homily prior to the destruction of the temple in Jerusalem nor a polemical concern to challenge those who were tempted by the temple service. Indeed, he never mentions the temple but employs the tabernacle as the basis for the extended comparison. Like Philo (*Moses* 2.72), the author regards the tabernacle as the appropriate symbol for a people who are looking for a homeland (cf. 3:7–4:11; 11:13–16).

Tracing the Train of Thought

The More Perfect Tent (9:1–14)

After declaring that the heavenly high priest attained a better ministry and better covenant (8:6), the author provides the foundation for this claim in chapter 9, continuing the comparison between heavenly and earthly ministries and explaining the relationship between the ministry and the covenant. This relationship is evident in the comment in 9:1 that the "first [covenant] had regulations for ministry and an earthly sanctuary." Here the context indicates that the reader must supply the term "covenant" to the author's omission. The construction in 9:1, 11 (*men . . . de*) signals a new contrast (cf. similar construction in 7:23–24; 8:4–6) between the regulations for ministry in the earthly sanctuary (9:1–10) and the work of Christ in the "greater and more perfect tent" (9:11), continuing the contrast between the true tabernacle and the shadow and copy (8:2, 5). In keeping with the *synkrisis* throughout the homily, the author can only demonstrate the extraordinary nature of this salvation through a comparison. Consequently, he presents the regulations for ministry in the earthly tabernacle (9:1–10) as a foil to the great work of Christ (9:11–14).

9:1–7. The negative foil in 9:1–10 is marked by an *inclusio* indicating that the point of comparison involves **regulations** (9:1, *dikaiōmata*) in the earthly sanctuary, which include the furnishings (9:1–5) and

---

Hebrews 9:1–10:18 in the Rhetorical Flow

Hearing God's word with faithful endurance (1:1–4:13)

Probatio: Discovering certainty and confidence in the word for the mature (4:14–10:31)

  Drawing near and holding firmly: following the path of Jesus from suffering to triumph (4:14–5:10)

  Preparing to hear the word that is hard to explain (5:11–6:20)

  Grasping the anchor in the word for the mature: the sacrificial work of Christ as the assurance of God's promises (7:1–10:18)

    The priesthood of Melchizedek as the anchor of the soul (7:1–28)

    The sacrificial work of Christ as the assurance of God's promises (8:1–13)

  ▶ The ultimate sacrifice in the heavenly sanctuary (9:1–10:18)

    The more perfect tent (9:1–14)

    Why did Jesus die? (9:15–28)

    The once-for-all sacrifice (10:1–18)

---

the ministry (9:6–10). The author includes only a brief summary of the tabernacle furnishings in 9:1–5, giving special focus to the aspects that will be important for the argument. The description of the tabernacle furnishings is based primarily on Exod 25 and 26, and the distinction between the holy place and the most holy place is found in Exod 26:33. Although he mentions the contents of the sanctuary briefly (see Introductory Matters), his special focus is on the division of the sanctuary into two sections. While the reference to a **first tabernacle** (9:2, 6) and a tabernacle **behind the second curtain** (9:3) could suggest two separate tents, the references elsewhere to the single tabernacle (8:2; 9:11, 23–24) indicate that the author envisions one tent divided into separate rooms. His language accents the separation of the two sections and the importance of the curtain separating them, preparing the way for the symbolic interpretation of the furnishings. This distinction between the two parts of the sanctuary will become a major focus of the argument, as the author depicts the entry of the exalted high priest behind the curtain (cf. 6:19; 10:19) into the heavenly world. Thus the outer court is a symbol for the material world, while the most holy place is a symbol for the heavenly world.

> ## An Outline of Hebrews 9:1–14
>
> The more perfect tent (9:1–14)
>
> The entrance of the high priest into the earthly tent (9:1–7)
>
> The way not yet opened (9:8–10)
>
> The entrance of Christ into the heavenly tent (9:11–12)
>
> The cleansing of the conscience (9:13–14)

The separation between sections in the tabernacle in 9:1–5 is the basis for the symbolic interpretation of the tabernacle ministry in 9:6–10, for the two sections of the tabernacle correspond to two types of ministry. In Greek, 9:6–10 is a lengthy periodic sentence introducing the themes for discussion in the remainder of the cultic section. The first half (9:6–7) describes the ministry in the tabernacle, creating a suspense that is solved in the second section (9:7–8; Cortez 2006, 533–34). Priests enter into the first tent **continually** (9:6, *dia pantos*) to carry out the ministry mentioned in 9:1, while only the high priest enters the second tent **annually** (9:7a, *hapax tou eniautou*). The sacrifices performed "continually" include the offering of the bread to God each Sabbath (Lev 24:5–9), the daily care for the lighting of the lamps (Exod 27:20–21), and the daily offering of incense (Exod 30:7). With the reference to the high priest's annual entrance into the second tabernacle, the author makes his first reference to the sacrifice of the Day of Atonement (*yom kippur*) in Lev 16, which becomes the dominant image for interpreting the sacrifice of Christ. On this day the high priest made atonement for himself (Lev 16:11–14), for the people (Lev 16:21), and for the sanctuary (Lev 16:33). With the inclusion of the comment **not without blood** (9:7b), the author mentions another major theme for the first time (cf. 9:12–13, 18–20, 25; 10:4; 11:28; 13:11), recalling that the priest sprinkled the blood of the animal on the mercy seat (Lev 16:14–15) and on the horns of the altar (Lev 16:18–19).

9:8–10. The significance of the ministry at the Day of Atonement becomes evident in 9:8–10, indicating that the cultic arrangements point beyond the actual tabernacle to a higher truth. With the introductory comment that **the Holy Spirit reveals** (9:8a; *dēlountos tou pneumatos*), the author indicates that the Holy Spirit not only provides divine oracles (3:7; 10:15) but also interprets them (cf. 12:27), revealing the deeper meaning of the text. *Dēloun* has the technical meaning of the revelation of hidden mysteries (Weiss 1991, 456) and is used for the interpretation of dreams (Dan 2:5–7) or scripture (Philo, *Flight* 157; *Migration* 85; Josephus, *Ant.* 3.187 interpreting the robe of the high priest). In this instance the Holy Spirit reveals the limitations of the ministry of the OT sacrificial system: **the way into the sanctuary has not yet been disclosed as long as the first tent still exists** (9:8b). The first tent belongs to the first covenant (8:7–13) that is becoming obsolete (8:13). The way into the sanctuary will not be open until Christ enters behind the curtain (10:19; cf. 6:19; 9:11), opening the path for others to follow. The people on the move cannot reach the goal of entry into the heavenly world until the forerunner opens the way (cf. 2:10; 3:7–4:11; 6:20). Inasmuch as the author speaks of the tabernacle rather than the temple, he is referring not to actual practices at the temple but to the situation without the work of Christ in opening up the way, for only he provides access to God.

The author indicates the deeper meaning of the Levitical system in 9:9, declaring that it is a **symbol** (*parabolē*) **of the present time** (9:9a) before the inauguration of the new covenant. Having described the new covenant as the ministry in which God would "remember sins no more" (8:12), the author concludes that as long as the old covenant was in force, gifts and sacrifices were offered that were not able to perfect the conscience of the worshiper. This claim is reminiscent of earlier statements that "the law made nothing perfect" (7:19; cf. 7:11) and the later claim that the sacrifices offered each year

Parabolē

Parabolē, whose etymology suggests "placing things side by side with each other," refers to various forms of metaphorical speech. In the LXX, the term is used as a translation of the Hebrew *mashal*, which has a wide range of meaning, including proverb and allegory. In the Synoptic Gospels, the term refers to both the extended stories and the similes of Jesus. In the Greek rhetorical tradition, the *parabolē* was one of the accepted proofs in the speech, meaning hypothetical example or comparison. The author of Hebrews uses the term in 11:19 to recall that, as a result of the sacrifice of Isaac, Abraham symbolically received the child from the dead.

were not able to perfect those who draw near (10:1). Just as the old covenant is replaced by the new covenant (8:7–13), the present time (9:9a) is eclipsed by **the time of reformation** (9:10c), which involves not only a temporal change but a qualitative change as well. The cultic ordinances pointed toward the ultimate removal of sin through the high priestly work of Christ but could not fulfill their ultimate goal.

Just as the author contrasted the imperfect priests who belonged to the sphere of the flesh with the heavenly priest (7:16), he now indicates the limitations of the earthly priests: their sacrifices were limited to the sphere of the flesh (9:10). The **foods, drinks, and washings** (9:10a; lit. "baptisms"; cf. 16:23–24; see Lev 10:9, 12–14; 11:2 for food and drink) could not perfect the conscience. This contrast between "flesh" and "conscience" suggests two dimensions of human existence corresponding to the earthly and heavenly tabernacles. As the *inclusio* of 9:1, 10 indicates, the earthly sanctuary (9:1; *hagion kosmikon*) has only **regulations of the flesh** (9:10b) but **cannot perfect the conscience** (*syneidēsis*) (9:9b). The earthly side of human existence can be cleansed with material offerings, while the whole person requires a superior sacrifice. *Syneidēsis* refers to the "consciousness" (10:2–4), which can be cleansed only by the entrance of Christ into the heavenly world (cf. 10:22). Thus the argument assumes not only that material sacrifices have been superseded but also that they are fundamentally ineffective (Thompson 1982, 109).

This claim would have been remarkable throughout the Jewish tradition, for the instructions in Leviticus maintain that the sacrifices make atonement for the people. Even those who, like Philo, interpreted the physical sacrifices symbolically and employed cosmic speculation to show that the sacrifices pointed beyond themselves never maintained that the sacrificial system was fundamentally ineffective and destined to become obsolete (cf. 8:13). The author's critique must be seen within the purposes of the homily. Since his purpose is not to engage in polemic against Judaism but to rebuild his community's confidence in its own confession, he is actually presenting a negative foil for his interpretation of the death of Christ. Using the common method of *synkrisis*, which he employs throughout the homily, he establishes the foil in 9:1–10 as the background for his claim that only the sacrifice of Christ provides access to God. Using the metaphysical argument against earthly securities (see Introductory Matters), he reminds his community that it has no need for earthly securities when it is in touch with the transcendent world. The critique would apply to the desire for any earthly means of dealing with the most basic human problem. This sets up the new section on the blood of Christ.

9:11–12. The critique of the ministry in the earthly sanctuary in 9:1–10 places the contrast in 9:11–14 in bold relief, for now the author contrasts the ministry of Christ with that of the earthly sanctuary, declaring that Christ has done what the Levitical regulations could not do. The **coming good things** (9:11) are the equivalent of the "time of reformation" (9:10) and of the new covenant anticipated by the first covenant (8:7–13) when God would "remember their sins no more" (8:12). This new situation occurs only **when Christ the high priest arrived** (9:11a, *Christos de paragenomenos archiereus*), entering the heavenly world. The compound aorist participle *paragenomenos* is an intensified form of the author's more customary *genomenos* (from *ginomai*, "become"), which he uses for the exaltation when Christ "became greater than the angels" (1:4) and an exalted high priest (2:17; 5:9; 6:20; 7:22, 26; see Weiss 1991, 464). When Christ arrived at God's right hand (1:3; 8:1), he entered through the greater and more perfect tent, opening the way that had previously been closed (9:8). As the author indicates later, the community now has access to the heavenly sanctuary because the high priest has gone through the curtain (10:19–20) that separates heaven and earth. Believers who are on their way to the heavenly homeland (3:7–4:11) may now draw near to God because their pioneer (2:10) and forerunner has entered behind the curtain, becoming the high priest according to the order of Melchizedek (6:20) and the source of eternal salvation (5:9).

The Day of Atonement ritual described in 9:1–10 provides the lens for interpreting the work of Christ in 9:11–14. Just as the Levitical high priest went through the curtain separating the two tents, the exalted Christ went through the greater and more perfect tabernacle, the equivalent of the true tabernacle (8:2; 9:23) and archetype that Moses saw on the mountain (8:5). It is the heavenly counterpart to the earthly tabernacle (9:1, *hagion kosmikon*). As a tabernacle **not made with hands** and **not of this creation** (9:11b), it is the one that the Lord made (8:2). The "better and more perfect tabernacle" belongs not to the world that is passing away (cf. 1:10–12; 8:13) but to the one that is invisible (11:1) and unshakable (12:27).

Just as the priestly service on the Day of Atonement was "not without blood" (9:7) but offered the blood of goats and bulls and calves, the heavenly high priest offered **his own blood** (9:12b; cf. 7:27), becoming both the priest and the sacrifice. The suggestion of the offering of blood in the heavenly sanctuary stretches the imagery to the limit, for Jesus actually shed his blood at the cross. The author has, however, collapsed the death and exaltation into one event, bringing together Good Friday and Easter. "Blood" is not a substance that the exalted Christ brings into the sanctuary but a metaphor for Jesus' sacrifice of himself. The offering of Jesus' blood is the ultimate Day of Atonement.

The sacrifice of Christ in the heavenly sanctuary was not continual, like the sacrifices of the Levitical priests (9:6), or annual, like that of the high priest (9:7), but **once for all** (9:12c, *ephapax*). As with the contrast between the many priests and the high priest according to the order of Melchizedek (7:23–24), the author contrasts the one and the many, knowing that the many suggests imperfection and incompleteness (cf. 10:1–4). The author insists repeatedly in this central section that the Christ event was "once for all" (*ephapax*, 7:27; 10:10; cf. *hapax*, 9:26). This theme, which was common in the Platonic tradition (see Introductory Matters), is the basis for the author's claim that only the exalted high priest **obtained an eternal redemption** (9:12d). "Redemption" (*lytrōsis*; cf. the related word *apolytrōsis*, 9:15), the common term for the ransoming of prisoners (BDAG, 606), was frequently used in Jewish literature for the deliverance of Israel from tyranny (Luke 1:68; 2:38). For the author (cf. also 1 Pet 1:18) it took on the meaning of redemption from the oppressive power of sin. Because he entered eternity in the heavenly sanctuary, he makes "eternal redemption" available to others.

9:13–14. In 9:13–14, the author supports the claim for the unique saving work of Christ, once more returning to the Levitical system to provide the lens for interpretation. In place of the goats and calves in 9:12, he refers to the **goats and bulls** in 9:13a, and then adds the **ashes of the red heifer**, which he derives, not from the Day of Atonement, but from the ritual in Num 19. The author has linked these two rituals because both involved purification through sprinkling. In the Day of Atonement ritual, however, only the furnishings are sprinkled (Lev 16:14), while the ritual of the red heifer involves the sprinkling of both the furnishings and the people (Num 19:17–19). The author may also be anticipating the description of the ritual establishing the covenant in 9:15–22, for he recalls that Moses sprinkled the scrolls and the people at the inauguration of the first covenant (9:19). Since the ritual of the red heifer involved the restoration of ritual purity for those who had become defiled by touching unclean things rather than the atonement for sins, as in Lev 16, it is also the background for the imagery in the acknowledgment that the ritual **sanctifies for the purification of the flesh** (9:13b), for both sanctification and purification are terms for the removal of the defilement that disqualifies one from access to the sanctuary.

As the author suggests in 9:9–10, the purification of the flesh does not adequately address the human dilemma, for what was lacking in earthly sacrifices was the perfection of the conscience. Arguing from the lesser to the greater (cf. 2:1–4; 10:26–31), the author concludes that only the blood of Christ, offered in a heavenly sanctuary, purifies the conscience, for the conscience is the heavenly side of human existence. Thus the work of Christ is the "eternal redemption" (9:12) that allows one to turn away from **dead works to minister to the living God** (9:14). The pastoral dimension of the argument is evident in the use of the first person plural: that we may "minister to the living God." The context suggests that the dead works are the cultic sacrifices on earth that do not **purify the conscience**. The listeners have the opportunity to turn from these dead works to the authentic ministry. In contrast to those who minister (*latreuousin*) vainly in the earthly sanctuary (8:5; 9:1), they may now "minister to the living God" (*latreuein theō zōnti*) because Christ has opened the way to the heavenly sanctuary. Most translations render the phrase "serve the living God"; the translation given here maintains the cultic terminology, indicating the parallel between the priests who "minister" in the sanctuary and the readers who also "minister" in their own context.

Why Did Jesus Die? (9:15–28)

The author recognizes that the climactic proclamation of the saving work of Christ in 9:11–14 will be persuasive to the listeners only if he addresses two questions. In the first place, he must demonstrate the relevance of this claim for the weary listeners. In the second place, he must answer the fundamental question that has occupied Christian theologians for centuries: Why did Jesus die? In 9:15–22, he seeks to answer those questions.

9:15. **Therefore** (*dia touto*) in 9:15 suggests that the author now draws a conclusion from the description of the ultimate Day of Atonement (9:11–14) and connects it with its relevance for the readers (9:15b). Having assured his readers earlier that Christ is the mediator of a better covenant (8:6) in which "they will remember sins no more" (8:13), he has shown in 9:1–14 that the sacrifice of Christ was the ultimate Day of Atonement that takes away sins (9:12). Therefore, the sacrifice of Christ announced in 9:11–14 is the inauguration of the new covenant mentioned in chapter 8. As the **mediator of the new covenant** (9:15a), he is analogous to Moses, the mediator of the first covenant. The "mediator" (*mesitēs*) in this instance is not the negotiator between two parties but the guarantor (7:22) of the covenant. This claim recalls the author's earlier assurance that the listeners can believe in the promise because God guaranteed (*emesiteusen*) with the oath (6:17). For listeners who now question the promises, the author reassures them, indicating that the sacrifice of Christ, which cleanses the innermost being of the person, is his guarantee of the new covenant.

The relevance of this saving act for the readers becomes clear as the author indicates the purpose of Christ's saving act: **in order that** (*hopōs*) . . . **those who have been called may receive the promise of the eternal inheritance** (9:15c). "Those who have been called" (*hoi keklēmenoi*) are the listeners (cf. 3:1, "partakers of a heavenly calling"), who have not become Christians at their own initiative but have responded to the invitation of God (cf. 1 Cor 1:9; 7:15, 17; 1 Thess 2:12; 4:7; 5:24). Having held before the readers the certainty of God's promise for an eschatological reward (4:1; 6:12, 15, 17), the author now says that the listeners may receive the promise because **a death has occurred** (9:15b) *thanatou genomenou*). Indeed, the saving significance of this death results in **redemption from the transgressions under the first covenant.** The "redemption from the transgressions" (*apolytrōsis tōn . . . parabaseōn*), the equivalent of the eternal redemption (9:12; *aiōnion lytrōsis*), evokes the image of release of prisoners (i.e., release for prisoners of war [Plutarch, *Pomp.* 24.4] or of slaves [*Epist. Ar.* 12;

An Outline of Hebrews 9:15–28

Josephus, *Ant.* 12.27]). It stands alongside the imagery of purification (1:3; "purification for sins"; cf. 9:13–14) to describe the saving effect of the work of Christ. What those who served at the altar could not do for "the transgressions of the first covenant," Christ has done. Thus the death of Christ is redemptive for "those who have been called" (Grässer 1993, 2:171). Only because of the saving work of Christ can the community have the assurance to receive the promises.

9:16–17. In order to make his case persuasive, the author must explain why the death of Christ was necessary to ensure that Christ is the mediator of the new covenant. In 9:16–22, he offers two explanations based on the nature of a "covenant" (*diathēkē*), a topic he introduced in 7:22 and 8:6–13. Here one may follow the author's argument best by noting his use of *diathēkē*. In the first place, in 9:16–17 he argues that **the death of the one who makes the covenant** (*diathēkē*) **must be established** (lit. "must be brought") (9:16); in 9:17 he elaborates, saying that a *diathēkē* is **valid at death** (lit. "valid over dead bodies"), since it does not remain in force as long as the one who made the *diathēkē* is still living. Thus 9:16–17 appears to be an argument based on a premise drawn from common legal practice. It corresponds to the frequent appeals to premises that he assumes are unquestioned by the readers (cf. *anankē/anankaios*, "must" or "of necessity," in 7:12, 27; 8:3; 9:23; cf. "beyond all dispute" in 6:16; 7:7).

Covenant and Testament

In antiquity and the OT, covenants were a common basis for relationships not based on kinship ties. The OT describes God's covenants with Noah (Gen 9:8–17), Abraham (Gen 15; 17:1–4), the priestly line of Phinehas (Num 25:10–13), and David (2 Sam 7). The Mosaic covenant (Hebrew *berith*) between God and the people is a relationship of mutual obligation in which God pledges faithfulness and protection, to which the people respond with obedience. Covenants in the OT are modeled after treaties in the ancient Near East between the king and his subjects. In the preamble to the covenant, the king declares his beneficence to the people and then gives the stipulations required of the people, as in the Ten Commandments (Exod 20:1–17). Thus the covenantal relationship is not between equals but between the sovereign and his vassals. With few exceptions, the LXX translators rendered the Hebrew *berith* with *diathēkē*, a word that in secular Greek meant "last will and testament." In both Old and New Testaments, *diathēkē* maintained the associations of the Hebrew *berith*. Only in Gal 3:15 and Heb 9:16 does the word contain the ordinary Greek meaning of will, or testament. Hebrews reflects on the meaning of *diathēkē* more than any other NT book. The word is used interchangeably with oath (7:20–22), law (7:19), and promise (8:6). The author's focus is not on human obligation but on God's faithfulness to the promise (cf. 10:23).

Like ancient orators, the author appeals to an aspect of common experience, using comparison (*parabolē*; cf. 9:8), a device that ancient rhetorical theorists considered effective (Backhaus 1996, 195; Grässer 1993, 2:172; cf. Quintilian, *Inst.* 5.11.22–29, 32, 34). The legal analogy is useful for the author because he wishes to insist that Jesus' death was the necessary basis for his becoming mediator of the new covenant. What the author suggests as a valid principle does not, however, hold true for covenants in the Bible, for death is not necessary for a covenant to be in force. Consequently, most translations render *diathēkē* as "testament" or "will," the common meaning in secular Greek. However, this general principle does not precisely fit Hellenistic law either, for in numerous instances the heirs received the bequest before the death of the testator (J. Hughes 1976–1977, 15–17). Thus the general principle in 9:16–17 is based on legal practice but has many exceptions. The author's oscillation between the two meanings of *diathēkē* is not unusual for someone who lives between the Jewish and Greek cultures (Backhaus 1996, 195), for it allows him to make an important play on words, adhering precisely to neither Jewish nor Greek law but reflecting the influence of both.

Undoubtedly the author's statement of a general principle in 9:16–17 looks ahead to the establishment of the Mosaic covenant described in 9:18–22, according to which the death of the sacrificial victim was the basis for the covenant. With this metaphor, Jesus is the one who "makes the will" (*diathemenos*) rather than the mediator (*mesitēs*). Both what is "necessary" (*anankē*) and what is "in force" (*ischyei*) are common terms for ordinances that are legally binding (cf. 7:12). A favorite term for the author is *bebaios/bebaia*, which, in legal parlance, refers to matters that are legally valid, but also have the connotation of those things that are unwavering and reliable (2:2; 3:6; 6:16, 19; 13:9; Backhaus 1996, 197).

The author has made similar appeals to legal practice earlier in the argument. In 2:1–4, he employs legal language, recalling that the first revelation was valid (2:2), but that the revelation in Jesus Christ was validated (2:3) and witnessed by God (2:4). His claim in 6:16–20 that an oath is for confirmation (*bebaiōsis*) and that Christians have a sure and steadfast (*bebaian*) anchor of the soul assures the readers that they have found in the exaltation of Christ the unwavering reality to which they can hold. In 9:16–17, he elaborates on that claim, indicating to his readers that the death of Jesus establishes a covenant that is reliable and steadfast.

9:18–22. The author moves without a transition from the argument from common legal practice to an argument from scripture in 9:18–22, providing a second reason why the death of Jesus was necessary. Just as the legal argument maintains that death is necessary for a law to be in force (9:16–17), the **first** (covenant) **was not inaugurated** (*enkekainistai*) **without blood** (9:18). Thus the focus is on the death of the mediator as the condition for inauguration (9:18), which the author demonstrates in 9:19–22 with an appeal to Exod 24:3–8, the one OT passage that links blood with a covenant.

Typology

Typology was the method of interpretation in Jewish literature and the NT in which events and people become the foreshadowing (types) of the events and people of the new era. Typology is rooted in the OT expectation of a prophet like Moses (Deut 18:15–18), a new creation (Isa 66:22), a new exodus (Isa 43:16–19), and a new covenant (Jer 31:31–34). In the NT, Paul describes Adam as a type of Christ (Rom 5:14) and the events in the wilderness as types for the church (1 Cor 10:6, 11). Typology is to be distinguished from allegory, in which the details of a text are not foreshadowings of future events but symbols for a moral or philosophical truth.

The author does not report everything from the ceremony, such as the response of the people ("all of the words that the Lord has spoken we will do," Exod 24:3, 8) or Moses' construction of the altar (Exod 24:4). Rather he relates the covenant ceremony in such a way as to prepare the reader for typological comparison to the work of Christ (9:11–14, 23–28). In 9:19 he follows the narrative of Exod 24:3–8 in recalling that Moses took **young calves** (*moschōn*; Exod 24:5 LXX *moscharia*) and **sprinkled the people** (Exod 24:8), but he adds to the narrative that Moses took **scarlet wool and hyssop** and **sprinkled the book of the covenant** as well as the people. (Many important manuscripts also add "and goats," combining the covenant ceremony with the Day of Atonement. This addition is most likely a scribal attempt to align the passage with 9:12.) The addition of "scarlet wool and hyssop" suggests that he has combined the ceremony of the red heifer (Num 19:6, 18) with the covenant ceremony, just as he had earlier (9:13) combined it with the Day of Atonement ritual (on the use of hyssop, see also Exod 12:22; Lev 14:4–6; Ps 51:7). The sprinkling of the book (i.e., the Ten Commandments [Exod 20:1–17] and the covenant code [Exod 21:1–23:33]) is not attested in the OT or Jewish literature and may be an inference from the claim that everything in the sanctuary was cleansed (9:21; Grässer 1993, 2:180).

As the citation from Exod 24:8 and the author's interpretation indicate in 9:20–22, his purpose is not to report the details of the covenant ceremony but to focus on the importance of a covenant inaugurated by the sprinkling of blood. In reporting that **the tabernacle and all the vessels for the ministry were sprinkled with blood** (9:21) before the tabernacle was actually constructed and that **almost everything** was **purified with blood** (9:22a), his purpose is to comment on the importance of purification with blood in the entire sacrificial system. He has probably combined OT rituals that speak of the sprinkling of blood to comment on the entire sacrificial system. The maxim **without the shedding of blood there is no forgiveness** (9:22b) corresponds to the earlier maxim that the death of the testator is necessary before a covenant is in force. Thus the author provides the lens for interpreting the death of Jesus as the ultimate "purification for sins" (1:3; 9:14) and demonstrates why the death of Jesus was necessary, preparing the way for the affirmation that the listeners have "hearts sprinkled clean from an evil conscience" (10:22).

9:23–28. In 9:23–28, as in 9:11–14, the author applies the general principles derived from the Levitical system to the Christ event, pulling together the threads of the argument derived from the Levitical priesthood. The opening phrase, **it was necessary that the copies of the things in the heavens be purified with these** (9:23a), summarizes the preceding argument, for the author has established that the Levitical priests minister in a copy of the tabernacle (8:5), purifying both the flesh (9:13) and all the vessels of the sanctuary (9:19) with the blood of animals. In asserting that these sacrifices were "necessary," the author appeals once more to a principle based on the nature of reality and common experience (cf. 2:10, 17; 7:12; 9:16) to which the law conformed (Thompson 1998, 314).

In his statement that **only better sacrifices could effect the purification of the heavenly things** (9:23b), the author introduces a claim that he develops in verses 24–28. The contrast between the purification of the "copies" and the "heavenly things" continues the metaphysical dualism that has shaped the entire argument, for the claim that Christians have a superior priest, a "better covenant," and better sacrifices rests on the dualism between heavenly and earthly realities. In keeping with this dualism, the author's distinction between the purification of the earthly "copies" and of the "heavenly things" has been puzzling to scholars, raising the question of what needed to be purified in the true tabernacle. The context suggests that the author has in mind not specific objects in the heavenly tabernacle but rather the cleansing of the conscience (9:14) from sin.

In 9:24–28, the author explains the nature of the better sacrifice, describing once more the heavenly counterpart to the sacrifice of the high priest on the Day of Atonement (cf. 9:6–14). The statement that Christ did not enter into a sanctuary **made with hands, a mere copy of the true one** (9:24), is a contrast to the entry of the Levitical high priest into the earthly sanctuary on the Day of Atonement (9:1–10; cf. 9:11–12) and the thesis that the author will develop in verses 25–28. The term for "copy" (*antitypos*) corresponds to the earlier comment that Moses saw the "archetype" (*typos*) of the tabernacle on the mountain (8:5), suggesting that the archetype is the true tabernacle in contrast to what is merely a "copy." The author has already indicated that the community has a high priest who has entered behind the curtain (6:19–20) into the heavenly world (cf. 9:11–12) and intercedes (7:25) for his people. Now he reiterates that claim with the statement that Christ **entered . . . to appear before the face of God for us** (9:24b). He has a special interest in the fact that "he entered" (cf. 6:19; 9:11–12; 10:19) through the curtain, for his entrance as forerunner opens the way for others to enter the heavenly world also (cf. 4:1, 3, 6, 10, 11). Thus the exposition of the high priestly work of Christ is no theoretical abstraction, for this work is the sign that the weary community has not been abandoned.

In the elaboration on this thesis in 9:25–28, the focal point of the contrast between the earthly and heavenly sacrifices is the contrast between the once-for-all sacrifice of Christ and the many sacrifices on earth, a reiteration of the earlier contrast between the many mortal high priests and the one exalted high priest (7:23–24). The Platonic assumption is evident: the one belongs to the heavenly world, while the many belong to the physical world that is always undergoing change (see Introductory Matters). Thus he is not like the Levitical priests who enter the sanctuary each year (9:7), for the repetition of their sacrifices reflects imperfection (cf. 10:1–4). If he had been a high priest on earth, **he would have had to suffer many times from the foundation of the world** (9:26a). In contrast to the Levitical high priests, he appeared **once for all** (*hapax*) **to take away sin** (9:26b). Indeed, the threefold use of *hapax* in 9:25–28 indicates the focus of the argument and the reason that Christ has offered a better sacrifice. A heavenly sacrifice is also eternal. Christians have an eternal redemption (9:12) because Christ, like all people (9:27), died once (9:26, 28).

Although the correlation of the dualism of heaven and earth with the one and the many reflects Platonic language, the author's Christian convictions are not totally compatible with Platonism, which had no place for a belief in a saving event effected by the death and resurrection of a savior at a particular moment in history. Thus the author employs the traditional language of Jewish apocalyptic to say that Christ appeared **at the end of the ages** (9:26, *epi synteleia tōn aiōnōn*; cf. Matt 24:3; 28:20) and **will appear a second time without sin for those who await him**. The community lives between the time when God spoke "in these last days" (1:1) through the death and exaltation of Christ and the time when the Son returns. In the meantime the listeners **wait** (9:28; cf. *apekdechesthai*, for eschatological waiting in Rom 8:19, 23, 25; 1 Cor 1:7; Gal 5:5; Phil 3:20) for God's promise, even when they see no signs of God's triumph (2:8). As they wait, the assurance of the finality of the eternal Christ sustains them in the midst of the temptations to drift away.

The Once-for-All Sacrifice (10:1–18)

In this section the author comes to the conclusion of the "word" that is "hard to explain" (5:11), preparing the way for the exhortation that begins in 10:19. Having attempted to rebuild the community's shattered world in this description of the high priestly work of Christ, his final words are not the occasion to break new ground but to summarize and draw a climactic conclusion. The argument continues the motif of *synkrisis* that has shaped it from the beginning. In 10:1–10, he again contrasts the Levitical sacrifices (10:1–4) with

**An Outline
of Hebrews 10:1–18**

The once-for-all sacrifice (10:1–18)

A shadow of the coming good things (10:1)

A reminder of sins (10:2–4)

I have come to do your will (10:5–10)

Perfected forever (10:11–18)

the sacrifice of Christ (10:5–10) before moving to a new contrast in 10:11–14. The quotation of Jer 31:33 in 10:15–17 forms an *inclusio* with the earlier citation of the same passage in 8:8–12, providing a frame for the entire discussion and indicating that the entire section is an explanation of the new covenant, under which God would remember sins no more (8:12).

10:1. The author begins the new comparison with a reiteration of the argument that he has consistently given. As the foundation for the sacrificial system (7:5, 12; 8:4; 9:19, 22), the law is **unable to perfect those who draw near** (cf. 7:11, 19; 9:9–10) because it has only a **shadow of the good things to come rather than the form of these things** (*eikona tōn pragmatōn*). As in the earlier parts of the argument, the language resonates with the Platonic antithesis between the shadow and the reality (8:2, 5; 9:1, 11–14, 24), although in this instance "form" (*eikōn*) is not a synonym for "shadow" (*skia*), as it was for Plato, but the actual reality. The claim that the sacrifices are unable to perfect those who draw near is a restatement of the earlier argument that sacrifices in the sphere of the flesh are unable to perfect the conscience (9:9). Those who draw near are not only the priests but all the worshipers who have no access to God (9:8), for only the listeners who benefit from the entry of Christ into the sanctuary can now draw near (4:16; 10:19).

The statement that the sacrifices are brought **each year** (*kat' eniauton*), an allusion to the ritual of the Day of Atonement (cf. 9:7, 25), is the focal point of the author's argument in 10:1–14, establishing the incompleteness of the Levitical sacrifices and the basis for the comparison to the finality of the work of Christ. Annual sacrifices that are offered **forever** (*eis to diēnekes*) provide the basis for the comparison to the one whose single sacrifice is "forever" (*eis to diēnekes*, 10:12, 14), indicating that nothing belonging to the physical world is eternal.

Despite the Platonic language of 10:1, the author is not consistently Platonic, for his contrast is not only between the heavenly and the earthly realities. In saying that the law has a "shadow of the good things to come," he is also making the familiar eschatological contrast between two successive ages. He has introduced this contrast at the beginning of the homily when he declared that God has spoken "in these last days" (1:1) and alluded to it again when he affirmed that the listeners have "tasted the powers of the coming age" (6:5) in which a new priesthood and a new covenant have replaced their older counterparts (7:11–12; 8:6, 13). Living between two worlds, the author has employed the language of both to declare that the ministry of Christ is both final and metaphysically superior to any alternative that may tempt the community, for only the ministry of Christ is ultimate.

10:2–4. In 10:2–4, the author reinforces the case for the limitations of the old sacrificial system, pressing the implications of sacrifices offered "each year." In 10:2–3, he draws the logical conclusion (cf. similar logical deductions in 4:8; 7:11; 8:6) that the repetition of sacrifices each year indicates their ineffectiveness at the deepest level. Inasmuch as those who are **once cleansed** (10:2; *hapax kekatharismenoi*), unlike the listeners (cf. 6:4, "those once enlightened," *hapax phōtisthentoi*), still have a **consciousness of sins** (*syneidēsis hamartiōn*), their purification is not once for all. Because the earthly sacrifices could not cleanse the conscience (*syneidēsis*, 9:9, 14), the worshipers in the Levitical system, in contrast to the listeners, continue to have an evil conscience (cf. 10:22). For the author, as for Philo (*Worse* 146), the conscience is the judge of one's acts of unrighteousness (Grässer 1993, 2:209).

The corollary to the conclusion that the sacrifices do not remove the consciousness of sins is that they are a **reminder of sins** (*anamnēsis tōn hamartiōn*) **each year** (10:3) rather than the removal of sins (9:26). The author may be alluding to the grain offering of remembrance administered to the suspected adulteress (Num 5:15) or occasions when sin is "brought to remembrance" (1 Kgs 17:18). His conclusion resembles Philo's statement that worshipers who come to God without kindly feeling or justice experience not a "remission but a reminder of past sins" (*Moses* 2.107). For Philo, however, this judgment applies only to the unrighteous who come before God, while for Hebrews this judgment extends to the entire sacrificial system.

The author moves from comments about the defects of the Levitical system (10:1–3) to the generic statement that **it is impossible for the blood of bulls and goats to take away sins** (10:4), which is unparalleled in the OT or Jewish literature. Although writers frequently noted that sacrifices were ineffective without appropriate conduct, no one made such an absolute claim as this. The statement is one of the author's frequent maxims indicating what is either "impossible" (*adynatos*, 6:4, 18; 11:6) or necessary (*anankē*, 7:12, 27; 9:16, 23), assuming that the readers will assent. In this instance, his categorical statement resembles the ancient Greek critique of material sacrifices. The Levitical sacrifices are ineffective because all material sacrifices are ineffective. This conclusion indicates that the author is engaged in a polemic not against Judaism but against all approaches to God that are alternatives to the sacrifice of Christ.

10:5–10. Just as the author has previously argued that the sacrifice of Christ is the alternative to ineffective sacrifices (9:1–14, 23–28), he again describes the work of Christ in 10:5–10 in a midrash on Ps 40:6–8 (39:7–9 LXX). **Therefore coming into the world, he says** (10:5a), is reminiscent of earlier quotations from scripture that are introduced as the words of Christ (2:12–13). His coming into the world recalls the incarnation, when he was "a little while lower than the angels" (2:9). Jesus is, therefore, the one who expresses the words of the psalm.

In the original context, Ps 40 (39 LXX), the psalmist expresses gratitude for God's mercy in saving him from death or severe illness (Ps 40:2). Although the usual response in such cases was a sacrifice of thanksgiving (Ps 50:23; 56:12; 107:22; 116:14, 18), the psalmist declares that God does not require the offering (cf. Amos 5:21–24; Hos 6:6). According to the Hebrew text, God has given the psalmist an open ear instead of demanding a sacrifice. The author's citation of Ps 40:6 (39:7 LXX) follows the LXX, **you have prepared a body for me** (10:5b). With this citation the author suggests that the body of Jesus has replaced all sacrifices of the Levitical cult. The "body" referred to here is reminiscent of the earlier reference to "the days of his flesh" (5:7) and to the suffering that culminated in the cross.

The author's interpretation of the citation in 10:8–10 indicates the primary focus of the citation. Jesus' statement, **I have come to do your will** (10:9a), supersedes the **sacrifices, gifts, and burnt offerings** (10:8) offered according to the law. The statement **he takes away one in order to establish another** (10:9b) appeals to the same hermeneutical method that the author has used earlier (4:8; 7:11; 8:6): the latter passage nullifies and replaces the earlier. Just as the new covenant replaces the old covenant (8:6, 13), the event in which Jesus did the will of God in his sacrificial death replaced the sacrifices of the Levitical covenant. This interpretation may rest on common legal practice, according to which a later codicil replaces the earlier testament. The relevance of this principle for the readers becomes evident when the author moves from abstract principles to the experience of the listeners, which is indicated by the first-person plural: **We**, unlike those who minister in earthly sanctuaries, **are being sanctified through the offering of the body of Jesus Christ once for all** (10:10). This sacrifice is not a perpetual "reminder of sins" (10:3), for we have reached the goal of the new covenant according to which God "will remember their sins no more" (8:12). In the claim that this event is "once for all" (*ephapax*), the author reaches the goal of this section, reiterating a major theme of the contrast between the one and the many (cf. 7:23–27; 9:25–28; 10:1–4). The sacrifice that is "once for all" is the alternative to the many animal sacrifices that remain imperfect and incomplete.

10:11–18. In 10:11–18, the author concludes this section with a final *synkrisis* in order to establish the finality of the Christ event, returning to the themes announced in chapter 8. He returns to the theme of the one and the many, contrasting **every priest** (cf. 5:1; 8:3) **offering sacrifices many times** (10:11) with Christ, who offered a single sacrifice **for all time** (10:14; *eis to diēnekes*; cf. 7:3). The author adds a new dimension to the argument, contrasting the priests who **stood** (10:11) with the one who **sat down at the right hand of God** (10:12), suggesting that the normal posture of priests (1 Kgs 8:11; 13:1; 2 Chron 29:11; 1 Esd 1:2, 5, 10; cf. Grässer 1993, 2:228) is a sign of the incompleteness of their work. With the citation of Ps 110:1 the author returns to the theme of exaltation of Christ (cf. 1:3; 8:1), which provides the frame for the argument that began with the declaration that the high priest according to the order of Melchizedek is "eternal" (*eis to diēnekes*, 7:3) because he is "at God's right hand." Thus, in contrast to the Levitical priests, he "sat down," indicating that his work is forever (*eis to diēnekes*).

Because the community cannot see the final triumph envisioned by Ps 110:1, as the author indicated earlier (cf. 2:8, "we do not see all things in subjection"), the further allusion to Ps 110:1 indicates that the exalted one continues to wait until all enemies are under his feet, just as the community continues to wait (cf. 10:36–40) for the final realization of the promise. Nevertheless, it has the assurance that by one sacrifice he perfected "forever" (*eis to diēnekes*) **those who are being sanctified** (10:14). The high priest who is "eternal" (7:3, *eis to diēnekes*) is, therefore, the one who has perfected "forever" (*eis to diēnekes*) "those who are being sanctified."

In 10:15, the author supports his final claim with a reiteration of Jer 31:33 (cf. 8:7–13). The final line of the prophecy has been the focal point of the "word" that is "hard to explain" (5:11) for it points to the time when God will **remember their sins . . . no more** (10:17). Having demonstrated that this prophecy has been realized in the sacrifice of Jesus in the heavenly sanctuary, the author concludes, where there is forgiveness of these things there is no longer a sacrifice for sins. Unlike the unfinished Levitical sacrifices, this sacrifice is complete; no other sacrifices are needed.

Theological Issues

The extended description of the sacrifice of the heavenly high priest is an elaboration of the promise of Jeremiah, "I will forgive their iniquity and remember their sins no more" (Heb 8:12). By interpreting the death of Jesus as the saving event, the author joins other NT writers in elaborating on the early Christian creed, "Christ died for our sins in accordance with the scriptures" (cf. 1 Cor 15:3). His interpretation both develops earlier images and explores new ways of interpreting the meaning of the cross. With earlier writers, the author affirms that the death of Jesus effects "redemption" (*lytrōsis*, 9:12; *apolytrōsis*, 9:15; cf. Matt 20:28; Luke 1:68; Titus 2:14; 1 Pet 1:18) and "forgiveness of sins" (*aphesis*, 9:22; 10:18; cf. Matt 26:28), and that the shedding of Jesus' blood is the basis for a new covenant (9:15–22; cf. 1 Cor 11:25). He also develops the images from the sacrificial system that he inherits from earlier tradition, expanding on the early Christian interpretation of Jesus' death as expiation (*hilastērion*, Rom 3:25), arguing that Jesus "made expiation for sins" (Heb 2:17), and elaborating on that theme in the central section of the homily. With this extended section, the author gives the most detailed interpretation of the death of Jesus in the NT.

The OT offers no precise theory as to how the animal sacrifice could remove sin and guilt for the community. Nor did NT writers, including the author of Hebrews, offer a comprehensive explanation of how the death of one took away the sins of many. Only in later centuries did theologians attempt to provide a coherent explanation of the necessity of Jesus' death. They produced two main answers. Some argued that the death of Jesus propitiated God's wrath, while others maintained that he averted the threat of the devil. The first employs legal metaphors, while the second employs the language of the battlefield to describe a victory over evil powers (Fiddes 1989, 69). John Chrysostom suggested that the death of Jesus softened the anger of God against sin and won him over to us (*Hom. Heb.* 29). Anselm of Canterbury gave classic expression to the satisfaction theory of atonement, according to which God demands satisfaction for the offense against the divine honor. Since humans cannot pay the debt, God sent Christ to give payment, "because only man *must* pay the debt of honor, and only God can *pay* it" (Fiddes 1989, 97). Calvin argued that Christ paid a debt to the justice of God by taking the punishment for humankind (*Institutes of the Christian Religion* 2.16.3–5). The battlefield metaphor has a long history in Christian thought. According to this view, the cross was the great battlefield where Christ, in his weakness, defeated Satan. Many early church figures, including Origen, Augustine, and Gregory of Nyssa, interpreted the cross as the battle against Satan.

The battlefield imagery in Heb 2:14–15, according to which "through death he destroyed the power of death, that is the devil," undoubtedly suggested an image that the church fathers developed. At the cross, Jesus "rescued those who live constantly in the fear of death." The author weaves this image into a broader tapestry that he gives in great detail in 8:1–10:31.

The death of Jesus was an act of solidarity on the part of the one who was "like his brothers in every respect" (2:17). With his "loud cries and tears" (5:7) he shared the human situation. His suffering was the path to perfection (2:10; 5:9). Thus the shedding of his blood in the heavenly sanctuary (9:11–14) involves both Good Friday and Easter as a single event in which Jesus shared human suffering as a prelude to his exaltation.

The Levitical cultus provided the author with the imagery for portraying the impact of the cross in taking away sin in a more profound way than the images from the law court or battlefield. The depiction of Jesus' death as the purification for sins (1:3) and the claim that he "made expiation for sins" (2:17) anticipate the extended description of the work of Christ in 8:1–10:18. The imagery, which is taken primarily from the celebration of the Day of Atonement (Lev 16), suggests that sin is uncleanness that must be blotted out by divine mercy in order to restore a relationship to God. Indeed, sin is so serious that only the shedding of blood can purify the stain (Heb 9:22–23;

10:2). Thus, when the author declares that Jesus sanctifies (2:11; 10:10, 29; 13:12) and purifies (9:14) through the shedding of his blood, he indicates the seriousness of sin and the extraordinary means of removing the stain. Indeed, in the claim that the death of Jesus purifies the conscience (9:14), he affirms that this act cleanses the innermost part of the person from the awareness of guilt that creates a separation from God.

The author makes a distinctive contribution to the interpretation of the sacrifice of Jesus in his focus on Jesus' death as the pathway of the Christian's access to God. The image of the way that was formerly closed (9:8) but is now open (10:19) because of the death and exaltation of Jesus is the basis for the invitation to "draw near" to God with a clean conscience (10:22). Only because the stain has been removed can the community come before God. The appropriate response to God's saving work is to worship (Long 1998, 68), knowing that Christ has taken away human guilt.

Although sacrificial language is familiar to people in many parts of the world, few readers in Europe and North America can envision the sights and smells that accompany an animal sacrifice. Nevertheless, by this imagery Hebrews addresses concerns that are universal. Hebrews indicates an acute awareness of the seriousness of sin and the futility of human attempts to address the most fundamental human problems. In cultures that are familiar with animal sacrifices, Hebrews indicates that the death of Christ is the ultimate sacrifice that puts an end to all other sacrifices (Bediako 2000). The claim that only the death of Jesus cleanses the conscience addresses the brokenness of other human societies, offering a reminder that the fundamental problem is the separation from God that results from human rebellion. The comparison between sacrifices that cleanse the flesh and the sacrifice that cleanses the conscience speaks to those who look for alternative means to heal human brokenness, claiming that only the death of Jesus removes the stain of sin. Although the author does not employ Paul's judicial imagery of justification by faith, he shares with Paul the conviction that only God's grace, and no human work, reconciles humanity to God (cf. Grässer 1976, 93).

Hebrews 10:19–31

Drawing Near and Holding Firmly
in an Unwavering Faith

Introductory Matters

The transition signaled by "having therefore" in 10:19 clearly marks the shift from exposition to exhortation and a major transition in the argument. Scholars debate, however, where both this unit and the central section of Hebrews ends and the last major section of Hebrews begins. Since the exhortation extends through 10:39 before a new rhetorical form begins, some scholars maintain that all of 10:19–39 belongs to the preceding section, drawing the implications from the exposition in 7:1–10:18. Others, however, maintain that 10:19 marks the beginning of the final section of Hebrews, an exhortation calling for the readers to be steadfast. Thus, although many scholars conclude that Hebrews has three major divisions, they do not agree about the precise boundaries of these sections. This uncertainty is a result of the author's rhetorical artistry, for he often moves smoothly from one topic to another, anticipating themes in one section before developing them in another.

Despite the difficulty of demarcating the divisions, two structural signals are important for ascertaining the author's purpose. In the first place, the *inclusio* of 4:14–16 and 10:19–25 suggests that these exhortations provide the frame for the central section on the high priestly work of Christ, dividing the homily into three sections. Both passages begin with "having therefore" (*echontes oun*) to point to the community's possession of a "great priest" ("great high priest" in 4:14) as the basis for the exhortations, "let us draw near" (4:16; 10:22) and "let us hold fast the confession" (4:14; 10:23). Both exhortations speak of the exaltation of Christ as the opening of the way for the community to enter the heavenly sanctuary with "boldness" (4:16; 10:19; *parrēsia*). The exhortation in 10:19–25 includes the additional exhortation, "let us stir one another up to love and good works" (10:24). In the second place, despite the new rhetorical form in chapter 11, this unit follows smoothly from 10:32–39, exploring the meaning of faith. Thus the central section concludes with the positive encouragement (10:19–25) and warning (10:26–31), summarizing the implications of the supreme sacrifice of Christ for the listeners. The final section of Hebrews begins in 10:32 with the call for faithfulness that dominates the last section.

The location of the lengthy treatment of the high priestly ministry of Christ (5:1–10:18) between parallel exhortations (4:14–16 and 10:19–25) indicates that the author's concern throughout the "word" that is "hard to explain" (5:11) has been to reestablish the community's original commitment. After providing the "solid food" that will give them the nutrition for their health and vitality, he now explores the practical implications for his wavering community. Just as Paul appeals to his readers to respond to the saving work of Christ by conducting themselves "worthy of the gospel" (Phil 1:27), the author urges his listeners toward the appropriate response to the work of Christ in the heavenly sanctuary.

In 10:26–31, the author elaborates on the warning of 6:4–6, describing the consequences of refusing the saving work of Christ in terms drawn from the OT. The "deliberate sin" recalls the distinction between those who commit unintentional sins (Lev 4:1–5:13; Num 15:22–29) and those whose offenses are committed "with a high hand" (Num 15:30–31). The latter will be cut off from Israel because they "despised the word of the Lord." This distinction is widely known in Jewish literature. The Dead Sea Scrolls (1QS 5.10–12) distinguish between deliberate and unintentional sins and develop an extensive set of regulations on the topic (1QS 6.24–7.25; 8.21–9.2; Grässer 1997, 3:35). Philo speaks of unintentional sins, which receive no punishment (*Unchangeable* 128; *Drunkenness* 162–163; *Posterity* 10), and the voluntary sins that outrage reason (*Posterity* 184). "The voluntary act, inasmuch as it was committed with forethought and of set purpose, must incur woes for ever beyond healing" (*Posterity* 11, trans. Colson and Whitaker 1929). While Jewish tradition identified the deliberate sin with blasphemy against the Torah or the deity, Hebrews identifies it with abandoning the community where God's saving gifts are received.

Tracing the Train of Thought

Entrance into the Sanctuary (10:19–25)

10:19–21. In 10:19 the author draws the full implications for the readers, addressing them directly as **brothers** (10:19a, *adelphoi*) for the first time since

3:1 and recalling the kinship language of 2:10–18. Here, as elsewhere (cf. 4:14; 8:1; 12:1–2), what "we have" as a result of the work of Christ is the basis for the exhortation "let us" (10:22). In the two objects of the verb, the author summarizes the argument of 7:1–10:18. "We have," in the first place, **boldness** (*parrēsia*). This boldness is no subjective feeling but the right of access to God (cf. 4:16), a gift to maintain (3:6) and not throw away (10:36). In keeping with the sacrificial imagery, it is the right of **entrance** (*eisodos*) into the sanctuary by the blood of Christ. *Eisodos* is not the term used in the LXX but is a common term in Philo (*Spec. Laws* 1.261) and Josephus (*Ant.* 19.332) for entry into the sanctuary. It echoes the description of the entry of priests (9:6, 12) into the Levitical sanctuary and the ultimate entry of Christ into the heavenly tabernacle (9:12) when he offered his blood (9:13–14). Thus in the boldness for entrance **into the sanctuary by the blood of Jesus** (10:19b), the community comes into the heavenly sanctuary, just as the Levitical priests once entered the earthly tabernacle.

This entrance is made possible because he **opened for us a new and living way through the curtain** (10:20a). To "open" (*enkainizein*) is literally to "dedicate" or "inaugurate" (BDAG, 272). The term is used in 9:18 for Moses' inauguration of the first covenant. In the OT, it is used both for the dedication of a new house (Deut 20:5) and the dedication of Solomon's temple (1 Kgs 8:63). The noun form *enkainia* was used for the rededication of the temple by Judas the Maccabee (1 Macc 4:42–59; 2 Macc 1:7–9, 18; 2:16; 10:1–8), and was celebrated as the Feast of Dedication (cf. John 10:22). Thus the image suggests that the heavenly high priest opened up a way that had been closed (9:8), accomplishing what the Levitical priests could not do. As the author has indicated earlier, at the exaltation, Jesus Christ went through the curtain into the heavenly world (6:19–20). The image of opening up the way also incorporates the author's earlier depictions of a people on the way following their pioneer (2:10) and forerunner (6:19–20) who opens up the way for others to follow.

Hebrews 10:19–31 in the Rhetorical Flow

Hearing God's word with faithful endurance (1:1–4:13)

***Probatio*: Discovering certainty and confidence in the word for the mature (4:14–10:31)**

  Drawing near and holding firmly: following the path of Jesus from suffering to triumph (4:14–5:10)

  Preparing to hear the word that is hard to explain (5:11–6:20)

  Grasping the anchor in the word for the mature: the sacrificial work of Christ as the assurance of God's promises (7:1–10:18)

▶ **Drawing near and holding firmly in an unwavering faith (10:19–31)**

  Entrance into the sanctuary (10:19–25)

    A new and living way (10:19–21)

    Let us draw near (10:22)

    Let us hold firm (10:23)

    Let us stir one another up (10:24)

    Not abandoning the assembly (10:25)

  Deliberate sin (10:26–31)

What the author means by "through the curtain," **that is, his flesh** (10:20b), is a matter of debate, for "flesh" is an unexpected appositive for "curtain." Some have tried to solve the unusual expression by suggesting that the genitive phrase "[of] his flesh" describes "the way" (i.e., "the way through his flesh"; Westcott 1890, 320–21; Spicq 1952, 2:316). A more likely reading is to recognize the parallelism in 10:19–20. The author affirms in 10:19 that the community has an entrance into the sanctuary by the blood of Jesus, and he reassures them in 10:20 that they have a way through the curtain by means of the "flesh" of Jesus (*dia tou katapetasmatos, tout' estin tēs sarkos autou*). Just as the English word "through" can be used to indicate both direction and means, the author has made dual use of *dia*. Similarly, in 9:11–12, he declared that Jesus "entered through (*dia* = direction) the greater and more perfect tent" and obtained eternal redemption "through (*dia* = means) his own blood." Thus Jesus opened up the way through the offering of his blood (10:19) and flesh (10:20).

The enigmatic phrase "through the curtain, that is, his flesh" is a summary of the author's portrayal of the saving significance of Jesus. As one who shared "flesh and blood" (2:14) with his brothers and sisters, he obtained glory and honor (2:9–10) only after the suffering of death. "The days of his flesh" (5:7) were filled with suffering, but they were the prelude to his entry behind the curtain as the forerunner of the people (6:20). He offered his blood in the heavenly sanctuary (9:11–14) and presented his body to God once for all (10:5–10). Thus the flesh and blood of Jesus, offered as a sacrifice, provide the entry of the people into the presence of God.

In the second place, the community has a **great priest over the house of God** (10:21; cf. Zech 6:11 for "great priest"), as the author has already demonstrated in 7:1–10:18, indicating the role of the priest as the one who draws near to God to intercede for the people (7:25). Although the "house of God" may recall the author's description of the tabernacle, the community is also God's house (3:6; cf. 1 Pet 2:4–10). As partakers in a heavenly calling (3:1), they belong to "the church of the firstborn whose names are written in heaven" (12:23). Thus, although they see only the deprivations associated with the house church, they have the assurance that they have a heavenly sanctuary.

This assurance is the basis for the exhortations that follow in 10:23–25, for without the knowledge that the community has "boldness to enter the sanctuary" and a "great priest over the house of God," the community would have no resource to prevent members from "fall[ing] away from the living God" (3:12; cf. 2:1–4; 6:4). In the three hortatory subjunctives in 10:22–25 ("let us draw near . . . let us hold fast . . . let us consider . . .") that follow the restatement of what the community "has" (10:19–21), the author challenges the readers to respond to the saving work of the exalted high priest with faith (10:22), hope (10:23), and love (10:24).

10:22. The challenge **Let us draw near** (10:22a) is an invitation for the whole community to come into the presence of God (cf. 4:16, "to the throne of grace") in the house of the great priest, doing what was once only the privilege of the high priest (cf. Lev 9:7–8; 21:17; 22:3). The community draws near in worship and prayer because the exalted one "is able to save always those who draw near" in order to intercede for them (7:25). The accompanying disposition of those who draw near indicates that the author is addressing the temptations that now face the community (Weiss 1991, 828). Instead of the "evil unbelieving heart" that was characteristic of the wilderness generation (cf. 3:10, 12), the community may now come before God **with a true heart**, for it lives in the time of the new covenant when God's will is written "on their hearts" (8:10; 10:16). Unlike the wilderness generation, which did not enter the promised land because of lack of faith (3:12, 19; 4:2), the listeners may now approach God **in the full assurance of faith** (10:22b). Furthermore, the listeners may now draw near **with hearts sprinkled clean from an evil conscience and their bodies washed with pure water** (10:22c), unlike the worshipers in the Levitical system, whose consciences were never cleansed by the earthly sacrifices (9:9–10; 10:1–4). While the Levitical sacrifices cleansed only the flesh (9:9), Christians now have experienced the once-for-all cleansing of both the conscience and the body (Weiss 1991, 529).

This event in the lives of the listeners is equivalent to the pivotal moment described in 6:4–5, according to which the readers had "once been enlightened, tasted the heavenly gift, become partakers of the Holy Spirit, tasted the good word of God and the powers of the coming age." The imagery of washing suggests that this pivotal moment came at baptism, an event that has permanent significance for them. Like the Levitical priests, who cleansed themselves before drawing near to God, the listeners have also been cleansed. The prophecy of the new covenant has become a reality in the death of Jesus (8:7–13; 10:15–18), and Ezekiel's prophecy of a time when God would "sprinkle clean water" on Israel and cleanse the people, removing from their bodies the heart of stone (Ezek 36:25–26), has occurred in their lives.

This defining event now has lasting effects as the community demonstrates "full assurance of faith" (*plērophoria pisteōs*), which is the equivalent of the "full assurance of hope" (*plērophoria tēs elpidos*) that the author previously challenged the community to demonstrate (6:11). As the author's definition of hope indicates (11:1), faith and hope are intertwined, for both terms point toward the promises of God that are yet to be fulfilled. The "full assurance" (*plērophoria*) is the "complete certainty" (BDAG, 827) that has no doubt or hesitation (Spicq 1952, 2:317) provided to the community by the saving work of Christ. As the author indicates in chapter 11, faith is no subjective feeling but the "conviction of things that are unseen" (11:1) that results in the endurance in all circumstances (10:36–39).

10:23. The second exhortation, **let us hold fast to the unwavering confession of hope** (10:23a), also suggests the lasting effects and the stable foundation of the community, for the "confession of hope" (*homologia tēs elpidos*) is probably the baptismal confession that the readers voiced at the beginning of their Christian existence (cf. 3:1). Indeed, the "word" that is "hard to explain" (7:1–10:18) is probably an elaboration on the baptismal confession in which the author has demonstrated the greatness of the saving work of Christ. Although most translations render the word "unwavering" (*aklinē*) as an adverb (i.e., "let us hold fast . . . unwaveringly"), the term can best be rendered as an adjective ("unwavering confession"), indicating the certainty of the community's faith (Weiss 1991, 532; Grässer 1997, 3:25). The term *aklinē(s)*, which appears nowhere else in the NT or the LXX, is a synonym for *bebaios* (Spicq 1952, 2:318), a term used frequently in Hebrews and translated "firm" or "valid" (cf. 2:2–3; 3:14; 6:19; 9:17). According to 6:19, the author assures his readers that they have a "firm and stable anchor of the soul" (*ankyran tēs psychēs asphalē te kai bebaian*). Having described this "unwavering confession" in 7:1–10:18, the author now insists that the community "hold on" to the confession rather than let it slip away. This exhortation reaffirms the author's earlier challenge for the community to "hold on (*katechein*) to the boldness and boasting of hope" (3:6), "hold on (*katechein*) to the firm beginning until the end" (3:14), to "hold fast (*kratein*) to the confession" (4:14), and to "hold fast to the hope" (6:18). Thus if the community is to avoid the present danger of drifting away (2:1) or falling away from the living God (3:12), it must "hold on" to the confession it has made, for God's great gifts require that the people grasp them. Like Philo of Alexandria, the author knows that only when people hold to a stable reality can they find stability for themselves. The "unwavering confession" offers the community a reality that the community can hold.

The ultimate reason that the community can "hold fast" is that **the (God) who has promised is faithful** (10:23b; on God's faithfulness, see Deut 7:9; 32:4; Ps 89:24; Isa 49:7 LXX; 1 Cor 1:9; 10:13; 2 Cor 1:18), as the author has demonstrated in 7:1–10:18. In the saving work of Christ, the God who cannot lie (6:18) has "guaranteed with an oath" (6:17). Consequently, the promise to enter into God's rest remains available (4:1–11) because the crucified and exalted Christ is the "guarantor of a better covenant" (8:6), enabling Christians to "receive the promise of the eternal inheritance" (9:15). Thus, like Abraham, the community can hold on in the midst of alienation and estrangement, knowing that "the one who promised is faithful" (11:11). The faithfulness of the community is thus the response to God's faithfulness.

10:24. Having called the community to faith (10:22) and hope (10:23), the author encourages the community, **Let us consider how to provoke one another to love and good works** (10:24), suggesting that members of the community cannot hold on to their confession alone. Having previously encouraged the readers to "consider (*katanoein*) Jesus," he now invites them to "consider (*katanoein*) one another," knowing that those who have lost familiar relationships and belongings (10:32–34) because of their confession can maintain their convictions only when they replace the familial relationships that they have lost. The Christian community is, therefore, a new family (2:10–13; 3:1–6), demonstrating cohesiveness in both a positive and a negative way (10:24–25). It demonstrates such positive aspects of solidarity as provoking others to "love and good works." The term *paroxysmos*, a medical term referring to a high degree of fever (Spicq 1952, 2:318; Galen, *Diff. febr.* 7.325.15–16; 7.336.14; etc.), normally has the negative sense of "irritation" or "provocation" (cf. Acts 17:16; 1 Cor 13:5 for the verb *paroxynein*; Acts 15:39 has the noun *paroxysmos*, "sharp disagreement") but can also have the sense of provoking someone to do good (Xenophon, *Mem.* 3.3.13), as it does in the appeal to provoke others "to love and good works." The author has recalled earlier the "work of love" exhibited by the community in the earlier days (6:9) as they "ministered to the saints." Undoubtedly the "work of love" includes the community's solidarity in response to persecution (10:32–34), when they "became partners" with those who suffered and showed sympathy for the prisoners. Now the author encourages them to reinvigorate the love that they had demonstrated in the past.

10:25. In the subordinate clause, **not abandoning the assembly of yourselves together, as is the practice of some** (10:25a), the author indicates in negative terms what community cohesion means, for no one can provoke others to love and good works without being present with the community. The author may be distinguishing between those who now "abandon the assembly" and those who have irrevocably fallen away (cf. 3:12; 6:4), suggesting that the abandonment of the assembly is a step toward the apostasy described earlier in the homily (2:1–4; 3:12; 6:4–6). The seriousness of abandoning the assembly is evident in the use of the word *enkataleipein*, which has the connotation of "leave in the lurch" (Johnson 2006, 261; cf. Matt 27:46 par. Mark 15:34 for Jesus' cry of abandonment; cf. also 2 Tim 4:10, "Demas has abandoned me"; Heb 13:5, "God will not abandon you"). To "abandon" the assembly is to reject the privilege of drawing near to God's sanctuary and to throw away the boldness (10:35) to enter the way opened up by Jesus, the high priest. The term "assembly" (*episynagōgē*), which is used in only one other instance in the NT (2 Thess 2:1), suggests that the author has chosen the word for the eschatological gathering of God's people (2 Macc 2:7), indicating that the gatherings in the house churches were nothing less than a gathering of a community that spans heaven and earth. Thus to abandon the assembly is to reject God's ultimate gift.

Although he does not tell why "some" are no longer present in the assembly, the most likely reason is that many have become weary with the seemingly unending pilgrimage that has brought disappointment and resulted in alienation from the society around them (10:32–34), leading them to wonder if their commitment to the Christian confession was worthwhile. In order to

---

The Day

Old Testament prophets spoke of the "Day of the Lord" (cf. Isa 2:12; 13:6; Joel 1:15; 2:31; Amos 5:18; Zech 14:1), a day of divine judgment. Since early Christians called Jesus "Lord," they spoke of the return of Christ (1 Cor 5:5; 1 Thess 5:2) as "the day of the Lord." In some instances, they spoke of "the day of the Lord Jesus Christ" (1 Cor 1:8), "the day of the Lord Jesus" (2 Cor 1:14), and "the day of Christ" (Phil 1:10; 2:16). In other instances the phrase is abbreviated to "the day" (2 Tim 1:12, 18; 4:8; Heb 10:25).

---

prevent this discouragement, the author once more calls on the members to **encourage one another** (10:25b; cf. 3:13) because the entrance into the promised land is not for isolated individuals but for communities whose members worship together and care for one another.

Although the community may be discouraged by the apparently endless waiting, the author assures them that their motivation to encourage one another is founded not only on what they have already (10:19) but also on the fact that they **see the day approaching** (10:25c). Indeed, the need for mutual encouragement is **all the more** urgent because the day is drawing near. The promise is not in the indefinite future but is now coming nearer. Like other early Christian writers, the author speaks of "the day" as an abbreviation for "day of judgment" (Matt 25:13; Luke 21:34; Rom 2:5, 16; 1 Cor 3:13) or "day of the Lord" (1 Cor 1:8; 2 Cor 1:14; Phil 1:6, 10; 1 Thess 5:2; 2 Pet 3:10). Like Paul in particular, he motivates his readers to intense ethical behavior by reminding them of the imminence of the final day (Rom 13:12; 1 Cor 7:29–31). Although he does not say when this "day" will come, he reminds his readers on several occasions of the certainty of the day of judgment (2:1–4; 3:13–19; 10:26–31; 12:25–29), when they will either enter the promised rest (4:1–11) or be excluded from God's promises.

The warning issued in 10:26–31, like the parallel in 6:4–6, has been one of the most perplexing passages of the homily for interpreters who have attempted to fit it within a comprehensive theology of apostasy and settle issues in the life of the church (see comments on 6:4–6). The author is not, however, offering a comprehensive theory but is attempting to maintain community cohesion and persuade the community to remain faithful on the pilgrimage to the final destination. This passage recapitulates earlier warnings about the consequences of falling away from God (2:1–4; 3:7–19; 6:4–6). Although the possibility that some will "sin deliberately" is very real, it remains hypothetical, for no member has yet abandoned the community totally. Thus rhetorical and sociological insights illuminate the passage. The warning is an example of *deinōsis*, the attempt to shock the audience with an appeal to fear (see p. 124). Like the warning in 6:4–6, the argument is a logical inference from the *synkrisis* in the central section (7:1–10:18), indicating that the finality of the work of Christ necessitates the finality of the readers' reception of the heavenly gift. That is, the greater the salvation, the greater the punishment for those who abandon it. The argument from the lesser to the greater is a common rhetorical device in Paul (cf. Rom 5:7–11; 2 Cor 3:7–11), Philo, and rabbinic literature, and it was recommended in the rhetorical handbooks (cf. Quintilian, *Inst.* 5.11.9–12). The author uses the argument consistently in exhortations (2:1–4; 7:26–28; 12:25–29) to persuade his readers to remain faithful.

Sociological realities also illuminate the author's attempt at persuasion. A community that is alienated from its society needs cohesion in order to survive. Because deviation from the symbolic world that the author has presented in 7:1–10:18 would undermine the fabric of the community, the warning serves "a therapeutic function, as a preventive measure acting on potential deviants to stay within the institutionalized definitions of reality" (Salevao 2002, 290). Having maintained consistently that this community is engaged in a pilgrimage toward the promised land (cf. 3:7–4:11), the author recognizes that the deviation of some members endangers the hope of the entire community.

Deliberate Sin (10:26–31)

10:26–27. The sacrifice of Christ confronts the readers with two alternatives: either they will "draw near" in prayer and commit themselves to the community (10:19–25), or they will **sin deliberately after receiving the full knowledge of the truth** (10:26a). The author warns of the consequences of rejecting the sacrifice of Christ (10:26–27) and offers logical support for the warning (10:28–29) before offering scriptural warrant for his claim (10:30–31). The readers received the "full knowledge of the truth" at conversion when they were "enlightened" (6:4; 10:32), and the author has explored this truth in depth (7:1–10:18), ensuring them of their access to this extraordinary revelation. To "sin deliberately," therefore, is to refuse to "draw near," to abandon the assembly where members encourage one another to love and good works, and to fail to endure until the end (10:36–39; cf. 3:12, "the deceitfulness of sin"). Because Jesus died once for all (10:11–14), **there is no longer a sacrifice for sins** (10:26b).

Similarly, the author declares that his community stands before the choice of expecting the promised reward (cf. 4:1–11; 11:1–40) or a **fearful expectation of judgment and raging fire that will devour the opponents** (10:27). Just as ancient Israel stood before the choice of blessings or curses (Deut 27–28), the readers face the choice between God's reward and judgment.

An Outline of Hebrews 10:26–31

Deliberate sin (10:26–31)

Fearful expectation of judgment (10:26–27)

Those who have trampled the Son of God (10:28–29)

Falling into the hands of the living God (10:30–31)

With images taken from the OT description of God's "fiery passion" (cf. Isa 26:11; Zeph 1:18; 3:8) that will judge God's enemies, the author indicates that those who "sin deliberately" will place themselves on the side of God's enemies.

10:28–29. The author supports his warning by appealing once more to the warrant of the scripture. Recalling that those who turned to idolatry were put to death "on the evidence of two or three witnesses" (Deut 17:6; cf. Num 35:30), he generalizes this law to indicate that **anyone who rejects the law of Moses dies without mercy upon the testimony of two or three witnesses** (10:28). Although the example is drawn from the ultimate rejection of the covenant in Deut 17:2–16, this passage lacks any reference to "without mercy," a phrase that is drawn from Deut 13:6–10, where the punishment of death is prescribed for those who tempt others to idolatry. This precedent becomes the basis for the conclusion that he draws. Having consistently declared the superiority of the Christian revelation, he employs the argument from the lesser to the greater to ask, **How much more severe punishment do you think will be determined for those who have trampled the Son of God, profaned the blood of the covenant in which they were sanctified, and outraged the Spirit of grace** (10:29)? Having demonstrated already that Jesus is greater than Moses (3:1–6) and has provided the great salvation, the author concludes that the greater the salvation, the greater the punishment for those who reject it.

These three parallel phrases give graphic depictions of deliberate sin and indicate the seriousness of the offense of abandoning the assembly. The preceding argument indicates the horror of the offense, for the author has established that God has given the ultimate revelation "in a Son" (1:1–2), who now sits at God's right hand (1:3), becoming greater than angels (1:4–13) and Moses (3:1–6). To "trample the Son of God under foot" is to respond to God's ultimate revelation in a Son (1:1–2) with contempt, the equivalent of "crucifying the Son of God and holding him up to contempt" (6:6). Having described the inauguration of the covenant through the blood of Christ (9:15–22), the author now indicates that to abandon the community is to "profane the blood of the covenant" (*to haima tēs diathēkēs koinon hēgēsamenos*; lit. "to regard the blood of the covenant as ordinary") in which they were sanctified (cf. 2:11; 9:14; 10:10; 13:12). Since only the blood of Christ, offered in the heavenly sanctuary, can cleanse the whole person (9:11–14), the ultimate disgrace is to treat it as ordinary. In the parallel phrase "outraged the Spirit of grace," the author is apparently referring to the Holy Spirit (cf. 6:4), which the community received at baptism. A rejection of this gift would be the supreme insult.

10:30–31. The author gives scriptural support for the warning in 10:30–31 with words taken from the Song of Moses (Deut 32:35–36), using the first line of each verse, which he separates for rhetorical effect with **again** (10:30; cf. 1:5; 2:13). In the original context the passage spoke of God's vengeance on Israel's enemies and his judgment on behalf of Israel (NRSV: "He will vindicate his people"; cf. Rom 12:19). The author cites the passage as evidence of God's judgment on the community that abandons God's gift. The concluding statement, **It is a fearful thing to fall into the hands of the living God** (10:31), concludes both the warning (note *phoberon* "fearful" in 10:27) and the central section in terms that are parallel to the ending of the first major section (4:13, "to whom we give an account").

Theological Issues

The author reaches the end of this extended word for the mature (4:14–10:31) with the exhortation, "not abandoning the assembly of yourselves together, as is the practice of some" (10:25) the only direct encouragement in the NT for believers to attend church. This challenge is not merely a mundane conclusion to the sublime message of the central section but a significant summation of the author's message, for it establishes the setting in which the community can continue toward the goal, indicating that theology is the basis for ethics—that God's saving deeds call for a response. Church renewal occurs only when the community acknowledges that it is the recipient of an extraordinary gift. Indeed, the invitation, "let us draw near," that provides the frame for the entire section (4:16; 10:22), challenges the community that awaits God's ultimate promise to approach God in the present. To "draw near" is a corporate venture of the people on the way. Thus the assembly is the occasion when the discouraged community sees beyond the painful realities of the present in order to "hold firmly to the confession" with the "full assurance of faith" (10:22).

The assembly is also the occasion for enriching the life of the whole community, for it provides the opportunity to encourage others to "love and good works" (10:24). Thus worship is not a retreat from the world but the occasion when those who "draw near" in their assemblies also find the resource to participate in a rich community life, acting as a social safety net for other members of the community. Only as the church gathers regularly can the community provide financial and physical support for weaker members and ensure the spiritual health of the whole.

The author's concluding warning in 10:26–31 returns to the theme that he has introduced earlier (2:1–4; 6:4–6), indicating that the God who has spoken a word of promise in the Christ event is also the judge who holds the people accountable. To "trample the blood of the Son of God" (10:29) is to reject God's supreme gift. Having concluded the first section with the reminder that God is "the one to whom we must give an account" (4:13), the author concludes the second section, "It is a fearful thing to fall into the hands of the living God" (10:31). Thus the author reminds the church of all ages that one may neither respond casually to God's gift nor take God's goodness for granted. One of the major distortions in the Christian view is to envision God as merely the one who is at our disposal to offer gifts and ensure our good fortune. As the author indicates, to hear the God who has spoken graciously is to recognize the urgency of the community's response.

Although the doctrine of original sin may be the one empirically verifiable Christian doctrine, only the community of faith confesses that the death of Jesus blots out sin. The author reminds those who have already accepted this Christian claim that no human deeds can provide atonement. This saving gift leaves the community with only two options. They may either "draw near" to God's throne of grace with a clear conscience (10:19–25) or reject the ultimate gift and "profane the blood of the covenant" (10:29). Because there is no other sacrifice, the community can now receive God's gracious gift with gratitude.

PART 3

Hebrews 10:32–13:25

On Not Refusing the One Who Is Speaking

In 10:32, the author reaches the final summation, or *peroratio*, of his sermon. The *peroratio* was critical for the effectiveness of the speech, for it was the speaker's last chance to persuade the audience to take the right course of action. It was the occasion for summarizing earlier parts of the speech, appealing to the emotions, and refreshing the memory of the audience (Quintilian, *Inst.* 6.1.1). Consequently, the author breaks no new ground but recapitulates what he has already said. The task now is to urge the wavering church to endure until it obtains the promise that the author has held before the community throughout the homily (4:1; 6:12, 17; 10:23).

The exhortation in 10:32–12:13 recapitulates the primary themes of 3:1–4:13. Whereas the earlier passage had challenged the community to remain faithful and recalled examples of unfaithfulness (3:12, 19), this passage challenges the readers to remain faithful and recalls examples of faithfulness. In 12:18–29, the author reaches the rhetorical climax of the presentation corresponding to 1:1–4, and he warns the community not to refuse the one who is speaking (12:25–29), reiterating the warning in 2:1–4. The sacrificial language of 4:14–10:18 reappears only in the closing words in 13:9–14. All the pieces of the exhortation come together in chapter 13 as the author again challenges the readers to follow the path of Jesus (13:9–14; cf. 2:10–18; 4:14–16; 10:19–23) from the place of suffering to the abiding city.

In the exhortation in 10:32–12:13, the author addresses the community's present experience of suffering, speaking directly to their situation in 10:32–39 and 12:1–13 and offering examples for imitation in chapter 11. The dominant theme is endurance (*hypomenein/hypomonē*) in the midst of pain (10:32, 36; 12:1–2, 7; cf. the opposite, *hypostolē*, "shrinking back," in 10:39), which the author illustrates with the heroes of faith (*pistis*) in chapter 11. The close relationship between faith and endurance is indicated in 10:36–39, where the author equates the two qualities.

Hebrews 10:32–39

Remembering the Faithfulness of Earlier Days

Introductory Matters

The exhortation in 10:32–39 provides the most specific indication of the history of the community in the entire homily. Soon after their conversion (*phōtisthentes*, "enlightened"; cf. 6:4), they "endured a hard struggle with sufferings." Undoubtedly, they suffered the fate that Christians experienced everywhere. Paul warns new converts in Thessalonica that they are destined for afflictions (1 Thess 3:3), and he encourages the Philippians not to be intimidated by their adversaries (Phil 1:28). Long before the emergence of persecutions sponsored by governmental authorities, Christian communities met local opposition everywhere because of their absolute loyalty to Christ and withdrawal from civic life (cf. 1 Pet 4:4). Greco-Roman society, because of its polytheistic nature, was tolerant of various deities and religious practices (DeSilva 1995, 147–48). Christians, however, denied the gods and claimed that the God of Israel alone was worthy of worship. Thus they disturbed the peace of ancient communities, often undermining family cohesion by converting members of the household (cf. 1 Pet 1:18; 2:18–3:7). "In their eagerness to save the world, Christians did not shy away from shattering the unity and sanctity of the family, the basic unit of society and thus of the state" (Fitzgerald 2006, 26; Aristotle, *Pol.* 1.2; Cicero, *Off.* 1.54).

Consequently, Tacitus (born ca. AD 56) called the Christian movement a "deadly disease" (*Ann.* 16.5) and accused the Christians of "hatred of the human race" (*Ann.* 15.44). Pliny (ca. AD 61–112) described it as a "wretched infection" (*Ep.* 10.96). Minucius Felix, a third-century Christian apologist,

215

records the complaint, "You do not go to our shows, you take no part in our processions, you are not present at our public banquets, you shrink in horror from our sacred games" (*Oct.* 12, cited in Wilken 1984, 66).

Verses 33–34 give specific examples of the "struggle with sufferings." The Greek construction *men . . . de*, often translated "on the one hand . . . on the other hand" (note the use in 7:20–24; 8:4, 6; 10:11–12), could suggest that some were singled out for public abuse, while others demonstrated solidarity with them. However, the more likely translation is "in part [BDAG, 630] being publicly exposed to insults and persecutions, in part being partners with those who were treated in this way" (NRSV, NIV have "sometimes . . . sometimes"). *Theatrizein*, literally "to act in the theater," takes on the metaphorical meaning of "expose publicly" (BDAG, 446) and focuses on the public disgrace. It suggests the image of the theater, the site not only for performances and games but also for public punishments. Philo describes an occasion when the Jews were put on public display in the theater and subjected to abuse (*Flaccus* 72, 74, 84–85, 95, 173; Thompson 1982, 64). Paul uses a related word when he declares, "We have become a spectacle (*theatron*) to the world, to angels, and to humankind" (1 Cor 4:9). The "insults" (*oneidismoi*) also indicate the public humiliation and shame associated with punishment; the word has connotations of mockery and scorn (cf. Ps 69:7, 9; Jer 15:15; 20:8 for the insults encountered for the Lord's sake; Spicq 1994, 2:585). "Persecutions" (*thlipseis*) include both physical and mental abuse that the community suffers for the sake of Christ (cf. Rom 5:3; 8:35; 12:12; 2 Cor 1:4, 8; 2:4; 4:17; 6:4; 7:4; 8:2, 13; Phil 1:17; 4:14; Col 1:24; 1 Thess 1:6; 3:3, 7). These images focus not only on the persecutions faced by the community but also on the community's loss of honor and experience of shame.

Although Paul experienced numerous imprisonments (2 Cor 6:5; 11:23), prior to the more comprehensive persecutions recorded in Revelation, only Hebrews mentions the imprisonment of members of the community and the confiscation of their property. These imprisonments are not only matters of the past but also a continuing reality for the readers (cf. 13:3). To show "sympathy with the prisoners" (*synepathēsate*) involved far more than the expression of concern. Under ancient prison conditions, prisoners depended on family and friends to supply them with food and clothing. Those who became "partners" (*koinōnoi*) shared the disgrace of the prisoners (DeSilva 1995, 159). The "confiscation of property" could come from an official act or be the result of local mob action. Philo records the plundering of Jewish property at a time of persecution in Alexandria (*Flaccus* 5, 53–57). Melito of Sardis (late second century) complains to the emperor Marcus Aurelius, "Shameless informers out to fill their own pockets are taking advantage of the decrees to pillage openly, plundering inoffensive citizens night and day" (Eusebius, *Hist. eccl.* 4.26.5, cited in DeSilva 1995, 161). This confiscation would add to the public humiliation by reducing people to total poverty.

Several scholars (Salevao 2002, 105; Lane 1991b, 296–301) have identified this vivid description of the community's experience with the persecution of Roman Christians by Nero (cf. Tacitus, *Ann.* 15.44). Inasmuch as the author indicates that no one in the community has died (12:4), this identification is unlikely, for victims of the Neronian persecution did not survive. Since harassment and humiliation of Christians were commonplace, the author is probably describing typical experiences rather than a specific event. His purpose is not historical precision but the presentation of an example to emulate (Grässer 1997, 3:63).

The author responds to the community's situation with language that echoes the literature of Hellenistic Judaism. With the memory that the community had endured a "great struggle with sufferings," he introduces the athletic image that will dominate this section. *Athlēsis* (great struggle) is literally an "athletic contest" (cf. BDAG, 24). The author develops this imagery further in 12:1–13, referring to the "great cloud of witnesses," the race (*agōn*) set before the readers, the struggle (12:4, *antagonizesthai*, "to struggle in a contest") with sin, and the training (*gymnazein*, lit. "to exercise," 12:11). The connection of the athletic metaphor with the repeated call for endurance suggests the athlete's pursuit of the goal to the point of exhaustion.

This metaphor has a long history in Greco-Roman literature. The nature of Greek athletics provided a rich metaphor, with its "rigorous preparation, conditioning, and self-denial followed by extreme exertion in an individual effort to achieve a superior performance" (Croy 1998, 43). Paul employs the metaphor frequently to describe his work (1 Cor 9:24–27; Phil 3:12–14; 1 Thess 2:2) and that of his readers (Phil 1:27; 4:3). Although several philosophers employ athletic metaphors (cf. Aristotle, *Eth. Nic.* 1.8.9; 2.2.6–7; 3.9.3–4; Dio Chrysostom, *Or.* 8.11–15), the Cynics and the Stoics especially equate the sage's capacity to overcome hardships with the work of the athlete (cf. Epictetus, *Diss.* 1.24.1; 3.15.1–7; 3.22.51; 3.24.113; 4.4.30; Seneca, *Ep.* 17.1; 34.2; 109.6). Philo also makes abundant use of the athletic image. In some instances he uses it to describe the training in philosophy characteristic of the sage (*Alleg. Interp.* 1.98; 3.14, 72; *Migration* 27; *Sobriety* 65). He also recognizes that suffering is a necessary part of the faithful life, arguing that one should receive blows like an athlete, not like a slave (*Alleg. Interp.* 3.201). In *Prelim. Studies* 164, he compares those who faint early in the contest with those who carry through the contest of life to its finish. According to *Joseph* 26, both Jacob and Joseph were athletes trained through suffering.

The use of the athletic metaphor in connection with endurance (*hypomonē/ hypomonein*, 10:32–34; 12:1–3) is rooted in the literature of Greek philosophy and the Jewish literature that was most influenced by philosophical discussions. In the LXX, *hypomonē* normally signifies expectant waiting or intense desire (Spicq 1994, 3:418), while in Greek literature it was commonly associated with courage (*andreia*), one of the four cardinal virtues, to describe the steadfastness

Cynics and Stoics

Diogenes of Sinope (ca. 400–325 BC) is widely recognized as the founder of the Cynic way of life. The name is derived from the Greek *kyōn* (dog) because of Diogenes' shameless behavior in public, living as a dog and doing what was natural. Diogenes adopted a life of self-sufficiency, keeping his needs to a minimum. The Cynic philosophers after Diogenes followed his example of the simple life. A particular emphasis of the Cynics was on frankness of speech, which they demonstrated by preaching to people in the marketplaces and wherever people gathered.

The Stoics developed the Cynic emphasis on living in accordance with nature. Founded by Zeno (ca. 335–263 BC), the Stoics developed a comprehensive philosophical system. Paul's argument for the cosmic order in nature (Rom 1:20) and the claim in the speech to the Athenian philosophers that "we are his offspring" (Acts 17:28) have Stoic overtones. Stoics of the first century AD were widely known as teachers of ethics. They maintained that happiness comes from living in accordance with nature (cf. Rom 1:26–27; 1 Cor 11:14) in a state of contentment that does not depend on outward circumstances (cf. Phil 4:11).

of those who "persevered in face of hostile forces" (*TDNT* 4:582). Endurance (*hypomonē*) in suffering (10:32, 36; 12:1–3, 7) was a major theme in Greek philosophical literature. The term, which was used for heroism in battle (Polybius, *Hist.* 29.17.4), was used in both athletic and moral spheres (Croy 1998, 64). Plutarch (ca. AD 50–120) contrasts athletes who cannot bear the strain of competition with "those who endure training resolutely" (*Quaest. conv.* 8.724–725). Stoic philosophers saw endurance as a vital part of moral development. Seneca maintained that one who endures torture is employing

Athletics

The frequent use of athletic metaphors in the New Testament (cf. 1 Cor 9:24–27; Phil 3:12–16; 2 Tim 4:6–8) reflects the central importance of athletic contests in Greek culture. The Greek ideal of human achievement involved not only education in music and the arts but also the development of the body. The beauty of the naked body was important in Greek life because it actualized the development of the whole person. Because the development of the mind required rigorous training and exercise, Greek philosophers frequently employed athletic metaphors to encourage their students to "train" and "exercise" the mind in the pursuit of philosophy. Socrates, for example (Plato, *Gorg.* 526d), described the whole of living the virtuous life as an *agōn* (athletic contest; cf. Phil 1:30; 1 Thess 2:2).

all the virtues (*Ep.* 67.10; Croy 1998, 64). Philo employed this metaphor frequently to describe biblical heroes. "One must bear, resist, hold fast, fortify one's resolution and barricade it with firmness and endurance (*karteria kai hypomonē*) drawn from within, the most potent of the virtues" (*Cherubim* 78). Philo claimed that the athlete, "by the constancy and vigor of his endurance, breaks the strength of his adversary until the victory is complete" (*Good Person* 26). Philo praises those who endure death (*Worse* 178; *Agriculture* 75; *Joseph* 226; *Moses* 2.206), torture (*Dreams* 2.84), captivity (*Unchangeable* 115), exile (*Cherubim* 2), and mistreatment (*Moses* 1.72, 90, 102, 106; other texts in Spicq 1994, 3:416). The word is sometimes used for "expectant waiting or of patience motivated by hope" (*Spec. Laws* 2.91; Spicq 1994, 3:417). Philo's concern is not with sports commentary (Croy 1998, 64), for he applies the image of endurance in athletic endeavors to the acquisition of virtue.

In order to encourage readers to emulate the virtues of the Maccabean martyrs, the writer of 4 Maccabees describes them as athletes who endured torture and death. The writer indicates that his philosophy "teaches us self-control . . . and trains us in courage (*andreia*), so that we will endure (*hypomenein*) any suffering willingly" (5:23). Faithful people endured torture (6:9; 7:22; 9:6, 22; 15:32; 16:1, 17, 19, 21; 17:7, 10), confirming their loyalty to the law (7:9) because they hoped to receive a reward (9:8; 17:12–13, 17–18). Those who endured were athletes in a noble contest. The author declares:

> Truly the contest in which they were engaged was divine, for on that day virtue gave the awards and tested them for their endurance. The prize was immortality in endless life. Eleazar was the first contestant, the mother of the seven sons entered the competition, and the brothers contended. The tyrant was the antagonist, and the world and the human race were the spectators. Reverence for God was victor and gave the crown to its own athletes. Who did not admire the athletes of the divine legislation? Who were not amazed? (17:11–16 NRSV)

The association of the community's suffering in Hebrews with the endurance of an athlete is indebted to the literature of martyrdom represented by 4 Maccabees. Like the author of 4 Maccabees, the author hopes to encourage his readers to endure sufferings by portraying them as athletes in a noble contest.

Having recalled the community's past endurance (10:32), the author turns to the present situation with "you need endurance" (10:36) in order to receive the promise, appealing to the witness of scripture in 10:37–38. The first line of the citation is an adaptation of Isa 26:20 LXX, "in a very little while" (*mikron hoson hoson*), which the author introduces with "for yet" (*eti gar*). The remainder of the citation is taken from Hab 2:3–4. In the original context, the latter passage responds to the prophet's complaint that the wicked persecute the righteous, promising that divine justice will come. "Look at the proud!

Their spirit is not right in them, but the righteous live by their faith." This passage has a long history of interpretation. In the LXX, which the author uses, the passage has taken on a different nuance: "The righteous one will live by *my* faith." Thus the Hebrew Bible (MT) emphasizes the faith of the people, while the LXX focuses on God's faithfulness. The citation in Hebrews does not correspond precisely to either reading but has elements of both. The author adds the definite article to the participle "coming" (i.e., the "coming vision"), giving it a messianic connotation (*ho erchomenos*, "the one who is to come," cf. Matt 11:3). Thus "the one who is to come . . . and will not delay" continues the thought of "the day that is drawing near" (10:25). The central verse for the author is "My righteous one will live by faith," which, like the MT reading, refers to the faithfulness of the people rather than God's faithfulness. The author omits phrases from the MT—"Look at the proud! Their spirit is not right in them" (NRSV)—and reverses the sequence of the LXX—"the righteous one will live by (my) faith" and "my soul is not pleased with anyone who shrinks back"—in order to comment on the latter phrase in 10:39.

Habakkuk 2:3–4 played an important role in Jewish literature. In the Dead Sea Scrolls, the passage is contemporized to refer to those members of the community who are faithful in keeping the law as interpreted by the Teacher of Righteousness. Paul uses the passage on two occasions to refer to the faith of Gentiles who are included in the faith community without keeping the works of the law (Rom 1:17; Gal 3:11). The context in Hebrews indicates that the author's focus is the antithesis of faith and shrinking back as he attempts to ensure that the community is composed of the people of faith. The context indicates the close relationship in the author's mind between "boldness" (10:35), "endurance" (10:36), and "faith" (10:38–39). The connection between endurance and faith is suggested by Habakkuk's phrase, "If it seems to tarry, wait for it" (*hypomeinon*, Hab 2:3 LXX), in which the author employs the verb that in Hebrews is translated "endure" (10:32). The passage marks a transition in the presentation from endurance to faith, which becomes the topic in the discussion of the heroes of faith in chapter 11. The author returns to the theme of endurance in 12:1–11.

Tracing the Train of Thought

The author's recollection of the sufferings the community experienced shortly after conversion reflects a careful rhetorical strategy, for he recalls how they "endured" (10:32; *hypemeinate*) at the beginning of their Christian existence before he declares that they "need endurance" (10:36) at the present. The appeal to memory was a common means of motivating an audience (Lausberg 1998, 432–33). The recollection of the community's exemplary conduct in the past is an attempt to gain their good will, a common practice of orators in the introduction of a speech (cf. Acts 24:2–4). The community's memory should have an emotional effect and motivate them to maintain conduct in the future that is similar to their conduct in the past.

10:32–36. Scholars have noted that the list of examples in chapter 11 stands apart from the rest of the homily, having a rhetorical quality of its own. Some have even argued that the author has taken chapter 11 from a source, interrupting the flow of thought of the homily. That is, while 10:32–39 and 12:1–11 focus on endurance, chapter 11 focuses on faith. However, a careful reading demonstrates that chapter 11 is integrally related to the exhortation in 10:32–12:11. In 10:32–39, the author's appeal to **remember the former days** (10:32a) is the basis for the exhortation to reinvigorate the same conduct in the present (10:35–39). Just as they endured sufferings shortly after they had been **enlightened** (10:32b), they **need endurance** now (10:36a). They **welcomed the confiscation of their possessions** (*harpagēn tōn hyparchontōn*) because they knew that they had a **better and abiding possession** (*hyparxin*) (10:34). This possession is the equivalent of the heavenly rest (4:1–11), the hope that is now available (6:18–19; cf. 3:6; 6:11; 7:19; 10:23), and the promise (6:12, 15, 17; 7:6; 8:6; 9:15). The author describes the possession with two adjectives that are central to the argument of the homily. It is "better" (*kreittona*) and "abiding" (*menousan*). Although the readers could not see this transcendent possession (cf. 2:8), the knowledge that Christ is better (1:4) than any object of comparison and that he is abiding (7:3, 24–25) has motivated them from the beginning. The "abiding possession," like the "abiding city" that the community awaits (13:14), belongs to the transcendent world. The community overcomes the shame and alienation of this world because of its access to the heavenly world. This outlook corresponds precisely to the perspective of the heroes of faith in chapter 11, all of whom endured alienation by looking to "things not seen" (11:1).

The imperative **Do not throw away your boldness, which has a great reward** (10:35), challenges the community to continue its past conduct. The "boldness" (*parrēsia*), as the author has already indicated, is the right of access to God that has been made possible by Christ (10:19; cf. 4:16). To "throw away" the boldness, therefore, is to fail to endure—the equivalent of "spurning the Son of God" and "profaning the blood of Christ" (cf. 10:29). The "great reward"

**Hebrews 10:32–39
in the Rhetorical Flow**

Hearing God's word with faithful endurance (1:1–4:13)

Probatio: Discovering certainty and confidence in the word for the mature (4:14–10:31)

Peroratio: On not refusing the one who is speaking (10:32–13:25)

  Enduring in hope: the faithfulness of Jesus and the faithfulness of the ancestors (10:32–12:13)

  ▶ Remembering the faithfulness of earlier days (10:32–39)

   The former days (10:32–36)

   Living by faith (10:37–39)

(*misthapodosia*) available for those who endure is the equivalent of the "better and abiding possession" (10:34) that motivated the readers in the past. *Misthapodosia*, which is used by no other NT writer, can refer either to a penalty (cf. Heb 2:2) or to a reward. Here the author refers to the reward of the heavenly rest described in 4:1–11 and anticipates the description of Moses as one who "looked to the reward" (11:26) as well as the statement that anyone who comes to God must believe that God "rewards those who seek him" (11:6).

In order to avoid throwing away the reward (10:35), the community needs endurance (10:36), the quality they demonstrated in the past (10:32), for only through endurance can they **do the will of God and receive the promise** (10:36b). This hope anticipates the author's description of the heroes of faith, who were "heirs of the promise" (9:15; cf. 11:9) and greeted the promise from afar (11:13). Thus the "better and abiding possession" (10:34), the reward (10:35), and the promise all refer to the ultimate salvation. Only those who endure (10:32, 36) rather than "throw away the boldness" (10:35) will attain the promise.

Just as the author had previously combined the warning of dire consequences, the memory of earlier days, and the promise of salvation (6:1–12) to motivate his community to endure, he once more motivates the readers by combining the severe warning of punishment (10:26–31) with the memory of former days (10:32) and the hope for the future reward (10:34–39). Knowing the power of examples to establish his case, the author recalls heroes who modeled the behavior that he encourages his readers to adopt. This appeal to examples of faithfulness recapitulates in a positive way the earlier recollection of Israel's example in the wilderness. Whereas the Israelites were examples of the lack of faith (3:12, 19; 4:2) not to be imitated, the heroes of chapter 11 exemplify the conduct that the author encourages in 10:32–39.

Reward and punishment play a central role throughout the homily. Like Joshua, who summoned the Israelites to choose between life and death, the author places two choices before the readers. The "great salvation" (cf. 2:3) made possible by the exalted Christ poses stark choices. Those who fail to endure to the end will not escape God's judgment (2:3–4). They will fail to enter God's rest (3:12–19), and thus they will stand under the judgment of God (10:29–31), while those who endure will inherit the promises (10:34–36).

10:37–39. In 10:37–39, the author assures his community that their time of waiting is not unlimited. He contemporizes the citation drawn from Isa 26:20 LXX and Hab 2:3–4, as he has done with other passages, indicating that it addresses his weary readers, promising that the time of waiting is **a very little while** and that **the one who comes will come and not delay** (10:37). Although the passage in the original context referred to the coming of God's justice, in the author's adaptation (see Introductory Matters) it refers to the return of Christ (cf. 9:28), which is drawing near (10:25). The focus of the citation is the assurance that **my righteous one will live by faith** rather than **shrink back** (10:38). As the transition from "boldness" (10:35) and "endurance" (10:36)

Faith and Faithfulness in Hebrews and Paul

Faith (*pistis*) is a central theme for both Paul and the author of Hebrews, both of whom quote Hab 2:4, "The righteous shall live by faith" (cf. Rom 1:17; Heb 10:37–38). However, the two authors employ the terms in different ways. Paul employs the verb *pisteuein* (to believe) to speak of believing in Christ (Gal 2:16), in God (Rom 4:3, 5, 17), in the message of the gospel (Rom 10:16), as well as believing that God raised Jesus from the dead (1 Thess 4:14). He frequently speaks of the "faith of Christ" (*pistis Christou*), which the translations render either as "faith in Christ" or "faith of Christ" (Rom 3:22, 26; Gal 3:22). For the author of Hebrews, *pistis* is the equivalent of patience (6:12) and endurance (10:37–39); unfaithfulness (*apistia*) is the failure to endure (3:12, 19). The author never speaks explicitly of faith in Jesus but instead presents Jesus as the example of faith (12:1–2) and endurance.

to "faith" indicates, the author employs these three words in overlapping ways. As the opposite of "shrinking back," faith has the connotation of the English "faithfulness."

The assurance, **We do not belong to those who shrink back to destruction, but to those who have faith for obtaining life** (10:39; *peripoiēsin psychēs*, lit. "saving of souls"; cf. 1 Thess 5:9, *peripoiēsin sōtērias*, "obtaining salvation"), like the earlier recollection of the community's past endurance (10:32), is an effective rhetorical device for motivating the readers. Echoing the distinction in the citation between those who "shrink back" and those who have "faith," the author expresses confidence that they will conduct themselves in the future as they have in the past. Despite the frequent warnings, he concludes that the readers will make the right choice and inherit the promise.

Theological Issues

In the graphic portrayal of the community's history in 10:32–34 and the description of its current situation in 12:4–11, the author gives the clearest indication in the homily of the problem that he seeks to address. From the beginning the readers have faced abuse, suffering, and marginalization. The athletic images suggest that the readers are like runners whose efforts have brought them close to exhaustion. Consequently, Christian experience is a matter of enduring. The need to endure was not unique to this community, for it was the common experience of Christian communities throughout the ancient world until Constantine declared Christianity the established religion in the Edict of Milan in 313. As Christianity has spread in the modern world, persecution of the church is not only a phenomenon of ancient times but occurs in many countries in the world today. As the Constantinian era comes to

Figure 8. Emperor Constantine.
This fourth-century marble head of Constantine by an unknown artist depicts the emperor whose name came to represent the close cooperation of church and state. Christians living in today's post-Constantinian world may find in Hebrews a reminder that in the beginning, Christianity had no secular status or power.

a close in Europe and North America, Christians increasingly discover that they no longer have a privileged place in society but face marginalization and loss of status.

Hebrews is a reminder that Christianity had no privileged place from the beginning, for its claims created hostility from the larger society. As H. Richard Niebuhr wrote in *Christ and Culture* (1951, 5), "Ancient spiritualists and modern materialists, pious Romans who charge Christianity with atheism and nineteenth-century atheists who condemn its theistic faith, nationalists, and humanists, all seem to be offended by the same elements in the gospel and employ similar arguments to defend society against it." As persecuted Christians in autocratic societies know, totalitarian regimes perceive Christians as a threat. Christians may also exist in tension with modern democratic societies for the same reason that ancient Roman society treated them with disdain: The confession that Jesus is Lord is an affront to pluralism and tolerance, for it gives absolute loyalty to the Christian confession. The call to values determined by the self-denial epitomized in the cross is a challenge to a culture that celebrates the freedom of individuals to create their own identities and morality.

The author does not envision that this house church will ever hold a place in the public square or have a privileged place in society. Instead, he holds before the community the vision of a marathon race in which the only solution is to endure to the end. What society considers objectionable about the Christian movement he offers as a resource. Christians are alienated from society because they see beyond the provisional solutions offered in this society to "things unseen." As the community's past experience (10:32) and the examples of the heroes (chap. 11) indicate, Christians can endure marginalization in this world because they see another reality. Indeed, they join the company of marginalized people that includes Jesus himself (12:1–2).

Hebrews 11:1–12:3

Remembering the Faithful Heroes of the Past

Introductory Matters

The appeal to heroes from the past in Heb 11 makes constant use of anaphora, the repetition of the same word or group of words at the beginning of a series of clauses or sentences, in this case, "by faith . . . by faith." Thus the style of this chapter is unlike any other section of Hebrews, leading some scholars to suggest that the author has employed a homily from a separate source (cf. Michel 1966, 371; Windisch 1931, 98; Weiss 1991, 554–55). However, since the themes are so well integrated into the homily (see Tracing the Train of Thought), this conclusion is unnecessary. The author has probably adapted a literary model that is well known in Greco-Roman and Jewish sources. A commonplace among Greco-Roman orators was the recollection of heroes from the past as examples worthy of emulation. In some instances, the orators gave lists of heroes (cf. Isocrates, *Antid.* 230–236; additional texts in Eisenbaum 1997b, 63–73). Nothing in Greek literature, however, approximates the length of the list in Heb 11. The OT and Jewish literature also provide models for the author's list of heroes. The lengthy summaries that show how God has led the people (Ps 105:8–44) or contrast God's faithfulness with Israel's disobedience (cf. Neh 9:6–31; Ps 78; 106; cf. Cosby 1988, 9–12) also indicate the place of summaries of the biblical narrative (cf. Josh 24). This model flourished in intertestamental literature, especially in Hellenistic Judaism. The earliest and longest example of the list of heroes is Sir 44–50 (ca. 180 BC), which, unlike the biblical summaries, focuses on the deeds of individuals arranged around a theme. Wisdom 10 arranges Israel's story around the theme of Wisdom, using a rhythmic style in the Greek text with the anaphoric repetition of "she" (Wis 10:5–6, 10, 13, 15, rendered by the noun "wisdom" in the NRSV) similar to "by faith" in Hebrews (Eisenbaum 1997b, 43). Philo appeals to historical examples frequently. In *Virtues* 198–227, he offers an extended series of heroes, and in *Rewards* 10–11 he uses the anaphoric repetition of "in hope . . . in hope." Each of these lists, however, is only a partial model for Heb 11, for none approximates the stylistic rhythm that is achieved by the author in chapter 11 in recalling the qualities of the heroes.

The Maccabean literature offers the primary model for the list of heroes in chapter 11. Under the persecutions unleashed by Antiochus Epiphanes (167–163 BC), Mattathias offers an eloquent speech in 4 Maccabees, urging continued faithfulness to the law by recalling Israel's heroes. In arranging his brief descriptions of eleven of Israel's heroes around the theme of faithfulness to the law, he organizes the narrative to make them the exemplars for those who suffer under persecution. This use of the list of heroes contains the closest parallel to Heb 11. Like the author of Hebrews, the author of this first-century work describes the heroes as athletes competing in the arena. In this instance they endured martyrdom rather than deny their faith. The aged Eleazar was "like a noble athlete" as he endured the tortures (4 Macc 6:9–10). The martyrs were "contestants for virtue" (12:14) in "an arena of sufferings" (11:20). The mother of the seven brothers describes the contest to which her sons are called to bear witness for the nation (16:16) and then recalls heroes of the past (Abraham, Daniel, and the three young men in the fiery furnace) as examples of those who endured in the face of death. Although Abraham was not a martyr, he fits within the list because he was prepared to offer Isaac (cf. 4 Macc 16:20). At the end of 4 Maccabees, the mother again recalls Israel's past heroes (18:11–19), reiterating the stories of those who died (Abel, 18:11), were zealous for the law (Phinehas, 18:12), were imprisoned (Joseph, 18:11; Daniel, 18:13), and were cast into the fire (Hananiah, Azariah, and Mishael in the fiery furnace, 18:12). In the two overlapping lists in 4 Maccabees, the author has selected heroes whose experience is a model for the readers as he arranges them around the theme of the larger work. Thus 4 Maccabees is parallel to Hebrews in several ways. Both writers place the list of heroes within the larger work to provide examples to follow, and both arrange their heroes around the theme that dominates the book. Both writers employ athletic imagery and related themes. Both writings focus on the endurance (*hypomonē*) of the athletes, which they equate with faith (*pistis*). Like Hebrews (10:34; 11:6, 13–16, 26), 4 Maccabees consistently describes the reward that follows the suffering. Both writers recall the ancient heroes as representatives of the same struggles that the readers are facing and use the examples to exhort the readers to remain faithful.

Both the unique understanding of faith and its association with specific heroes have close analogies to the thought of Philo of Alexandria. Both the author and Philo present Abraham as an example of a migrant in this world (*Migration* 9; *Alleg. Interp.* 3.83; *Confusion* 75–82), and both transform his journey to the promised land as a quest for a heavenly homeland (Heb 11:13–16; Philo, *Abraham* 69–71; Thompson 1982, 59). This theme was especially popular among diaspora Jews and a common subject in the philosophical literature of the time (Feldmeier 1992, 72). Similarly, both writers employ the imagery of "seeing the invisible" (cf. Heb 11:27) to describe the motivating force that enables faithful people to live as aliens in the world. Abraham surpassed the Chaldeans because he could see what was invisible to them (*Heir* 98). Those who are wise are especially able to "see the invisible" (*Unchangeable* 3; *Posterity* 15–16; *QG* 4.96). Thus, although the author of Hebrews may not be dependent on Philo, his distinctive understanding of faith suggests that he and his readers are familiar with the thought world of the Hellenistic Judaism represented by Philo and the author of 4 Maccabees.

Tracing the Train of Thought

The introduction of faith in 10:38–39 marks the transition to the major development of this theme in chapter 11. Despite the distinctive literary form of chapter 11, this section is not a digression in Hebrews but a part of the climax of the homily. Having already indicated the importance of examples (3:7–4:11; 6:12–15), the author offers models that will inspire the readers to endure to the end (10:38–39; cf. 3:14). The call for faithfulness in chapter 11 resumes the discussion in 3:1–4:11, in which the author contrasts the faithfulness of Jesus (3:1–6) with the unfaithfulness of the Israelites (3:7–4:11). Thus he indicates that the bleak assessment of Israel's history is only a part of the story, for heroic individuals provide positive examples for the readers to follow. This recollection of heroes is sandwiched between the challenges to endure through suffering in 10:32–39 and 12:1–11 because the heroes of faith faced circumstances similar to those that now confront the community.

The author's list of names was not determined by specific OT references to the faith of the ancestors. Indeed, the one passage that explicitly associates one of the heroes with faith is not mentioned (Gen 15:6). Moreover, the faithfulness of some of these heroes is doubtful. Some of the names appear routinely among lists of heroes. Abraham appears regularly (Sir 44:19; 1 Macc 2:52; 4 Macc 16:20). The names of Isaac, Joseph, Moses, Daniel, and the three young men in the fiery furnace appear in other lists (Sir 45:1–5 includes Moses; 1 Macc 2:53 includes Joseph; 4 Macc 18:12–13 has Daniel and the three young men). A noteworthy feature of the list in Heb 11 is the absence of such important figures in Israelite history as Aaron (cf. Sir 45:6–22), Joshua (Sir 46:1–10), and Phinehas (1 Macc 2:54), and the presence of Abel (Heb 11:4) and Rahab (11:31). Pamela Eisenbaum observes that the list includes only those who preceded the settlement in the land. All the heroes are outsiders who have no land of their own (Eisenbaum 1997b, 142). Having compared his people to Israel in the time before the entry into the promised land throughout the homily, the author concludes the list with the conquest.

The author has carefully structured the list of examples. The references to receiving testimony through faith in 11:1–2 and 11:39–40 form an *inclusio* (Attridge 1989, 305) marking the beginning and end of the examples. Like ancient philosophers, the author begins with a definition (11:1; cf. Plato, *Symp.* 186c; Philo, *Prelim. Studies* 79; Plutarch, *Curios.* 518c; Attridge 1989, 307) before elaborating on the subject. His list of heroes is preceded by the general statement about ancestors who were witnesses to the truth of the definition (11:2) and the community's own faith in creation (11:3). He begins the rhythmic recitation of the heroes, each introduced with the anaphoric "by faith," moving sequentially through scripture from Abel (11:4) to Rahab (11:31). He alternates the pace of the list of heroes by interspersing summary statements about the nature of faith (11:6, 13–16, 39–40). In 11:32, he changes the pace, giving only names in rapid succession.

11:1–2. The author's definition is not comprehensive in scope but establishes the characteristics of faith that will be the focus of the examples that follow. Continuing the statement that "we are

... of faith" (10:39), the author elaborates, **but faith is** (11:1a), completing the sentence with two parallel phrases that are "rich with rhetorical adornment" (DeSilva 2000, 381) created by the repetition of sounds (*st* in *pistis . . . hypostasis*; cf. *elpizomenōn . . . blepomenōn*), but a challenge for translators. The initial clause indicating that "faith is the *hypostasis* of things hoped for" is the first challenge. Translators have rendered *hypostasis* as "substance" (KJV),

---

Hebrews 11:1–12:3 in the Rhetorical Flow

Hearing God's word with faithful endurance (1:1–4:13)

Probatio: Discovering certainty and confidence in the word for the mature (4:14–10:31)

Peroratio: On not refusing the one who is speaking (10:32–13:25)

　Enduring in hope: the faithfulness of Jesus and the faithfulness of the ancestors (10:32–12:13)

　　Remembering the faithfulness of earlier days (10:32–39)

　　▶Remembering the faithful heroes of the past (11:1–12:3)

　　　Defining faith (11:1–2)
　　　From creation to Enoch (11:3–5)
　　　The necessity of faith (11:6)
　　　Noah (11:7)
　　　Abraham's journey (11:8–10)
　　　Abraham's progeny (11:11–12)
　　　The better country (11:13–16)
　　　Abraham's sacrifice (11:17–19)
　　　The patriarchs (11:20–22)
　　　Moses (11:23–26)
　　　The exodus (11:27–29)
　　　Taking Jericho (11:30–31)
　　　The victors (11:32–35a)
　　　The martyrs (11:35b–38)
　　　Not yet (11:39–40)
　　　The pioneer and perfecter of faith (12:1–3)

229

Hypostasis, Substance, and Trinity

Of the five occurrences of *hypostasis* in the NT, three are in Hebrews (1:3; 3:14; 11:1; cf. 2 Cor 9:4; 11:17). Like the Latin *substantia*, the root word *hypostasis* (derived from *hyphistēmi*), refers to the solid foundation that stands under the feet. The word became an appropriate metaphor in philosophical literature to refer to reality in contrast to mere appearances and to a "subsistent" as opposed to an "accident." In legal discourse it referred to a title deed or guarantee (Spicq 1994, 3:423).

Later Christian writers used the word *hypostasis* in discussions of the Trinity. When Origen said that Father, Son, and Spirit were three *hypostaseis*, he meant three realities: Father, Son, and Spirit really exist. Writers in the fourth century and beyond continued to use the word but became concerned lest "three substances" should be taken to mean three gods. By the end of their extended discussion, *hypostasis* was no longer synonymous with *ousia*; *ousia* was used for "substance," while *hypostasis* referred to a particular concrete expression of an *ousia*. Thus the orthodox tradition refers to one substance (Greek *ousia*) and three *hypostaseis* (sometimes *prosōpa*, whence Latin *personae* and English "persons").

In Heb 11:1, which predates these developments, *hypostasis* may be translated "substance" (in a nontechnical sense) or "reality."

"assurance" (RSV, NRSV; cf. NIV "being sure"), and "reality" (Attridge 1989). It suggests that faith is no subjective feeling but **the reality of things hoped for** (11:1b). Indeed, it is both the reality and the "realization" of things hoped for. The author has offered an example of this faith already in his recollection of the community's past when they suffered the loss of possessions because they knew that they had a better and abiding possession (10:34). That is, they recognized that "reality" was not found in material things or in one's present situation, but in the transcendent world.

The parallel expression indicates that faith is not only the "reality (*hypostasis*) of things hoped for" but also the **proof** (*elenchos*) **of things not seen** (11:1c). *Elenchos*, a term used nowhere else in the NT, means "reproof" or "accusation" in the LXX but here means "proof." Thus the parallel terms "reality" and "proof" both indicate the certainty and stability of faith that gives one the capacity to endure. This focus corresponds to the author's consistent claim that Christians have access to a firm reality to which they can hold fast. To have faith is thus to stand on solid ground rather than "shrink back."

The author addresses a community that does "not see all things in subjection" to the Son (2:8) with the affirmation that "things hoped for" and "things not seen," not the world around them, are the reality on which they can build their lives. The "things hoped for" echo the emphasis throughout the homily on the "full assurance of hope" (6:11) and the "better hope through which we draw near to God" (7:19), which the community may now grasp (6:19; 10:23) as a result of the entrance of Christ into the heavenly sanctuary. The reference to "things hoped for" and "things not seen" reflects the author's use of the categories of both the Hebrew scriptures and Greek philosophy (Thompson 1982, 72). "Things hoped for" presuppose the story world of the Hebrew scriptures, according to which the community waits with anticipation for future blessings, while "things not seen" belong to the Platonic distinction between the visible and the invisible world (Plato, *Phaedo* 79a; *Rep.* 6.509d; 7.524c). Just as the author attempted to motivate his audience earlier with the assurance that they are "heirs" (1:14) for whom the promise of heavenly rest remains open, he holds before them the things hoped for and things not seen, which are the equivalent of the "better and abiding possession" (10:34), the promised inheritance (6:12, 17; 9:15), and the unshakable kingdom (12:28). The entrance of Christ into the true heavenly sanctuary "not made with hands" (9:11, 24) also opened the community's access to the things not seen in the transcendent world. Thus the community can take a firm stand, knowing that reality is in the heavenly world.

Although the author employs philosophical language to define faith, he is more a pastor than a philosopher, for his purpose is to address the crisis in a community living in the uncertainty caused by the fact that they do "not see all things in subjection" to the Son (2:8). Since all that they see is alienation and disappointment, they are in danger of falling away (3:12) or shrinking back (10:38–39). By directing them to **things not seen** (11:1c), the author reassures the community that it can take its firm stand on the invisible reality. The emphasis on certainty in 11:1 is reminiscent of the author's earlier assurances. They have an anchor that is "secure and firm" (*asphalē kai bebaian*, 6:19), the certainty (*bebaiōsis*) provided by God's oath (6:16), and a guarantee (*engyos*) of a better covenant (7:22). Indeed, the primary purpose of the exposition on the high priestly work of Christ (7:1–10:18) is to demonstrate that the community places its trust not in earthly matters but in the work that Christ accomplished in the invisible world. Consequently, the author challenges them consistently to hold firm (3:14, *bebaian katechein*) and to "hold firm unwaveringly" (10:23) to the promise. His definition in 11:1 indicates that they have a place to stand in "the reality of things hoped for, the proof of things unseen."

The author introduces the list of heroes with the declaration **in this** (i.e., through faith) **our ancestors were confirmed** (11:2). As the narrative in chapter 11 indicates, the perspective in 11:1 guided the ancestors in all circumstances. The narrative is not merely about heroes of faith, however, for the *inclusio* in 11:2, 39 indicates the author emphasizes that they "were confirmed" (11:2, *emartyrēthēsan*; 11:39, *martyrēthentes*). The passive of *martyrein* indicates that they were "confirmed" by God. Abel was "confirmed" (11:4, *emartyrēthē*), and it was "confirmed" that Enoch was well pleasing to God (11:5). Thus the great "cloud of witnesses" (*nephos martyrōn*) are those who have been "confirmed" by God. God attested that those who had abandoned every earthly assurance in favor of the invisible reality were faithful.

11:3–5. The anaphoric list of those who acted by faith begins appropriately with creation in 11:3. The author does not mention the ancestors here, however, but describes the community's own faith. **By faith we know** (11:3a) is an elaboration of the earlier phrase "but faith is," suggesting the cognitive dimension of faith (cf. 10:34). **That the worlds were created by the word of God** (11:3b) was commonplace in biblical thought (Gen 1:3–26; Ps 33:6; Wis 9:1). "Worlds" (*aiōnes*) may refer to both the invisible and the visible world here and in 1:2. The focus of the author, who has mentioned the creation already in the homily (1:2, "through whom he made the worlds"; cf. 2:10), is primarily on the implication of this fact (here the Greek *eis to* does not mean "so that" but "and so"). Thus the author declares, **and so what can be seen originated from things that do not appear** (11:3c; *mē . . . ek phainomenōn*). The translation "so that what is seen was not made out of what was visible" (NIV) is also possible; the author's point remains the same. With his pastoral concern for his readers, he affirms that they orient their lives to the "things that do not appear," the equivalent of "things hoped for" and "things not seen" (11:1). What "we know" was also known to the ancestors, who were models of the same orientation.

Between the author's identification with his community, as suggested by "we know" in 11:3 and "apart from us" in 11:40, he turns from the first-person plural to describe the ancestors who were models of the orientation that he has described in 11:1–3. He introduces Abel (Gen 4:1–16) as the first example of the ancestors who were "confirmed" (cf. 11:2) by their faith. Since Abel was neither a major hero in Jewish literature (remembered elsewhere in 4 Macc 18:11) nor recalled as a man of faith, his appearance at the beginning of the list is surprising. Although the author employs the LXX consistently, his description of Abel is not derived from the LXX text, which mentions neither a **better sacrifice** (11:4a) offered by faith nor his being **confirmed as righteous** (11:4b; *dikaios*). This description may reflect the author's use of Habakkuk's statement that the "righteous will live by faith" (Hab 2:4), cited in 10:38. The statement that **though dying, he still speaks** (11:4c) is probably derived from God's word to Cain, "The voice of the blood of your brother cries out" (Gen 4:10). The story of Abel undoubtedly caught the imagination of the author, who affirms that the community has drawn near to one whose "blood speaks better than the blood of Abel" (12:24). While the author may have more than one reason to recall the story of Abel, including his role as one who both offered a sacrifice and was a victim, his primary reason is to show that Abel, the victim, overcame death. Beyond his death were "the things hoped for." If he speaks beyond death, he has overcome death. Thus the voice of Abel, as the author indicates later (12:24–25), speaks to the temptations of a suffering community, telling them of the reality beyond death. As in 4 Macc 18:11, Abel is the righteous martyr, and his situation is analogous to that of the readers, who now suffer alienation.

Like Abel, **Enoch** (11:5) demonstrated the reality of "things not seen." The author's reflections are based not on the extensive literature on Enoch but only on Gen 5:24, which he follows closely. Although Enoch did not, like Abel, experience a violent death, both he and his predecessor were **confirmed** (*memartyrētai*) before God (11:4, 5), and both built their lives on "things not seen," for neither of the ancestors was defeated by death.

11:6. In 11:6, the author breaks the pattern to offer a general principle, as he does frequently in the homily. Insofar as Enoch was "well pleasing to God" (11:5; *euarestēkenai tō theō*), he exemplified the principle that **without faith it is impossible to please (God)** (11:6a). The general principle recalls the author's frequent use of axiomatic principles describing what is "impossible" (*adynaton*, 6:4, 18; 10:4) and necessary (*dei*, cf. 2:1; *anankē*, 7:12, 27; 9:16, 23). Having invited the community to "draw near" (*proserchesthai*, 4:16; 7:25; 10:22) in worship to the heavenly sanctuary, the author now indicates that **the one who draws near to God must believe that God is and that he rewards those who seek him** (11:6b). In speaking of the necessity of believing that God "is," the author is probably not alluding to the possibility of atheism, which was rare in the ancient world, but to the basic teaching that all new converts received (cf. 6:1, "faith in God"). To believe that God rewards those who seek him conforms to the working definition of faith in 11:1, for to believe in God's reward is to believe in "things hoped for" and "things not seen." Indeed, Moses "looked to the reward" (11:26), exemplifying the nature of faith.

11:7. As in other Jewish lists (cf. Sir 44:17; *Jub.* 10.17), Noah follows Enoch in the list of heroes (Heb 11:7). In both the OT and Jewish tradition, Noah was remembered as a righteous man who pleased God (Gen 6:9; Wis 10:4; Philo, *Migration* 125). However, the author does not mention this aspect of Noah's life, although it would correspond to the memory that Abel was righteous (11:4) and that Enoch was pleasing to God (11:5). Nor does he, like the author of 1 Peter (3:20–21), express an interest in the parallel between Noah's family and the church (Attridge 1989, 319). Instead, he interprets the story of Noah to fit the working definition of faith in 11:1. Like Moses (cf. 8:5), he received a divine command (*chrēmatistheis*). When he was warned **about things not yet seen, Noah responded reverently** (*eulabētheis*) (11:7a). The word *eulabein* (to be reverent) is related to *eulabeia* (reverence), which Jesus demonstrated in the context of his "loud cries and tears" (5:7). As a result Noah **built an ark for the salvation of his house** (11:7b). Although what was "not yet seen" was the flood, the author alludes also to "things not seen" (11:1), making Noah an example of the faith that acknowledges the reality of the heavenly world. As a result of his attention to "things not yet seen," Noah **condemned the world** (11:7c). While the immediate reference may be to those who refused to heed Noah's preaching of repentance, the context indicates that the author sees beyond that original setting, for a consistent theme in chapter 11 is that those who build their lives on the unseen world become aliens in this world. At the conclusion of the list, the author summarizes that "the world was not worthy" (11:38) of these heroes. This theme is especially important for the author's attempt to address the alienation of his readers. Just as their faith has created alienation (10:32–34) from the world around them, the great heroes of faith were also separated from their world.

The consequence of Noah's faith was that he became **an heir of the righteousness according to faith** (11:7d). Although the language sounds Pauline (cf. Rom 1:17; 3:21–26), the author does not have in mind the Pauline doctrine of the righteousness of God. Instead, he emphasizes consistently that the readers are "heirs of the promise" (6:17; cf. 1:14; 6:12; 9:15), and he presents the heroes of faith as people who have an inheritance (11:8) of eternal salvation. Thus Noah is the example of one who was alienated from this world but the heir of God's promise.

11:8–10. Abraham (11:8) belongs to all the lists of heroes, as authors use the stories about him for their own rhetorical purposes. According to both 1 and 4 Maccabees, when he was tested at the sacrifice of Isaac, he became the example of faithfulness (1 Macc 2:52; 4 Macc 16:20). Sirach portrays him as the example of one who kept the law (Sir 44:20). Paul recalls the one incident in which "Abraham believed God" (Gen 15:6) as an example of one who was saved by faith apart from works of the law (Rom 4:3; Gal 3:6), while James recalls Abraham as the example of deeds that accompany faith (Jas 2:21). In Hebrews, the story of Abraham occupies a major part of this recitation of heroes. Out of the lengthy Genesis narrative (12–25), the author paraphrases the story of Abraham's early migration (11:8–12), comments on the narrative (11:13–16), and recalls the sacrifice of Isaac (11:17–19) before concluding with brief comments about Isaac, Jacob, and Joseph (11:20–22).

Although the story of Abraham occurs in all the lists of heroes, only Hebrews focuses on the beginning of the narrative (Gen 12:1–4). Like other writers, the author paraphrases the story to indicate his own rhetorical purpose. According to Genesis, God said, "Go out from your land . . . to the land that I will show you" (Gen 12:1), and so "Abraham went" (12:4). The author paraphrases, **by faith, Abraham, being called, obeyed to go out to a place that he was about to receive as an inheritance** (11:8a), equating Abraham's response to that of Noah. Just as Noah received a divine command (11:7), Abraham was "called." Just as Noah responded reverently, Abraham "obeyed." Noah became an "heir of the righteousness by faith," and Abraham went out to receive an inheritance. In both instances, therefore, the faithful response is to heed the divine voice.

Although the author's paraphrase is not inaccurate in its recollection of the story of Abraham, it heightens the drama and focuses the attention on the

Figure 9. Abraham's Journey.

This painting by Jozsef Molnar (1821–1899) depicts Abraham's travels. Hebrews says the ultimate goal of Abraham's pilgrimage was the heavenly city prepared by God for his faithful people.

one dimension that serves his pastoral purpose. The author twice indicates that Abraham **went out**, elaborating on Abraham's insecurity by indicating that **he did not know where he was going** (11:8b). Whereas, according to the Genesis account, God will show Abraham a land, the author speaks of the "place that he was about to receive as an inheritance."

The author elaborates on Abraham's migration in 11:9–10, further emphasizing the patriarch's transient status. Although he arrived in Canaan, the land to which God directed him, he **lived as a stranger** (*parōkēsen*) **in the land of promise as in a foreign land** (11:9a). Although the Genesis narrative indicates that Abraham migrated frequently, "lived as a stranger" (*parōkēsen*) among various groups (12:10; cf. 23:4, "I am a stranger" [*paroikos*]), was an alien (*parepidēmos*), and dwelled in tents, the author recalls the story for his own purpose. According to his interpretation, even in the land of promise Abraham was a "stranger" in a "foreign" (*allotrios*) land. The fact that he **lived in tents** (11:9b) further emphasizes his transient status. Thus as the author maintained earlier in the homily (3:7–4:11), Canaan was not the ultimate land of promise. Even in the place where God led Abraham, the patriarch did not find the security of a homeland.

Only in 11:10 does the author indicate what the ultimate promise is. Abraham had not reached his goal in Canaan; he abandoned all earthly securities because **he waited on a city that has foundations whose maker and builder is God.** The fact that he "waited" (*exedecheto*) suggests that the ultimate promise remained unfulfilled. Just as the author's community lives in a period of "waiting" (10:13; *ekdechomenos*) until all enemies are vanquished, Abraham

235

waited for the "city" (*polis*) that God has built. This city, as the author indicates elsewhere (cf. 11:16; 12:22; 13:14), is the heavenly world, the equivalent of the heavenly rest described in 4:1–11 and the promise that the author has mentioned repeatedly, and the place of the heavenly sanctuary. Thus Abraham exemplifies the principle in 11:1 that faith is "the reality of things hoped for, the proof of things not seen." The city prepared by God remains invisible to Abraham's eyes. Nevertheless, the author knows that it was the reality that served as the anchor of his life and enabled him to live as a migrant.

11:11–12. The author's portrayal of Abraham moves to a second pivotal moment in Abraham's life in a reflection on the birth of Isaac in 11:11–12. Although neither Abraham nor Sarah is the model of faith in the Genesis narrative (16–19), the author, like Paul (cf. Rom 4:19), recalls that event as an example of faith. This example, however, has perplexed interpreters for centuries, for the wording leaves unclear whether Abraham or Sarah is the subject of the sentence. If Sarah is the subject of the sentence, the statement is problematic, for the complete sentence would be rendered "By faith Sarah, who was barren, received the power to deposit seed," thus associating Sarah with the masculine role in procreation. The KJV and ASV, along with several church fathers, maintain that Sarah is the subject but assume that "received the power to deposit seed" (*dynamin eis katabolēn spermatos elaben*) is an elliptical expression meaning that Sarah "received the power to conceive" (see Attridge 1989, 325, for ancient texts). Others have observed that many people in antiquity assumed that women also deposited seed (Eisenbaum 1997b, 158).

The masculine language for procreation in 11:11 and the continued reference to Abraham as the subject of the sentence in 11:12 suggests an alternative rendering of 11:11, according to which Abraham "received the power to deposit seed." If Abraham is the subject, the interpreter has two possibilities for rendering the words "herself Sarah barren" (*autē Sarra steira*). One possibility is to emend the reading by adding iota subscripts denoting the dative case in order to render the phrase "with Sarah, who was barren." The more likely solution is to regard the reference to Sarah as a parenthetical statement indicating that both Sarah and Abraham were unlikely to become parents in their old age. That is, **by faith he—Sarah herself being barren—received the power to deposit seed** (11:11a). Although the description **past the normal age** (*para kairon hēlikias*) could apply to both Abraham and Sarah, the author's focus on Abraham as "as good as dead" (11:12) suggests that his primary reference is Abraham. Despite the appearances, Abraham **regarded the one who promised as faithful** (11:11b). In the two examples that the author has offered, Abraham is characterized as one who waits, even in the absence of the immediate signs of fulfillment, because he believes in the promise. Thus he exemplifies the author's definition of faith, standing firm because he believes "in things hoped for."

The memory of the remarkable birth of Isaac in 11:11 is the basis for the conclusion that **they were born from one man** who was **as good as dead**

(11:12a). This reference to Abraham's age reinforces the emphasis on his vulnerable existence, indicating that he was not only a migrant (11:8–9) but near death. Like other heroes of faith who die or come near death, Abraham had no resources other than the promise of God (cf. Eisenbaum 1997b, 159; Swetnam 1981a, 89). Although God promised that his descendants would be **as many as the stars of the heaven and as innumerable as the sands on the seashore** (11:12b; Gen 15:5–6; 22:17; 32:12), Abraham never lived to see the fulfillment of the promise.

The author has shaped the paraphrase of the narratives about Abraham in 11:8–12 as an appeal to a community that shares Abraham's vulnerability. Because of their Christian confession, the readers also live as strangers in a foreign land. Although they have not, like Abraham, left their homeland, they have abandoned the security they once had in their own cities (10:32–34). As they experience the discouragement of waiting for God to fulfill the promises, they complain that they do not see the world in subjection to Christ (2:8). Because Abraham was motivated by the promises that remain unseen and unfulfilled, he is the model for the readers. In the two pivotal events described by the author in 11:8–12, he builds his life on "things hoped for" and "things unseen," waiting endlessly for the fulfillment of God's promise.

11:13–16. In 11:13–16, the author interrupts the rhythmic recitation of those who lived "by faith" (*pistei*) with the summary and commentary that focuses the readers' attention on the specific features that address their situation. The reference to the one who was "as good as dead" (11:12) provides the transition to the summation, **These all died in faith without receiving the promises** (11:13a). Like the readers, they experienced the frustration of not seeing the fulfillment of their hopes. The author's comment stands in tension with the earlier statement that Abraham patiently endured and "obtained the promise" (6:15) and the reference to Enoch, who did not see death (11:5). His rhetorical purpose in this instance is to place before a community faced with alienation and death (cf. 2:8) the memory of those who endured with unfulfilled hopes until the day they died. After the recitation of additional heroes in the remainder of chapter 11, the author concludes, "They did not receive the promise" (11:39).

Those who did not receive the promise were models of the orientation that the author encourages the readers to adopt. Instead of abandoning their commitment, the ancestors **saw the destination and greeted it from a distance** (11:13b). Although the object of faith is "things unseen" (11:1), they saw the invisible (cf. 11:27) with their own powers of perception, even if only from a distance. As they "greeted it from a distance," they were like pilgrims who recognize their destination from afar. The image may recall Moses, who looked over the promised land before he died but did not enter it (Deut 34:4; Grässer 1997, 3:137). In contrast to the Genesis narrative, where Abraham says, "I am a stranger and an alien among you" (Gen 23:4), these ancestors who did not reach their destination made it clear **that they were strangers and aliens on the earth** (11:13c). Like Philo and the Platonists, the author indicates that the earth is no homeland for those who belong to the heavenly world.

The author reinforces the pastoral comments in 11:14–16a, concluding that those who are "strangers and aliens" are filled with a strong desire for another place. They do not look back to their place of origin (11:15) but **long for** (11:14; *oregontai*) a heavenly home (11:16a). Only Hebrews describes the ultimate salvation as a **homeland** (11:14; *patris*), which is parallel to the heavenly city. As the author indicates in 11:16a, this homeland is **better** than other objects of human longing because it is **heavenly**. Thus it is the equivalent of "things hoped for, things unseen." Although the faithful people have not received the promise, **God is not ashamed to be called their God, and he has prepared for them a city** (11:16b). Those who died without receiving the promise ultimately reached the homeland for which they had longed throughout their lives.

11:17–19. After the commentary in 11:13–16, the author resumes the list of those who acted by faith in 11:17, concluding the section on Abraham with the event in his life that appears most frequently in other lists of heroes. Recalling that "God tested Abraham" in the Genesis account (Gen 22:1), the author says, **by faith, Abraham, when he was tested, offered Isaac as a sacrifice** (11:17a), and then adds, **he was about to offer the firstborn son as a sacrifice** (11:17b). The twofold use of *prospherein*, the term used regularly to mean "offer a sacrifice" (5:1, 3, 7; 7:27; 8:3–4; 9:7–14, 25, 28; 10:1–2, 8, 11, 12; 11:4), in 11:17 reflects the paradox in the author's own perspective (Grässer 1997, 3:145). The perfect tense, "he offered a sacrifice" (*prosenēnochen*), indicates that Abraham completed the sacrifice, while the imperfect may be rendered "he was about to offer a sacrifice" (*prosepheren*). The author indicates the full extent of this test with the reminder that **the one who received the promise** (11:17c) was about to offer the child born when "he was as good as dead" (11:11), the one hope for the fulfillment of the promise (11:18; cf. 11:12) of future descendants. The indication that Abraham completed the sacrifice corresponds to the author's interpretation: Abraham **considered that God was able** (*dynatos ho theos*) **to raise someone from the dead** (11:19a). That God is the one "who gives life to the dead" is a fundamental conviction in Jewish literature (cf. Rom 4:17; Deut 32:39; 1 Sam 2:6), which the author applies to the sacrifice of Isaac because, **figuratively speaking** (*en parabolē*), **he recovered him** (*auton . . . ekomisato*) **from the dead** (11:19b). Although he, like the other patriarchs, died without receiving the promise (11:13, 39), in a figurative way Abraham exemplified the promise that the author has made to his readers: that those who endure "receive the promise" (10:36, *komisēsthe tēn epangelian*). Thus for the author the sacrifice of Isaac, like the other stories in the list, is an indication that people continue to live by faith in God's promises, despite the reality of death. In his willingness to sacrifice Isaac, Abraham never abandoned the promise but staked his life on "things hoped for, things unseen." Thus he is a model of faithful endurance for the readers who are also now being tested (cf. 2:18; 3:8–9; 4:15) by the delay in the fulfillment of God's promises.

11:20–22. In the brief accounts of the generations that followed Abraham (11:20–22), the author reinforces the principle that the heroes of faith exemplified the definition of faith in 11:1. He chooses the final moments in the lives of Isaac, Jacob, and Joseph, indicating that, even at the point of death, they looked beyond the immediate circumstances to "things hoped for." The author recalls that Isaac **blessed Jacob and Esau** (11:20b; cf. Gen 27:27–29, 38–40) without mentioning the intrigue surrounding the story, the conflict between the brothers (Gen 27:41), or the fact that Esau is the negative example of one who chose to fill his appetite in the present rather than look to the future (Heb 12:15–17). Indeed, the aged Isaac promises only hardship for Esau (Gen 27: 39–40). Instead, the author indicates that Isaac offered the blessing **by faith in things to come** (11:20a, *peri mellontōn*), suggesting that Isaac anticipated the "world to come" (2:5, *tēn oikoumenēn tēn mellousan*) and the "city that is to come" (13:14; cf. 10:1, "the good things to come") as the ultimate fulfillment of God's promises.

Similarly, the author recalls that **by faith, when Jacob was dying, he blessed each of the sons of Joseph** (11:21a; cf. Gen 48:15–22), but does not mention the blessing to all the sons of Jacob (Gen 49). The statement that he **bowed in worship over the top of his staff** (11:21b), which appears only in the LXX (Gen 47:31), actually occurs in the Genesis narrative before the blessing of the sons of Joseph. This act of worship suggests the total trust in God's promise by one who was near death (Grässer 1997, 3:159).

The author's omission of Jacob's other sons is noteworthy, as he proceeds from Joseph's sons to Joseph himself. In keeping with his interest in patriarchs who were aliens, he departs from other ancient lists by omitting those who were prominent in the settlement of the land or in the national institutions of Israel (Eisenbaum 1997b, 142). As the one who speaks the last words in Genesis, he is the transition to Moses, who also occupies a major place in the author's list of heroes. Like Isaac and Jacob, Joseph also looked to the future when he was dying. In this instance, his dying words did not come in the form of a blessing (Gen 50:24–26). **By faith Joseph, when dying, reflected on** (*emnēmoneusen*) **the exodus of the sons of Israel and gave instructions about his bones** (11:22; cf. Gen 49:29–32 for the same instruction from Jacob), looking forward to the fulfillment of God's promises. Although he, like the others, "died in faith" (11:13), he was firm in the conviction about "things not seen" and a model for a community that now questions the outcome of its situation.

Just as the discussion of the faith of Abraham (11:8–19) is a development of an earlier description of the patriarch's faith (6:13–15), the discussion of Moses in 11:23–31 continues the earlier treatment of him as the one who was "faithful in all God's house" (3:2; cf. 8:5). In giving the major attention to the two great leaders, the author establishes a parallel between them that is evident not only in the comparable length of the two portraits but also in the addition of brief narratives about the successors of each one (11:20–22, 29–31). Moreover, neither was at home in the promised land. Abraham lived there as a stranger, and Moses never reached it. Both are appropriate models for the author's theme of the pilgrim people of God.

11:23–26. As Israel's founding leader, Moses has a regular place in Jewish lists of heroes. The other lists recall his miracles and the exodus event that followed (Wis 10:16–17; Sir 45:3) as well as his role as lawgiver. Philo, Josephus, and numerous other writers magnify his role with extended discussion (Eisenbaum 1997b, 167). However, the author does not mention the events for which Moses is most remembered. Instead, he gives a series of parallel statements, each of which begins with "by faith," recalls an event illustrating that faith, and concludes with a commentary indicating the nature of that faith (D'Angelo 1979, 27). The sequence ends with the exodus, omitting the entire period of the wilderness wanderings. The author's primary text is Exod 2:2–15 for the early years and 12:21–23 and 14:22–27 for the events connected with the exodus.

In the first of the parallel episodes, the author refers to the circumstances of Moses' birth without telling of Pharaoh's edict for male children to be slain, assuming that the audience is familiar with the story. Although he begins with **by faith Moses**, he actually recalls the faith of Moses' parents: **when born was hidden by his parents for three months** (11:23a), following the account in Exod 2:2. The author also follows the LXX in recalling that the parents hid the child **because they saw that the child was beautiful** (*asteios*) (11:23b). *Asteios* can mean "handsome" or "full of grace and charm" (BDAG). The term is used for those who are especially gifted and called by God (cf. Judg 3:17 LXX; Jdt 11:23). The author emphasizes their power of perception, indicating that "they saw" (*eidon*) the greatness of the child (cf. 11:26, "he looked" [*aneblepen*] to the reward"; 11:27, "as seeing the invisible one"). Thus by faith Moses' parents knew that the infant was an extraordinary child. Although the **edict of the king** (11:23c) undoubtedly created terror among the Hebrews, because of their faith **they did not fear** it, anticipating Moses' own fearlessness (11:27) in a terrifying situation. By faith they recognized that the future role of Moses was more real than the threats of the king.

The second pivotal moment described by the author is Moses' killing the Egyptian who was beating a Hebrew (Exod 2:11–12). Once more the author does not tell the story, apparently assuming that it is familiar to the audience, but depicts the scene as a major choice in Moses' life. Verses 24–26 are an extended sentence interpreting the event with assumptions that were common in Jewish literature but not derived from the OT text. According to the main clause (v. 24), the incident is evidence that **by faith Moses ... refused to be called the son of Pharaoh's daughter** (11:24; cf. Exod 2:10). The author is undoubtedly echoing the numerous Jewish speculations about Moses as the grandson of Pharaoh, adopted into the royal house. As the alien adopted into the royal house, he refused the ultimate chance for status, demonstrating his disdain for earthly glory. The author may have in mind the kind of interpretation that Josephus records: "On his daughter's account, in a pleasant way (Pharaoh) puts his diadem upon [Moses'] head; but Moses threw it down to the ground, and, in a puerile mood he wreathed it round, and trod upon it with his feet" (*Ant.* 2.33, cited in DeSilva 1995, 192).

The author indicates why Moses made the decisive choice in the two parallel phrases in 11:25–26 that describe the alternatives Moses faced: **choosing to be mistreated with the people of God rather than to enjoy the temporary pleasures of sin** (11:25). To have stayed in Pharaoh's house would have involved the temporary pleasures of sin and the treasures of Egypt. The author's reference to pleasures of sin as "temporary" (*proskairos*) indicates Moses' values. The term is the opposite of "abiding" (*menōn*), a central theme in Hebrews. The author has insisted throughout the homily that the exalted Christ is the abiding one (1:10–12; 7:3, 24–25) and that Christians can endure abuse and the loss of possessions because they have an "abiding possession" (10:34) and an unshakable kingdom that "abides" (12:27–28). Although the author does not specify the nature of the "pleasures of sin," his references to sin elsewhere in the homily suggest that he refers to the failure to persevere to the end (3:13; 4:15; 12:1) and the refusal to accept the pain of enduring.

Moses' choice is an inversion of ordinary human values, for he chose to be mistreated with his people and **counted the abuse suffered for Christ greater wealth than the treasures of the Egyptians** (11:26a). Thus, like Abraham, he is a marginalized figure in the land, for he abandoned his place in society. Undoubtedly the author emphasizes this dimension of Moses' life because it parallels the experience of the readers, who have also made difficult choices. They have "endured sufferings" (10:32) and the loss of property. Insofar as Moses knew that the abuse suffered for Christ is greater wealth than the treasures of Egypt, he preceded the community that endured the loss of possessions because they knew the greater possession (10:34). To say that Moses endured the "abuse of Christ" may be, strictly speaking, an anachronism, but the author wants to emphasize the community of suffering that spans the centuries. "Abuse" (*oneidismos*) suggests not only physical suffering but verbal abuse, disgrace, and mockery as well. Indeed, this expression is probably the complaint of the psalmist (Ps 69:9 [68:8 LXX]; 89:50–51 [88:51–52 LXX]), "Remember, Lord, the mockery (*oneidismos*; NRSV "taunts") directed against your servant." The author has already recalled the "abuse" (*oneidismos*) suffered in earlier days (10:33), and he concludes the homily with the challenge to the community to follow Jesus "outside the camp, bearing his abuse" (13:13). Inasmuch as faith led Moses to suffer temporary disgrace and to challenge the values of his world, he is a model for a community that bears the abuse associated with its alien status.

Moses was able to reject the securities of this world because **he looked to the reward** (11:26b), demonstrating that those who endure hardship will also receive a "reward" (10:35) and taking his stand on "things hoped for" and "things unseen." The fact that he "looked to (*apeblepen*) the reward" suggests the special powers of perception that accompany faith. The use of the imperfect tense is important, suggesting that Moses looked continually at the reward, never letting it out of his sight (Grässer 1997, 3:172). His abandonment of earthly security and the acceptance of disgrace for the sake of a reward is a model for members of the community who face the same situation. Like Philo of Alexandria, the author indicates that faithful people can see beyond the realities of the physical world to the ultimate reward (*Abraham* 69–79).

11:27–29. The author turns to the next pivotal moment in Moses' life when **by faith he left Egypt** (11:27a) but does not specify which of two departures from Egypt he has in view. According to Exod 2:15, Moses fled to Midian after he killed the Egyptian and then returned. His second departure was at the exodus (Exod 14). If 11:27 is a reference to the exodus, the author has reversed the sequence between the exodus and the Passover (Heb 11:28). If he is referring to the departure for Midian, his statement that Moses went out **not fearing the king** (11:27b) is not consistent with the report in Exodus that Moses was afraid (Exod 2:14). The author's primary concern, however, is not historical reporting but the encouragement of his readers. He does not distinguish between the two departures because he wishes to emphasize that he left Egypt, becoming an alien like Abraham (cf. 11:8–12). Insofar as he did not fear the wrath of the king, he followed the example of his parents, who "did not fear the edict of the king" (11:23).

He left Egypt for the same reason that he abandoned the wealth of the royal court: **he endured as seeing the invisible one** (11:27c). The author summarizes Moses' choice by recalling that he "endured" (*ekarterēsen*). The term recalls the frequent references in the Maccabean literature to the endurance of the martyrs in the context of suffering (4 Macc 9:8, 30; 10:10). Moses, like the martyrs, endured because of his capacity to see the invisible one. This account of Moses' faith is the clearest example in the list of heroes of the definition of faith in 11:1. As in the examples of Moses' parents and Moses' rejection of the treasures of Egypt (11:23–26), the author focuses on the capacity to "see" beyond temporal realities. Although Moses first saw the "invisible one" at the burning bush (Exod 3:1–6), he was also a visionary in the extended sense that his faith enabled him to "see" the "things hoped for, the things unseen" (11:1).

Undoubtedly the author shapes the story of Moses in order to speak to a community that does not "see all things in subjection to the Son" (2:8) as they observe the realities around them. He presents Moses as the example of one who saw beyond temporary alienation and, like the readers, experienced shame because of his faith. Moses is a demonstration that those who see the unseen and eternal world can reject ephemeral pleasures and endure temporary suffering in this world.

The author concludes the series of examples from the life of Moses with the events surrounding the exodus in 11:28–29. When he says that **by faith Moses kept the Passover and the sprinkling of blood** (11:28a), he summarizes Exod 12 (especially verses 7, 13, 21–23). The perfect tense "kept" (*pepoiēken*) indicates Moses' role in a lasting institution (Grasser 1997, 3:176). The reference to the sprinkling of blood emphasizes that Moses, like Abraham (11:17–19), was involved in a sacrificial act with confidence in the future. The purpose of the sprinkling of blood was to ensure **that the destroyer did not touch the firstborn of the Israelites** (10:28b). Thus when, to all appearances, the people were destined for destruction, "the sprinkling of blood" expressed confidence in God's promises.

In the final three examples (11:29–31), the author no longer mentions Moses, although he is the leader of the exodus. As in the story of Abraham (cf. 11:21–22), he adds the accounts of Moses' successors in 11:30–31. Although the exodus narrative describes the Israelites' fear and the resistance to their departure from Egypt (Exod 14:11–14), the author depicts people who demonstrated their belief in God's promises by taking extraordinary risks. Without describing the drama associated with the exodus, the author indicates only that **they went down to the Red Sea as if on dry land,** and that **the Egyptians made an attempt to do so and were drowned** (11:29). Similarly, the author does not mention the name of the one who led Israel around the walls of Jericho (cf. Josh 6:14–16) but attributes the faith to the people.

11:30–31. The list of those who acted "by faith" ends before the conquest of the land, suggesting that the heroes of faith have always been without the security of an earthly homeland. The author has deliberately drawn the list to a close with **Rahab the prostitute** (11:31) by reversing the sequence between the collapse of **the walls of Jericho** (11:30; cf. Josh 6:14–16) and the role of Rahab (11:31; cf. Josh 2:1–14). Rahab does not appear in other Jewish lists, but has an honored place in Christian literature (Matt 1:5; Jas 2:25; *1 Clem.* 12.1; cf. Eisenbaum 1997b, 173). Besides Sarah (11:11) and others who are not named (11:35), she is the only woman in the list. She too is an outsider who demonstrates her faith by risking her security for the sake of the promises to Israel. Unlike the other inhabitants of Jericho, she acknowledges that the Lord has given the Israelites the land (Josh 2:9), a reality that remains unseen in her own time.

11:32–35a. In 11:32–40, the author reaches a rhetorical climax, as he no longer lists those who acted "by faith" but now recalls events in which heroic people, many of whom remain unnamed, acted **through faith** (11:33). Both the rhetorical question **What should I say?** (11:32a) and the phrase **time will run out if I tell you** (11:32b) are rhetorical commonplaces, suggesting that the list could run forever (cf. BDAG, 375; cf. Philo, *Sacrifices* 27; Josephus, *Ant.*

20.11.1; further texts in Attridge 1989, 347). The list is arranged in two sections. In 11:32–35a, it involves heroic deeds, many of which involve military accomplishments. The list in 35b–38 recalls the sufferings of faithful people that extend from the conquest of Canaan into the Maccabean era, signifying that the alienation of the people of God did not end with the conquest of the land but continued throughout Israel's history. The unifying thread in the list of military heroes and martyrs is the endurance of the people of God as they struggled in the firm conviction of "things hoped for."

Although the listing of Israel's judges in 11:32 follows naturally from the reference to Rahab in 11:31, the author does not list the judges in sequence. **Barak** appears in Judges (4:6–22) before **Gideon,** and **Samuel** appears before **David** (1 Sam 1–24). Of this list, only David and Samuel appear in other lists. Gideon defeated the Midianites (Judg 6:12–24; 7:1–8:3; cf. Ps 83:9), and Barak, inspired by Deborah (Judg 4:6–11), defeated Sisera. **Samson** defeated the Philistines (Judg 13–16), and **Jephthah** defeated the Ammonites (Judg 11). The author describes none of David's exploits but reverses the sequence with Samuel in order to link the latter with the prophets (cf. 1 Sam 3:20 for Samuel as a prophet).

The author proceeds from mentioning names apart from deeds to a series of deeds accomplished "through faith" without identifying the heroes in 11:33–35a. The first list is filled with active verbs indicating the intensity of the heroes' struggle. The absence of names in several instances suggests that these events are not all limited to one person. At the beginning of the list he recalls those who **conquered kingdoms** (11:33a; *katēgōnisanto basileias*), using an athletic image (cf. *agōn*, "contest," 12:1; *athlēsis*, 10:32) as an example for the readers in their own struggle. Those who **established righteousness** (11:33b) by maintaining God's laws included several ancient leaders (Ps 14:2 LXX; 15:2; 119:121; cf. 1 Kgs 3:6; Isa 64:5). Those who **received promises** (11:33c) are not, strictly speaking, a part of the list but include all the heroes of faith. Although they "did not receive the promise" (11:13, 39) of the heavenly city, they saw the positive outcome of their struggles (cf. 6:15). Daniel, who **shut the mouths of lions** (11:33d; Dan 6:2–29), and the young men who **extinguished the fire's power** (11:34a; Dan 3) are examples of endurance and faith both here (11:33–34a) and in other Jewish lists of heroes (1 Macc 2:59–60; 4 Macc 16:21–22). Those who **escaped the edge of the sword** (11:34b) included Elijah (1 Kgs 19:2–3, 10) and Elisha (2 Kgs 6:32) as well as Mattathias and his sons (1 Macc 2:28). The heroes who **became strong in weakness** (11:34c) could have included Samson (Judg 16:17) as well as others (cf. Hezekiah in Isa 38:1–8). Numerous heroes of the OT and Maccabean period **became strong in war** (11:34d; cf. David in 1 Sam 17:49–51; all Israel in 1 Sam 17:52) and **put foreign armies to flight** (11:34e; cf. Exod 14:10–18; Judg 4:16; 8:11; 1 Macc 3:17–25; 4:6–11, 30–33). The author may have in mind the events of the Maccabean war, which will play an important role in 11:35b–38. He concludes the first part of the list with the recollection of **women who received their dead by resurrection** (11:35a), an apparent reference to the deeds of Elijah (1 Kgs 17:17–24) and Elisha (2 Kgs 4:32–37).

11:35b–38. The second part of the list comes in 11:35b–38, moving from the memory of victors to the memory of the martyrs, who include both the prophets and faithful people of the Maccabean period (cf. 2 Macc 6:18–7:42). By including no names of the martyrs, the author may be suggesting that this suffering was commonplace. Eleazar, the seven brothers, and their mother are the primary examples of those who **were tortured** (11:35b, *etympanisthēsan*; cf. *tympanon* "rack" as instrument of torture, 2 Macc 6:19) in the course of their martyrdom (2 Macc 6:18–7:42; 4 Macc 5:1–7:23; 8:1–18, 24). Eleazar, who chose not to eat swine's flesh rather than live in shame (2 Macc 6:18), is an example of one who died **rather than receive freedom** (11:35c; 2 Macc 6:22, 30; cf. 7:24–25). In his readiness to meet death in order that he might **attain a better resurrection** (11:35d; cf. 2 Macc 7:9, 14), he stands in the tradition of those who staked their lives on "things not seen" (11:1) and serves as an example for those who now have a "better hope" (7:19) and a "better possession" (10:34).

The **others** who **experienced mocking and scourging** (11:36a; *empaigmōn kai mastigōn*) include not only the brothers in the Maccabean war (2 Macc 7:1, 7; 4 Macc 6:3, 6; 9:12) but other faithful people in the Hebrew scripture (cf. 2 Chron 36:16), Jesus (Matt 27:29 par. John 19:1), and those who follow him (Acts 22:24). **Chains and imprisonment** (11:36b) are also the legacy of faithful prophets (Micaiah in 1 Kgs 22:27; Hanani in 2 Chron 16:7–10) and of the disciples of Jesus (Acts 5:21; 12:6, 19; 2 Cor 11:23).

The author recalls the kinds of death suffered by faithful people in 11:37a. Those who **were stoned** included not only those who broke Israel's laws (Lev 20:10; 24:16; Deut 22:22–24) but those who were executed for their faithfulness (2 Chron 24:20–22; Matt 23:34–35; Acts 7:58–59). According to tradition, Isaiah was **sawn in two** (*Mart. Isa.* 5.1–11; cf. Sus 59 for this method of execution) because he stood firm when other Israelites turned away. Those who **died by the edge of the sword** included many prophets (1 Kgs 19:10; cf. Jer 2:30) and James the son of Zebedee (Acts 12:2). When the author concludes that they **went about in sheepskins and goatskins** (11:37b), he refers to the distinctive attire of the prophets (1 Kgs 19:13, 19; 2 Kgs 2:8, 13–14), who abandoned refined dress for the sake of their mission, but focuses on the fact that they "went about" (*periēlthon*) as migrants without a homeland. The legacy of faith, as the author has indicated in the memory of Abraham (11:8–16) and Moses (11:23–29), is the life of an alien in the land. This vulnerable existence of the alien is suggested in the concluding participles recalling that they were **in need, oppressed, and tormented** (11:37c; *hysteroumenoi, thlibomenoi, kakouchoumenoi*).

The alien existence is further evident in that **the world was not worthy** (11:38a) of the heroes of faith. Just as Noah "condemned the world" when he built the ark (11:7), those who recognized the reality of the unseen world lived as aliens in their own world. When the author recalls that they **wandered about in deserts and mountains and caves and holes in the ground** (11:38b), he further emphasizes the alienation of the people who have no homeland. Neither the OT nor the Jewish tradition records all the locales mentioned by the author, whose primary interest is the memory of those who "went about" (11:37) and "wandered" (11:38) because, like Abraham and the other patriarchs, they were "strangers and aliens" (11:13) on the earth.

It is clear from this and other lists of heroes that the ancient writers shaped the lists in order to communicate specific values to the readers. The author of Hebrews has shaped a story of alienation to address a community that has been repeatedly tested by its alienation from the society. As a people who have lost possessions (10:32–34) because of their faith, their continued endurance is in doubt. The author recalls Israel's story as a narrative of others who have "gone out" from the security of a homeland, abandoning their possessions, because they acknowledged a reality greater than their loss.

11:39–40. The conclusion in 11:39–40 that **these all were confirmed** (*martyrēthentes*) **through faith** (11:39a) forms an *inclusio* with the introduction in 11:2, indicating that the ancestors in 11:4–38 were not only examples of faith; the passive voice of *martyrein* indicates that God "bore witness" to them in a legally binding way (Weiss 1991, 563). Nevertheless, the author concludes the recollection of the ancestors in a surprising way. Instead of providing a positive ending to the story, he indicates that **they did not receive the promise** (11:39b), repeating the words of 11:13. Although many "received promises" (plural in 11:33; singular in 6:15), they did not enter into God's rest (3:11, 19), come to their homeland (11:14), or enter the city prepared by God (11:16), for only those who have been cleansed by the perfect sacrifice receive the promised inheritance (9:15). Until their death the ancestors lived by faith in "things hoped for" and "things not seen" (11:1), but they could see only through the eyes of faith (11:26–27). Thus the author reminds readers who now suffer because they "do not see" the world in subjection to the exalted Son that their experience does not undermine their confession but confirms that they now share in the legacy of faith.

According to 11:40 they did not receive the promise because God was **foreseeing something better for us** (11:40a; *peri hymōn kreitton ti problepsamenou*). What is "better" (*kreitton*), as the author has consistently maintained, is the "abiding possession" (10:34) and the heavenly homeland (11:14–16) made possible by the superior sacrifice of Christ (9:23). As the author indicates by his resumption of the first-person plural, set aside after 10:39, the better promise (cf. 8:6) is "for us," for the possibility of entering God's rest remains (4:3–11) for those who will demonstrate the same endurance as the ancestors whom God confirmed. However, the promise is not "for us" apart from our ancestors insofar as **without us they would not be made perfect** (11:40b). The context suggests that the ancestors will be "made perfect" only when they reach the heavenly city, which they could see only in the distance during their lifetime (11:13). As the author indicated at the beginning of the homily, the community stands in continuity with those ancestors to whom God spoke in many and various ways in the past (1:1–2), for God's plan will be fulfilled only when the faithful people throughout the ages reach the heavenly homeland together. Consequently, the completion of God's plan requires that the people endure to the end (cf. 10:35), joining those who persevered through circumstances far more difficult than those of the readers.

The surprising conclusion to the list of heroes in 11:39–40 indicates that the narrative is not complete, for those who were "confirmed in faith did not receive the promise" (11:39). The inclusion of the readers in the words "without us" (11:40) marks the transition to "therefore we" in 12:1, indicating the responsibility of the readers in the incomplete narrative. The repetition of the verb "endure" (*hypomenein*, 12:1–3, 7), the noun "endurance" (*hypomonē*, 12:1), and their opposites (12:3), "be weary" (*kamnein*) and "be exhausted" (*eklyein*), indicate that the author now renews his call for endurance (10:36–39) in 12:1–11 after providing examples in chapter 11 of those who endured alienation and suffering.

12:1–3. The author reaches the culmination of the narrative of faithful people in 12:1–3, marking the transition and motivating the audience with the familiar movement from what "we have" ("having therefore," v. 1) to "let us" (cf. 4:14–16; 10:19–25; 13:12–13). Thus what "we have" as a result of God's work is the basis for the community's response. In this instance, **we, therefore, having such a great cloud of witnesses surrounding us** (12:1a) is the motivation for the exhortation that follows. The "cloud of witnesses" (*nephos martyrōn*) includes the heroes who "were confirmed" (*emartyrēthēsan*) by God for their faithfulness (11:2, 4–5, 39) and stand as guarantors of God's promises. The "cloud" is a familiar image for a numberless throng (BDAG, 670) of people. The fact that the witnesses are now "surrounding" (*perikeimenon*) the community suggests the imagery of a stadium in which "witness" has the dual meaning of one who both "bears witness" and is a "spectator" in the arena (Croy 1998, 61). This imagery is especially striking in 4 Maccabees, which describes the heroic martyrdom of Eleazar and the brothers while "the world and humanity were the spectators" (17:14; see Croy 1998, 62, for additional texts).

The author's athletic image becomes explicit with the challenge, **putting away every weight and entangling sin, let us run the race that is set before us with endurance** (12:1b), which suggests that the readers are involved in a distance race. The image of "putting away every weight" could allude either to the athlete's loss of body fat in order to maintain proper conditioning or the stripping for the race (Croy 1998, 63). With the epexegetical "ensnaring sin," the author is referring to the discouragement and sluggishness (5:11) that now hinders them from reaching the goal. Like other ancient writers, especially those who write of martyrdom, the author describes it as a "race set before us." The image of the race (*agōn*) communicates the intense struggle to reach the goal. It is "set before us" (*prokeimenon*) insofar as it is not a misfortune but the destiny of those who belong to the narrative of faith. The author renews the call for "endurance," which the community demonstrated in the past (10:32) and now needs in the present (10:36).

In keeping with the metaphor of the race, the participial phrase, **looking intently on Jesus, the pioneer and perfecter of faith** (12:2a), suggests that believers run behind the leader, focusing on the path ahead and nothing else, for to "look intently" (*aphoran*) is literally "to look away" from any distraction (cf. 4 Macc 17:10, "looking to God"). The "pioneer and perfecter" (*archēgos kai teleiōtēs*), as the roots *arch-* and *tel-* suggest, is the one who both initiates and brings to a conclusion. That is, Jesus was both the forerunner (6:19) who opened the way into the heavenly sanctuary (10:19) and the one who "was made perfect" (cf. 2:10; 5:9) by completing his journey. Thus, when the author encourages the readers to "hold the beginning of the reality firm until the end" (3:14), he alludes to the fact that Jesus both initiated the journey to the promised land and will bring it to an end.

Contrary to numerous translations, the author does not say that Jesus was the "pioneer and perfecter of *our* faith." "Faith" here has a definite article (lit. "the faith"), and in Greek a definite article can substitute for a personal pronoun (thus "our faith")—but that translation misses the point here. Nor does the author present Jesus as the object of faith. Rather, Jesus is the ultimate *example* of faith, the culmination of the list of heroes in chapter 11. The nature of Jesus' faith becomes clear in the summary of the story of Jesus in 12:2b, which is stated in a rhythmic manner similar to the introduction in 1:1–4. Although interpreters agree that the author motivates his readers by summarizing the story of Jesus, the opening phrase has been problematic. Inasmuch as *anti* can mean "in place of" as well as "for the sake of," some interpreters render the phrase, "In place of the joy set before him, he endured the cross," suggesting that Jesus, faced with the choice between earthly joy and the cross, chose the latter (Lane 1991b, 413–14). Two considerations suggest that the more plausible reading is **for the sake of the joy set before him, he endured the cross** (12:2b), meaning that the "joy" stood on the other side of the cross. The author uses *anti* in the sense of "for the sake of" in the illustration in 12:16, where Esau gave up his birthright "for the sake of food." Moreover, the chiastic structure of 12:2b–d suggests that Jesus went to the cross "for the sake of the joy":

A the joy set before him
  B he endured the cross
  B′ despising the shame
A′ is seated at the right hand of God

Thus Jesus attained the "joy set before him" at the right hand of God after he had endured the cross. This summary of the story of Jesus recapitulates the introduction in 1:1–4.

The author's primary concern in recalling the story of Jesus as the ultimate example of faith is to demonstrate that Jesus models the very qualities that he encourages the readers to maintain. Just as they need to endure in faith (10:36–39), Jesus was the model of faith when he "endured the cross." Readers who have experienced mockery and abuse (10:33–34) can look to the one who **despised shame** (12:2c) by going to the cross, the ultimate example of shame. Thus Jesus, having no regard for the popular evaluations of honor and shame, was the ultimate example of faith. Like Moses and others who chose to abandon earthly security for the sake of God's call, he endured mockery because of his choice (11:26).

However, Jesus is not only the culminating example of the mockery and abuse that accompany faith. As the end of the story indicates, the shame of the cross led to the place **at the right hand of the thone of God** (12:2d) and to "the joy set before him," which the ancestors only saw in the distance (11:13, 39). Just as the alienated community has a "race set before them" (*ton prokeimenon agōna*) as their destiny, Jesus took the path of "the joy set before him" (*anti tēs prokeimenēs charas*) at the end of the journey, ensuring the author's readers that the path for them and for the ancestors before them is now open (cf. 11:40).

With the exhortation to **consider the one who endured such hostility from sinners against him** (12:3a), which is parallel to "looking intently to Jesus" (12:2), the author reinforces the two dimensions of the story of Jesus that speak to his own audience. Like the readers, Jesus faced hostility. Since he went to his death, a fate no one among the readers has experienced (12:4), he endured to the absolute limit. The author recalls that story of endurance **in order that [they] not become fatigued, giving out** (12:3b) like athletes in a long-distance race.

Theological Issues

A distinctive contribution of Hebrews is the depiction of the nature of faith. Although the author shares with other NT writers the focus on the singular importance of faith as a response to God, he never speaks of faith *in Jesus*. Instead, he describes faith as the "reality of things hoped for" and "evidence of things not seen" and offers examples of those who embodied this definition. As the author indicates in 10:36–39 and 12:1–11, faith is inseparable from endurance. Those who see another reality can endure the deprivations created by their Christian commitment.

This capacity to see beyond temporal realities creates distance from the perceptions of others. As the community has already demonstrated (10:32–34), the knowledge that their abiding possession lies in the future creates the refusal to accept materialistic solutions to human problems. This knowledge empowers Christians to see beyond crass commercialism and consumerism and to recognize that material goods are not the ultimate value. The fact that Christians are seeking a homeland (11:13–16) also separates the Christian movement from nationalistic and political answers to ultimate human questions. Because Christians take their stand on "things not yet seen," they refuse to accept provisional solutions to human problems. As Karl Barth wrote, "[The church] exists to set up in the world a new sign which is radically dissimilar to [the world's] own manner and which contradicts it in a way which is full of promise" (Barth 1962, 4.3.2:779).

This alternative perception can be sustained only in solidarity with others, as the author indicates in 10:32–34. The church runs the exhausting race together, looking out for those who falter along the way (12:12–13). They support each other, encourage each other with the reminder of the alternative reality, and demonstrate their convictions with the generous support of others. Their community includes not only those who gather in the house church but also the great "cloud of witnesses" (12:1) that has preceded them. This community serves as a constant reminder that their marginalized existence is not a misfortune but a response to the call of God. As the author indicates in 11:40, the list of marginalized people is not complete. Christians of every age join the community of the faithful who serve, knowing that they have an ultimate loyalty in "things hoped for." Thus the author's open-ended list of heroes is a reminder of the ever-expanding community of witnesses who challenge the church to become witnesses in the midst of suffering and alienation.

Hebrews 12:4–13

Enduring Faithfully in the Midst of Suffering

Introductory Matters

The interpretation of the readers' suffering also indicates the author's interaction with the literature of Hellenistic Judaism. He moves from the argument from examples to the direct voice of scripture, citing Prov 3:11–12 almost verbatim. The scriptural statements, "do not take lightly the discipline [*paideia*] of the Lord" and "for whom the Lord loves, he disciplines [*paideuei*]," introduce an educational metaphor to accompany athletic images in the discourse (10:32; 12:1–4, 11). This metaphor is the central focus of 12:4–11. *Paideia* has a wide range of meanings, including education, training, discipline, and punishment. In Greek literature, the term was commonly used for education and culture. Consistent with the common view in the Wisdom literature that punishment plays an important role in the formation of the child (Prov 23:13–14), the word in Prov 3:11–12 refers to punishment. Jewish literature frequently interpreted the people's sufferings as God's "discipline" (*paideia*). Moses tells the Israelites that God is the father who tests and disciplines (*paideuei*) his children in the wilderness (Deut 8:2–5 LXX). The theme that suffering is God's *paideia* is developed in other texts, especially in the Wisdom literature (Wis 12:19–22; Sir 4:17). In the Maccabean literature, the people interpret their suffering in persecution as the discipline (*paideia*) of God (2 Macc 6:12; 7:33; 10:4). Whereas the author of 2 Maccabees regarded suffering as God's punishment on Israel's sins, the author of 4 Maccabees interpreted the persecutions as educational and formative (Croy 1998, 103). When the third brother is near death, he declares, "We suffer these things for the sake of education [*paideia*] and the virtue of God" (4 Macc 10:10).

Philo also acknowledges the educational value of suffering. Although Philo speaks of *paideia* on numerous occasions, one passage is especially noteworthy as a background to Hebrews. In *On the Preliminary Studies*, Philo has a lengthy discussion of affliction. He argues that prosperity causes one to forget God's laws (159–160), while affliction breeds virtue. Philo describes the period in the wilderness as a time of testing for Israel, concluding that some are "like weary athletes," for "they drop their hands in weakness and determine to speed back to Egypt and enjoy passion" (164). Others, however, "finish the contest of life" (165). Like the author of Hebrews, Philo cites Prov 3:11–12, concluding that affliction is a sign of a kinship with God (175; see Croy 1998, 212).

Philo's reflections on suffering as education (*paideia*) are indebted not only to the OT but to Greek philosophy, for this was a common theme in Stoic reflection on the meaning of adversity. Seneca's comments are especially significant as a background to Philo and to Heb 12:4–11. In *On Providence*, Seneca maintains that God "rears" the wise person like a son (2.5). Those whom God loves are disciplined (2.6; 4.7). He uses athletic imagery to depict the meaning of suffering, indicating that brave people regard suffering as training (2.2). Similar athletic imagery is employed by Epictetus (*Diss.* 3.22.57; 3.24.113) to describe suffering (Croy 1998, 150–51).

This background is significant for the interpretation of Heb 12:4–11, for the author's reflections rely not only on Prov 3:11–12 but on images current in philosophical discussion in his own day. Like the Stoics, the author combines educational and athletic metaphors to interpret suffering. The reference to the "struggle against sin" (12:4) at the beginning of the discussion employs an athletic metaphor (*antagōnizomenoi*, lit. "struggle in an athletic contest"), as does the concluding line in verse 11 (*gegymnasmenois*, lit. "to those being trained"). The interpretation of persecution as suffering is indebted to the Maccabean literature described above. Thus the author, who earlier paraphrased a well-known Greek maxim, "He learned from what he suffered" (*emathen aph hōn epathen*, 5:8; cf. Aeschylus, *Ag.* 177–178; 250–251), concludes the interpretation of the community's suffering by using the resources of philosophical reflection and the Jewish martyr tradition. The author shares the educational interpretation of the community's suffering and the call to endure.

Tracing the Train of Thought

The exhortation not to "give out" (*eklyein*, 12:3) is the transition to a theological rationale for the community's continued endurance in 12:4–11, which the author provides in the form of a midrash on Prov 3:11–12, a passage that encourages the one who suffers not to "give out" (*mēde eklyou*, Heb 12:5). This theological rationale provides the basis for the exhortation to "lift your drooping hands and strengthen your weak knees" in 12:12–13. With this call not to give out, the author concludes the call for endurance (*hypomonē*) that began in the exhortation in 10:32–39 (especially 10:32, 36). Faith, as the author has shown, is demonstrated through endurance (cf. 10:36–39; 12:1–3).

12:4–6. Both the introduction of the midrash in 12:4–5 and the conclusion in 12:11 indicate the relevance of Prov 3:11–12 for the audience. The author develops the athletic imagery further, explaining that the community continues to "wage a battle" (12:4) and to be "trained" (12:11) through suffering. Unlike Jesus, who endured suffering to the point of death (12:1–2), the community has **not yet resisted to the point of shedding blood in its battle with sin** (12:4), although it has suffered physical and verbal abuse (10:32–34) in the past. "Battling against sin" (*tēn hamartian antagonizomenoi*) is not the confrontation with various vices but a struggle with the "deliberate sin" of apostasy (10:26), which the author describes elsewhere as the "deceitfulness of sin" (3:13) and the "entangling sin" (12:1) of despair (cf. 10:39).

The comment that the community has "not resisted to the point of shedding blood" (12:4) and the statement that **you have forgotten the encouragement that speaks to you as sons** (12:5a) are not criticisms of the readers but prepare them to hear encouragement from Prov 3:11–12. Indeed, as one who describes this homily as a "word of exhortation" (*logos tēs paraklēseōs*, 13:22), the author introduces the citation as "exhortation" (*paraklēsis*), a term that has connotations of both consolation and encouragement. Having already called on community members to "exhort one another" (3:13; 10:25), the author now speaks of scripture as exhortation addressed to the community as "sons" (see p. 72 regarding inclusive language). Scripture, therefore, addresses the community in its present circumstance. Just as it speaks directly with words of warning (3:7–11) as a "two-edged sword" (4:12–13), it now speaks words of exhortation to those who are in danger of abandoning the race to the finish line.

Hebrews 12:4–13 in the Rhetorical Flow

Hearing God's word with faithful endurance (1:1–4:13)

Probatio: Discovering certainty and confidence in the word for the mature (4:14–10:31)

Peroratio: On not refusing the one who is speaking (10:32–13:25)

  Enduring in hope: the faithfulness of Jesus and the faithfulness of the ancestors (10:32–12:13)

    Remembering the faithfulness of earlier days (10:32–39)

    Remembering the faithful heroes of the past (11:1–12:3)

    ▶ Enduring faithfully in the midst of suffering (12:4–13)

      Encouragement for God's children (12:4–6)

      The Lord's discipline (12:7–11)

      Drooping hands and weak knees (12:12–13)

The adaptation of **my son** in the citation (12:5b; cf. Prov 3:11) to an address to "sons" is central to the author's argument, for it indicates that the passage speaks to people alienated from their own society with the assurance that they have a special relationship to God. The author has established earlier in the homily that God "brings many sons to glory" through the work of the Son, who is not ashamed to speak of his brothers (2:10–14), and he has reassured the readers, "We are his house" (3:6). This special relationship to God allows the community to interpret its sufferings as a sign not of abandonment but of a special relationship to God.

The focus of the author's interpretation of Prov 3:11–12 is the **discipline of the Lord** (12:5b, *paideia tou kyriou*), as the author's repeated references to "discipline" (*paideia*; cf. also *paideuein*, "to discipline," and *paideutēs*, "instructor" or "one who disciplines") indicate in 12:7–11. In Prov 3:11–12, the author compares the discipline given by human fathers to the discipline of the Lord. Although *paideia* in Greek literature was the common word for education or culture (*TDNT* 5:597) that parents provided for their children, the term in the OT commonly has an association with the chastisement carried out by parents in the course of raising children (Prov 4:13; 13:24; 22:15; 23:13). The parallelism of Prov 3:11 indicates that suffering is the equivalent of **being punished** (12:5c, *elenchomenos*) and "chastised," as in the phrase **he chastises** (*mastigoi*, lit. "whips") **every son** (12:6). Thus the original text of Proverbs interprets suffering with the divine punishment that is analogous to a father's punishment of an errant child, maintaining that punishment is a sign of God's love.

12:7–11. The author interprets the passage in 12:7–11, declaring first that suffering is a sign of divine sonship (12:7–8) before describing the benefits of the divine discipline in 12:9–11. His repeated use of forms of "discipline" (*paideia*) in 7–11 contains no suggestion that suffering is a punishment for the community's sins; it is instead the paternal discipline necessary to train (12:11) them in order that they may attain the goal. Just as Jesus "learned from what he suffered" (5:8), the community is now being educated by its suffering. Consequently, after the citation the author interprets their situation, **It is for discipline that you endure** (12:7a), connecting this interpretation of the passage with the call for endurance that began in 10:32–39 and the example of Jesus, who "endured" the cross (12:2–3). The author supports the interpretation in 12:7a with a syllogism in 12:7b–8. Drawing on the premise, "The Lord [i.e., God] disciplines those whom the Lord loves" (12:6), he maintains that **without the discipline** (12:8a) that they are now experiencing they would be **illegitimate and not sons** (12:8b), and thus unloved by God. He concludes, **God is dealing with you as with sons** (12:7b). Although they are abused by society, they are the recipients of God's love.

In 12:9–11, the author develops this assurance with a comparison between human and divine parents, once more appealing to rational argumentation and human experience. In 12:9, he contrasts the discipline **we had** (*eichomen*; the imperfect tense suggests a continuing experience) from **earthly parents** (*tēs sarkos hēmōn pateras*; lit. "fathers of the flesh") with that given by the **father of spirits,** continuing the dualistic distinction between the sphere of the flesh (cf. Heb 5:7; 7:16; 9:10, 13) and the transcendent world that he has assumed throughout the homily. This dualistic distinction is the basis for the argument from the lesser to the greater (cf. 2:1–4; 10:26–31), which contrasts two responses to suffering. The author assumes as a common human experience that **we respected** human "disciplinarians" (*paideutas*), drawing the logical conclusion that we will do more than "respect" our divine disciplinarian: **we will be subject** (*hypotagēsometha*) to the latter by enduring suffering rather than abandoning the race. Only those who endure the divine discipline **will live.**

In 12:10, the author reinforces the contrast between natural parents (*hoi men*, "they") and God (*ho de*, "he"), pointing to two dimensions of the superior benefit of the divine discipline, which he contrasts in parallel lines:

They (natural parents) disciplined for a few days as they thought best.

He (disciplines) for our good so that we may share his holiness.

The human discipline is "for a few days," while the divine discipline is lasting, "that we may share his holiness." Furthermore, human parents disciplined "as they thought best," while God disciplines "for our good," which the author defines as sharing God's holiness. Thus, having placed before the readers the ultimate goal of entry into the heavenly city (cf. 11:13–16), the author reassures the suffering community that, like Jesus, they will reach the goal only through the path of suffering, which is now disciplining them for the future in which they will participate in the nature of God.

The author concludes the midrash with a general rule that was at home in philosophical circles: **all discipline** (*paideia*) **seems to be sorrowful rather than joyful in the present, but afterward yields peaceful fruit of righteousness to those who are being trained** (12:11; cf. Diogenes Laertius, *Vit.* 5.18). As the athletic metaphor suggests (*tous gegymnasmenous*, "those who are being trained"), the present suffering, like the disciplined training of the athlete, is the necessary condition for reaching the goal. To say that it is not "joyful" in the present recalls the community's earlier suffering, in which they endured sufferings "with joy" because they had an abiding possession (10:34), Moses' abandonment of the treasures of Egypt for the sake of the reward (11:25–26), and Jesus' path to the cross "for the joy set before him" (12:2).

After challenging the community to endure (10:36; 12:1) despite the abuse that it has suffered, the author has provided a theological rationale, appealing to both Greek and Jewish interpretations of suffering. The assurance that suffering is a sign of the favor granted by God to beloved children reminds the readers who have been rejected by society that they have a place of honor with God. The athletic metaphor reminds them that suffering is a discipline that trains them for the ultimate reward. This encouragement from scripture (12:5) is the foundation for the call for endurance (DeSilva 1995, 301).

12:12–13. The exhortation **strengthen** (*anorthōsate*; lit. "straighten") **your drooping hands and your weak knees** (12:12) continues the language of the race (12:1–11) in terminology derived from the wisdom tradition (Isa 35:3; Sir 2:12; 25:23; Job 4:3). Anyone who endures rigorous training (12:1, 11) to reach the finish line must ensure that the limbs are not bent over from fatigue. The term *anorthoun* is used in Luke 13:13 for the crippled woman who "stood erect" after she was healed. Thus to "strengthen" the hands and knees is to restore them to their original condition in order that the readers can once more endure suffering as they did in the past (Grässer 1997, 3:280).

The image of the people on the move is strengthened by the additional imperative, **make straight paths for your feet** (12:13a), which is also derived from the Wisdom literature (Prov 4:26). The purpose for making the paths straight is ambiguous, since *ektrepein* can mean either "turn away" or "be dislocated" (cf. NIV, NRSV). In keeping with the image of the distance race, the more likely rendering is **in order that the lame may not be dislocated** (i.e., as with a sprained ankle), **but rather be healed** (12:13b). This metaphor suggests that the "lame" are the members of the community who suffer from lethargy and despair. Just as the entire community actively encourages other members (cf. 3:12–14; 10:24–25) along the way, they take responsibility to ensure that no one leaves the path that leads to the destination (Weiss 1991, 659).

Theological Issues

The description of suffering as discipline in 12:4–11 is not an attempt to explain why bad things happen to good people. Nor is it advice to those who are suffering in abusive relationships to endure passively. Taken out of context the message that suffering is educational could be destructive for those who are confronted each day with illness or abuse. Instead, the author speaks encouragement to a vulnerable community in a specific situation, offering hope that their suffering is not the end of the story. To follow Jesus in suffering is also to follow him into the presence of God. In using the wisdom tradition, the author is not making a categorical statement that all suffering results in education but encouraging the readers to see that God can work in their circumstances to train them to be faithful. His encouragement is a challenge, especially to Christians in affluent societies, to recognize that the Christian confession offers no guarantee of ease or comfort but rather an invitation to follow the suffering of Jesus, who "learned from what he suffered" (5:8). Although not all suffering is educational, this exhortation indicates that participation in the suffering of Jesus is a component of the path of discipleship.

Mother Teresa of Calcutta, founder of the Missionaries of Charity, describes the role of suffering in *Suffering into Joy* (Egan and Egan 1994). Members of her order not only take vows of poverty, chastity, and obedience but also vow to serve the poorest of the poor, recognizing the place of suffering in their ministry. Mother Teresa wrote, "Without our suffering, our work would be just social work—it would not be the work of Jesus Christ, not part of the redemption" (Egan and Egan 1994, 24; Moessner 2003, 288).

Hebrews 12:14–29

Listening to the One Who Is Speaking from Heaven

Introductory Matters

As part of the *peroratio*, the unit in 12:14–29 recapitulates the argument of the homily, reaching a rhetorical crescendo in the careful parallelism of 12:18–24 and the eschatological urgency of 12:25–29. The author maintains the theme of the people on the move, locating them in the wilderness as he has throughout the homily. The exhortation "pursue peace with everyone" (12:14) is drawn from early Christian paraenesis (cf. Rom 12:18; 14:19; 2 Tim 2:22; 1 Pet 3:11) and based on the words of the psalmist (Ps 33:15 LXX; 34:15 MT), "seek peace and pursue it." Inasmuch as the author has indicated repeatedly that the community is "being sanctified" (*hagiazomenoi*, 2:10) by the blood of Christ (9:13; 10:10, 29; 13:12), the exhortation to "pursue holiness" (*hagiasmos*) is a challenge to pursue what God has given. "Without which no one will see God" corresponds to the promise that the pure in heart "will see God" (Matt 5:8). In contrast to the philosophical literature, the OT speaks not of the invisibility of God but of the fact that ordinary mortals are not permitted to see God. Job hopes to "see God" after his death (Job 19:26; Grässer 1997, 3:288). Like other NT writers (cf. 1 Cor 13:12; 1 John 3:2), the author envisions the eschatological moment when those who have pursued what God has given "will see God."

The author specifies the means for seeking peace in the series of three parallel clauses introduced by "seeing to it" (*episkopountes*) in 12:15. *Episkopein* (lit. "oversee"), which has the connotation of caring for others, is used in many manuscripts of 1 Pet 5:2 for the role of church leaders who care for the community. In the noun form it is used as a title for church overseers (*episkopoi*, Phil 1:1; cf. 1 Tim 3:2). For the author, however, the act of caring (*episkopountes*) is the task of the entire community. In the parallel construction in 12:15–16, the threefold phrase "that not any" (*mē tis*) indicates their communal responsibility (cf. 3:12–14; 10:24–25). The first clause, "that not any one fall back from the grace of God," continues the theme of the people on the way, using imagery sometimes associated with the sheep "falling back" (*hysterōn*) from the rest of the flock (BDAG). The second clause, "that not any bitter root grow up and cause trouble" is almost a verbatim rendering of Deut 29:17 (*enochlē*, "cause trouble," appears in Hebrews in place of the LXX *en cholē*, "in wrath"). "Bitterness" is a traditional image for sexual offenses and idolatry (Deut 29:18; 32:32; Jer 2:21; Amos 6:12; cf. Eph 4:31; Braun 1984, 425). The concern that "the many be defiled" normally has a cultic connotation, signifying the desecration of things that are holy (cf. John 18:28). The term is used for the desecration of the temple by Antiochus Epiphanes (1 Macc 1:46).

The use of Deuteronomy is not limited to one phrase, for the exhortation in 12:14–17 draws on the larger context of Deut 29, in which Moses addresses the people prior to the entry into the promised land, warning them about the danger of idolatry and instructing them to ensure that "no one" (*mē tis*) is an idolater and "no one (*mē tis*) is a bitter root springing up" to pollute the people. Moses warns the community that "the Lord will be unwilling to pardon them" and that all the "curses of the book of the law will come upon them" (Deut 29:20).

Thus the warning of irrevocable consequences for those who are "defiled," drawn from Deut 29, marks the transition to the example of Esau, whose fate was determined by his choice. In the third clause, he urges vigilance "lest anyone be a sexually immoral and worldly person like Esau, who gave up his privilege as firstborn son for a single meal." In Jewish tradition Esau exemplified one who turned away from God. The claim that Esau was "sexually immoral" (*pornos*) is drawn not from the OT but from Jewish haggadic tradition, which interpreted Esau's marriage to Hittite women (Gen 26:34–35) as an example of sexual immorality. According to *Gen. Rab.* 63.9 on Gen 25:27, Esau was guilty of homosexuality and sexual intercourse with a betrothed woman (63.12, on Gen 25:29; cf. Löhr 1994, 127–28). According to the *Targum Pseudo-Jonathan*, Esau was a hunter who killed not only animals but humans as well (comments on Gen 25:27), including Nimrod and Enoch. Philo interpreted Esau's abandonment of his privilege as firstborn as an example of his indulging "without restraint the pleasures of the belly and the lower lying parts" (*Virtues* 208; cf. *Sobriety* 26) and his "craving that pursues evil"

(*Sacrifices* 120; cf. 81). Esau "exercised himself in the basest things" (*Migration* 153) and was a hunter after passions (*Alleg. Interp.* 3.2), exhibiting a "savagery that knows no discipline" (*QG* 4.242).

The author does not pursue the sexual dimension of Esau's sin, as the example of the abandonment of the birthright indicates (12:16). The phrase "sexually immoral or worldly" (*pornos ē bebēlos*) and the example of the abandonment of the birthright indicate that the author's primary focus is on Esau's inverted values. *Bebēlos* is the opposite of the holy or sacred (Spicq 1994, 1:284). When Esau gave up his birthright, he committed a sacrilege, for he disregarded the holy.

In the conclusion in 12:17, "you know that afterward when he wished to inherit the blessing, he was rejected," the author combines the example of the birthright with the later account of the blessing (Gen 27:1–40), and again apparently draws on Jewish haggadic traditions to supplement the Genesis narrative. That "he was rejected" is not explicitly stated in Genesis but is probably an interpretation of Gen 27:38–39, which recalls the occasion when Isaac informed Esau that Jacob had inherited the blessing. That Esau "sought a place of repentance, but did not find it although he sought it with tears" is also not stated in Genesis but is probably an interpretation of Esau's plea for a blessing when he "lifted up his voice and wept" (Gen 27:38). The author mentions neither the intrigue surrounding the blessing nor the role of Esau's parents in the story. By combining the two stories of Esau, he has portrayed him as one who attempted to repent of his inverted values. Contrary to the NIV, the "opportunity for repentance" (*metanoias . . . topos*, lit. "place of repentance") refers not to a change of Isaac's mind but to the opportunity for Esau to repent of the worldliness evident in his giving up the birthright for a meal. By combining the two stories in the life of Esau, the author has offered an example that is the opposite of the heroes of faith in chapter 11 and has shaped the story to correspond to the theme of the impossibility of repentance (6:4–8; 10:26–31).

In 12:18–24, the consistent comparison of the community's experience to the pilgrimage of Israel through the wilderness under the leadership of Moses (cf. 3:7–4:13; 8:5) reaches a rhetorical climax in the comparison between those who approached Mount Sinai and the community that has come to Mount Zion. In the OT and Jewish literature, the Sinai theophany was the defining moment in Israel's story, for here the people witnessed the power of God and received the divine revelation. The rabbinic appreciation of the story is reflected in Rabbi Simeon ben Lakish's statement: "If that multitude had not seen the thunder, flames, lightning, quaking mountains, and sound of the trumpet, they would not have taken the kingdom of God upon themselves" (cited in Strack and Billerbeck 1926, 2:586; cf. Thompson 1982, 46). This event shaped the imagination and became the model for Jewish reflection on the end time, according to which God would repeat in the messianic age all of the signs done in the wilderness (Hos 2:14–16; Isa 40:3–5; 41:17–20; 48:20–21; 52:11–12; see Eichrodt 1963, 34). Two of these signs were the hearing of the voice (cf. Exod 20:18) and the shaking of the earth.

Mount Zion shaped the imagination of Israel no less than Mount Sinai, for it is the place of God's new revelation (cf. Isa 2:2–4). If Mount Sinai was the place of Israel's infancy (Levenson 1985, 89), Mount Zion was the place where Israel's ultimate hopes would become realized. The return of the peoples to Zion symbolizes the return of the world to God and the establishment of the new covenant and the worship of the restored community (Jer 31:6; Son 2005, 48–49). In apocalyptic literature, the heavenly Mount Zion is the place of God's presence, which will appear at the end of time (cf. *4 Ezra* 2.15–22, 42–48). It was also commonly associated with the heavenly temple where the archangel offers sacrifices on behalf of the righteous (cf. *T. Levi* 3.4–10).

The parallel phrases "you have not come to what may be touched . . . you have come to Mount Zion" probably draw upon traditional contrasts between Mount Sinai and the new Jerusalem (cf. *Jub.* 4.26; Gal 4:25–26; Rev 21:1–2). Inasmuch as Sinai was the place for the giving of the Levitical covenant, Zion now becomes the place of the new covenant (cf. 8:7–13). The carefully balanced list of the distinguishing features of Sinai and Zion are probably also taken from traditional apocalyptic imagery describing the correspondence of the events of Sinai and the events of Mount Zion.

The author combines the narratives of Exod 19:12–18 and Deut 4:11 to describe the Sinai events. The "blazing fire," "darkness," "whirlwind," and "sound of words" are derived from Deut 4:11; the author has added "gloom" (*zophos*) to "darkness" (*gnophos*) for rhetorical effect. The "sound of the trumpet" recalls Exod 19:16, and the warning that "even if a beast touch the mountain it will be stoned" is based on the divine decree forbidding either animal or human being to touch the mountain (Exod 19:12–13). The author expands on the comment that "all who were in the camp trembled" (Exod 19:16), adding that "those who heard begged that no further word be spoken" and "could not bear the command." He also adds the response of Moses, "I am trembling with fear" (cf. Deut 9:19), which is derived not from the narrative of the theophany but from the description of Moses' descent from the mountain.

The author's interpretation of that event becomes evident in the way he has shaped the narrative. He speaks not of the presence of God but of the phenomena associated with Mount Sinai. Furthermore, he does not speak specifically of Mount Sinai but refers to the place as "what may be touched" (*psēlaphōmenō*, 12:18). Although this description may be derived from the command not to touch the mountain (12:20; Exod 19:12), the author employs the word to describe the entire Sinai theophany. The contrast between "what may be touched" and Mount Zion in 12:22 indicates that the author is distinguishing between the "palpable," material nature of the Sinai theophany and the immaterial nature of "Mount Zion, the city of the living God, the heavenly Jerusalem" (12:22). This distinction is consistent with the contrast between the "earthly sanctuary" (9:1) and the sanctuary "not made with hands, that is, not of this creation" (9:11; cf. 9:23) earlier in the homily. Just as the author has distinguished between things that are "seen" and "unseen" (11:1, 3, 26–27) and points his readers to the unseen world, here he points the readers to "what may not be touched." The "thunder, lightning, earthquake, trumpet and voice of many words" are only "natural phenomena" (Schierse 1955, 24), the basis for comparison to the superior features of Mount Zion (12:22–24).

The author reinforces his evaluation of the Sinai event by describing the manifestations at Sinai as a "spectacle" (*to phantazomenon*), emphasizing the visible aspects of the event. Thus he locates the Sinai event in the sphere of sense perception. This evaluation of the Sinai event corresponds to the perspective of the Platonic tradition, according to which that which is touchable belongs to the sphere of sense perception (*Phaedo* 99e; *Tim.* 28b, 31b; Thompson 1982, 45). This negative evaluation of the Sinai event has its closest analogies in the Alexandrian tradition of Philo of Alexandria and his predecessor, Aristobulus. Both Jewish philosophers see a conflict between the account in Exod 24 and their convictions about the transcendence of God (Thompson 1982, 47). Both Philo (*Decalogue* 33) and Aristobulus (Eusebius, *PE* 13.12.3) are troubled by the idea of the audibility of God's voice to human ears. Consequently, Philo concludes that the voice was "invisible" (*Decalogue* 33) and that "there was the appearance of flame, not a veritable flame" (*QE* 2.47). Thus Philo is concerned about the "sense perceptible" nature of the event and attempts to minimize the material nature of the event, while the author of Hebrews draws attention to the palpable and visible aspects of Israel's experience at Mount Sinai in order to contrast it with Christian experience at Mount Zion.

The author's careful arrangement of the Sinai theophany also indicates his interpretation of the event. His list of phenomena culminates in the "sound of words" (12:19), his primary focus. He recalls not the giving of the Ten Commandments at Mount Sinai but only the terror associated with the "sound of words" (Wider 1997, 93). This word evoked such terror that "those who heard begged (*parētēsanto*) that no other word be given," and even Moses said, "I tremble with fear." The author interprets Israel's response as a refusal to hear God's voice, as indicated by the exhortation to the community, "do not refuse (*paraitēsasthe*) the one who is speaking" (12:25). Thus the author focuses on the terror of hearing God's word, anticipating the comparison to the church's hearing of the divine voice at the heavenly Mount Zion (12:25).

The contrasting "But you have come to Mount Zion, the city of the living God, the heavenly Jerusalem" suggests that the author contrasts the Christian listeners with "those who heard" at Mount Sinai. The list of inhabitants of the heavenly world suggests a contrast to the earthly phenomena of Mount Sinai. The author has attempted to integrate images from apocalyptic imagery into his own message. In Jewish tradition, "myriads of angels in a festal gathering" are the inhabitants of the heavenly world (cf. Dan 7:10 LXX; Rev 5:11; *1 En.* 1.9; 14.22). The "festal gathering" (*panēgyris*; cf. Ezek 46:11; Amos 5:21; Hos 2:13; 9:5 for the earthly counterpart) may suggest the joy of the heavenly community in contrast to the terror of Mount Sinai (Weiss 1991, 677). The "assembly of the firstborn who are enrolled in heaven" is also a commonplace of apocalyptic literature (on the concept of the heavenly books, see Exod 32:32–33; Isa 4:3; Dan 7:10; 12:1; *1 En.* 47.3; 98.6–8); for the author it may refer to all those who are now participants in a "heavenly calling" and share in the blessings of the age to come (cf. 3:1; 6:4; Weiss 1991, 679). The "judge of all" is God, to whom the community must give an account (4:13; 10:31). Reference to the "spirits of the just made perfect" is also commonly found in apocalyptic literature, describing the deceased who have completed the journey (cf. 3:14). The fact that the image does not correspond well to the author's comment that "without us they would not be made perfect" (11:40) may suggest that the author has not integrated the apocalyptic image into the rest of the homily. The "mediator of the new covenant" and the "sprinkled blood that speaks better than that of Abel" are most likely the author's own summation, for they recall the earlier claim that Jesus is the "mediator" (*mesitēs*) of a better covenant (8:6; 9:15). That his blood "speaks better" than the blood of Abel recalls the statement in 11:4 that Abel's blood "still speaks." Thus the author concludes this series, as he did the first series, with a reference to the word event of Christian experience, contrasting the "sound of words" (12:19) with the word that is "better" than the cry of Abel. The term "better" (*kreitton*) links the description of the divine word to the author's consistent use of the term to describe the greatness of the saving event effected by the exalted Christ.

The contrast between the terrifying word spoken at Sinai and the one who speaks "better than Abel" at Mount Zion (12:24) is the basis for the exhortation in 12:25–29, in which the author develops the implications of the comparison. He maintains the dualistic distinction between refusing the warning "on earth" and rejecting the warning "from heaven" (12:25), using the familiar argument from the lesser to the greater (cf. 2:1–4; 10:26–31) to indicate that the greater the message, the greater the consequences for refusing. Although 12:18–21 does not say that "the voice shook the earth," the author is apparently recalling the report in Exod 19:18 that "the earth shook violently." This earthquake is the basis for the comparison to the eschatological earthquake described in the citation of Hag 2:6 in 12:26. According to the Haggai passage, the Lord says, "Once more I will shake the heaven and the earth and the sea and the dry land." This passage was frequently cited in the apocalyptic literature to speak of the final eschatological earthquake (*2 Bar.* 59.3; *4 Ezra* 6.11–17; 10.25–28; Thompson 1982, 48). The author has adapted the passage for his own purposes with the citation, "Once more I will shake not only the earth but also the heaven," adding "not only" and omitting "the sea and the dry land" from the original passage. This adaptation corresponds to the author's dualistic distinction between the two spheres of reality. Unlike the voice that only "shook the earth" at Sinai, the voice from heaven will shake the entire cosmos. The author interprets the passage from Haggai in a way consistent with the argument of the homily, adapting "I will shake" (*seisō*) to a contrast between "things that cannot be shaken" (*ta mē saleuomena*) and "things that can be shaken" (*ta saleuomena*). The latter are the equivalent of "things that have been made" (*ta pepoiēmena*). In his comment that the "things that cannot be shaken remain," the author once more builds his argument on the Platonic distinction between the two spheres of reality, suggesting the equivalence between what "may not be touched" and "the things that cannot be shaken" in contrast to the material world. This distinction corresponds to the view of Plato and his successors that only the ideal world remains in eternity, while the physical world is subject to destruction and decay. Thus the author has combined the eschatological images of the heavenly city and the end of the world with the Platonic distinction between the temporal and the eternal to indicate that the community is in contact with ultimate reality.

Tracing the Train of Thought

The exhortation "pursue peace with everyone and holiness" (12:14a) both continues the thought of 12:1–13 and marks the transition to the climactic depiction of the community's approach to "Mount Zion, the city of the living God" in 12:18–24, maintaining the focus on the people's journey through the wilderness to the heavenly Jerusalem (12:18). The promise that those who "make straight paths" for their feet will receive "peaceful fruit" (12:13) provides the transition to the exhortation to pursue peace with all (12:14). This advice probably reflects also the influence of Prov 4:26–27 LXX, according to which "God himself will make your paths straight" and "lead your ways forth in peace" (cf. Lane 1991b, 432).

Care for Each Other (12:14–17)

12:14–15. Within the context of Hebrews, **peace with everyone** (12:14a) is to pursue the harmonious relationship with the community that is now wandering in the wilderness. To pursue **holiness** is to maintain the gift that God has given, and to **see the Lord** (12:14b) will be the fulfillment of the promise that the author has consistently held before the community. The author elaborates on the exhortation to "pursue peace with everyone" in 12:15–16, suggesting once more the communal responsibility of members for one another. He does not mention the role of church leaders until chapter 13 (cf. 13:17–18) but assumes (cf. 3:12–14) that community members will help the stragglers along the way. **See to it** (12:15a), he says, using *episkopountes*, the term used elsewhere for the function of elders (1 Pet 5:2), suggesting that each is a "bishop" (*episkopos*) to the other, caring for the weaker members. The author's frequent use of *tis* (anyone, no one) suggests the concern for the whole community (cf. 3:12–13; 4:1). With the careful arrangement of the three parallel clauses, each beginning with *mē tis* (lest anyone) in a pattern of increasing length, he describes those who fall away and the consequences of their apostasy. In the first clause, the instruction that the community is responsible for taking care **lest anyone forfeit** (*hysterōn*) **the grace of God** (12:15a) reinforces the earlier concern to ensure straight paths for the lame (12:13) and the challenge to take care "lest anyone of you fail" (*hysterēkenai*) to enter into God's rest (4:1). Those who have received God's grace (cf. 2:9; 10:29) must now be encouraged to remain within in it as they "draw near to the throne of grace" (4:16) in anticipation of God's ultimate gift.

The second clause describes those who fall away with imagery drawn from Deut 29:17, reiterating Moses' concern **lest any bitter root spring up** (12:15b)

Hebrews 12:14–29 in the Rhetorical Flow

Hearing God's word with faithful endurance (1:1–4:13)

Probatio: Discovering certainty and confidence in the word for the mature (4:14–10:31)

Peroratio: On not refusing the one who is speaking (10:32–13:25)

  Enduring in hope: the faithfulness of Jesus and the faithfulness of the ancestors (10:32–12:13)

    Remembering the faithfulness of earlier days (10:32–39)

    Remembering the faithful heroes of the past (11:1–12:3)

    Enduring faithfully in the midst of suffering (12:4–13)

▶ Listening to the one who is speaking from heaven (12:14–29)

    Care for each other (12:14–17)

      That no one fall (12:14–15)

      The failure of Esau (12:16–17)

    Sinai and Zion (12:18–24)

    Do not refuse the one speaking (12:25–29)

      The unshakable reality (12:25–27)

      Acceptable worship (12:28–29)

---

among them and adding the consequences of such a failure. These people become an infection by which **the many** who have been made holy by the blood of Christ **are defiled** (12:15c). That is, a defection from the pilgrim people would be a loss not only for the individual but also for the holy community, which would become contaminated by the evil in its midst. Thus the community's own situation determines this reading of the scripture, for the author recognizes that the attrition of any members would undermine the cohesion of the community.

12:16–17. In the third clause, the author describes the additional consequence of falling away, instructing the community to take care **lest anyone be sexually immoral or worldly like Esau** (12:16a). The author's primary concern is not, however, with problems of sexual morality within the community, for the phrase *pornos ē bebēlos* (sexually immoral or worldly) places the emphasis on Esau's disregard for the holy, as the illustration from the combination of two narratives about Esau indicates. According to the Genesis account, Esau **gave away the privileges of the firstborn** (12:16b; Gen 25:33), to which the author adds, **for a single meal**, emphasizing Esau's worldliness and disregard for the ultimate good. The juxtaposition of "a single meal" (*brōsis*) with the "privileges of the firstborn" (*ta prōtotokia*) corresponds to the contrast between "food and drink" (9:10; cf. 13:9) and heavenly realities, suggesting that Esau's choice of a "single meal" was the ultimate inversion of proper values. Unlike the heroes of faith, who denied the pleasures of the moment for the sake of the later inheritance (11:8; cf. 11:26), Esau epitomizes the inverted values of those who choose the material world over the eschatological promise. In his failure to find a **place of repentance** (12:17) for his worldly outlook, Esau also exemplifies the irrevocable consequences of rejecting God's promise. The author has depicted Esau in this manner because his community, composed of those who do not see the world in subjection to the Son, is now in danger of choosing this world over the promise of entering God's rest. The author's interpretation of Esau is a warning against disregarding the ultimate gift for the sake of immediate relief from the alienation that the community now experiences.

Sinai and Zion (12:18–24)

In 12:18–29, the author reaches the rhetorical climax of the *peroratio* and of the entire homily, summarizing the content of the message with the same rhetorical intensity with which it began. The carefully crafted periodic sentences in 12:18–24 correspond to the artistry of 1:1–4. The parallelism and rhyme—for example, **darkness and gloom** (12:18, *gnophos kai zophos*)—give the passage a rhetorical effect similar to the opening words. The contrast between God's "speech" in the past and "in these last days" (1:1–2a) corresponds to the focus on the word delivered at Sinai (12:19, 25) and the "better" message (12:24) that "speaks" from heaven (12:26). Moreover, the contrast between the ephemeral world and the abiding son (10:10–12) anticipates the promise that the material world will be removed and that the abiding reality will remain (12:27–28).

The distinctive rhetorical pattern of the homily is also present here. The affirmation of the superiority of the word in 12:18–24 appears between the warnings in 12:14–17 and 12:25–29. The author speaks with assurance of the community's participation in heavenly realities (12:22–24, 27–28) and warns of the consequences of the refusal of a great salvation (12:25). The memory that the earlier hearers "did not escape" and the warning of even greater consequences for those who refuse the voice "from heaven" (12:25) reiterate the author's earlier question, "How shall we escape if we neglect such a great salvation?" (2:3).

The passage cannot be separated from the preceding warning, as **for** (*gar*) in 12:18 indicates. Thus the people should not, like Esau, give up their inheritance for the sake of material things because they **have not come** (*ou proselēlythate*, "you have not come") to a sanctuary in the world of the senses that **can be touched** (12:18; *psēlaphōmenō*) or seen (12:21, *to phantazomenon*). For people who looked to the Sinai theophany as the religious encounter par excellence, the author boldly categorizes it as palpable and visible, belonging to the world of the senses. The author employs the same verb (*proserchesthai*) that he has employed earlier to encourage the people to "draw near" (4:16; 10:19; cf. 7:22) to the heavenly sanctuary but now speaks in the perfect tense to describe an event that has occurred already (12:18, 22). Thus he reassures a community that suffers because it cannot "see the world in subjection" to the exalted Christ (2:8) but desires palpable and visible assurances, "we have not come to what may be touched."

As with the comparisons throughout the homily, the author's purpose is not to engage in a polemic with Judaism or to denigrate Israel's sacred institutions but, like the ancient orators, to use the *synkrisis* to demonstrate the greatness of the Christian experience in comparison to all alternatives. In the comparison between Sinai and Zion, the author employs the same dualistic framework that he has employed throughout the homily to affirm the superiority of the exalted Christ. If Mount Sinai and the phenomena surrounding it can be described as "what may be touched," the author's affirmation that **we have come to Mount Zion, the city of the living God, the heavenly Jerusalem** (12:22) suggests that this untouchable and invisible city is the homeland and city that Abraham could see only from a distance (11:13–16), the "things not seen" (11:1), and the heavenly rest that Israel did not enter (3:7–19). The community has approached this heavenly world because Christ, the forerunner, opened up the way for his people to enter the heavenly sanctuary (6:20; 10:19).

The author does not indicate the moment when "we have come" to the heavenly city. Some scholars interpret the reference to the community's corporate worship. More likely he is recalling the community's conversion, in which they were "enlightened" (6:4; 10:32) and experienced "the powers of the coming age" (6:5). In becoming "partakers of a heavenly calling" (3:1), they came to the heavenly world, and they continue to draw near to the throne of grace in their worship.

The author maintains the distinction between God's word in the past and in these last days (cf. 1:1–2a) in 12:18–29, focusing on the contrast between Israel's hearing of the word at Sinai (12:19–21) and the community's hearing of the word in the heavenly sanctuary that **speaks better than (the blood of) Abel** (12:24). He focuses only on the warning that not even a beast could touch the mountain without being stoned. The author's focus is especially evident in his addition to the ancient narrative. Both the community's response in begging **that no further word be spoken** (12:19) and Moses' statement, **I tremble** with fear (12:21), indicate the awesome power of God's word of warning and establish the basis for comparison with the word that "speaks better than the blood of Abel" (12:24).

Do Not Refuse the One Speaking (12:25–29)

12:25–27. The practical consequences of the community's hearing of this word become evident in 12:25–29. Just as God's word has addressed the community as both warning and promise throughout the homily (cf. 3:7–4:13; 6:13–20; 10:26–39), the author concludes the comparison of the words spoken at Sinai and Zion with both warning (12:25–26) and promise to the community (12:27–29). **Do not refuse** (*mē paraitēsēsthe*) **the one who is speaking** (12:25a): the author refers to the blood of Jesus that speaks (12:24) and contrasts his listeners with those listeners at Sinai who "begged" (12:19, *parētēsato*) that no further word be spoken, interpreting their response as a refusal. Their response is the basis for the extended comparison of the consequences of refusing the "voice from heaven." The author assumes that those who refused the voice **did not escape** the one who warned (*ton chrēmatizonta*; cf. *chrēmatizein* in 8:5 for the divine instructions to Moses) in the material realm **upon earth** (12:25b), a fact not explicitly mentioned in the narrative. He then argues from the lesser to the greater, **How much more those who reject the voice from heaven?** (12:25c). The voice that speaks from the heavenly realm is thus "greater" than the voice from the earthly realm (12:24). The author concludes here, as he has earlier in the homily, that refusal of the greater salvation has corresponding consequences. He recapitulates the similar argument from the lesser to the greater that he has given earlier in the homily (2:1–4; 10:26–31). Thus if God's word at Sinai was a severe word of warning, God's ultimate word is even more severe. The ultimate voice has ultimate consequences for the listeners.

God's voice comes as both warning and promise, as the author has indicated throughout the homily (cf. 3:7–4:13). Continuing the theme of God's voice, the author introduces the citation from Hag 2:6 with the phrase **now he has promised** (12:26a), suggesting once more that the community, like the heroes of faith, stands before a promise (cf. 4:1; 6:12–13, 17; 10:23; 11:9, 13, 17). With his alteration of the passage (see Introductory Matters) and his interpretative words in 12:27, the author reassures the community. With the omission of the "sea and dry land" from the passage and the addition of "not only" (the earth) and "but" (the heaven), the author cites the promise **Once more I will shake not only the earth, but also the heaven** (12:26b), integrating it into his dualistic distinction between heaven and earth. That is, unlike the voice that shook the earth at Mount Sinai (Exod 19:18), the voice that the community hears comes from outside the material realm and anticipates the final moment that will greatly exceed the earthquake at Mount Sinai. This event corresponds to the occasion when "the one who is coming will come and not delay" (10:38; cf. 9:27).

The author's interpretation indicates the significance of that event for the struggling community. The **once more** in the Haggai passage **signifies** (*dēloi*) **the removal** (*metathesis*) **of those things that can be shaken** (*tōn saleuomenōn*), that is, **those things that are made** (*tōn pepoiēmenōn*), **in order that the things that cannot be shaken abide** (*meinē ta mē saleuomena*) (12:27). The author has taken the traditional apocalyptic image of the eschatological earthquake and shaped it for his own practical purpose. His concern is not to satisfy the curiosity of the readers over the nature or time of the end. He employs Platonic language, distinguishing between the material and the unshakable reality that abides, in order to assure the discouraged community that it has come to the eternal realities of the heavenly world. Those things that can be shaken, like the mountain "that can be touched" (12:18), belong to the world that will not last. The exalted high priest who abides (*diameneis*, 1:11; *menei*, 7:3, 24) provides the community with an abiding possession (*hyparxin menousan*, 10:34). Thus the stability of the heavenly world provides the foundation for the community's continued existence. The community's access to the world that does not pass away functions as an anchor (6:19).

12:28–29. Assurance of the future promise is the basis for the exhortation in 12:28. **Therefore receiving an unshakable kingdom** (12:28a) employs the imagery of "receiving a kingdom," which is used elsewhere for a ruler's entrance into power (2 Macc 10:11) and for the apocalyptic hope that "the holy ones of the most high will receive the kingdom and possess the kingdom forever and ever" (Dan 7:18). The author emphasizes that the kingdom is "unshakable" and therefore belongs to the stable, heavenly world. When all the material things that they see and touch have been removed, the "unshakable kingdom" will remain. Thus a community searching for a firm possession can recognize now, as they did in the past (10:34), that they find stability for themselves by receiving an "unshakable kingdom."

On the basis of this transcendent possession, the author challenges the community, **Let us give thanks, and thus** (*di' hēs*, lit. "by which") **let us worship God in an acceptable way** (12:28b) rather than refuse the one who is speaking (12:25). Using the cultic word *latreuein*, which he has employed repeatedly to indicate the inability of the Levitical cult to perfect the worshiper (*ton latreuonta*, 9:9; 10:2; cf. 8:5; 13:10), the author has indicated that only the work of Christ in the heavenly sanctuary has cleansed the conscience, enabling the people to "worship the living God" (*eis to latreuein theō zōnti*, 9:14). In the same way, those who receive the "unshakable kingdom" may now "worship acceptably" **with awe and reverence** (12:28c). Although this worship may include the assembly (cf. 10:25) in which the people offer up a sacrifice of praise (13:15), it also includes good deeds (13:16), the common life of the community, and the ethical life described in 13:1–6.

The parallel of the community's experience at the heavenly Mount Zion with Israel's experience at Sinai suggests that the "awe and reverence" (*eulabeia kai deos*) expressed by the community corresponds to the surpassing greatness of their entry into the heavenly world. If the "blazing fire" and the voice at the earthly Sinai evoked fear among the listeners and even Moses (12:21), those who draw near to the heavenly city now respond with "awe and reverence," recognizing that **God is a consuming fire** (12:29; Deut 4:24). Therefore, the community stands before both God's promise and God's judgment. As the rhetorical conclusion to the homily, this reminder that "God is a consuming fire" reiterates the author's earlier warnings about the judgment of God. According to 4:13, God is the one "to whom we give an account." According to 10:31, "It is a fearful thing to fall into the hands of the living God."

Theological Issues

Just as the author offers models of faithful people who could see beyond temporary satisfaction in this world (chap. 11), in Esau (12:16–17) he offers the example of one who recognized only temporary gratification. The believing community perpetually faces the choice between the heroic examples of faithfulness and the failures of those who could only recognize the reality that is perceptible to the senses. Only those who staked their lives on the invisible reality had the courage to build for the future or resist the power of evil. Esau's heirs have always chosen immediate gratification over ultimate reality.

The author offers a resource to the community by which it can avoid Esau's choice. In the words, "You have not come to what may be touched . . . but you have come to Mount Zion, the city of the living God, the heavenly Jerusalem" (12:18, 22), he reassures the struggling community that the unseen reality is not only in the distant future but is already a present reality. Although this affirmation may refer to all their Christian experience, the language also indicates that the communal assemblies provide the occasion for recognizing the reality beyond "what may be touched." Indeed, the comparison between two assemblies—the extraordinary assembly at Sinai and the more extraordinary heavenly assembly—is a reminder to the house church that its worship is a participation in a heavenly reality. Thus he concludes, "Let us worship with reverence and awe" (12:28). This worship empowers the church to overcome the inverted values of Esau, which is the constant temptation of a society overwhelmed by consumer goods and material satisfaction.

The description of the assembly speaks to many issues of the contemporary church in its continuing debate over the nature of worship. At the heart of the author's depiction of worship is the community's experience of awe in the presence of God. Moses said, "I tremble with fear" (12:21), and the author describes God as a "consuming fire" (12:29). Worship is not a consumer product designed to attract outsiders or satisfy the competing desires of the worshipers but an encounter with the "consuming fire." As Vic Pfitzner has said, "To replace the central mystery with a peripheral concern for personal satisfaction ('I got something out of it') is an unwitting kind of idolatry" (2003, 79). The appropriate response in worship is "reverence and awe."

The focus of this awesome event is the hearing of a word that comes from the God who refuses to be domesticated into the church's routine. The Israelites could not bear this word and begged that no more words be spoken (12:20); the church hears a voice that speaks better than that of Abel (12:24). The author warns the church not "to refuse the one who is speaking" (12:25), indicating that no one escapes the voice of God. Although "God has spoken" (1:1) in the entire story of Jesus Christ, the worship service is the occasion for the communal listening to the divine voice. The reading of scripture and its exposition remind the church that it is accountable to a voice that continues to speak with words of warning and promise. Because biblical faith is especially a religion of hearing rather than seeing, the exposition of scripture holds an important place in Christian worship. To hear "The word of the Lord," after the reading of scripture and respond "Thanks be to God" is to recognize an authority that summons the community to obedience.

Hebrews 13

Bearing with the Word of Exhortation

Introductory Matters

Because Heb 12:18–29 is the rhetorical climax of the homily with parallels to chapter 1 in both style and content (see above), it would be an appropriate ending to the author's summons to respond to the divine message (1:1–2a; 12:25–29) with endurance. However, a series of loosely connected imperatives in 13:1–6 follows the rhythmic style of 12:18–29, and new topics appear in chapter 13 that have not been addressed in the first twelve chapters. "Let brotherly love continue" (13:1) follows without transition from "Our God is a consuming fire" (12:29). Whereas the author's singular challenge to the community throughout chapters 1–12 is to "hold firm" (3:6, 14; 6:18; 10:23) in the midst of the temptation to fall away, the staccato style of 13:1–6 calls for specific ethical behavior that he has scarcely mentioned in the first twelve chapters. Indeed, the style of these unconnected imperatives resembles the paraenetic sections of the Pauline letters (cf. 1 Thess 5:12–24), and the specific instructions belong to the common storehouse of early Christian paraenesis. "Brotherly love" (*philadelphia*, 13:1) is common in early Christian exhortation (cf. Rom 12:10; 1 Thess 4:9; 1 Pet 1:22; 2 Pet 1:7). As an example of brotherly love, "hospitality" (*philoxenia*, 13:2) also had an important place in Christian instruction (cf. 1 Pet 4:9), especially in instructions about leaders (cf. 1 Tim 3:2; Titus 1:8). New converts were commonly given instructions about marital fidelity (13:4; cf. 1 Thess 4:3–8). The injunction "not to be greedy" (*aphilargyros*, 13:5) addressed one of the common concerns in early Christian paraenesis (cf. 1 Tim 3:3; 6:10; 2 Tim 3:2). Only the instruction to "remember the prisoners" has no parallel in the other exhortations in the NT. The instructions in 13:1–6 appear to be so general that they could have been spoken to any early Christian congregation (Michel 1966, 478), and the transition from chapter 12 to chapter 13 appears to mark the change from the genre of the homily to the genre of the letter.

The closing (13:18–25) also closely resembles the ending of Pauline letters. The request "pray for us" (13:18) is reminiscent of Paul's pleas for prayers (cf. Rom 15:30), and the author's desire to be restored to the community soon (13:19) is a familiar theme in Pauline correspondence (cf. Rom 15:22; 1 Cor 16:5–9; Phil 2:24; 1 Thess 3:11; Phlm 22). The reference to Timothy's release (13:23), the final greetings (13:24), and the benediction (13:25) all echo familiar components of Pauline letters.

Chapter 13 is divided into three units. Whereas 13:1–6 and 3:18–25 have the common characteristics of a Pauline letter, 13:7–17, which is demarcated by an *inclusio* ("remember your leaders," "be obedient to your leaders"), recapitulates much of the argument of the homily. It continues the cultic discourse of 7:1–10:18 in 13:9–13, and it maintains the familiar style of chapters 1–12, which alternates between reminders of what "we have" (13:10, 14) and the hortatory subjunctive, "let us" (13:13, 15). Thus, while 13:1–6 and 13:18–25 resemble the conclusion of a Pauline letter, 13:7–17 maintains the style of the first twelve chapters and recapitulates the argument of its central section (7:1–10:18).

The distinctiveness of chapter 13 has raised questions about the relationship of this unit to chapters 1–12. Some scholars argue that either all or part of chapter 13 was added by a later hand in imitation of the Pauline letters. A. J. M. Wedderburn (2004, 403–5) suggests, for example, that chapter 13 is the work of a later author, who wrote the thirteenth chapter in an attempt to apply the message of chapters 1–12 to a new situation. Erich Grässer (1997, 3:409) argues that 13:22–25 is the work of a Pauline imitator who added the ending to give apostolic status to the homily. Otto Michel (1966, 78) maintains that chapter 13 is by the author himself, but that it is an appendix rather than an integrated part of the homily. Other scholars regard the section as the appropriate culmination of the argument or the key to the entire homily (Filson 1967, 82–84; Lehne 1990, 115).

Despite the abrupt stylistic changes in chapter 13, the most compelling conclusion is that 13:1–21 concludes the *peroratio* that began in 10:32, drawing the ethical consequences of the argument (13:1–6) and recapitulating its major themes (Koester 2001, 554; Backhaus 1996, 61). The *inclusio*—"let us worship in a pleasing way" (*euarestōs*, 12:28) and "with such sacrifices God is pleased" (*euaresteitai*, 13:16)—suggests that 13:1–16 gives concreteness to the author's call for acceptable worship (Weiss 1991, 697). The instructions in 13:1–6 develop the earlier exhortation to "love and good works" (10:24; Backhaus 2005, 161). "Let brotherly love continue" (13:1) elaborates on the author's earlier description of the community as a family (2:10–18; 3:1). The exhortation to "remember the prisoners" (13:2) recalls the community's past deeds for prisoners (10:34). Although the exhortations to marital fidelity (13:4) and the appropriate attitudes toward money (13:5–6) belong to the common stock of early Jewish and Christian instruction, they further indicate the common ethical outlook that holds the community together. Thus the exhortations define the community cohesion that is necessary for the community to survive.

The final cultic section in Heb 13:9–14 is one of the most complex and disputed passages in Hebrews. The author speaks elliptically, expecting the reader to fill in the blanks, in an extraordinary concentration of evocative images that continue to perplex interpreters. He refers to "diverse and strange teachings" without identifying them. He warns against "foods" and "those who serve in the tent" and offers as an alternative the fact that "we have an altar" and challenges the listeners to follow "Jesus outside the camp." F. J. Schierse has correctly said that "there is scarcely a concept . . . in verses 9–14 that can be reduced to a clear, generally-recognized view" (1955, 184).

Most interpreters have attempted to discover the coherence of this passage by assuming that the strange teachings involve food laws, to which the author offers an alternative. Since the early church faced numerous issues over foods (cf. Acts 15:20; Rom 14:17; 1 Cor 8:8; Gal 2:11–14), interpreters have suggested numerous possibilities. Many in the ancient church interpreted "those who serve in the tent" as Jews who advocated "strange teachings" involving foods. They maintained that the "altar" is the Eucharist (see Grässer 1997, 3:377 for texts), from which the Jews were excluded. According to this view, to go "outside the camp" is to leave Judaism. Variations on this view are widely held today (cf. Young 2002, 255; Lindars 1991, 11; Salevao 2002, 147). Others hold that the author is warning against either pagan or Jewish-syncretistic cultic dining practices as guarantees of salvation (Braun 1984, 462; Theissen 1969, 77). Inasmuch as Hebrews engages in explicit polemic against false teachings nowhere else in the homily, 13:9–14 is not likely a polemic against a particular heresy but rather a continuation of the homily's use of *synkrisis*, according to which cultic practices provide the foil for the reaffirmation of the Christian confession.

In his reference to the bodies of sacrificial animals that priests burned "outside the camp," the author resumes the interpretation of the death of Jesus as the ultimate Day of Atonement, which he developed in 9:1–10:18. His focus now moves beyond the offering of blood (9:7, 14, 18, 21, 22) in the tabernacle to the disposal of the bodies of the sacrificial animals "outside the camp" described in Lev 16:27. Inasmuch as "outside the camp" was also the place for executions (Lev 24:14, 23; Num 15:35), the author has probably combined images from the Day of Atonement and the execution of offenders in recalling that Jesus "suffered outside the gate."

Outside the Camp

The phrase "outside the camp" has several associations in the OT. Not only the sacrifice on the Day of Atonement but also the carcasses from other sacrifices are burned outside the camp (cf. Lev 4:12, 21; 6:11; 8:17; 9:11). Those who had leprous skin or other impurities were required to remain "outside the camp" for a period of time before reentering the city (Lev 13:46; 14:3, 8; Num 31:19). It was also the place where Moses pitched his tent and met God (Exod 33:7). Thus it could be both a place of impurity and a place for encountering God.

Just as the central section of Hebrews (4:14–10:31) rebuilds the community's symbolic world, the recapitulation of the argument in 13:9–14 also builds the intellectual foundation for the community's survival. In the claims that "we have an altar" (13:10) and "we wait for a city" (13:14), the author once more orients the struggling community to the alternative reality of the heavenly world (Backhaus 2005, 167). The affirmation that the community is seeking the city that is to come (13:14) connects the community to the ancient heroes who were looking for a heavenly city (11:16). The statement that "it is good for the heart to be strengthened (*bebaiousthai*) by grace rather than foods (*brōmasin*)" in 13:9 continues the author's consistent emphasis on the firm (*bebaios*) possession of the community in the heavenly world (cf. *bebaia*, "firm," 3:14; 6:19; 9:17; *bebaiōsis*, "validity, certainty," 6:16), and the references to foods as symbols of the material world (9:10; 12:16). The call to bear the shame of the crucified Christ (13:13) recapitulates the earlier statement that Moses endured the "abuse of the Christ" (11:26) and the claim that the community looks to the one who "despised the shame" (12:2). Indeed, the conclusion that fellowship and good deeds are the sacrifices that are pleasing to God (13:16–17) is an appropriate summary of the homily's consistent claim that earthly sacrifices are not able to perfect those who draw near to God (9:9).

The ending in 13:18–21 adds a personal touch that is not present in the earlier part of the homily. The author speaks in the first-person singular, indicating his relationship to the community for the first time. In his appeal to his personal relationship with the readers (13:19) and benediction (13:20–21), he brings the *peroratio* to an appropriate conclusion, conforming to the ancient orator's appeal to the emotions and emphasis on personal integrity (Quintilian, *Inst.* 6.1.34; Backhaus 1996, 61).

The conclusion of the homily in 13:22–25 is an epistolary postscript offering a rare glimpse into the setting of this homily and the author's relationship to the community. He describes the entire work as a "word of encouragement" (*logos tēs paraklēseōs*), a term that is used elsewhere for the synagogue homily (Acts

13:15; see pp. 11–12 for the characteristics of this genre). The author has indicated earlier the importance of exhortation among the members, whom he challenges to "encourage one another" (3:13; 10:25). *Paraklēsis*, which can mean either "comfort" (2 Cor 1:3–7) or "encouragement," was a term commonly used for Christian preaching (cf. 1 Thess 2:3; 1 Tim 4:13). The author has indicated earlier that scripture speaks "encouragement" (12:5) to the community (cf. Rom 15:4, "the encouragement of the scriptures"). The claim that one has "written briefly" is common in ancient communication (cf. 1 Pet 5:12; 2 Macc 2:31; *Barn.* 1.5).

The information that "our brother Timothy has been released" (*apolely-menon*) and that the author will join him in seeing the readers "if he comes in time" closely resembles the concluding travelogues in Paul's letters (cf. Rom 15:22–30; 1 Cor 16:5–12; 2 Cor 12:14; 13:1). Indeed, the reference to Timothy is reminiscent of Paul's frequent references to Timothy's travels to the churches (1 Cor 4:17; 16:10–11; Phil 2:19–24). Grässer (1997, 3:411–12) maintains that this reference is evidence that 13:22–25 is the work of a later writer who added the reference to the future travels of Timothy and the author to bring the homily into conformity with Paul's writings. However, if Timothy has been released from prison, as the verb *apolelymenon* (meaning also "let go" or "send away"; BDAG) suggests, it does not conform to the Pauline letters, which make no explicit reference to the imprisonment of Timothy. The reference to Timothy may suggest that the author and readers belong to a second generation of communities influenced by the work of Paul. If 13:22–25 were the work of a scribe attempting to make this work more Pauline, one must ask why the redactor did not place the Pauline stamp on this unit more clearly (Weiss 1991, 38).

Reciprocal greetings (13:24) and final benediction (13:25) are also common features at the conclusion of Pauline letters. The greetings of the people "from Italy" offer the only indication of the location of either the author or readers. The phrase is, however, ambiguous. "From Italy" (*apo tēs Italias*) can refer to those who came from Italy and are now living somewhere else, as with the case of Aquila and Priscilla, who came to Corinth "from Italy" (Acts 18:2; note analogous references to those who are "from" another location in Matt 21:11; Mark 15:43; John 1:44; 21:2; Acts 6:9; 21:27; 24:18; Koester 2001, 581). It can also refer to those who remain in Italy (cf. *apo* "from" to designate those who remain in the city of origin, John 11:1; Acts 10:23; cf. 17:13; Koester 2001, 581). Although recent scholars (Koester 2001, 581; Lane 1991a, xviii–xix) argue that Hebrews was written to Rome, the grammar remains inconclusive for determining the location of the author or readers.

Tracing the Train of Thought

Despite the apparent change in genre in chapter 13, the final words of the homily are not an appendix unrelated to the first twelve chapters but a challenge to the community to live out the implications of the homily. Indeed, the exhortation in 12:28, "let us worship God acceptably" (*latreuōmen euarestōs tō theō*) marks the transition to the final part of the homily insofar as it invites the community to worship (*latreuein*) as the culmination of the homily's consistent focus on the inability of the worship (*latreia*, 9:1) in the tabernacle to perfect the worshipers (*latreuousin*, 8:5; *ton latreuonta*, 9:9; 10:2; cf. 13:10). Chapter 13 elaborates on the meaning of worshiping "in a pleasing way" (*euarestōs*). According to 13:16, good work and fellowship are the sacrifices with which God is pleased (*euaresteitai ho theos*). In the final petition (13:21), the author prays that God will equip the community to do the will of God, "what is pleasing (*euareston*) in his sight." Thus chapter 13 describes the nature of worship that is "pleasing" to God.

Everyday Worship (13:1–6)

Although the specific instructions like those in 13:1–6 are common in early Christian paraenesis, within the context of the argument of Hebrews they indicate the practical consequences of the author's theological argument. The imperative "Let brotherly love continue" (13:1) serves as the heading for the instructions that follow, indicating that the community's worship involves their care for one another (cf. 13:16). Although the author has given few specific directives, he has anticipated these concrete instructions in chapters 1–12. The theological sections have opened up a symbolic universe that separates the people from the world around them, exposing them to shame and ridicule (10:32–34). The author has established that the community is held together by the bonds of kinship (2:10–14; 3:1–6), and he has addressed them repeatedly as "brothers and sisters" (3:1, 12; 10:19; 13:22). He has motivated them by recalling the love that they had demonstrated for each other in the past (6:9–10) and encouraged them to "stir one another up to love and good works" (10:24) within the context of their assemblies (10:25). The author's challenge for the people on the way to look out for those who lag behind (see 3:12–14; 12:12–17)

Hebrews 13 in the Rhetorical Flow

Hearing God's word with faithful endurance (1:1–4:13)

Exordium: Encountering God's ultimate word (1:1–4)

Narratio: Hearing God's word with faithful endurance (1:5–4:13)

Probatio: Discovering certainty and confidence in the word for the mature (4:14–10:31)

Peroratio: On not refusing the one who is speaking (10:32–13:25)

Enduring in hope: the faithfulness of Jesus and the faithfulness of the ancestors (10:32–12:13)

Listening to the one who is speaking from heaven (12:14–29)

▶ Bearing with the word of exhortation (13:1–25)

Everyday worship (13:1–6)

Ethics of the family (13:1–4)

Being content with what you have (13:5–6)

A life that is pleasing (13:7–17)

Prayers and exhortations (13:18–25)

---

indicates that this minority community will survive only with group cohesion. Thus the exhortations introduced by "let brotherly love continue" indicate that community cohesion requires care for others and shared moral practices.

The inner coherence of the commands for brotherly love (13:1), hospitality (13:2), care for prisoners (13:3), marital fidelity (13:4), and the absence of greed (13:5–6) become evident within the context of the ancient church's attempt to live as a minority group in a hostile society. The passage is illuminated by Lucian of Samosata's satire *The Passing of Peregrinus*, which describes the charlatan Peregrinus, who claimed to be a Christian prophet, accepted the hospitality of Christians, and was finally put in prison by the authorities (Lane 1982, 267–70; Backhaus 2005, 162). Lucian describes the Christians' attention to the needs of Peregrinus during his imprisonment. "From the very break of day aged widows and orphan children could be seen waiting near the prison, while their officials even slept inside with him after bribing the guards" (12, trans. Harmon 1915). He adds, "Much money came to him from them by reason of his imprisonment, and he procured not a little revenue from it." Then he explains, "Their first lawgiver persuaded them that they are all brothers of one another after they have transgressed once for all by denying the Greek gods and by worshipping that crucified sophist himself and living under his laws" (13, trans. Harmon 1915). He concludes that "if any charlatan and trickster, able to profit by occasions, comes among them, he quickly acquires sudden wealth by imposing upon simple folk." Lucian's description suggests the linkage among the instructions in 13:1–6. The minority community, despised by the dominant culture, is a family practicing brotherly love through hospitality, care of prisoners, and financial support. These practices and marital chastity (13:4) distinguish the community from the dominant culture.

13:1–4. The author has indicated in 10:23–24 the close relationship between the call to "hold firm to the confession" and the exhortation "to stir up one another to love and good works." Thus they can endure (10:36) only as they **let brotherly love continue** (13:1), renewing the practices that had sustained them in the past (6:10). One dimension of "brotherly love" (*philadelphia*) is **hospitality** (13:2; *philoxenia*), which enabled early Christians to travel from city to city and created a web of interconnected communities. Alluding to the ancient narratives about the inadvertent accommodation of divine guests (cf. Gen 18–19; Ovid, *Metam.* 8.620–724), the author suggests a community that extends into heaven (Backhaus 2005, 163).

Just as the community had "sympathized with prisoners" (10:34) by demonstrating full solidarity with them, the author now urges them to **remember the prisoners** (13:3). The parallel phrase, **and those who are mistreated** (*tōn kakouchoumenōn*), recalls not only the "reproaches and afflictions" experienced earlier (10:32–33; Attridge 1989, 386) but also the past heroes who were also mistreated (11:37). To "remember" is not only to consider them but to practice brotherly love with concrete deeds of solidarity, as in the case with

Peregrinus. The author offers parallel reasons for this solidarity: to remember prisoners as (*hōs*) **fellow prisoners** (*syndedemenoi*) and those who were mistreated as (*hōs*) **being yourselves in a body**. The two phrases indicate the vulnerability and absolute sympathy (cf. 10:34) of the people for their Christian siblings. "As fellow prisoners" and "as being yourselves in a body" are both metaphorical. By taking care of the prisoners, the members share the vulnerability to imprisonment and the weakness of bodily existence with the prisoners.

Although some commentators (cf. Grässer 1997, 3:353) argue that the author turns from communal existence to private life in 13:4–6, the instructions, **Let marriage be held in honor and the bed undefiled** (13:4a) and "conduct yourselves without greed" (13:5) are not merely private concerns, for they also define the communal ethos (Backhaus 2005, 164). Indeed, the author assumes, with other NT writers, that family stability is a vital element of the existence of the new family of faith (cf. Eph 5:21–6:9; Col 3:18–4:1; 1 Thess 4:3–8; 1 Tim 3:4–5) and an essential feature of its countercultural existence. Once more the author gives a reason for this Christian conduct in the fact that **God will judge the sexually immoral and adulterers** (13:4b), echoing the earlier description of Esau, the sexually immoral person who was unable to repent of his deeds (12:16–17). As in the case of Esau, to be subject to the sexual appetites is the epitome of an existence oriented to the present moment rather than to the unseen world.

13:5–6. In the same way as community members demonstrated in the early days when they suffered the loss of their possessions "with joy" (10:34), they will demonstrate their orientation to the heavenly world if they live **without greed** (*aphilargyros*), **being content with** (their) **possessions** (13:5a). The author shares the common early Christian condemnation of the love of money (cf. 1 Tim 3:3), the "root of all evil" (1 Tim 6:10), challenging the readers to follow the heroic example of the pilgrim heroes, who had no possessions. Moses, for example, chose the "abuse of Christ" over the treasures of Egypt (11:26) because he looked to the reward. As Lucian's account of the story of Peregrinus indicates, the financial generosity of the Christians enabled them to support the victims of persecution. In keeping with the tone of the entire homily, the author motivates his readers by appealing to both fear of judgment and divine assurance. Whereas he concluded the exhortation to marital fidelity with the reminder, "God will judge sexually immoral people and adulterers" (13:4), he assures those who do not place their trust in possessions, **I will not leave you or forsake you** (13:5b), in words derived from Moses' assurance to Israel (Deut 31:6, 8). As a result the community **is bold to say** the words from Ps 117:6 LXX, **The Lord is my helper, I will not be afraid; what can people do to me?** (13:6). Like other ancient texts that speak to the community (cf. 3:7–19; 12:5–11), this psalm speaks to a vulnerable minority church, inviting them to see beyond the threats to their existence (cf. 10:32–34) and share the insecure life of the heroes of faith who did not fear overwhelming forces (cf. 11:23, 27).

A Life That Is Pleasing (13:7–17)

In 13:7–17, the author returns from the series of separate ethical norms to the style and themes that have characterized the first twelve chapters, thus providing a final summary in his appeal to the marginalized community. This unit is framed by the appeal for an appropriate response to the "leaders" (*hēgoumenoi*) of the past (13:7) and present (13:17). This section maintains the alternation between the theological affirmation of the community's possession ("we have," 13:10; "we do not have," 13:14) and the hortatory subjunctive ("let us," 13:13, 15) as the author returns to the argument based on the Levitical sacrificial system. Thus this section is an appropriate conclusion to the *peroratio* of the argument.

The reference to "leaders" (*hēgoumenoi*) is new to the homily, for the author has consistently described the whole community as responsible for the welfare of the people (cf. 3:12–14; 10:24–25; 12:12–14). *Hēgoumenoi*, which is used for leaders only rarely in Christian literature (Luke 22:26; Acts 15:22; *1 Clem.* 1.3; 21.6), refers to a variety of tasks, including those of a political or administrative nature (cf. Acts 7:10; 1 Macc 9:30; *1 Clem.* 5.7; 32.2). That the term designates the personal qualities of individuals rather than a title (Grässer 1997, 3:368) is suggested by the portrayal of Paul as the "chief speaker" (Acts 14:12; *ho hēgoumenos tou logou*). Although the instruction to acknowledge the community's leaders is common at the conclusion of letters (1 Thess 5:12–14; 1 Pet 5:5), the reference to past and present leaders is significant for framing the final instructions in Hebrews, for the role of the leaders is to maintain the cohesiveness of the community on its pilgrimage. While leaders of the past apparently founded the community, the leaders in the present take responsibility for them.

13:7–8. The imperative **Remember your leaders, who spoke to you the word of God** (13:7a) continues the homily's focus on the hearing of God's word. These leaders are the links in a chain of tradition from the message delivered by the Lord and "confirmed to us by those who heard him" (2:3). Through these leaders the community received "the word of hearing" (4:2), and because of them they now stand before the word that is "sharper than any two-edged sword" (4:12). As the author has indicated earlier in the homily, examples from the past provide both negative and positive examples for imitation (cf. 4:11; 11:1–40). Consequently, the author instructs the community, **as you observe the outcome of their way of life, imitate their faith** (13:7b), suggesting that the message of the past leaders conformed to their way of life. They belonged to the heroes of faith, who endured until the end.

The declaration **Jesus Christ is the same yesterday, today, and forever** (13:8) is the conviction that unites the community with the past leaders and sustains them in a time of trial. That Jesus Christ is "the same" recalls the author's earlier contrast between the exalted Son, who is always "the same" (1:12), and the transient creation. "Yesterday, today, and forever" indicates the link between the death of Jesus once for all ("yesterday") and the "today" (cf. 3:13) when the community continues to hear the word of God. To say that he is "forever" (*eis tous aiōnas*) is to recall the author's repeated assurances that the exalted Son "abides forever" (cf. 1:10; 7:3, 24–25; cf. 10:14). As the author has insisted throughout the homily, the marginalized community finds its only stability in the unseen and eternal reality that does not change, even when death separates them from their leaders.

> **An Outline of Hebrews 13:7–17**
>
> A life that is pleasing (13:7–17)
>
> Jesus is the same (13:7–8)
>
> We have an altar (13:9–10)
>
> Outside the camp (13:11–12)
>
> Bearing his shame (13:13–14)
>
> A sacrifice of praise (13:15–16)
>
> Your leaders (13:17)

13:9–10. The author addresses the community's need for stability in an insecure environment in 13:9, contrasting two alternatives that confront them. They may either **be carried away** (13:9a; *parapheresthe*) in instability or have the **heart made firm** (13:9b; *bebaiousthai*). The frequent use of forms of *bebai-* (firm, stable) indicates the importance of stability for the wavering community (cf. 2:2–3; 3:6; 6:16, 19; 9:17). *Parapheresthe*, a term suggesting the image of one who is "carried away" by the winds (cf. the nautical image, "drift away" in 2:1), was used for those who were vulnerable to strange ideas (Jude 12; Plato, *Phaedrus* 265b; Thompson 1982, 143). In this instance, **diverse and strange teachings** (13:9a) probably does not refer to any particular threat, inasmuch as the author does not explicitly mention false teaching anywhere else in the homily. Indeed, "diverse" (*poikilos*) is not the term that one would have expected if the author had been combating a specific heresy. His real concern is to ensure that the readers "strengthen the heart."

The author also describes two alternatives by which one might seek to "strengthen the heart": either **by grace** (13:9b) or **by foods, in which those who were engaged did not benefit** (13:9c). The reference to "foods" is undoubtedly elliptical, leading scholars to fill in the blanks of the author's reference with suggestions about heresies confronting the readers (see Introductory Matters). However, the meaning becomes more evident if one observes that the author is alluding to the earlier argument. Whereas "grace" (*charis*) is the summary word for all the benefits of Christ described in 7:1–10:18, "foods" is most likely a metonymy for all the earthly alternatives that do not bring stability (cf. 9:9; 12:16). The statement that foods "did not benefit" (*ouk ōphelēthēsan*) those who participated in them is reminiscent of the earlier memory that the ancient message "did not benefit" (*ouk ōphelēsen*) the listeners (4:2) and the argument that the Levitical priesthood was "weak and useless" (*anōpheles*, 7:18).

281

The author indicates the content of this grace (13:9) with the affirmation, **We have an altar from which those who serve in the tent do not have the right to eat** (13:10), which suggests that the "altar" is a synonym for God's "grace." Thus the two alternatives—we who have an altar and those who serve in the tent—correspond to the alternatives of grace and food in 13:9. This metaphorical language has puzzled interpreters, but the wider context of Hebrews indicates that the author speaks symbolically. The "altar," as the explanatory comments in 13:11–12 demonstrate, is the atoning death of Jesus. "We have an altar" is the equivalent of "we have a high priest" (8:1; cf. 4:14; 10:19). It is the work of Christ in the heavenly sanctuary that gives an anchor of stability (6:19) to wavering people. "Those who serve in the tent," as the author has indicated throughout the argument (cf. 8:1–5; 9:9; 10:1), are the priests who offer sacrifices in the Levitical sanctuary. This description, as the author has indicated earlier, is metaphorical (9:9), inasmuch as the tent no longer exists. As a recapitulation of the earlier argument, the author reassures his community that its altar—the place of salvation—is not located in the transience of the physical world. Only the heavenly altar can give the wavering community the stability that it needs.

13:11–12. In 13:11–12, the author elaborates on the "grace" (13:9) at the heavenly "altar" (13:10), returning once more to a comparison between the sacrificial work of Levitical priests and the death of Jesus derived from his interpretation of the Day of Atonement ritual recorded in Lev 16. In contrast to the emphasis on the offering of blood in the sanctuary in 9:1–14, the author now turns to **the bodies of those animals** (*zōon*; the author generalizes the LXX "bull" and "goat") that **are burned outside the camp** (13:11), paraphrasing the instructions of Lev 16:27–28, according to which those who burned the animals were required to wash themselves before entering into the camp.

As in 9:1–14, the Levitical practice becomes the basis of the comparison to the work of Jesus. However, in contrast to the earlier passage, the focus is not on Jesus' entrance into the heavenly sanctuary to "sanctify" (9:13; cf. 2:11; 10:10, 29; 12:14) the people but on the fact that he, **in order to sanctify the people through his own blood, suffered outside the gate** (13:12). Although in both instances the author recalls Jesus' death as the event of sanctification, in this instance the author alludes to Jesus' death "outside the gate" of the city of Jerusalem (cf. John 19:17, 20), suggesting the correspondence of this event to the burning of the bodies of sacrificial animals "outside the camp." The focus is not, however, only on historical reminiscence of Jesus' death, as the exhortation in 13:13 indicates. Furthermore, inasmuch as the author says not that Jesus *died* "outside the camp" but that he *suffered*, he suggests the paraenetic focus of this memory, for he writes to a community that has "endured a great struggle of sufferings" (10:32), and he has emphasized Jesus' solidarity with his people in suffering (2:9–10).

13:13–14. That the author's memory of Jesus' suffering "outside the gate" is not only a historical fact but also a metaphor becomes clear in the exhortation **Therefore let us go out to him outside the camp** (13:13a). Jesus' suffering "outside the gate" was also his entrance into the heavenly sanctuary at the exaltation (6:19; 9:12), where he shed his blood. Like Philo, who interpreted the pitching of Moses' tent "outside the camp" as the departure from "the objects dear to the body" (*Alleg. Interp.* 2.54–55; 3.46; *Worse* 160), the author's metaphorical language indicates that he collapses Good Friday and Easter into one event. Just as he has previously encouraged the community to "draw near" to the heavenly sanctuary to follow Jesus the forerunner (6:10; 10:19), he now invites the community to "go out to him outside the camp," once more challenging the community to maintain solidarity with the one who demonstrated his solidarity with them (cf. 2:10–18). To "go out to him outside the camp," therefore, is one dimension of drawing near to him in the heavenly sanctuary.

As the author indicates with **bearing his abuse** (13:13b), one undeniable dimension of the cross is the reproach of being "outside." To "draw near" to the heavenly sanctuary is also to experience the reproach of being an outsider. Indeed, as the author has indicated already, the heroes of faith were wanderers who had no firm place in their own society. If the community follows Jesus in "bearing his abuse," they follow the heroes of the past, including Moses, who bore "the abuse suffered for Christ" (11:26), and Jesus, who "despised the shame" of the cross (12:2). Thus the author brings the *peroratio* to a ringing conclusion in challenging a wavering community to "go out to him outside the camp." This existence will involve continuing to endure (cf. 10:36) the abuses they have faced in the past (10:32–34). Like the past heroes, they will find stability for their marginalized existence in knowing that the shame of their minority status is nothing less than solidarity with other outsiders who were on a pilgrimage but were sustained by knowing that "outside the camp" of social acceptability was also access to the throne of God (8:1; 10:19–23).

As the author indicates in 13:14, the motivation for continuing the pilgrimage is the acknowledgment that **here we do not have an abiding city** (13:14a; *menousan polin*), for those things that "abide" belong to the transcendent world (cf. 10:34; 1:10–12; 7:3, 24). Like the heroes of faith, the community now seeks **the city that is to come** (13:14b; cf. 11:10, 16), to which it has already "drawn near" (12:22) in anticipation of the ultimate fulfillment of God's promises. Only this city abides (12:27); it alone will "strengthen the heart" (13:9) and provide the firm anchor (6:19) for the community.

13:15–16. To follow Jesus "outside the camp, bearing his abuse" is, as the author has indicated repeatedly, a corporate endeavor (cf. 3:12–14; 12:12–15) sustained by the communal assembly (10:24–25) in which members remind one another of the alternative reality that separates them from the surrounding culture. Thus, the exhortation **Therefore let us offer up a sacrifice of praise continually to God, the fruit of the lips that confess his name** (13:15) and the instruction not to **forget doing good and fellowship** (13:16) bring the *peroratio* to a suitable end, for the author describes both actions as a sacrifice to God. As the preceding argument indicates, the community has no need for material sacrifices in an earthly tent (9:1) but offers the acceptable worship described in 12:28 in the assemblies, where its members confess the name of Christ (13:15), and in daily life, where they are involved in the same good deeds for others within the community that distinguished them in the past (cf. 6:9–12; 10:32–34). Whereas it was once the task of priests to "offer up a sacrifice," now the whole community has taken over that role. In their access to the heavenly world they see what the dominant culture does not see. They will only endure as they sustain the common life in worship.

13:17. The community's leaders (*hēgoumenoi*) play an important role in ensuring the continued focus on "good works" and "fellowship" (13:15–16) by the pilgrim people. Like Paul, who insists on the dialectical relationship between the task of the whole community (1 Thess 5:14) and of leaders ("those who are over you and labor among you and admonish you," 1 Thess 5:12), the author assumes a similar view of the pastoral care of the people. Adding to his earlier admonition for all the members to look out for others (3:13–14; 12:12–17) he instructs the community, **be persuaded** (*peithesthe*) **by your leaders and submit** (*hypeikete*) **to them** (13:17). These leaders not only belong to the past (13:7) but have a continuing role. Their authority rests, not on their title, but on their function, for **they watch over** the souls of the people, ensuring their ultimate salvation (cf. 10:39, "for the salvation of the soul"). The author mentions neither a liturgical role for them nor their place as guardians of orthodox teaching but focuses on their pastoral role. In using a term that is used nowhere else for the role of leaders (*agrypnousin*) but is used elsewhere in warnings to "be on guard" in the presence of eschatological peril (BDAG, 16; cf. Mark 13:33; Luke 21:36), he indicates the seriousness of their task: they ensure that the pilgrim people continue to endure in response to the saving work of Christ and will ultimately "give an account" (*logon apodōsontes*) like a steward entrusted with the management of the account of his master (cf. Luke 16:2). Consequently, the community's submission will serve the mutual interests of both the leaders and those who are led: on the one hand, it will allow the leaders to serve **with joy rather than sighing**; on the other hand, to make life difficult for them **would not be helpful** (*alysiteles gar . . . touto*) to the people. Thus the community's submission to the leaders is necessary for ensuring that the community endures to the end.

Prayers and Exhortations (13:18–25)

After recapitulating the argument of the homily in 13:7–17, the author concludes in 13:18–25 with the epistolary form (cf. 13:1–6) and topics (see Introductory Matters) that appear at the end of the Pauline letters. The author speaks for the first time in the first-person singular (*parakalō*, "I appeal," 13:19,

22), indicating his relationship to the readers. The concluding benediction followed by "amen" in 13:21 suggests that the author concludes the *peroratio* in 13:21 before adding a postscript (Übelacker 1989, 224) in 13:22–25. Contrary to Grässer (1997, 3:409), the concluding words in 13:22–25 are not the addition of a later hand but the author's own personal note to the congregation that he knows well.

An Outline of Hebrews 13:18–25

Prayers and exhortations (13:18–25)

Pray for us (13:18–19)

The God of peace (13:20–21)

My word of exhortation (13:22)

Future plans (13:23–25)

13:18–19. The request **pray for us** (13:18a) . . . **I appeal that you especially do this** (13:19a), marks the transition to the final words, insofar as it corresponds to the previous instruction, "Be obedient to your leaders" (13:17), suggesting that the author is himself a leader who has been separated from the community. The assurance **We are persuaded that we have a good conscience, in all things conducting ourselves well** (13:18b) corresponds to the speaker's claim of credibility that was common in the *peroratio* of a speech. According to ancient rhetorical theorists, effective persuasion includes not only proof based on rational argument (*logos*) but also the speaker's character (*ethos*) and the emotional bond with the listeners (*pathos*). The urgency of the appeal for their prayers (*perissoterōs*, "especially") and the author's desire to be restored to the readers adds a note of both the author's ethos and the pathos that unites him to the community.

13:20–21. The prayer of blessing in 13:20–21 reflects the style and the language of the ancient liturgy. **May the God of all peace** (13:20a) echoes the benedictions that conclude Paul's letters (cf. Rom 16:20; Phil 4:9; 1 Thess 5:23; cf. 2 Cor 13:11, "The God of love and peace"; 1 Pet 5:10, "the God of grace"). The combination of the dependent clause introduced by the relative pronoun "who" (*ho*; cf. 1 Pet 5:10, "May the God of grace, who called you . . .") followed by the request is apparently a common liturgical form. The author has, however, integrated this form into the message of the homily. Indeed, the request indicates the author's desire to assure the community that he reciprocates the requests that they will make on his behalf (13:18–19). The clause **who brought up from the dead the great shepherd of the sheep, our Lord Jesus, by the blood of the eternal covenant** (13:20b) paraphrases Isa 63:11 LXX, according to which Moses "brought up the shepherd of the sheep from the earth," while God "led" (*ēgages*) the people (Isa 63:14). For "brought up" (or "led up"), the author uses the participle *anagagōn*, from a verb that is elsewhere employed with "from the dead" for the resurrection (cf. Rom 10:7, *ek nekrōn anagagein*). Although the phrase refers to the resurrection, within the context of Hebrews the author is undoubtedly speaking also of the exaltation of Christ to God's right hand, a central theme of the homily (cf. 1:3, 13; 8:1). Indeed, he has reminded the readers of Jesus' "suffering of death" (2:9) and his death as the destruction of the power of death (2:14) as the necessary prelude to his exaltation. The one who "led Jesus up from the dead" is also the one who "leads (*agagonta*) many sons to glory" (2:10; Weiss 1991, 756).

The reference to the "blood of the eternal covenant" and the request **may God make [you] complete for every good work in order to do his will, producing among us what is pleasing in his sight** (13:21) also connects the benediction to the argument of the homily. The author has established that the death of Jesus results in an "eternal redemption" (9:12) in which Jesus is the mediator of a new covenant (9:15). The petition is an appropriate end to the homily, as it summarizes the response that the author has called for repeatedly (cf. 13:1–6). "What is pleasing" (*euareston*) forms an *inclusio* with 12:28, linking the petition with the exhortation to "worship God in a pleasing way."

13:22. The reciprocity of prayer and the claim of personal integrity in 13:18–21 prepare the way for the author's final request, **I appeal to you to bear with the word of exhortation** (13:22a). The request to "bear with (*anechesthai*) the word of exhortation" may suggest the author's uncertainty over the hearing that this homily will receive and explain the need for him to appeal to his personal ethos in 13:19. This "word of exhortation" indicates that the author envisions his own continuity with leaders who spoke the word of God in the past (13:7; 2:3). In his interpretation of scripture, he has demonstrated that this word addresses the community "today" (3:13) as warning (3:12–19; cf. 2:1–4; 6:4–6; 10:26–31; 12:14–17), promise (4:3–11; 6:13–20), and encouragement (*paraklēsis*, 12:5). To ask that they "bear with the word of exhortation" is to reiterate the frequent summons to the community to "pay attention" (2:1), "hear his voice" (3:7), and not to "refuse the one who is speaking" (12:25; Übelacker 1989, 204).

The author's apologetic tone may also be evident in the added comment, **for I have written to you briefly** (13:22b), which appears to conflict with the earlier statement, "There is much to say" (i.e., a long speech; see 5:11 and comments). "Long" and "brief" are relative concepts (cf. Tholuck 1850; cited in Übelacker 1989, 206: "Threatening letters are always too long, love letters are always too brief"). The author's comments indicate that he recognizes ancient hearers' appreciation of brevity. Thus he indicates, as he has previously in the homily (cf. 9:5; 11:32), that he could have spoken in detail, but he appeals to the goodwill of the audience by indicating that he has said only what is essential (cf. 1 Pet 5:12; 2 Macc 6:17), following a common practice by ancient orators (cf. Lausberg 1998, 881).

13:23–25. The concluding words in 13:23–25 correspond to the conclusion of Pauline letters and suggest that the author and readers belong to a wider Pauline circle that is familiar with **Timothy** (13:23; see Introductory Matters for the historical situation). The reference to future visits by Timothy and the author and the exchange of greetings in 13:24 reflect not only historical fact and common practice but also the author's attempt to develop the personal bonds that will gain a hearing for his "word of exhortation." Similarly, the final benediction, **Grace be with all of you** (13:25), echoes the liturgy and expresses the author's concern for the health of the community.

Theological Issues

When Justin Martyr wrote to Emperor Antoninus Pius to prove the unreasonableness of persecution, he spoke of the change produced in the lives of Christians:

> We formerly rejoiced in sexual immorality but now love only chastity. We also used magic arts but have now dedicated ourselves to the good and unbegotten God. We loved resources of money and possessions more than anything, but now we actually share what we have and give to everyone who is in need. We hated one another and killed one another and would not share hearth and table with those who were not of our own tribe, but now, since the manifestation of Christ, we have a common life and pray for our enemies and try to win over those who hate us unjustly. (*1 Apol.* 14)

He then gives a summary of the moral habits and values that characterized the Christians, indicating that the Christian confession had transformed their lives. Justin maintained that these shared values defined the cohesion of a community that was united only by its loyalty to Christ.

Although the ethics described by Justin were not unheard of in ancient society, the distinctive feature was his claim for the cohesion of a community united not only by a shared confession but also by shared moral conduct. Similarly, the specific instructions in Heb 13:1–6 describe the cohesion of the alien community that is united by love, the sharing of goods, and shared views with regard to sexuality and material goods. This community did not reduce moral issues to the private sphere where autonomous individuals make their own choices. To be within the community was to share moral commitments with others.

The author's advice indicates important aspects for Christian ethical practice. As the placement of the ethical advice in Hebrews indicates, Christian ethics is one dimension of worship. By placing this advice between "Let us worship God acceptably" (12:28) and "these are the sacrifices that are acceptable to God" (13:16), the author indicates that the sphere of worship is not limited to the Christian assembly but extends to the Christian's ethical conduct. Worship occurs in familial care within the home, in loving acts toward others, and in the selfless use of possessions.

The precepts in 13:1–6 are not exhaustive, but they illustrate the communal behavior of aliens and exiles. The author offers a more comprehensive understanding of Christian conduct in the final summation of the homily in 13:7–17. Recalling that Jesus died "outside the gate" of Jerusalem at the place of shame, the author invites the community to follow the crucified one "outside the camp" and share the shame of the cross. As a final challenge to the community, he calls for an ethic of discipleship that takes the people outside the comforts of the public square. If the Christian faith began "outside the gate," those who follow Jesus the outsider can only expect to share the abuse of Christ. This challenge addresses Christians in a post-Constantinian world with the memory that Christian faith takes believers into uncomfortable territory where they will be exiles in their own lands. Christian faith began and thrived without a privileged place in society in the first centuries. As it returns to its original place of marginalization, the author's challenge to follow Jesus "outside the camp" addresses Christians in the contemporary context. Like the heroes of faith, they are sustained by the vision of the city that is to come (13:14).

Bibliography

Aitken, Ellen Bradshaw. 2003. "The Hero in the Epistle to the Hebrews: Jesus as an Ascetic Model." In *Texts, Traditions, and Symbols: Essays in Honor of François Bovon*, edited by David H. Warren, Ann Graham Brock, and David Pao, 179–88. Biblical Interpretation Series 66. Leiden: Brill.

Anderson, R. Dean. 1999. *Ancient Rhetorical Theory and Paul*. Rev. ed. Leuven: Peeters.

Andriessen, Paul. 1974. "La communauté des 'Hébréux': Etait-elle tombée dans le relachement?" *Nouvelle revue theologique* 96:1054–66.

Attridge, Harold. 1986. "The Use of Antitheses in Hebrews 8–10." *Harvard Theological Review* 79:1–9.

———. 1989. *The Epistle to the Hebrews*. Hermeneia. Philadelphia: Fortress.

Backhaus, Knut. 1996. *Der neue Bund und das Werden der Kirche: Die Diatheke-Deutung des Hebräerbriefs im Rahmen der frühchristlichen Theologiegeschichte*. Neutestamentliche Abhandlungen, n.s., 29. Münster: Aschendorff.

———. 2001. "Das Land der Verheissung: Die Heimat der Glaubenden im Hebräerbrief." *New Testament Studies* 47:171–88.

———. 2005. "How to Entertain Angels: Ethics in the Epistle to the Hebrews." In *Hebrews: Contemporary Methods—New Insights*, edited by Gabriella Gelardini, 149–75. Leiden: Brill.

Barrett, C. K. 1956. "The Eschatology of the Epistle to the Hebrews." In *The Background of the New Testament and Its Eschatology*, festschrift for C. H. Dodd, edited by W. D. Davies and D. Daube, 363–93. Cambridge: Cambridge University Press.

Barth, Karl. 1962. *Church Dogmatics*. Vol. 4, *The Doctrine of Reconciliation*. Edinburgh: T. & T. Clark.

Bateman, H. W. 1997. *Early Jewish Hermeneutics and Hebrews 1:5–13*. New York: Lang.

Bauer, W., F. W. Danker, W. F. Arndt, and F. W. Gingrich. 2000. *Greek-English Lexicon of the New Testament and Other Early Christian Literature*. Rev. ed. Chicago: University of Chicago Press.

Bediako, Kwame. 2000. *Jesus in Africa*. A Kropons-Akuapem, Ghana: Regnum Africa; Carlisle: Paternoster.

Berger, Klaus. 1977. *Exegese des Neuen Testaments*. Uni-Taschenbücher 658. Heidelberg: Quelle & Meyer.

———. 1984. "Hellenistische Gattungen im Neuen Testament." In *Aufstieg und Niedergang der Römischen Welt* pt. 2, vol. 25, pt. 2, edited by W. Haase, 1031–1432, 1831–85. Berlin: W. de Gruyter.

Black, C. Clifton. 1988. "The Rhetorical Form of the Hellenistic Jewish and Early Christian Sermon: A Response to Lawrence Wills." *Harvard Theological Review* 81: 1–18.

Bornkamm, Günther. 1963. "Das Bekenntnis im Hebräerbrief." In *Studien zu Antike und Christentum*, 188–203. 2nd ed. Munich: Kaiser.

Braun, Herbert. 1984. *An die Hebräer*. Handbuch zum Neuen Testament 14. Tübingen: Mohr.

Brawley, R. L. 1993. "Discoursive Structure and the Unseen in Hebrews 2:8 and 11:1: A Neglected Aspect of the Context." *Catholic Biblical Quarterly* 55:81–98.

Bruce, F. F. 1990. *The Epistle to the Hebrews*. Rev. ed. Grand Rapids: Eerdmans.

Busch, Peter. 2000. "Der mitleidende Hohepriester: Zur Rezeption der mittelplatonischen Dämonologie in Hebr 4,14f." In *Religionsgeschichte des Neuen Testaments: Festschrift für Klaus Berger zum 60. Geburtstag*, edited by A. von Dobbeler et al. Tübingen: Francke.

Butler, H. E., trans. 1920. *Quintilian: Institutio Oratoria*. Loeb Classical Library. Cambridge, MA: Harvard University Press.

Caplan, Harry, trans. 1954. *Ad C. Herennium de ratione dicendi (Rhetorica ad Herennium)*. Loeb Classical Library. Cambridge, MA: Harvard University Press.

Charlesworth, James. 1983. *The Old Testament Pseudepigrapha*. 2 vols. New York: Doubleday.

Colson, F. H., and G. H. Whitaker, trans. 1929. *Philo, with an English Translation*. Loeb Classical Library. Cambridge, MA: Harvard University Press.

Cortez, Felix. 2006. "From the Holy to the Most Holy Place: The Period of Hebrews 9:6–10 and the Day of Atonement as a Metaphor of Transition." *Journal of Biblical Literature* 125:527–47.

Cosby, Michael R. 1988. "The Rhetorical Composition of Hebrews 11." *Journal of Biblical Literature* 107:257–73.

———. 1989. *The Rhetorical Composition and Function of Hebrews 11*. Macon, GA: Mercer University Press.

Croy, N. C. 1998. *Endurance in Suffering: Hebrews 12:1–13 in Its Rhetorical, Religious, and Philosophical Contexts*. Society for New Testament Studies Monograph Series 98. Cambridge: Cambridge University Press.

D'Angelo, Mary Rose. 1979. *Moses in the Letter to the Hebrews*. Missoula, MT: Scholars Press.

Deichgräber, G. 1967. *Gotteshymnus und Christushymnus in der frühen Christenheit.* Studien zur Umwelt des Neuen Testaments. Göttingen: Vandenhoeck & Ruprecht.

———. 1994. *Gotteshymnus und Christushymnus in der frühen Christenheit.* Studien zur Umwelt des Neuen Testaments. Göttingen: Vandenhoeck & Ruprecht.

Deissmann, Adolf. 1965. *Light from the Ancient East.* Grand Rapids, Baker.

DeSilva, David A. 1994. "The Epistle to the Hebrews in Social-Scientific Perspective." *Restoration Quarterly* 36:1–21.

———. 1995. *Despising Shame: Honor Discourse and Community Maintenance in the Epistle to the Hebrews.* Society of Biblical Literature Dissertation Series 152. Atlanta: Scholars Press.

———. 2000. *Perseverance in Gratitude: A Socio-Rhetorical Commentary on the Epistle "to the Hebrews."* Grand Rapids: Eerdmans.

Dey, L. K. K. 1975. *The Intermediary World and Patterns of Perfection in Philo and the Epistle to the Hebrews.* Missoula, MT: Scholars Press.

Dittenberger, G. 1920. *Sylloge Inscriptionum Graecarum.* Leipzig: Hirzelium.

Egan, E., and K. Egan. 1994. *Suffering into Joy: What Mother Teresa Teaches about True Joy.* Ann Arbor, MI: Charis.

Ego, Beate. 1989. *Im Himmel wie auf Erden.* Wissenschaftliche Untersuchungen zum Neuen Testament 2.34. Tübingen: Mohr.

Eichrodt, W. 1963. "Is Typological Exegesis an Appropriate Method?" In *Essays on Old Testament Hermeneutics*, edited by C. Westermann, 224–45. Atlanta: John Knox.

Eisenbaum, Pamela. 1997a. "Heroes and History in Hebrews 11." In *Early Christian Interpretation of the Scriptures of Israel*, edited by Craig A. Evans and James A. Sanders, 380–96. Journal for the Study of the New Testament Supplement Series 148. Sheffield, UK: Sheffield Academic Press.

———. 1997b. *The Jewish Heroes of Christian History: Hebrews 11 in Literary Context.* Atlanta: Scholars Press.

———. 2005. "Locating Hebrews within the Literary Landscape of Christian Origins." In *Hebrews, Contemporary Methods—New Insights*, edited by Gabriella Gelardini, 213–37. Leiden: Brill.

Ellingworth, P. 1993. *The Epistle to the Hebrews.* New International Greek Testament Commentary. Grand Rapids: Eerdmans.

Elliott, John. 1981. *A Home for the Homeless.* Philadelphia: Fortress.

Enns, Peter. 1997. "The Interpretation of Psalm 95 in Hebrews 3.1–4.13." In *Early Christian Interpretation of the Scriptures of Israel*, edited by Craig Evans and James A. Sanders, 352–62. Journal for the Study of the New Testament Supplement Series 148. Sheffield, UK: Sheffield Academic Press.

Feld, H. "Der Hebräerbrief: Literarische Form, religionsgeschichtlicher Hintergrund, theologische Fragen." In *Aufstieg und Niedergang der römischen Welt* pt. 2, vol. 25, pt. 4, edited by H. Temporini and W. Haase, 3522–3601. Berlin: W. de Gruyter.

Feldmeier, Reinhold. 1992. *Die Christen als Fremde: Die Metapher der Fremde in der antiken Welt, im Urchristentum, und im 1. Petrusbrief.* Wissenschaftliche Untersuchungen zum Neuen Testament 64. Tübingen: Mohr.

Fiddes, Paul S. 1989. *Past Event and Present Salvation: A Study in the Christian Doctrine of Atonement.* Atlanta: Westminster John Knox.

Filson, Floyd. 1967. *"Yesterday": A Study of Hebrews in the Light of Chapter 13.* Naperville, IL: Allenson.

Fitzgerald, John. 2006. "Early Christian Missionary Practice and Pagan Reaction: 1 Peter and Domestic Violence against Slaves and Wives." In *Renewing Tradition: Studies in Texts and Contexts in Honor of James W. Thompson,* edited by Mark W. Hamilton, Thomas H. Olbricht, and Jeffrey Peterson, 24–44. Princeton Theological Monograph Series. Eugene, OR: Wipf & Stock.

Fitzgerald, Robert, trans. 1963. *Homer: The Odyssey.* New York: Anchor.

Frankowski, J. 1983. "Early Christian Hymns Recorded in the New Testament: A Reconsideration of the Question in Light of Heb 1:3." *Biblische Zeitschrift* 27:183–94.

Freese, John, trans. 1939. *Aristotle: The "Art" of Rhetoric.* Loeb Classical Library. Cambridge, MA: Harvard University Press.

Friedrich, G. 1962. "Das Lied vom Hohenpriester im Zusammenhang von Hebr. 4:14–5:10." *Theologische Zeitschrift* 18:95–115.

Gheorghita, Radu. 2003. *The Role of the Septuagint in Hebrews: An Investigation of Its Influence with Special Consideration of the Use of Hab 2:3–4 in Heb 10:37–38.* Wissenschaftliche Untersuchungen zum Neuen Testament 2.160. Tübingen: Mohr Siebeck.

Gieschen, Charles A. 1997. "The Different Functions of a Similar Melchizedek Tradition in *2 Enoch* and the Epistle to the Hebrews." In *Early Christian Interpretation of the Scriptures of Israel,* edited by Craig A. Evans and James A. Sanders, 364–79. Journal for the Study of the New Testament Supplement Series 148. Sheffield, UK: Sheffield Academic Press.

Grässer, Erich. 1965. *Der Glaube im Hebräerbrief.* Marburg Theologische Studien 2. Marburg: Elwert.

———. 1973. "Zur Christologie des Hebräerbriefes." In *Neues Testament und christliche Existenz,* edited by H. D. Balz and L. Schottroff, 195–206. Tübingen: Mohr.

———. 1976. "Rechtfertigung im Hebräerbrief." In *Rechtfertigung,* edited by J. Friedrich, W. Pöhlmann, and P. Stuhlmacher, 79–93. Tübingen: Mohr.

———. 1985. "Moses und Jesus." In *Der alte Bund im Neuen: Eine exegetische Vorlesung,* 290–316. Wissenschaftliche Untersuchungen zum Neuen Testament 35. Tübingen: Mohr.

———. 1986. "Das wandernde Gottesvolk: Zum Basismotiv des Hebräerbriefes." *Zeitschrift für die neutestamentliche Wissenschaft* 77:160–79.

———. 1990, 1993, 1997. *An die Hebräer.* Vols. 1–3. Evangelisch-Katholischer Kommentar. Neukirchen: Benziger.

Gray, Patrick. 2003a. "Brotherly Love and the High Priest Christology of Hebrews." *Journal of Biblical Literature* 122:33–351.

———. 2003b. *Godly Fear: The Epistle to the Hebrews and Greco-Roman Critiques of Superstition.* Academica Biblica 16. Atlanta: Society of Biblical Literature.

Greer, Rowan. 1973. *The Captain of Our Salvation: A Study in the Patristic Exegesis of Hebrews.* Beiträge zur Geschichte der biblischen Exegese 15. Tübingen: Mohr.

Gummere, Richard, trans. 1920. *Seneca: Epistles.* Loeb Classical Library. Cambridge, MA: Harvard University Press.

Guthrie, George H. 1994. *The Structure of Hebrews: A Text-Linguistic Analysis.* Grand Rapids: Baker Academic.

Hahn, Scott W. 2005. "Covenant, Cult, and the Curse-of-Death: *Diathēkē* in Heb 9:15–22." In *Hebrews: Contemporary Methods—New Insights,* edited by Gabriella Gelardini, 65–88. Leiden: Brill.

Harmon, A. H., trans. 1915. *Lucian.* Loeb Classical Library. Cambridge, MA: Harvard University Press.

Harnack, Adolf von. 1929. "Zwei alte dogmatische Korrekturen im Hebräerbrief." *Sitzungsberichte der preussischen Akademie der Wissenschaften,* Philosophisch-historische Klasse, 62–73.

Heen, Erik M., and Philip Krey. 2005. *Hebrews.* Ancient Christian Commentary on Scripture. Downers Grove, IL: InterVarsity.

Hegermann, Harald. 1988. *Der Brief an die Hebräer.* Theologische Handkommentar zum Neuen Testament 16. Berlin: Evangelische Verlagsanstalt.

Hengel, Martin. 1983. "Hymns and Christology." In *Between Jesus and Paul,* 74–96. Philadelphia: Fortress.

Hofius, Otfried. 1970a. "Inkarnation und Opfertod Jesu nach Hbr 10:19f." In *Der Ruf Jesu und die Antwort der Gemeinde: Exegetische Untersuchungen Joachim Jeremias zum 70. Geburtstag gewidmet von seinen Schülern,* edited by Eduard Lohse, Christoph Burchard, and Berndt Schaller, 132–41. Göttingen: Vandenhoeck & Ruprecht.

———. 1970b. *Katapausis: Die Vorstellung vom endzeitlichen Ruheort im Hebräerbrief.* Wissenschaftliche Untersuchungen zum Neuen Testament 11. Tübingen: Mohr.

———. 1970c. "Das 'erste' und das 'zweite' Zelt: Ein Beitrag zur Auslegung von Hb 9:1–10." *Zeitschrift für die neutestamentliche Wissenschaft* 61:271–77.

———. 1972. *Der Vorhang vor dem Thron Gottes.* Wissenschaftliche Untersuchungen zum Neuen Testament 14. Tübingen: Mohr.

———. 1973. "Die Unabänderlichkeit des göttlichen Heilsratschluss: Erwägungen zur Herkunft eines neutestamentlichen Theologoumenon," *Zeitschrift für die neutestamentliche Wissenschaft* 64:135–45.

———. 1991. *Der Christushymnus Philipper 2,6–11.* 2nd ed. Wissenschaftliche Untersuchungen zum Neuen Testament 17. Tübingen: Mohr.

———. 1994. "Biblische Theologie im Lichte des Hebräerbriefes." In *New Directions in Biblical Theology,* edited by Sigfred Pedersen, 108–25. Leiden: Brill.

Holmes, Michael W. 2006. *The Apostolic Fathers in English.* 3rd ed. Grand Rapids: Baker Academic.

Horbury, W. 1983. "The Aaronic Priesthood in the Epistle to the Hebrews." *Journal for the Study of the New Testament* 19:43–71.

Hughes, G. 1979. *Hebrews and Hermeneutics: The Epistle to the Hebrews as a New Testament Example of Biblical Interpretation.* Cambridge: Cambridge University Press.

Hughes, John J. 1976–1977. "Hebrews IX 15ff and Galatians III 15ff: A Study in Covenant Practice and Procedure." *Novum Testamentum* 21:27–96.

Hughes, Philip. 1977. *A Commentary on the Epistle to the Hebrews*. Grand Rapids: Eerdmans.

Hughes, W. Graham. 1979. *Hebrews and Hermeneutics*. Society for New Testament Studies Monograph Series 36. Cambridge: Cambridge University Press.

Hurst, L. D. 1990. *The Epistle to the Hebrews: Its Background of Thought*. Society for New Testament Studies Monograph Series 65. Cambridge: Cambridge University Press.

Isaacs, Marie E. 1992. *Sacred Space: An Approach to the Theology of the Epistle to the Hebrews*. Journal for the Study of the New Testament Supplement Series 73. Sheffield: JSOT Press.

————. 1997. "Hebrews 13:9–16 Revisited." *New Testament Studies* 43:268–84.

Jenkins, Philip. 2002. *The Next Christendom: The Coming of Global Christianity*. Oxford: Oxford University Press.

Johnson, Luke Timothy. 2003a. "Hebrews' Challenge to Christian Christology and Discipleship." In *Preaching Hebrews*, edited by D. Fleer and D. Bland, 11–28. Rochester College Lectures on Preaching 4. Abilene, TX: ACU Press.

————. 2003b. "The Scriptural World of Hebrews." *Interpretation* 57:237–50.

————. 2006. *Hebrews: A Commentary*. New Testament Library. Louisville: Westminster John Knox.

Käsemann, Ernst. 1982. *Kirchliche Konflikte*. Göttingen: Vandenhoeck & Ruprecht.

————. 1984. *The Wandering People of God: An Investigation of the Letter to the Hebrews*. Minneapolis: Augsburg.

Kiley, M. 1980. "A Note on Hebrews 5:14." *Catholic Biblical Quarterly* 42:501–3.

Klauck, Hans-Josef. 2006. "Moving In and Moving Out: Ethics and Ethos in Hebrews." In *Identity, Ethics, and Ethos in the New Testament*, edited by Jan G. Van der Watt, 417–43. Beihefte zur Zeitschrift für die neutestamentliche Wissenschaft 141. Berlin: W. de Gruyter.

Kobelski, Paul J. 1981. *Melchizedek and Melchiresa*. Catholic Biblical Quarterly Monograph Series 10. Washington, DC: Catholic Biblical Association.

Koester, Craig R. 1989. *The Dwelling of God: The Tabernacle in the Old Testament, Intertestamental Jewish Literature, and the New Testament*. Catholic Biblical Quarterly Monograph Series 22. Washington, DC: Catholic Biblical Association.

————. 2001. *Hebrews*. Anchor Bible. New York: Doubleday.

Kurianal, James. 1999. *Jesus Our High Priest: Ps 110,4 as the Substructure of Heb 5,1–7,28*. Frankfurt: Peter Lang.

Lane, W. L. 1982. "Unexpected Light on Heb 13:1–6 from a Second Century Source." *Perspectives in Religious Studies* 9:267–74.

————. 1991a. *Hebrews 1–8*. Word Biblical Commentary. Dallas: Word.

————. 1991b. *Hebrews 9–13*. Word Biblical Commentary. Dallas: Word.

Laub, Franz. 1980. *Bekenntnis und Auslegung: Die paraenetische Funktion der Christologie im Hebräerbrief*. Biblische Untersuchungen 15. Regensburg: Pustet.

Lausberg, Heinrich. 1998. *Handbook of Literary Rhetoric: A Foundation for Literary Study*. Leiden: Brill.

Lehne, Susanne. 1990. *The New Covenant in Hebrews*. Sheffield: JSOT Press.

Levenson, Jon D. 1985. *Sinai and Zion: An Entry into the Jewish Bible*. San Francisco: Harper & Row, 1985.

Lindars, Barnabas. 1989. "The Rhetorical Structure of Hebrews." *New Testament Studies* 35:382–406.

———. 1991. *The Theology of the Epistle to the Hebrews*. Cambridge: Cambridge University Press.

Loader, William R. G. 1981. *Sohn und Hohepriester: Eine traditionsgeschichtliche Untersuchung zur Christologie des Hebräerbriefes*. Neukirchen: Neukirchener Verlag.

Löhr, H. 1994. *Umkehr und Sünde im Hebräerbrief*. Beihefte zur Zeitschrift für die neutestamentliche Wissenschaft 73. Berlin: W. de Gruyter.

———. 2005. "Reflections on Rhetorical Terminology in Hebrews." In *Hebrews: Contemporary Methods—New Insights*, edited by Gabriella Gelardini, 199–210. Leiden: Brill.

Lohse, Eduard. 1973. "Deus dixit: Wort Gottes im Zeugnis des Alten und Neuen Testamentes." In *Die Einheit des Neuen Testaments,* edited by E. Lohse, 9–28. Göttingen: Vandenhoeck & Ruprecht.

Long, Thomas. 1998. "Bold in the Presence of God: Atonement in Hebrews." *Interpretation* 52:53–69.

Mackie, Scott D. 2007. *Eschatology and Exhortation in the Epistle to the Hebrews*. Wissenschaftliche Untersuchungen zum Neuen Testament 2.223. Tübingen: Mohr.

März, Claus-Peter. 1991. "Vom Trost der Theologie." In *Denkende Glaube in Geschichte und Gegenwart*, edited by W. Ernst and Konrad Feieres, 260–76. Erfurt theologische Studien 63. Leipzig: Benno.

———. 2003. "'Wir haben einen Hohenpriester . . .': Anmerkungen zur kulttheologischen Argumentation des Hebräerbriefes." In *Liebe, Macht und Religion*, edited by M. Gielen and J. Kügler, 237–52. Stuttgart: Katholisches Bibelwerk.

Meier, John P. 1985. "Structure and Theology in Heb 1:1–14." *Biblica* 66:168–89.

Michel, Otto. 1966. *Der Brief an die Hebräer*. Kritisch-Exegetischer Kommentar über das Neue Testament. Göttingen: Vandenhoeck & Ruprecht.

Mitchell, Alan C. 1992. "The Use of *prepein* and Rhetorical Propriety in Hebrews 2.10." *Catholic Biblical Quarterly* 54:681–701.

———. 1996. "Holding on to Confidence: *Parrēsia* in Hebrews." In *Friendship, Flattery, and Frankness of Speech*, edited by J. T. Fitzgerald, 203–26. Supplements to Novum Testamentum 82. Leiden: Brill.

———. 2005. *Hebrews*. Sacra Pagina. Collegeville, MN: Liturgical Press.

Moessner, Jeanne. 2003. "The Road to Perfection: An Interpretation of Suffering in Hebrews." *Interpretation* 57:280–90.

Moffatt, James. 1924. *A Critical and Exegetical Commentary on the Epistle to the Hebrews*. International Critical Commentary. Edinburgh: T. & T. Clark.

Moffitt, David M. 2007. "Passing through the Veil: Reassessing the Relationship between the Veil and Jesus' Body in Hebrews 10:20." Paper presented at the international meeting of the Society of Biblical Literature, July 24, 2007.

Motyer, Stephen. 1999. "The Psalm Quotations of Hebrews 1: A Hermeneutic-Free Zone?" *Tyndale Bulletin* 50:3–22.

Moxnes, Halvor. 1980. *Theology in Conflict: Studies in Paul's Understanding of God in Romans.* Supplements to Novum Testamentum 53. Leiden: Brill.

Nauck, Wolfgang. 1960. "Zum Aufbau des Hebräerbriefes." In *Judentum, Urchristentum, Kirche: Festschrift für Joachim Jeremias,* edited by Walther Eltester, 199–206. Berlin: Alfred Töpelmann.

Neeley, Linda Lloyd. 1987. "A Discourse Analysis of Hebrews." *Occasional Papers in Translation and Textlinguistics* 3–4:1–146.

Neyrey, J. H. 1991. "'Without Beginning of Days or End of Life' (Hebrews 7:3): Topos for a True Deity." *Catholic Biblical Quarterly* 53:4399–55.

Niebuhr, H. Richard. 1951. *Christ and Culture.* New York: Harper.

Nissilä, Keijo. 1979. *Das Hohepriestermotiv im Hebräerbrief: Eine Exegetische Untersuchung.* Schriften der finnischen exegetischen Gesellschaft. Helsinki: Oy Liiton Kirjapaino.

Nongbri, Brent. 2003. "A Touch of Condemnation in a Word of Exhortation: Apocalyptic Language and Graeco-Roman Rhetoric in Hebrews 6:4–12." *Novum Testamentum* 45:265–79.

Olbricht, Thomas H. 1993. "Hebrews as Amplification." In *Rhetoric and the New Testament,* edited by Stanley E. Porter and Thomas H. Olbricht, 375–89. Journal for the Study of the New Testament Supplement Series 90. Sheffield: JSOT Press.

Peterson, David. 1982. *Hebrews and Perfection: An Examination of the Concept of Perfection in the 'Epistle to the Hebrews.'* Society for New Testament Studies Monograph Series 47. Cambridge: Cambridge University Press.

Pfitzner, Victor. 2003. "Where Tradition and Context Meet: The Christology of Hebrews as a Theological Paradigm." In *God Down Under,* edited by Winifred Wing Han Lamb and Ian Burns, 63–80. Adelaide: ATF Press.

Rad, Gerhard von. 1958. "Es ist noch eine Ruhe vorhanden dem Volk Gottes." In *Gesammelte Studien zum Alten Testament,* 101–8. Munich: Kaiser.

Riggenbach, E. 1922. *Der Brief an die Hebräer.* Leipzig: Deichert.

Runia, David T. 1993. *Philo in Early Christian Literature.* Philadelphia: Fortress.

Salevao, Iutisone. 2002. *Legitimation in the Letter to the Hebrews: The Construction and Maintenance of a Symbolic Universe.* Journal for the Study of the New Testament Supplement Series 219. London: Sheffield Academic Press.

Schenck, Kenneth L. 1997. "Keeping His Appointment: Creation and Enthronement in Hebrews." *Journal for the Study of the New Testament* 66:91–117.

———. 2001. "A Celebration of the Enthroned Son: The Catena of Hebrews 1." *Journal of Biblical Literature* 120:469–85.

———. 2005. *Understanding the Book of Hebrews: The Story behind the Sermon.* Louisville: Westminster John Knox.

Schierse, F. J. 1955. *Verheissung und Heilsvollendung: Zur theologischen Grundfrage des Hebräerbriefes.* Microcard Theological Studies 9. Munich: Zink.

Schille, G. 1955. "Erwägungen zur Hohepriesterlehre des Hebräerbriefes." *Zeitschrift für die neutestamentliche Wissenschaft* 46:81–109.

Scholer, John M. 1991. *Proleptic Priests: Priesthood in the Epistle to the Hebrews.* Sheffield: JSOT Press.

Schröger, Friederich. 1968. *Der Verfasser des Hebräerbriefes als Schriftausleger.* Biblische Untersuchungen 4. Regensburg: Pustet.

Schunack, Gerd. 1999. "Exegetische Beobachtungen zum Verständnis des Glaubens im Hebräerbrief: Eine kritische Anfrage." In *Text und Geschichte: Facetten theologischen Arbeitens aus dem Freundes-und Schülerkreis; Dieter Lührmann zum 60. Geburtstag,* edited by Stefan Maser and Egbert Schlarb, 208–32. Marburger theologische Studien 50. Marburg: Elwert.

Scott, J. Julius. 1986. "*Archēgos* in the Salvation History of the Epistle to the Hebrews." *Journal of the Evangelical Theological Society* 29:47–54.

Shorey, Paul, trans. 1930. *Plato: The Republic.* Loeb Classical Library. Cambridge, MA: Harvard University Press.

Smillie, Gene R. 2004a. "ὁ λόγος τοῦ θεοῦ in Heb 4:12–13." *Novum Testamentum* 46:19–25.

———. 2004b. "'The One Who Is Speaking' in Hebrews 12:25." *Tyndale Bulletin* 55:275–94.

———. 2005a. "Contrast or Continuity in Hebrews 1:1–2." *New Testament Studies* 51:543–60.

———. 2005b. "'The Other *Logos*' at the End of Heb 4:12." *Novum Testamentum* 47:19–25.

Söding, Thomas. 1991. "Zuversicht und Geduld im Schauen auf Jesus: Zum Glaubensbegriff des Hebräerbriefes." *Zeitschrift für die neutestamentliche Wissenschaft* 82:214–41.

Son, Kiwoong. 2005. *Zion Symbolism in Hebrews: Hebrews 12:18–24 as a Hermeneutical Key to the Epistle.* Paternoster Biblical Monographs. Waynesboro, GA: Paternoster.

Spicq, Ceslas. 1952. *L'Épitre aux Hébreux.* 2 vols. Paris: Librairie Lecoffre.

———. 1977. *L'Épitre aux Hébreux.* Sources bibliques. Paris: Librairie Lecoffre.

———. 1994. *Theological Lexicon of the New Testament.* 3 vols. Translated and edited by James D. Ernest. Peabody, MA: Hendrickson.

Stanley, Steven. 1994. "The Structure of Hebrews from Three Perspectives." *Tyndale Bulletin* 45:245–71.

———. 1995. "Hebrews 9:6–10: The 'Parable' of the Tabernacle." *Novum Testamentum* 37:385–99.

Sterling, Gregory. 2001. "Ontology versus Eschatology: Tensions between Author and Community in Hebrews." *Studia Philonica Annual* 13:190–211.

Strack, H. L., and Paul Billerbeck. 1926. *Kommentar zum Neuen Testament aus Talmud und Midrasch.* Munich: Beck.

Strecker, Georg, and Udo Schnelle. 1996. *Neuer Wettstein: Texte zum Neuen Testament aus Griechentum und Hellenismus,* Band 2, *Texte zur Briefliteratur und zur Johannesapocalypse.* Berlin: W. de Gruyter.

297

Swetnam, James. 1981a. *Jesus and Isaac: A Study of the Epistle to the Hebrews in the Light of the Aqeda*. Rome: Biblical Institute Press.

———. 1981b. "Jesus as Logos in Hebrews 4,12–13." *Biblica* 62:214–24.

Theissen, Gerd. 1969. *Untersuchungen zum Hebräerbrief*. Gütersloh: Gerd Mohn.

Theobald, Michael. 1997. "Vom Text zum 'lebendigen Wort' (Hebr 4.12): Beobachtungen zur Schrifthermeneutik des Hebräerbriefs." In *Jesus Christus als die Mitte der Schrift: Studien zur Hermeneutik des Evangeliums*, Festschrift for O. Hofius, edited by Christof Landmesser, Hans-Joachim Eckstein, and Hermann Lichtenberger, 751–90. Beihefte zur Zeitschrift für die neutestamentliche Wissenschaft 86. Berlin: W. de Gruyter.

Tholuck, August. 1850. *Kommentar zum Briefe an die Hebräer*. Hamburg: Berthes.

Thompson, James W. 1982. *The Beginnings of Christian Philosophy*. Catholic Biblical Quarterly Monograph Series 13. Washington, DC: Catholic Biblical Society.

———. 1998. "The Appropriate, the Fitting, and the Necessary: Faith and Reason in Hebrews." In *The Early Church in Its Context*, Festschrift for Everett Ferguson, edited by Abraham J. Malherbe, Frederick W. Norris, and James W. Thompson, 302–17. Supplements to Novum Testamentum 90. Leiden: Brill.

———. 2007. "Ephapax: The One and the Many in Hebrews." *New Testament Studies* 53:566–81.

Übelacker, Walter. 1989. *Der Hebräerbrief als Appell: Untersuchungen zu exordium, narratio und postscriptum (Hebr 1–2 und 13,22–25)*. Stockholm: Almqvist & Wiksell.

———. 2004. "Paraenesis or Paraclesis—Hebrews as a Test Case." In *Early Christian Paraenesis in Context*, edited by James Starr and Troels Engberg-Pedersen, 319–52. Beihefte zur Zeitschrift für die neutestamentliche Wissenschaft 125. Berlin: W. de Gruyter.

Vanhoye, Albert, SJ. 1976. *La structure littéraire de l'épître aux Hébreux*. Rev. ed. Studia Neotestamentica 1. Paris: Desclée de brouwer.

Wedderburn, A. J. M. 2004. "The 'Letter' to the Hebrews and Its Thirteenth Chapter." *New Testament Studies* 50:390–405.

Weiss, Hans-Friedrich. 1991. *Der Brief an die Hebräer*. Kritisch-exegetischer Kommentar über das Neue Testament. Göttingen: Vandenhoeck & Ruprecht.

Westcott, B. F. 1890. *The Epistle to the Hebrews*. London: Macmillan.

Westfall, Cynthia Long. 2005. *A Discourse Analysis of the Letter to the Hebrews: The Relationship between Form and Meaning*. Edinburgh: T. & T. Clark.

Wettstein, J. J. 1962. *Novum Testamentum Graecum*. Graz: Akademische Druck und Verlagsanstalt. Facsimile of the 1751–1752 ed.

Wider, David. 1997. *Theozentrik und Bekenntnis: Untersuchungen zur Theologie des Redens Gottes im Hebräerbrief*. Beihefte zur Zeitschrift für die neutestamentliche Wissenschaft 87. Berlin: W. de Gruyter.

Wilken, Robert L. 1984. *The Christians as the Romans Saw Them*. New Haven: Yale University Press.

Williamson, Clark. 2003. "Anti-Judaism in Hebrews?" *Interpretation* 57:266–79.

Williamson, Ronald. 1970. *Philo and the Epistle to the Hebrews*. Leiden: Brill.

Wills, Lawrence. 1984. "The Form of the Sermon in Hellenistic Judaism and Early Christianity." *Harvard Theological Review* 77:277–99.

Windisch, Hans. 1931. *Der Hebräerbrief*. Handbuch zum Neuen Testament 14. Tübingen: Mohr.

Wray, Judith Hoch. 1998. *Rest as a Theological Metaphor in the Epistle to the Hebrews and the Gospel of Truth: Early Christian Homiletics of Rest*. Society of Biblical Literature Dissertation Series 166. Atlanta: Scholars Press.

Wrede, William. 1906. *Das literarische Rätsel des Hebräerbriefes*. Forschungen zur Religion und Literatur des Alten und Neuen Testaments. Göttingen: Vandenhoeck & Ruprecht.

Young, Norman H. 1981. "The Gospel according to Hebrews 9." *New Testament Studies* 27:198–210.

———. 2002. "'Bearing His Reproach' (Heb 13.9–14)." *New Testament Studies* 48: 243–61.

Subject Index

Index of Modern Authors

Index of Scripture
and Ancient Sources

311

Deuterocanonical Books

New Testament

313

314

315

Other Early Jewish, Christian, and Gnostic Corpora

Anonymous Ancient Works